THREE CENTURIES OF HARVARD
1636-1936

THREE CENTURIES
OF HARVARD
1636–1936

BY

SAMUEL ELIOT MORISON

CLASS OF 1908

THE BELKNAP PRESS OF

HARVARD UNIVERSITY PRESS

CAMBRIDGE, MASSACHUSETTS
AND LONDON, ENGLAND

Library of Congress Catalog Card Number 36-14160
ISBN 0-674-88890-1 (cloth)
ISBN 0-674-88891-X (paper)

PREFACE

THIS volume, covering in some measure the entire history of Harvard University from her founding to the present year, is a private venture of the author and the publishers. The official Tercentennial History has reached four volumes, and will be continued until the present gap between 1723 and 1869 is filled; but in this little volume I am writing as an individual, and not as the official historian. Readers indignant with my sins of omission and commission may therefore abuse me instead of the Corporation, and I hope that they will exercise that right to the full. For no one can be more aware than myself of the shortcomings of this brief history. The earlier chapters, to be sure, are digests of larger researches made in preparation for the Tercentennial History; but those covering the last century and a half have been thrown together very hastily, in the midst of many distractions, in order that Harvard graduates and others may have something of this scope to read in 1936.

The greater part of the space is devoted to Harvard College, whose birthday we are celebrating this year. Treatment of the graduate and professional schools, and the multifarious institutes, museums, and the like, is very sketchy. More details on these may be found in the volume *The Development of Harvard University*, which I edited. Financial history has been almost wholly neglected, for want of time and capacity to explore it properly. Few members of our legion of benefactors have been so much as mentioned. For this is not intended as a reference book, or a treatise; it has been written to be read and enjoyed.

S. E. MORISON

May 10, 1936

CONTENTS

THE PURITAN AGE
1636–1707

AARON'S ROD
1708–1806

THE AUGUSTAN AGE
1806–1845

THE AGE OF TRANSITION
1846–1869

THE OLYMPIAN AGE
1869–1933

'THE AGE THAT IS WAITING BEFORE'

THE PURITAN AGE
1636–1707

PRESIDENTS AND ACTING PRESIDENTS

'FIRST FLOWER OF THEIR WILDERNESS'

IN THE year of Our Lord, 1636. Several summers had passed since Governor Winthrop led the vanguard of the great puritan emigration to New England. Some fifteen to eighteen thousand English were now seated along the seafront from Old York in the Province of Maine to Narragansett Bay; and the new colony of Connecticut was already taking shape along the fertile river meads between Springfield and Hartford. Most of these communities were in a relatively prosperous condition for new settlements, finding a ready market for their corn, cattle, and fish among the newcomers fleeing to this new Land of Canaan from the persecution of the high Anglicans. Yeomen for the most part, and artisans from the towns, they included a sprinkling of gentlefolk and (by 1640) over a hundred alumni of Oxford and Cambridge, mostly puritan parsons who had chosen to obey 'God's Ordinances' in the New World, rather than knuckle down to Bishop and King in Old England.

Enthusiasm for education was one aspect of that desire to know and do the will of God that bound the puritans together, and led them to brave the sea, the wilderness, and the New England climate. Their Congregational churches must have a learned clergy, cost what it might. A puritan minister must be able to expound the Sacred Scriptures from the original Hebrew and Greek, and be cognizant of what the Church Fathers, the Scholastic Philosophers, and the Reformers had written, in Greek and Latin. Newly launched colonial commonwealths needed men broadened by education to guide them through the perils of Indian diplomacy, English colonial policy, and the ambitions of England's rivals, before they reached the deeps, when plain people might perhaps be allowed to take the quarterdeck. New Englanders were no less English for being puritans. A firm determination to transplant English civilization as a whole was bound up with their desire to purify it in the translation of all 'corruptions,' in order that sober and God-fearing people of English speech might lead a life at once civilized and Christian. Comfort, decency, and culture were as much a part of the puritan scheme of things as Congregational churches and responsible government. Education and learning should be fostered by schools and colleges, lest the rising generation relapse into uncouth ways and barbarian ignorance.

Harvard College was the acme of a series of cultural efforts in the 1630's and 1640's, made by the ruling class of New England and supported by the people at large. Common schools, compulsory education laws, grammar schools such as the Boston Latin, and the Cambridge printing press, belonged in the same category. Circumstances compelled a rough-hewn temporary structure, rather than a harmonious building, well planned from cellar to ridgepole. Gentlefolk and ambitious yeomen with bright lads growing up could not afford to wait many years for a college corresponding to those of Oxford and Cambridge. Every newly settled frontier town wanted at least one learned minister, and if things continued to go hard with the puritans in England, a collegiate foundation of Cambridge standards, starting fresh without expensive futilities and useless survivals, might well attract the benefactions and the offspring of godly families in the Old Country. For every person that emigrated to New England there were hundreds of the same mind who could not bring themselves to face the ocean journey and the separation from home; such families might well send their hopeful young men overseas to a new seat of English culture.

These were doubtless matters of common conversation in Boston and the settlements round about, from 1634 on. We glean snatches of it from letters and other documents of the time. Finally, in 1636, came the time for action. The Great and General Court of Massachusetts met under the presidency of twenty-three-year-old Governor Harry Vane, late of Magdalen Hall, Oxford. Among the forty-three members were six alumni of Cambridge and one of Trinity College, Dublin, besides eight or ten who were sons, brothers, or nephews of English university men. The Court assembled on September 8 (corresponding to the 18th of our present calendar), sat a few days, and adjourned to October 25. On the fourth day of that session, October 28, it passed the legislative act that founded Harvard College. As Mr. Secretary Nowell recorded it, 'The Court agreed to give 400*l* towards a schoale or colledge, whearof 200*l* to bee paid the next yeare, and 200*l* when the worke is finished, and the next Court to appoint wheare and what building.'

This is the event we celebrate in 1936 — the first official and recorded step toward the establishment of the earliest collegiate foundation in the English colonies. It was not the earliest in the New World. The Spanish had founded two noble universities, at Mexico City and Lima, in the previous century, and a third at Córdoba in 1613. A Jesuit college for children was already open at Quebec, and within thirty years it was giving instruction of university grade. But the Indian College and University planned in 1618 by the Virginia Company had come to nothing; and no other European colony managed actually to establish a college of liberal arts so shortly after its foundation as the Colony of Massachusetts Bay.

Over a year elapsed before anything was done to carry into execution the generous vote of October 28, 1636.

The causes of the delay, one infers, were twofold — the Hutchinsonian faction, which preferred inspired exhortation to learned exposition of the Bible, and the short but ferocious war with the Pequot Indians. On November 15, 1637, within two weeks of the banishment of Anne Hutchinson, 'the colledg' was 'ordered to bee at Newetowne,' and five days later a committee of six magistrates and six ministers (including eight Cantabrigians and one Oxonian), the first Board of Overseers, was appointed by the Court 'to take order for a colledge at Newetowne.'

Any stranger who in 1936 is hurled out to Harvard Square by subway or taxicab may well wonder why the puritan fathers in their wisdom chose 'Newetowne' (renamed Cambridge when the College was at the point of opening) as the site. And his wonder will increase when he learns that Salem offered a tract of three hundred acres on the borders of Marblehead, with an ocean frontage of a good quarter-mile, which was rejected in favor of a house and lot measuring slightly over an acre among the cowyards of Cambridge. One reason, doubtless, was desire to do something for the New Town which had already been once emptied of its inhabitants by the emigration to Connecticut, and abandoned by Massachusetts as the colonial capital. Another reason, explicitly stated by contemporaries, was the personality of Thomas Shepard, the young minister of the New Town, a Master of Arts of Cambridge who had a winning way with young men (among whom he had once, by his own confession, been somewhat of a hellion), and who had kept his parish clean of the Hutchinsonian heresy with which Boston was still tainted. And we should like to think that the winding Charles, reminiscent of Cam and Isis, and the plain smooth as 'a bowling green' that sloped to it, had something to do with the choice, even though the College turned her back on the river for over two centuries.

American frontier history can be told largely in terms of cattle; and Cambridge, in 1636, was still in the cow country. The present Cambridge Common is merely the apex of a great triangle of cow pasture that extended to the borders of the township. In days when wolves and other 'varmints' were still plentiful, it was not profitable to leave cattle unattended at night; so in two or three parts of Cambridge there was a row of cowyards, where the animals were parked at night. The principal 'Cow-yard Row' occupied the southern half of the present College Yard; it had doubtless been placed there because 'Watch-House Hill,' on the eastern side of the present Harvard Square, offered a good vantage point from which the town watch, if he kept awake, could guard the herds. Along the southern edge of Cow-yard Row were three dwelling houses: Goodman Goffe's, Goodman Peyntree's, and the Reverend Mr. Shepard's. Peyntree had gone to Connecticut, and (unless there was an intervening owner) it was from him that the Overseers of the College, late in 1637 or early in 1638, purchased the house with its eighth-of-an-acre house-lot and one-acre cowyard behind. This little slip of land was promptly christened the College Yard, to distinguish it from the cowyards on either side; within a year it was enclosed in a six-foot pale fence, and thirty apple trees were set out. Around this nucleus the Harvard Yard slowly accrued until, a century ago, it attained the present dimensions.

Before the end of 1637, the Overseers had also secured a master for their College. That summer an important group of London puritans came to Boston. It was led by Theophilus Eaton, Deputy-Governor of the Eastland Company of London, and by his friend and pastor, John Davenport. A thirty-year-old Master of Arts of Emmanuel College, Cambridge, named John Harvard, probably came in the same ship with Theophilus Eaton and his younger brother, Nathaniel, a gentleman of about the same age as John Harvard, and his contemporary at the University of Cambridge. After leaving Trinity College, Nathaniel had studied at the University of Franeker in the Netherlands, under William Ames, a celebrated English puritan who had been forced into exile. He had there published a Latin dissertation on the Sabbath, and after leaving Holland he taught school for a time in England.

The Eaton group were regarded as highly desirable citizens by the Massachusetts people, and were offered their choice of a place for settlement. But, as Londoners and traders, they wanted a good harbor for a trading town; and after carefully examining the coast line they decided that Massachusetts had nothing so good to offer as Quinnipiac, which they purchased from the Indians and named New Haven. In the meantime John Harvard and Nathaniel Eaton had settled in Charlestown and decided to stay in Massachusetts; the first, because he was candidate for assistant minister of the church there, and the second, because he had been chosen master of the new College.

The exact date when alterations were completed in the Peyntree House, and the College was opened there, we do not know. Early in May the Town of Cambridge granted two lots to Eaton personally, and one to Eaton for the College. The only one that the College managed to secure was that part of the present College Yard which includes the sites of Harvard, Hollis, Stoughton, and Holworthy. Master Eaton and his wife moved to Cambridge in May or early June, and on September 7 a prominent neighbor reported to a friend in England that the College had opened. It was probably in July or August, 1638, that Master Eaton held the first recitations of the first freshman class, which graduated in 1642.

We may assume that John Harvard rode over from Charlestown to Cambridge in the early summer of 1638, and was sufficiently impressed with what was going on to help the good work along. And although death came speedily, in death John did not forget the College. We have no details of his last illness; we only know that on September 14, 1638, John Harvard died at Charlestown of tuberculosis. By an oral will, dictated doubtless in his last hours, he left half his property and all his library to the College. As Thomas Shepard wrote, 'The man was a Scholler and pious in his life and enlarged toward the cuntry and the good of it in life and death.'

Of John Harvard's library of four hundred volumes we fortunately have a contemporary short-title catalogue; but his 'estate' is still wrapped in mystery. According to the College records, our 'moiety' of the estate amounted to £779 17s 2d; but I cannot find that more than £375 3s of it was actually received, and this was used for building. The balance, says Thomas Shepard, 'mr Eaton did lauish out.' Nor can it now be ascertained whereof the estate consisted. John Harvard left a childless widow who inherited his land in Charlestown, but he still owned real estate in London, and it is a likely conjecture that the Queen's Head Tavern in Southwark, near his old home on the south side of London, provided most of the legacy that the College secured. However, the Harvard benefaction was easily the largest gift that the College had yet received, and for that reason the General Court on March 13, 1639, 'ordered, that the colledge agreed vpon formerly to bee built at Cambridg shalbee called Harvard Colledge.'

The trust placed in Nathaniel Eaton by the community was hardly justified. Very little is known of the single academic year in which he conducted the College, in the former Peyntree House, and that little is not to his credit. 'He was a *Rare Scholar* himself, and he made many more such,' wrote Cotton Mather; the studies were, one infers, of English freshman grade; but Eaton was too prone to drive home lessons with the rod. At the opening of the second academic year, in August, 1639, the Master made the mistake of beating his assistant so briskly with a walnut-tree cudgel, 'big enough to have killed a horse,' that Thomas Shepard rushed in from the parsonage next door to save the poor man's life, and the magistrates haled Eaton into court for assault. On that occasion there was a general ventilation of complaints against Eaton for brutality, and against his wife for the quality of food and quantity of drink dispensed to her boarders. The magistrates, who had been whipped themselves in school or college, were not disposed to dismiss Eaton for an occasional flogging. But the food question was more serious. Englishmen of the seventeenth century considered themselves starved without plenty of beef, bread, and beer; but Mrs. Eaton confessed that she had never given the students beef (although she denied that she served ungutted mackerel); she admitted that the bread was sometimes 'made of heated, sour meal' (although 'goat's dung in their hasty pudding' was 'utterly unknown' to her); and she made the grave admission of 'their wanting beer, betwixt brewings, a week or half a week together' — she 'should tremble' to do so again. The magistrates did not give her the chance. Eaton was promptly dismissed, and fled the country, and after sundry adventures in Virginia, Italy, and England, died in debtors' prison at Southwark, hard by his friend Harvard's birthplace.

For a whole academic year (1639–40) Harvard College was deserted; and it must have seemed to many pessimists that it would never reopen. The students dispersed to their several homes, and tutored with the local minister, or enjoyed themselves. It was almost equivalent to a second founding when the Overseers on August 27, 1640, engaged as President of Harvard College one Henry Dunster, a thirty-year-old graduate of the University of Cambridge who had just arrived at Boston.

In comparison with Eaton, Dunster was undistinguished both in family and in academic record; a Lancastrian farmer's son, he had worked his way through Magdalene College, and subsequently served as curate and schoolmaster in his native place. The youngest in the long line of Harvard presidents, he proved to be one of the greatest. But for his faith, courage, and indomitable energy, Harvard College might have become a mere boarding school, or have closed altogether during the gloomy depression that settled over New England before he had been in office a year. It was the Civil War in England that caused this: puritans stopped emigrating; many already in New England returned home to get into the fight; and without the weekly arrivals of hungry hordes of well-to-do people, the bottom fell out of the stock market. Ruined planters skipped the country to escape their debts, and for a few years, until Yankee ships found new markets in the West Indies, New England had the depressing aspect of a boom town that has fallen flat. Yet under these conditions Dunster went confidently ahead, not only building a college, but pinning to it the high standards of those at Oxford and Cambridge. The only bright side of the depression for the College was the fact that Cambridge went out of the cattle business, so that the College Yard and building were no longer impregnated with stockyard atmosphere.

Dunster recalled to Cambridge as many of Eaton's former pupils as would take the chance of his proving a second flogger, and called them the junior sophister class. A new freshman class of four entered that fall. A three-year course in the Liberal Arts, the Three Philosophies, and the Learned Tongues was instituted for the Bachelor's degree; the lectures, recitations, and other exercises being so arranged that the President could conduct them all. And his best efforts were concentrated on completing the college building that had been framed in Eaton's administration. For the founders of Harvard insisted that Harvard be a real college, in the English sense of the word: a society of scholars, where teachers and students lived in the same building under common discipline, associating not only in lecture rooms but at meals, in chambers, at prayers, and in recreation. It was not that they knew no other way of conducting a school of higher learning, for the Dutch universities, where Eaton and several other New Englanders had studied, allowed undergraduates to live in town and took little care of their social and spiritual concerns. Governor Winthrop was advised from England to let Harvard take that very form: one might hire ministers to deliver lectures in their spare time, and let the students board around Cambridge. But, as Cotton Mather wrote, 'the Government of *New-England*, was for having their Students brought up in a more *Collegiate* Way of Living.'

Cost what it might, a real college, in the Oxford and Cambridge sense, they would have. The early beginning and ambitious dimensions of the first building show that the Overseers were of that mind; and Dunster bravely pushed the building to completion, in the midst of depression. How he obtained the money, for the building cost about £1000, we do not know. John Harvard's legacy (such part as Eaton did not make off with) was plowed into it; the 'Countrys gift' (the original £400 granted by the General Court) was doled out by instalments as the bills came in; and individual planters gave donations ranging from a few shillings up to £40. A committee sent to England to obtain funds for the impoverished colony gathered a few hundred pounds for the College, including our first scholarship fund, £100 from Lady Anne (Radcliffe) Mowlson, as well as £150 for other purposes, which the General Court appropriated for a presidential lodge on the site of the Peyntree House. At length, just before the first Harvard Commencement, in 1642, President Dunster had the satisfaction of gathering his pupils, till then 'dispersed in the town and miserably distracted in their times of concourse,' under one roof. The 'Old College,' or simply 'Harvard College,' as this building was called, stood in the Yard behind the Peyntree House, almost on the site of Grays Hall. It was the pride of the Colony, an edifice 'very faire and comely within and without, having in it a spacious Hall (where they daily meet at Commons, Lectures, Exercises), and a large Library with some Bookes to it, the gifts of diverse of our friends, their Chambers and studies also fitted for, and possessed by the Students, and all other roomes of Office necessary and convenient.' The plan, closely resembling that of a part of Eton College (where John Wilson of the Board of Overseers had gone to school), was E-shaped. The main part, a rectangle facing Massachusetts Avenue, contained the college hall for prayers, lectures, and meals, and the buttery, on the ground floor; a library and a 'long chamber' for freshmen overhead. Two wings extending north contained the kitchen and five large chambers for students. Access to the upper stories was by a square staircase turret that projected from the centre, like the short bar on a capital E. With its many jogs and gables and 'euill contrivall' of sills resting on the ground, the 'Old College' was unsuitable for the New England climate. It cost the College dear in repairs, and was abandoned after thirty-five years' use; but it had all the facilities for collegiate life on the English pattern, and made a brave showing. 'By some,' says a contemporary chronicler, it was thought 'to be too gorgeous for a Wilderness.' The complaint of college boys being pampered by luxury began early!

It was a triumph to move into this 'Old College' in 1642, there to celebrate the first Commencement in English academic style, with Latin and Greek orations and disputations, dinner spread for fifty in the new hall, and the conferring of degrees on nine young men according to the immemorial rite. But President Dunster now had a new 'burthen . . . to bee their steward, and to Direct their brewer, baker, buttler, Cook, how to proportion their commons.' No more than his predecessor did Dunster escape complaints at the commons, but the college beer, at a halfpenny a quart, appears to have given satisfaction. For many years, until the Colony went on a specie basis, the students paid their term bills, commons, and sizings (bread and beer) largely in commodities: beef, mutton, and cattle on the hoof; wheat, corn, rye, and barley; malt, flour, and meal; butter, eggs, and cheese; turnips, apples, and parsnips; even boots and shoes, various sorts of cloth, boards and hardware, and, in single instances, a saddle and a sword. Such of these commodities as the College Steward was unable to turn into drinkables and eatables he had to sell, somehow. Half Cambridge was shod with the shoes that John Glover, a merchant's son, turned in for his college expenses.

Finance was undoubtedly Dunster's greatest problem. He must have had the faith that moves mountains. Every college of the British Isles was well endowed at the start with lands, rents, and tithes sufficient to maintain a dozen or more fellows (who were paid extra for teaching) and a number of poor scholars, and to keep the buildings repaired. Harvard had no endowment; revenue-producing legacies and gifts came in very slowly; and the colonial governments refused to assume the burden of support. The General Court of Massachusetts did celebrate Dunster's accession by granting the College the revenues of the Boston-Charlestown ferry (the shortest route to Cambridge), which brought in £30 to £40 a year, payable mostly in wampumpeag (the small change of the Bay Colony), and 'badd and unfinished peague' at that.

Dunster complained that all the fake wampum in New England found its way into the college treasury. Modern college treasurers as they check over their securities and contemplate handsomely engraved certificates of Wildcat Oil and Kreuger & Toll may sympathize with President Dunster and Treasurer Danforth, picking over sundry fathoms of ferry wampum in the hope of salvaging a few bushels of genuine merchantable shell.

A committee of the General Court that audited the college accounts in 1654 reported that Dunster had run Harvard College for twelve years on an average annual budget of £175, of which he kept £55 as salary. This budget included the tuition fees of £1 6s 8d per annum, and the Commencement fees, which (according to the custom of Cambridge colleges) were £3 for each B.A. or M.A.; but not commons, which were self-supporting. And the only way that Dunster obtained these inconsiderable sums to dispose of was through the generosity of the plain people of New England. Thomas Shepard appealed in 1644 to the New England Confederation of Massachusetts Bay, Connecticut, New Haven, and Plymouth Colonies; and they recommended that 'for advance of learneing' each family in New England contribute a peck of wheat or a shilling in money to Harvard College, for fellowships and scholarships. The colonies 'chearfully embraced' this scheme; and for eight years enough came in through this 'Colledge Corne,' as it was called, to support the entire teaching staff of the College, except the President, and to assist ten or twelve poor scholars. Gradually the 'Colledge Corne' petered out; and in 1654 the General Court of Massachusetts began to raise by taxation £100 per annum for the President's salary, which released other slender funds for supporting scholars and paying the teaching fellows.

Nevertheless, the financial structure of the College remained precarious until near the end of the century, when Sir Matthew Holworthy's bequest of £1000 eased for a time the Treasurer's problem. This particular donation, like many others of the century, came from England, where Harvard was in high favor among dissenters, and where a little nucleus of graduates, ministers for the most part of dissenting chapels, kept interest alive in the overseas college. The rents of a farm in Norfolk, donated by a London merchant named Pennoyer in 1670, continued to be paid to Harvard College until 1903, when the farm was sold and the proceeds funded. Most of the colonial gifts and bequests to the College were (for want of any suitable medium for investment) in wild land, which could seldom be rented and was often as not seized by squatters; but the College Farm at Billerica, joint gift of the Town of Cambridge and of President Dunster in 1649, paid annual rent until its sale in 1775; and the 'College Marsh,' a tract of salt meadow in what is now Revere, devised by John Cogan of Boston in 1652 'for the use benifitt and behoofe of the President and fellows of the sayd Colledg,' paid from £4 to £25 a year until its sale in 1831. On extraordinary occasions community subscriptions were made; a group of ten merchants of Portsmouth, New Hampshire, guaranteed the College £60 a year for seven years, in 1669, and made good with lumber products that the College Treasurer sold; and in 1672 a subscription was circulated for a new college building. Although an Indian war interrupted, the several towns of Massachusetts, New Hampshire, and Maine provided almost £2000 to build Old Harvard Hall, first occupied in 1677.

A lucky windfall from an unexpected quarter in the Bahamas enabled President Dunster to enlarge the Yard and buildings in 1651. A group of needy puritan exiles from Bermuda, who had settled on the island of Eleuthera in the Bahamas, were sent a shipload of provisions by the people of Boston and neighboring towns, and Nathaniel White (A.B. 1646), son of the Eleutheran pastor, was sent down as supercargo. The people of Eleuthera returned the ship laden with 'ten Tuns of Brasiletto wood . . . as a stock for your Colledges use . . . that wee may expresse how sensible wee are of Gods love and tender Care of us manifested in yours; and avoid that foule sin of ingratitude so abhorred of God, so hatefull to all men.' The Brazil wood fetched £124, which was used to buy the Goffe house and cowyard adjoining the College Yard on the west, and possibly also to obtain the lot on which Holyoke House stands. 'Goffe College,' as it was renamed, was fitted up with chambers and studies for students, who were already taxing the resources of the Old College; and several other studies were contrived in lean-tos to the President's Lodge. From 1638 to 1794 the eastern boundary of the Yard ran from the site of the east end of Holworthy to the east end of Grays. The estate next adjoining on the east, a combination of several cowyards and pasture lots, belonged to the successive ministers of Cambridge until acquired by President Leverett, and afterwards to the two Professor Edward Wigglesworths. On the other side of this Leverett-Wigglesworth estate was a small parcel whose history offers the first example of Harvard men clubbing together to purchase property for Alma Mater. John Bulkeley and George Downing of the Class of 1642, and Samuel Winthrop and John Alcock of the Class of 1646, purchased it when still a cowyard, set out apple trees, and named it the 'Fellows' Orchard' — Bulkeley and Downing being the first teaching fellows of the College. It had all been deeded or bequeathed to Harvard College by 1649.

In 1650 President Dunster was able to obtain from the General Court the Charter under which Harvard University still operates. The President and Treasurer and five fellows were incorporated as the President and Fellows of Harvard College ('The Corporation' as we still call it), and given perpetual succession. It was doubtless Dunster's intention that all five fellows should receive stipends to teach or study, as in the English colleges of the time; but the state of the college funds forbade. The Charter of 1650 continued the Board of Overseers, as organized in 1642, as a second governing board; and, composed as it was of magistrates and ministers, the Board of Overseers remained the dominant governing board until 1686, when it was temporarily suspended by a change in government.

The constant interference in the affairs of the College by the Overseers was resented by Dunster, and the failure of the community to give the College more adequate support preyed on his mind. Around 1654 there were about fifty or sixty students in College, including graduates studying for the Master's degree; boys had been sent to Harvard from Bermuda, Virginia, and New Amsterdam as well as from England, where Harvard degrees had been accepted by Oxford and Cambridge as equivalent to their own. Dunster had a right to feel that as far as standards and quality were concerned he could do no more, and a committee of the General Court, appointed to investigate the financial affairs of the College, reported that he had managed the affairs of the House with complete integrity and the most rigid economy. Still, there were no funds to maintain more than two teaching fellows, and these with such miserable stipends — not more than £12 a year — that the tutorial turnover was too rapid for efficient teaching. Ministers who neither taught nor received stipends sometimes had to be elected fellows in order to maintain a quorum on the Corporation.

It is possible that these difficulties would have been surmounted, and that Dunster would have lived long enough to gather the harvest of his early efforts, if he had not embraced what his contemporaries in New England regarded as an abominable heresy — the historically correct belief that infant baptism is 'unscriptural' and that, following the primitive Church practice, only adult believers should be christened. He refused to allow his youngest child to be baptized, and interrupted the public baptism of another Cambridge infant. The news that the President of Harvard had gone 'antipaedobaptist' aroused as much consternation in the community as if President Conant should announce his adherence to the Third International. For the orgies of the Baptist pioneers in Germany had affected the English mind much as the exploits of the Russian Bolsheviki have created in the American mind a fearsome image of Communism. There was a law on the statute books of Massachusetts against questioning infant baptism, and several respectable citizens, for professing the objectionable tenet in a less offensive manner than the Harvard President, had been deported to Rhode Island, the home of religious liberty. So the only alternative for Dunster was to resign, or recant. He was treated with a consideration rare in that era of religious intolerance — labored with by fellow-ministers, and begged by the Overseers to stay, on the sole condition of keeping quiet on religious topics; but he was man enough to stand up for the faith that was in him, and in October, 1654, proffered his resignation, which was regretfully accepted. Shortly after, he retired to Scituate in the Plymouth Colony, where a small Baptist congregation was tolerated; and there he died in 1659, after declining an invitation to become minister of a Congregational church in Ireland.

Dunster's genius for organization was such that the curriculum, the forms, and the institutions established under his presidency long outlasted his time, and even his century. Harvard University grew out of the Liberal Arts college as Dunster left it; and the Charter of 1650 that he obtained, and in all probability drafted, still serves as constitution of the modern University.

II

SCHOOL OF THE PROPHETS

THE organization, the life, and the studies of Harvard College in the seventeenth century are difficult for a modern college graduate to appreciate, or even to grasp. Just as our New England puritans, despite their 'anti-popery,' were much nearer in thought, feeling, and doctrine to the Catholic Church than to most of their own descendants, so Harvard in the puritan century was far closer to a college of medieval Paris or Oxford than to the Harvard that even the oldest reader of this book can remember. *Tempora mutantur*, and especially in America the universities have been forced *mutare in illis*; but many ancient ceremonies and ways of doing things which have been preserved in the English colleges long after they had lost their meaning or purpose, have been scrapped at Harvard in the name of efficiency, or simply blown up by expansion. The University of Cambridge in 1636 had almost as many colleges as she has today, and not far from as many students; but Harvard confers more A.B.'s every year nowadays than she did in the entire seventeenth century, and as many more of other and higher degrees. Ancient as the buildings in the Harvard Yard seem, in comparison with those of most American universities, there is not one that dates further back than 1720; and of early Harvard institutions, little is left save the Charter, the Governing Boards, the names of the four undergraduate classes, and the ceremony of Commencement.

The choice of Cambridge has proved irrevocable, although there was talk in the 1670's of shifting to Boston, and the War of Independence required a temporary sojourn at Concord. At no time in three centuries have the Harvard authorities anticipated the need for physical expansion. University grounds have been added to bit by bit as the need arose — mostly by purchase, rarely by gift. At Dunster's death, as we have seen, the Yard consisted of a strip about 110 feet wide running through from Braintree Street (the lane since widened, at the expense of the Yard, into Massachusetts Avenue) to the Charlestown Path, at the point where its present equivalent, Kirkland Street, is joined by Cambridge Street. At the southern end of the Yard were the three college buildings: the monumental though prematurely mouldy Old College at about the site of Grays; the President's Lodge, on or in front of the site of Wadsworth House; and Goffe College, the transformed dwelling just west of it. The Indian College, built shortly after Dunster's departure, completed this informal open quadrangle. The Fellows' Orchard on the site of part of Widener, and the site of Holyoke House, were the only other grounds that the College owned. In Chauncy's time the Betts cowyard just west of Goffe was purchased from money given and bequeathed by the Paines of Ipswich; and when it was decided to replace the Old College and Goffe by a new brick building, Old Harvard Hall was constructed on the northern end of this lot, on the exact site of the present Harvard Hall. Old Harvard, first occupied in 1677, was a four-storied brick building, with a gambrel roof and twelve gables. It contained all the necessary public rooms such as hall, library, buttery and kitchen, two tutors' chambers, and twelve chambers with corner studies for students.

Old Harvard became the focal point for a re-orientation of the college buildings into the open quadrangle shown on the well-known 'Prospect of the Colledges in Cambridge' published in 1726. The Spencer orchard north of Harvard was purchased in 1697, but almost a

century elapsed before any more of the present College
Yard was added. In 1699 Stoughton College (not to be
confused with the present Stoughton Hall) was built at
right angles to Old Harvard to the southeast, completing
the new open quadrangle with Old Harvard and a new
President's Lodge, which in turn was replaced by Massachusetts Hall, our oldest existing building, in 1720. These
'colleges,' as they were collectively called, were built of
the best materials and in the best style of which the colonists were capable. They contained every comfort known
to the times, for the notion that college students should
'live like gentlemen' came over with our founders.

The purpose that established and maintained early
Harvard at such pains and sacrifice is not very different
from that which makes the University an object of energy,
devotion, and benevolence today; only the emphasis has
changed from the religious to the secular. Harvard was a
religious college, but emphatically not a 'divinity school'
or a seminary for the propagation of puritan theology —
although the Mathers would have made her just that.
The difference was very nearly that between a Catholic
university of today and a Catholic diocesan seminary.
Harvard was founded, and in the seventeenth century
supported, as a college of English university standards for
the liberal education of the young men of New England,
under strict religious discipline. 'Several worthy persons
in our primitiue times,' declared the General Court in
1671, were stirred up by 'our Gratious God of his Diuine
favour . . . to lay the foundaitons of Good Learning and
Literature at Harvard Colledge.' President Oakes addressed a graduating class in 1677 as *liberi liberaliter edu-
cati*, 'gentlemen, educated like gentlemen.' And in 1721
the resident fellows declared, 'Now the great End for
which the College was founded, was a Learned, and pious
Education of Youth, their Instruction in Languages,
Arts, and Sciences, and having their minds and manners

form'd aright.' Manners (mark you!) as well as minds; the old formula with which the President presented seniors to the Overseers declared that they were sufficient *tam doctrina quam moribus* — 'as much in Learning as in Manners' — to be laureated Bachelors of Arts.

The Charter of 1650 nowhere mentions the training of ministers. The purposes of Harvard College stated in that fundamental document are 'the aduancement of all good literature artes and Sciences'; and making 'all other necessary prouisions that may conduce to the education of the English and Indian Youth of this Country in knowledge and godlines.' And 'New Englands First Fruits,' the pamphlet of 1643 that is equivalent to an official statement of the founding fathers, strikes a nice balance between the general purposes of the College and the dynamic motive of founding it: 'to advance *Learning* and perpetuate it to Posterity; dreading to leave an illiterate Ministry to the Churches.' A learned clergy was the immediate and pressing social need that Harvard was expected to supply; but the advancement of learning, both on the part of individuals and in respect to the world's stock of knowledge, was the broad purpose of the College; and prospective parsons, up to the Bachelor's degree, were given exactly the same Liberal Arts course as other boys who had no such ambition. Many students were so ambitious. In seventeenth-century New England, as in medieval Europe, the Church offered the most attractive career to a scholarly young man, especially to one who wished to rise in the world. Medicine was not yet a learned profession, and the law not even a profession. A New England parson was *ex officio* a gentleman and a member of the ruling class. He was, to be sure, ineligible for political office; and there were no deaneries or bishoprics in the Congregational Church; but consideration, respect, and even veneration, were his to a degree that a modern Protestant minister can hardly imagine. Until nearly the end of the century, the ablest young men of each class generally proceeded M.A. after three years and entered the Congregational ministry. In reference to this favorite profession of the typical Harvard man of the century, and to a medieval tradition that the Hebrews founded the first universities, the College was often referred to as 'the School of the Prophets,' and Harvard men were called 'the Sons of the Prophets.'

The early emphasis on a *liberal* education and the *advancement* of learning has never been lost sight of; although it was not until the last century that the University was able to contribute much to the enlarging of man's domain of knowledge. Harvard College, non-vocational (at least in intention), emphasizing the Liberal Arts, has always been central to Harvard University. Recently, at a time when many American universities were mangling their undergraduate department into junior colleges or inferior vocational schools, President Lowell put some of his best efforts into revitalizing the ancient conception of a liberal education. And in part this was effected by restoring the tutorial system and 'collegiate way of living' that the founders had established, and the nineteenth century nearly forgotten.

An important, and, as many will think, an essential, ingredient of this early liberal education was the religious spirit of Harvard. Our founders brought over this medieval Christian tradition undiluted. The Harvard student's day began and ended with public prayer: daily he heard a chapter of Scripture expounded by the President; Saturday was given up to catechizing and other preparations for the Sabbath, which was wholly devoted to worship, meditation — and surreptitious mischief. Harvard students were reminded in their college laws, and by their preceptors, that the object of their literary and scientific studies was the greater knowledge of God; and that the acquisition of knowledge for its own sake, without 'laying

Christ in the bottome, as the only foundation,' was futile and sinful. 'In Christi Gloriam' appeared on the college seal of 1650; and 'Veritas' on the original design of the college arms undoubtedly meant (as it did to Dante) the divine truth. President Dunster's Harvard was so closely modelled on English university colleges (where the religious emphasis was equally strong) that, but for the distance, it might well have been affiliated with one of the English universities when they came under puritan control. This meant, for one thing, that 'young gentlemen' of no serious scholastic intentions were welcome, as well as serious students; even 'fellow-commoners' who paid double tuition, dined with the fellows, and alone of undergraduates were addressed as 'Mr.,' were invited by Dunster; and as one-third of this privileged class took no degree, one suspects that, as in England, special courses of light and gentlemanly reading were arranged for them. Everyone who wished to graduate had to follow a rigidly prescribed course; there was no flexibility as in England, where the university requirements were a bare minimum to which the colleges added as they saw fit.

From England, too, came the names of the four classes: freshman, sophomore, junior sophister, and senior sophister. The last three long since became obsolete in England, but in their abbreviated form have spread throughout the United States. 'Sophomore' originally meant a student who was doing his 'sophomes' or college disputations, the successful performance of which made him *sophista*, sufficiently learned in Logic to take part in the public disputations. These battles of wit in Latin, according to a traditional pattern, were as much a feature of seventeenth-century Harvard as of Paris in the days of Abélard; every sophister had to dispute twice a week, and senior sophisters must be ready to perform publicly at Commencement. Just before they graduated, the seniors were called 'Questionists' at Harvard, because one of the duties of the medieval candidate for the baccalaureate was to reply to a question out of Aristotle's Prior Analytics; M.A. candidates were called *Inceptores* or Inceptors (Commencers), because the medieval Commencement was for Masters only. The English universities had already put their greatest stress on the course for the B.A., leaving the M.A. candidates to study by themselves for three years, and return to the university to go through some new paces before obtaining the second degree in Arts. Harvard followed their example, and made a precedent for all later American universities by regarding the date of the *first* degree as the date of graduation.

Harvard students were mostly prepared for college at one of the grammar schools on the English model, of which there were several in New England, the most famous being the Hopkins of New Haven, the Boston Latin, and the Cambridge Grammar School, to which boys were often sent from a distance for preparation. Others were 'fitted for college,' as the old phrase ran, by a local minister. The earliest entrance requirements were extempore translation of Cicero and ability to write and speak Latin *suo ut aiunt Marte* (by one's own skill), and a little Greek grammar; this was enlarged under Chauncy to include parsing 'ordinary Greeke, as in the Greeke Testament, Isocrates, and the minor poets,' the payment of a quarter's expenses, and filing a bond against evading bills in future. The oral examination was held by the President and tutors shortly after Commencement; if everything was in order, the candidate made a copy of the college laws, to which the President signed his *admittatur*. He was assigned to a chamber with two or three other students, one of them generally a classmate, and one, if it could be so arranged, a resident B.A. or senior sophister; and from these chamber-fellows or chums the freshman doubtless learned as much as from his books.

Usually it was not until sophomore year that he rented a study, one of the little four-by-six closets let into the angles of the chamber; but after Old Harvard was built, everyone had a study. As late as the 1830's, Harvard students paid the College 'study rent'; a place in a chamber was theoretically gratis.

Our freshman next paid the Steward a shilling to have his name posted in the buttery, and became a member of the House, as Harvard College was familiarly called. His order in the list of names on the 'buttery table' (bulletin board) was a matter of great pith and moment, for the order of seniority there shown determined the student's precedence through college, and even in the catalogue of graduates, unless he lost place by neglecting his studies or by misbehavior. Originally Harvard 'kept' throughout the year, like the English colleges; but late in the century there was a vacation after Commencement, which stretched out to six weeks.

Once entered, the freshman found that besides his studies he was expected to play errand-boy and unpaid servant to the sophisters. These 'abuses' in sending freshmen upon 'private Errands' were complained of by the Overseers as early as 1667, and ordered to be eradicated; but by that time freshman fagging had become an old college custom. One of his first duties was to procure bread and beer for his seniors at the buttery hatch; for 'morning bever,' as breakfast was called, consisted of nothing else, and was consumed in the students' chambers or in the Yard, if the weather was warm and pleasant.

Morning bever was preceded by college prayers at five o'clock, and followed by a study hour before the eight o'clock lecture. Lectures were generally of the medieval sort: the class tutor read aloud from some prescribed textbook in Latin, and the students took notes, or followed the reading in a text of their own. Dinner came at eleven, or at noon late in the century. It was a formal feast in the college hall (which had been used for lectures all the morning), preceded by 'asking a blessing' and concluded by 'giving thanks.' Resident fellows and fellow-commoners sat at a head or high table adorned by silver, with the 'great salt' (still owned by the College) in the centre; the undergraduates eating from wooden trenchers, drinking beer from pewter 'cue-cups,' and providing their own knives and spoons. Forks were still a luxury beyond scholars. A peculiar Harvard custom was the wearing of one's hat in commons; it was a form of punishment to dine uncovered.

After dinner came the recreation hour; then recitations in your tutor's chamber, where you were quizzed on the morning lecture, or disputations in hall for the sophisters, moderated by the President. Around half-past four or five the college bell tolled for 'afternoon bever,' and the welcome creak of the buttery hatch opening was heard, as the graduate-student butler stood ready to serve out more 'sizings' of bread and beer. Evening prayers came at five; then a study hour; and supper at half-past seven. A recreation hour extended after supper until nine; and except in summer it was probably spent around the hall fire, talking and smoking. 'Taking tobacco,' at first allowed only with parent's permission on doctor's orders, became so general before 1660 that the Steward sold the baneful herb.

In an era of tallow dips, students were not expected to study at night, and most of them were probably ready to retire at the ringing of the nine o'clock bell; but they might if they chose 'watch' — that is, stay up with a light in their studies — until eleven.

The intention of the college laws was to confine Harvard students to the College and the Yard twenty-four hours in the day; they were forbidden to frequent taverns, leave Cambridge, join a military company, or 'frequent the company and society of such men as lead an ungirt and dissolute life.' The college authorities were fairly liberal in letting students visit their homes for a few days in term time; and an occasional drowning accident indicates the prevalence of bathing in Fresh Pond or the Charles in summer, and skating in winter. There are some suggestions that gunning and fishing might occasionally be indulged in; but at best, until a century ago, Harvard students were too much cloistered and confined for their health and well-being. Youthful spirits broke out in an occasional brawl with the townspeople, or among the students, with consequent damage to the college windows. The 'Scholars of the House,' in return for an annual stipend of £5, were supposed to aid in preventing disorders, and check up on damages when they occurred. In the late 1670's, the post-war period of the century, there was an epidemic of turkey stealing with the connivance of unsavory Cambridge characters, followed by a midnight supper in college chamber or town alehouse; and the new fiery beverage known as 'Rumme or Kill-Devil' began to give trouble. A student's notebook of the year 1671 records the tradition of a dirty trick played on President Dunster. A group of scholars, having previously smeared the hand-holds on the staircase with 'sir reverence,' made a row in the top of the turret to call the President up. 'Who did this foul deed?' thundered the President. 'Whoever did it, it seems you had a hand in it!' said a bold wag.

In the prescribed course for the B.A., which varied very slightly from Dunster's day to Leverett's, one can discern three elements: the 'Seven Liberal Arts' and 'Three Philosophies' as studied in the medieval universities; the reading of *bonae litterae* or classical belles-lettres; and the study of the 'learned tongues.' The last two elements had entered university curricula at the Renaissance. Harvard put special emphasis on Logic and Rhetoric, Greek and

Hebrew, Ethics and Metaphysics; she was distinctly weak in Mathematics, as the English universities were until the age of Newton; and (until the close of the century) in Natural Science, as all universities were outside the Netherlands. A knowledge of Latin was taken for granted, and almost all the textbooks, even the Greek and Hebrew grammars, were in that tongue.

This curriculum was well adapted for a general education in the seventeenth and early eighteenth centuries. Through Logic (which was studied from Ramus, Milton, Keckermann, and sundry other manuals supposed to be an improvement on Aristotle) the freshman's mind was 'broken in to keep thought's beaten track.'[1] Rhetoric, studied from classical texts, manuals, and collections of *flores*, and practised constantly by declamations in English and Latin, taught him how to speak and write with 'clearness, force, and elegance.' In Greek the students went much further than the New Testament, with which freshmen were supposed to be familiar after 1655. The usual books read were gnomic or edifying authors, especially Isocrates, whose shrewd advice for getting on in the world was combined with high moral precepts in a manner peculiarly acceptable to the New England character. Homer and Hesiod were also read, and some students owned an anthology of Greek lyrics and idylls.

The only new or peculiar feature of the Harvard curriculum in comparison with that of Oxford and Cambridge was the attention given to Hebrew and allied languages. The humanists had urged that Hebrew, as the reputed *Ursprache* of the western world, be placed beside Greek; but seldom had this been accomplished. The emphasis at Harvard may have been due to a desire to give every educated man the key to the Old Testament; but the real reason, one suspects, was the fact that Presidents Dunster and Chauncy were Hebraists. In Dunster's programme,

[1] Goethe, *Faust*, ll. 1910–15.

the freshmen study Hebrew Grammar; the junior sophisters, the Aramaic books of the Old Testament; the senior sophisters, the Syriac New Testament. The same requirements are found in the Jesuit *Ratio Studiorum* of 1599.

In Ethics, the Harvard students used Aristotle and manuals based on him; and, late in the century, Henry More's *Enchiridion Ethicum*; their Metaphysics was largely Aristotelian; Astronomy and Physics (which then comprehended almost all Natural Science) in Dunster's day were purely Aristotelian; but the Copernican system replaced the Ptolemaic before 1660, and in 1686 a manuscript manual of science by Charles Morton, which included scientific discoveries of the century, replaced Magirus's dismal manual of scholastic physics. There appear to have been no experimental facilities until the next century, with the exception of the college telescope presented by Governor John Winthrop, F.R.S., in 1672; with this Thomas Brattle (A.B. 1676) made observations of the comet of 1680 that won the commendation of Newton in his *Principia*. Slight and generally obsolete as was the science studied at Harvard in the seventeenth century, the annual New England almanacs, compiled largely by tutors and resident B.A.'s, informed the farming population on the discoveries of Galileo, Kepler, and Gassendi.

The intellectual life of the College was not confined to prescribed studies. A few students' commonplace books that have come down to us, dated between 1650 and 1680, indicate that some of the undergraduates read widely in the English poets and prose-writers of the Elizabethan and Jacobean ages, and copied ballads, of an amorous and even facetious nature, that they either read or heard sung. There are even a few hints of music being played, and part singing, apart from the metrical psalms that formed a part of divine service; but no effort was made to teach music until the nineteenth century. The

College Library, old as the College itself, played very little part in the undergraduate's course. He was admitted to it only on sufferance, and obtained his books from his college predecessors, or from Boston booksellers. Joseph Browne, a fellow-commoner of the Class of 1666, began in college to accumulate a 'gentleman's library'; and within a decade we find several students having printed *ex libris* struck off for them, like those that President Dunster had printed for himself when a student at the University of Cambridge. The College Library, predominantly though not overwhelmingly theological and philosophical, was used mostly by graduate students.

All four undergraduate classes were instructed in a body, like grades in grammar school, although there must have been much individual attention when a class of ten was large, and tutors shared their chambers with pupils. The tutorial method of instruction, which dates back to the fourteenth century at Oxford and Cambridge, could not be reproduced in its entirety for want of revenue to support a sufficient number of tutors. Harvard, by necessity, continued the medieval tradition that the proper teacher for undergraduates was a young man who had just been through the mill, and that each teacher should instruct in every subject of the curriculum.

Written examinations are of comparatively recent date in university history, and courses are of yesterday. Early Harvard students were promoted or demoted on their tutor's report of their industry and ability. Degrees were a more serious matter; and the senior sophisters had to go through a form of examination inherited from the middle ages. For a couple of weeks from June 10 they had to sit in the college hall from nine to eleven in the forenoon, and on certain afternoons, 'to bee examined by all Commers' (which in practice meant certain Overseers) in the subjects of the curriculum. This was called 'sitting solstices,' and with some modifications lasted until 1870.

Theoretically, any Master of Arts might drop in and quiz the 'questionists' (as the B.A. candidates were called); actually, the examining (or 'Visitation' as it was called) seems to have been done by the university alumni on the Board of Overseers, who either asked questions or pitted two or more students against each other in a disputation. If no visitor showed up, the President probably set the ball a-rolling. Latin disputations, another medieval legacy, were an important educational method for which no effective substitute has been found in modern times. The Harvard students were continually practising them; and the final performance came on Commencement Day,[1] which in the seventeenth century generally came in July or August.

For some weeks beforehand the Steward had been laying in spices, sack, and substantial provisions for the Commencement feast, to which all university graduates and all magistrates and ministers of the New England Colonies were invited. 'Turnspit Indians' were engaged to see that the beeves were properly roasted before the great kitchen fireplace. The cost of this lavish entertainment fell by ancient usage on the graduating class, each member of which paid £3, more than a year's tuition, with additional tips to Steward and cook. The morning ceremonies were for the Bachelors. A local clergyman delivered a Latin salutatory oration; chosen seniors orated in the learned tongues; and disputations were held among the others on theses (propositions) selected from the printed thesis sheet, a broadside compiled by the graduating class, dedicated in flowery Latin to the as-assembled dignitaries, and printed at the seniors' expense on the college press. This practice apparently

---

[1] The word came from Cambridge, and is simply a translation of *Inceptio*, the 'beginning' of one's being a member of the Masters' gild in medieval Paris. The ceremony was a form of initiation, the original purpose of the commencement parts being to allow the graduates to 'show their stuff,' as it were.

came from the University of Edinburgh, where it was customary for learned members of the audience to catch the moderator's eye and challenge one of the printed propositions, which some degree candidate then had to defend. There is record of this happening once or twice at Harvard, but usually the programme went through without interruption. At the end of it the President proposed the candidates' names to the Overseers, in a formula which may be translated:

> Honourable Gentlemen and Reverend Ministers, I present to you these youths, whom I know to be sufficient in learning as in manners to be raised to the First Degree in Arts, according to the custom of the Universities in England. Doth it please you?

The Overseers replied *placet*, and the President then conferred the degrees individually, at the same time handing each candidate a book (which had to be promptly returned):

> I admit thee to the First Degree in Arts, namely to reply to the Question, according to the custom of the Universities in England. And I hand thee this book, together with the power to lecture publicly on any one of the Arts which thou hast studied, whensoever thou shalt have been called to that office.

Both formulae and the ceremonies were combinations of several parts of the very complicated, prolonged, and expensive baccalaureate ceremonies at the University of Cambridge, and more telescoping was done by having the Masters' Commencement in the afternoon of the same day.

The Master's degree was taken at the traditional space of three years after the Bachelor's; and, as in England, the requirements for it were so slight that a large majority of B.A.'s proceeded M.A. in course. It was not even necessary to reside in college; one only had to return to Cambridge before Commencement in time to discuss a philosophical problem or give a 'commonplace' (sample sermon), to hand in a synopsis of Arts, and to reply to a question (prepared beforehand, and the subject printed) at Masters' Commencement in the afternoon. The B.A.'s who were planning to become ministers resided in college if they could afford it, or received a scholarship or fellowship; but they paid no tuition, and received no instruction, unless from the President. They were supposed to spend their time reading Theology and Philosophy in the College Library, which existed largely for their benefit. M.A. candidates not intending to embrace a clerical career replied on a medical or philosophical or literary *quaestio* at Commencement. This practice of taking the second degree in course was rendered progressively easier until in the nineteenth century it was a saying that all a Harvard man had to do for his Master's degree was to pay five dollars and stay out of jail. The sudden falling off of M.A.'s after the Class of 1869 in the printed Catalogue of Graduates marks the abandonment of this last vestige of the *septennium* considered necessary to make a full-fledged 'Artist.'

The granting of degrees was the boldest thing President Dunster and the first Board of Overseers did; for the conferring of academic titles was a jealously guarded prerogative of sovereignty, to be exercised only by express grant from pope, emperor, or king. It raised Harvard from the status of a collegiate school to a university college; and gave a new incentive to the students, especially after Oxford and Cambridge had recognized Harvard degrees as equivalent to theirs. And in spite of the decline in members just following the mid-century, and the very slow increment of endowment and revenue, New Englanders rightly regarded their College with pride and satisfaction. As President Mather wrote in 1688:

The *Colledge* by Ingenuous and Civil Education hath had its proper Influence. The *Colledge* which *we* say was a *Noble* and *Necessary* Work, and therefore deserves all Encouragement and Promotion. *Noble*; for where is the Like in all the English America? where, even among those that in wealth do far Exceed the poor Laborious New-Englanders, is there any such thing? And *Necessary* too; for else the Rising Generations would have soon become Barbarous; because neither would their Estates reach to seek Education in *England*; neither would any person of worth goe from hence (unless driven by Persecution) so far off to seek Employment when he might have it nearer home. 'T was therefore a brave and happy thought that first pitched upon this *Colledge.* . . .

III

DECLINE AND REVIVAL

CHARLES CHAUNCY, who succeeded Dunster as President in 1654, was a much older and more experienced man than his predecessor. Member of an ancient landed family of Hertfordshire, he entered Westminster School a few weeks before the memorable gunpowder plot, and was elected scholar to Trinity College in the year that Dunster was born. From Trinity, already the richest and most famous Cambridge college, he took both Arts degrees near the head of his class, and as a fellow of Trinity received one of the two lectureships in Greek, George Herbert having the other. These appointments indicate that Chauncy became a puritan only after he had left the University and obtained an ecclesiastical living. During the reign of Charles I his tender conscience in the matter of ceremonies got him in trouble with the authorities; and after suspension from office and a short term in prison, he emigrated to the Plymouth Colony. There, his insistence on the total immersion of infants in baptism proved 'not so conveniente' (as Governor Bradford complained) 'in this could countrie,' and after his colleagues had ruled against him he was about to return to his English parish, when the Harvard Overseers induced him to accept the presidency on condition that he keep his peculiar ideas on baptism to himself. More logical and accommodating than Dunster, he reflected that college presidents had no occasion to administer baptismal rites, and accepted.

Chauncy was a learned and devoted President, no innovator or organizer, and content to walk in the footsteps of his predecessor. It was not Chauncy, but growing materialism, that brought about a decline of numbers in the student body, compared with the relatively high enrolment of Dunster's last days. Ascetic in his life (despite the six sons, all of whom took both Harvard degrees), and a glutton for pious observances, he imposed on the students a stiff regimen of prayer, catechism, and repeating sermons; yet he was also interested in modern science, and stamped with his approval the almanac compiled by Zechariah Brigden (A.B. 1657), in which the Ptolemaic astronomy was ridiculed and the Galilean system recommended to the farmers of New England. And in his last year of office Harvard acquired her first telescope, the means of making original scientific observations.

President Dunster bequeathed to his successor all his 'mathematicke bookes' and the 'great press in the hall chamber' of the President's Lodge. A less welcome legacy was the experiment of Indian education. A persistent delusion of English colonists, from the early days of Virginia to the founding of Dartmouth College, was the notion that the proper way to civilize an Indian was to catch him and send him to college. President Dunster himself undertook to prepare some promising young redskins for Harvard, but they never managed to make the grade. He did, however, prepare the way for a relatively large-scale educational experiment by inducing the English Society for Propagation of the Gospel in New England to build and subsidize an 'Indian College' in the Harvard Yard. This building, a neat two-story brick structure, with chambers and studies for twenty Indian students, was erected about 1655 just west of the Old College, across the site of the southern end of Matthews Hall. A dozen or more Indian youths were sent to Master Corlet of the Cambridge Latin School to be prepared for college; but not more than four or five ever managed to enter, and of those but one, Caleb Cheeshahteaumuck, took his degree; and he died of tuberculosis within a year.

His classmate Joel Iacoomes, like him from Martha's Vineyard, would have appeared in the Catalogue of Graduates after Caleb but for an unfortunate accident. On a visit home shortly before Commencement his vessel ran ashore on Nantucket, where the heathen Indians plundered the wreck and murdered Joel. President Chauncy dutifully undertook to instruct these 'nasty salvages' (as he once described them), since the tutor specially provided for them turned out idle and drunken; and doubtless he was relieved when, after 1665, no more came. The Indian College was turned over to pale-faces, and to the printing press, until its demolition in 1698.

In a lower room of the Indian College flourished the first American university press, after its removal from the President's Lodge around 1655. Originally imported in 1638, with the notion of printing puritan tracts prohibited in England, this press was enlarged at the expense of the English society with the long name, in order to print John Eliot's Indian translation of the Bible. In addition to a considerable Indian library, the college press produced almanacs, law books, broadsides, catechisms, psalm books, sermons, an occasional reprint of an English work, and a few books of poetry by New Englanders such as Anne Bradstreet, Michael Wigglesworth, and President Oakes. Until 1675, this and a local offshoot were the only printing presses in the English colonies; but after that date, when John Foster (A.B. 1667) set up a press in Boston, the printing business of New England gravitated to the metropolis.

President Chauncy's salary of £100, paid largely in country produce, did not suffice to support his large family; but after two gentle pleas for more consideration from the General Court, and a grant of wild land that was of no use to him, he kept silent and carried on to his eightieth year. Although disappointed in most of his efforts to obtain money, and disheartened by the low enrolment (the average size of graduating classes, 1661–1670, was seven), he was doubtless cheered by what one of its members called the 'great and yet civill' Class of 1671, eleven strong. In his day were graduated two of his successors, Increase Mather and Samuel Willard; Samuel Sewall, the diarist and judge; Abraham Pierson, the first Rector of Yale; Governor Joseph Dudley of Massachusetts, and Governor Nathaniel Higginson of Madras, who once headed a petition to Queen Anne to retire Governor Dudley from office; and Elisha Cooke, provincial politician who was a thorn in the side of Increase Mather. Among the more noted clergy of the Chauncy vintage were John Hale of Beverly, Solomon Stoddard of Northampton, and Moses Noyes of Old Lyme.

Chauncy died in 1672; and thirty-five years elapsed before the College obtained another President who combined such learning, devotion, and competence. His immediate successor, Leonard Hoar (A.B. 1650), started off with high hopes, but speedily came to grief. Hoar was one of the several Harvard graduates of Dunster's day who obtained ecclesiastical livings in England under Cromwell, only to be turned out of them in 1662 for declining to veer with the wind like the Vicar of Bray. Dr. Hoar was fortunate in having private means and medico-scientific interests; becoming friendly with some of the *virtuosi* who were patronized by Charles II, he was created Doctor of Medicine by the University of Cambridge at the King's command. At the same time he kept in touch with the dissenters, and his *Index Biblicus* was considered so scholarly that he was invited to come to Boston to be minister of the Old South Church. Shortly after Chauncy's death he arrived, bearing letters of recommendation from several dissenting ministers of London (some of them Harvard graduates) suggesting that he be elected President of the College. This was done; whereupon

President Hoar wrote an enthusiastic letter to his friend Robert Boyle proposing to establish a chemical laboratory, a botanic garden, and a mechanical workshop, 'for readings or notions only are but husky provender.' This was in line with the most advanced educational thought of the day; and if President Hoar had succeeded in his worthy ambition, Harvard would have been the first university college in the English-speaking world to incorporate this essential apparatus for the new experimental science.

The event proved otherwise. Dr. Hoar had not been President many months before symptoms of disgust and even revolt manifested themselves among the tutors and students. Contemporary allusions to the affair are exasperatingly indefinite. It was hinted, and may well be true, that Urian Oakes, the minister of Cambridge, was disappointed at not obtaining the presidency, and played trouble-maker. Yet it is doubtful if even he could have wrecked an administration that began with such promise; and the Overseers supported Hoar consistently. Probably, like many men of greater learning, he was temperamentally unsuited to administration; possibly his long sojourn in England had engendered a conceit that made him difficult to work with, overbearing to the young Fellows of the College, and unduly severe to the students. The flogging of one of them at the hands of a prison-keeper who was later dismissed for cruelty was hardly the way to establish discipline, even in the puritan century. Certainly there must have been something pompous or ridiculous about Hoar, since the students (wrote Cotton Mather, who was one of them) 'set themselves to Travestie whatever he did and said, and aggravate every thing in his Behaviour disagreable to them, with a Design to make him Odious.' Tutors resigned, and it was difficult to secure successors. The General Court held a hearing and tried to smooth out the difficulties; but in the winter of 1674–75 the students as a body deserted the College. In March, 1675, President Hoar resigned in despair, and not long after died of a broken heart. But he established one Harvard institution that has only recently come to an end: the series of triennial and quinquennial catalogues of graduates, arranged by classes. The *Sobolis Harvardinae Catalogum* of 1674 on a single sheet, dedicated to Governor Leverett, listing two hundred graduates by classes, and concluding with a Latin poem by the President on the infant *Academia in sylvis surgens*, is direct ancestor of the ponderous Quinquennial of 1930, with 65,584 names of holders of Harvard degrees.

After Hoar's experience, the College found great difficulty for the next thirty-four years in procuring a President. A clergyman was thought to be essential as head of the College; but New England parsons were supposed to remain a lifetime in the parishes that elected them as young men, unless released; and those considered presidential timber were generally so strongly attached to their parishes that they neither desired nor could obtain dismissal. Consequently, unless a parson could be captured on the fly, like Chauncy, or imported, like Hoar, only second-raters were available.

President Hoar's successor was his putative rival Urian Oakes (a.b. 1649). Like Hoar, he had been a minister in England under the Cromwellian Protectorate, and had returned to New England to succeed Jonathan Mitchell as minister of Cambridge. Oakes was elected President in 1675, within three weeks of Hoar's resignation, but consented to take the office only on the understanding that it was a temporary arrangement and that he need not resign his Cambridge pulpit. After five years of president-hunting had proved fruitless, Oakes consented to be President *de jure* as well as *de facto*, only to die in the summer of 1681.

Oakes was a little bit of a man, cram-full of learning,

intolerance, and choler. No mean poet in English, and a writer of vigorous prose, he has left on record a series of lengthy Latin Commencement orations that are models of academic punning and classical wit. On one occasion, for instance, he compared his presidency with the consulate of C. Caninius Rebilus who was consul for only part of a day, and of whom it was remarked that he neither ate nor slept during his term of office. 'I shall do better than that,' said Oakes, 'for I hope you won't fall asleep during this discourse, and I assure you that Commencement Dinner will be served promptly at its conclusion!' As King Philip's War came during his presidency, the graduating classes were reduced in numbers to a maximum of six and a minimum of three. Yet, through the charity of the people of Massachusetts Bay, and the energetic drumming up of subscriptions by the country clergy and others, Old Harvard Hall was completed in 1677 to replace the Old College. This building was the scene of the amusingly disparaging account of Harvard by two Dutch travellers in 1680. Approaching it from the Charlestown road (Kirkland Street), all was silence; but on rounding the corner of Old Harvard by the present Johnston Gate, they heard so much noise in an upper chamber that it seemed a disputation was going on. Entering, and ascending the stairs, they found 'eight or ten young fellows, sitting around, smoking tobacco' in a room so full of smoke that they thought it must be a tavern, not a college! The Dutchmen questioned the boys as best they could in halting English, since (as the visitors alleged) they 'knew hardly a word of Latin.' [1] After this imperfect conversation, and a visit to the Library, 'where there was nothing particular,' the students

---

[1] This is hardly credible, as we find students punished subsequent to this date for not speaking Latin in the College precincts. Undoubtedly the Dutchmen spoke Latin with the continental pronunciation, and the Harvard students with the English

drank a glass of wine with their visitors, who departed with a comfortable sense of superiority.

After the death of President Oakes, in the summer of 1681, almost nine months elapsed before John Rogers (A.B. 1649) of Ipswich was elected President; another twelvemonth passed before he consented to move to Cambridge and be inaugurated; and within a year he died, during a total eclipse of the sun. Once more the Corporation went a-begging for a President. After at least two ministers had declined, the Reverend Increase Mather of the Second Church in Boston consented to take it on the same terms as had Oakes: that he should not be expected to give up his church, but would devote such time as he could to the College until a permanent and resident President could be found. Yet, although he never resided more than a few months in Cambridge, Mather's presidency stretched out into the next century.

On May 14, 1686, not quite a year after Mather's presidency began, Joseph Dudley (A.B. 1665) received a royal commission as President of the Council for New England, superseding the Massachusetts Bay Charter under which the Colony had been governed since 1629. Dudley (although he later reversed his opinion) regarded the College Charter voided with that of the Colony — 'the Calf died in the Cow's belly,' as he put it bluntly. The government of the College was now at the disposal of the King and his Viceroy. But neither Dudley, who was a loyal son of Harvard, nor his successor Sir Edmund Andros, who was not, had any desire to interfere with the free functioning of Harvard College, or to twist it away from the puritan tradition. President and Council for New England requested Mather to continue as head of the College, with the title of Rector, and confirmed in office the existing tutors, Leverett and Brattle.

The public appears to have had such confidence in the Rector and tutors that enrolment, which showed some

signs of improvement under Rogers, took a decided up-
swing: the Class of 1690 was 22 strong, a new record
equalled in 1695, but not broken until 1719. Among the
graduates of this period, 1684–1701, who have achieved a
certain fame are: Gurdon Saltonstall and Jonathan Law,
Governors of Connecticut; Jonathan Belcher, Governor
of Massachusetts and of New Jersey; John Winthrop
(A.B. 1700), second of that name to be elected Fellow of
the Royal Society; Paul Dudley, F.R.S. and Chief Justice
of Massachusetts; colonial justices Benjamin Lynde, Edmund Quincy, and Peter Burr; Dudley Woodbridge,
Judge of Admiralty in Barbados; John Read, one of the
fathers of the New England bar; President Wadsworth of
Harvard and Timothy Cutler, Rector successively of
Yale and of Christ Church, Boston; Benjamin Colman,
herald of liberal Congregationalism; and William Vesey,
first Rector of Trinity Church, New York.

Increase Mather was easily the most distinguished man
that the College had for President before the nineteenth
century; yet, by treating the presidency as a part-time job,
he proved one of the least useful of Harvard presidents.
During four full years (1688–92) he was absent in England on a political mission, and then resumed his Boston
ministry, attending to the College only in his spare time.
He was keenly interested in the new science and other intellectual movements of the day; in a recorded Commencement oration he praised the 'liberal mode of
philosophizing' in vogue at Harvard, and advised the
young men to make the attainment of *Veritas* their goal.
Yet he had little understanding of youth and a decided
dislike for college life, and his policy was directed toward
making Harvard a mere feeder for the Congregational
churches. He conceived of the College as a bulwark of
things-as-they-were (or rather, as they had formerly been)
in a world where everything was in a state of change,
flux, and readjustment. Consequently, it was very fortu-

nate for Harvard's future that, instead of giving the College his undivided attention, and a too strong impress of his vigorous personality and positive views, Increase Mather left the management of it to the two tutors, John Leverett and William Brattle. These two scions of Boston mercantile and magisterial families were classmates in 1680, and from 1686 to 1697 they were the sole tutors and resident fellows of the College. Although their experience was confined to New England, they were more liberal and broad-minded than the President, and of a character that had deep and lasting influence on the young men whom they taught. Brattle remained faithful to his post during the smallpox epidemic of 1690–91, nursing sundry students until he came down with it himself; Leverett was praised for his 'enlarged Catholic spirit'; and both, while maintaining good order, imparted such a happy atmosphere to the College, and encouraged such good conversation, that many graduates stayed on even after taking their Masters' degree, in order to enjoy the pleasant intellectual society. President Mather apparently did not realize the extent of their liberalism until 1697, when both married and gave up their fellowships, Brattle becoming the minister of Cambridge and Leverett entering the law and politics. Even then, both resided within the present Yard, and the tutors who succeeded them, both their pupils, continued their policy of acquainting young men with the best in literature and divinity, regardless of puritan prejudices. It is largely owing to Brattle as tutor and to Leverett both as tutor and President that Harvard was saved from becoming a sectarian institution, at a time when the tendency of most pious New Englanders was to tighten up and insist on hundred-per-cent puritanism in the face of infiltrating ideas that heralded the Century of Enlightenment.

Increase Mather's return to Boston in 1692 inaugurated a decade of charter-mongering for the College. He

found the Charter of 1650 in force once more, by virtue
of a temporary restoration of the Colony Charter by a
provisional government. But calf and cow alike were
speedily returned to the grave. Mather brought to Boston
a new Province Charter for Massachusetts Bay, and the
new General Court proceeded to reincorporate the College. In this, as in several subsequent short-lived college
charters, Mather's object was to keep the College under
control of the Congregational Church, and free of political influence. To that end the various charters and
charter bills of 1692–1700 did not revive the Board of
Overseers, which as a semi-political body would have
included a certain number of Anglicans and perhaps
members of other sects not of the New England establishment. The government of the College was placed in
the hands of a President and a relatively large Corporation, eight to fourteen fellows, of whom only two were
resident tutors and the rest Congregational ministers.

The Charter of 1692 remained in force until 1697,
when it was disallowed by the King in Council on the
ground that it reserved no power of visitation to the
Crown. This at once raised a constitutional point which
the colonial legislature would not yield: they did not
wish to give the Royal Governor, who represented the
Crown in Massachusetts, the right to intervene in college
affairs, as college 'visitors' were wont to do in England.
And the Crown was equally insistent on its prerogative.

In the next college charter, passed in 1697, a compromise was effected: the power of visitation was conferred
on the Governor and Council. This Charter, which went
into effect immediately, awaiting the King's pleasure, had
a curious history. The Solicitor-General in London was
about to recommend its acceptance to the Privy Council
when a letter from President Mather requested a suspension until he could come to London and explain matters.
A voyage to London, where he had spent the four happi-

est years of his life, had been the object of Mather's private prayers and public intrigues for some years; but his letter evinced such ill-timed eagerness to 'explain,' that the English authorities read the Charter of 1697 and saw the joker in it. The power of visitation was not reserved to the Crown, or the Royal Governor, but to the Governor and Council; and the Council, in Massachusetts, was an elected body. So that charter was disallowed.

The next attempt of the General Court to pass a college charter, in 1699, was properly vetoed by the Royal Governor because at Mather's insistence a clause was inserted to the effect that nobody should be President or Fellow unless an adherent of orthodox New England Congregationalism. This first attempt to impose a test oath on Harvard (the first that succeeded was in 1935) was prompted by Mather's discovery of Leverett-cum-Brattle liberalism. Thomas Brattle, elder brother of the tutor, and for many years Treasurer of the College, had helped other broad-minded and well-to-do people in organizing a liberal Congregational Church in Boston, the minister of which, a former pupil of Leverett named Benjamin Colman, indulged in a peppery pamphlet exchange with Increase and Cotton Mather. So keen was President Mather for this illiberal exclusion of all but rigid puritans from the College government, that he preferred that the College be without a charter, and consequently lose the power of granting degrees and become a mere theological seminary, rather than abandon the religious qualification.

Fortunately, few were of his mind. The General Court next tried passing a 'Draught of a Charter,' sending it to London with the request that His Majesty be pleased to make it a charter indeed. In the meantime, President Mather and the Corporation named in this draft (from which Leverett and Brattle had been excluded) were ordered to act as the College Corporation *de facto*. This legislative manoeuvre forced a show-down on the question of presidential residence. The General Court required Mather either to resign his ministry and move to Cambridge, or resign the presidency. He had always claimed that his church would never, never let him go; but now that all hope of a trip to England had faded, he had to decide one way or the other. He chose Cambridge. But six months' residence in the college town in hired lodgings (for the President's Lodge had long since been fitted up for students) proved so disgusting to eminent Mr. Mather that he gave it up after Commencement, 1701, and returned to Boston, where the church (by pre-arrangement no doubt) had kept his seat warm.

The clever politicians in the General Court, led by Mather's arch-enemy Elisha Cooke (A.B. 1657), now discovered that, whilst the *President* of Harvard College must legally reside in Cambridge, there was no law as to where the *Vice-President* must reside. The House therefore resolved that the presidency was vacated by Dr. Mather's return to Boston, and voted that the Reverend Samuel Willard of the Old South Church in Boston, Vice-President of the *de facto* College Corporation, be invited to take charge. To the Mathers' intense disgust and annoyance, Willard accepted; and Harvard had a second commuting President.

Unquestionably the founding of the Collegiate School of Connecticut in 1701, named Yale College at the suggestion of Cotton Mather in 1718, had some connection with the feeling among New England conservatives that Harvard was slipping; but the movement for a college at New Haven had begun almost as soon as Harvard was founded. A dream of John Davenport, pastor of Eaton's company and member of the first Harvard Board of Overseers, it was slow to be translated into fact because the New Haven Colony was not rich enough to support a college of her own. (Similarly, Governor Bradford of the

Plymouth Colony planned a rival 'Academy' to Harvard at Duxbury, with Charles Chauncy as president, but the other Pilgrim Fathers thought it too much of a luxury.) All the founders of Yale were Harvard graduates in the Connecticut Valley or on Long Island Sound; among the original donations of 'books with which Yale was founded' were several from President Chauncy's library; and the Harvard of Chauncy's day was the ideal set up by the Yale founders as their standard. From the first the relations between the two New England colleges were friendly; students frequently transferred from one to the other, and each admitted the other's graduates *ad eundem gradum*, if they came to live near the sister institution. But Yale from the first was more cautious and less adventurous than her ancient rival.

The draft charter of 1700 became lost somewhere in the various offices, boards, and bureaux at Whitehall, and everyone forgot about it. The General Court had had its fill of charter-mongering; Joseph Dudley (A.B. 1665), the new Royal Governor of Massachusetts, was a brother-in-law of Vice-President Willard, who filled amiably and acceptably (for he was a learned man with good horse sense) the rôle of stopgap for six years. The *de facto* College Corporation undertook to fill vacancies that occurred, and by this means the Brattle brothers and John Leverett were readmitted to a share in the College government. In the summer of 1707, a few days after the liberals had obtained a definite majority in the Corporation, Vice-President Willard was taken seriously ill, and resigned. The way was now clear to conclude this twenty years of presidential paltering, and obtain a new head who would spend his entire time and energy on Harvard College.

AARON'S ROD

1708–1806

PRESIDENTS AND ACTING PRESIDENTS

1708–1724 JOHN LEVERETT
1725–1737 BENJAMIN WADSWORTH
1737–1769 EDWARD HOLYOKE
1770–1773 SAMUEL LOCKE
1774–1780 SAMUEL LANGDON
1781–1804 JOSEPH WILLARD
1804–1806 ELIPHALET PEARSON, *Acting President*

IV

THE GREAT LEVERETT

ON OCTOBER 28, 1707, a few weeks after Willard's death, the *de facto* Corporation met and elected John Leverett President of Harvard College. Their power to choose a President was questionable, since they were not a legal corporation, but a group of men charged by the General Court with a temporary expedient; and they invited trouble by choosing a layman and a liberal to an office always filled by an orthodox puritan parson. Leverett's friends, anticipating the rage of the Mathers, cannily circulated a petition to the General Court signed by thirty-nine ministers of the Bay Colony, half of them Leverett's former pupils, commending his wisdom, piety, and learning, and praying the Court to confirm the choice by granting him an honorable salary. Although this did much to counteract the gossip and slanderous letters that outraged conservatives circulated against the appointment, Leverett would hardly have got in but for a political deal inspired by his friend Governor Dudley. That astute politician proposed that if the legislature would grant Leverett a proper salary, he would agree to put a final quietus on the royal charter movement, and declare the old Charter of 1650 in force again. So notable an abdication of royal prerogative bowled the politicians over. They voted the President a salary of £150 a year, and by joint resolve declared that the old college charter had never been legally void, and was now to be considered in full vigor. The arrangement had the further merit of reducing the number of Fellows of the Corporation from fifteen to five, eliminating those who were unfriendly to Leverett.

To the presidency, Leverett brought vigor, integrity, and complete devotion, with a worldly experience, as member and Speaker of the House, lawyer, judge, and councillor, and envoy of the provincial government to New York, such as no other Harvard President had before Josiah Quincy. He was liberal in his attitude toward religion, conservative in politics, and withal a man with an innate sense of government, a majestic manner of speech, and a deportment that 'struck an Awe upon the Youth.' Nathaniel Cotton (A.B. 1717) describes President Leverett with hands in his pockets being consulted by the two Cambridge deacons standing with hats in hand, and making low obeisances at parting. He completely dominated the town, where he had resided constantly since 1685, as well as the College. His pupil Nathaniel Appleton, the minister of Cambridge, described him after his death as a 'great and generous Soul' designed by God for posts of honor and difficulty; and in his lifetime Benjamin Colman, the liberal minister of Boston, wrote of Leverett's character with such enthusiasm to White Kennett, Dean of Peterborough, that this learned prelate expressed a desire to open correspondence with 'the President of Harwarden College.' At the suggestion of another former pupil, Henry Newman (A.B. 1687), Leverett and William Brattle were elected Fellows of the Royal Society. He continued to reside in his mansion — the old Shepard parsonage and later Wigglesworth house — which with its garden and back pasture occupied the central sector of the present College Yard from Massachusetts Avenue to Kirkland Street.

President Leverett revived the ancient formalities which had fallen into desuetude during the charter's abeyance. His inauguration took place in Old Harvard Hall. Governor Dudley took President Leverett 'by the hand and led him down into the Hall,' where the keys, seal, records, and charter were lying on a table, and where the Councillors (who now became *ex officio* Overseers) were assembled. The senior fellow, the Reverend Nehemiah Hobart of Newton, made a 'very serious and suitable,' and doubtless very long, prayer. Sir Sewall delivered an oration in Latin; Governor Dudley, in a short Latin speech, delivered to the President the keys, charter, and seal as emblems of his office; Leverett made a suitable acknowledgment in Latin; Sir Holyoke, who would one day be President, delivered a Latin oration. The Reverend Mr. Danforth prayed, and then the entire company, led by Paul Dudley (1690), sang the One-hundred and thirty-second Psalm, *Memento Domine*, a most appropriate choice:

> For Sion does in God's esteem
>   all other seats excel;
> His place of everlasting rest,
>   where he desires to dwell.
> Her store, says he, I will increase,
>   her poor with plenty bless;
> Her Saints shall shout for joy, her priests
>   my saving health confess.
>
> There David's power, shall long remain
>   in his successive line,
> And my anointed servant there
>   shall with fresh lustre shine.
> The faces of his vanquished foes
>   confusion shall o'erspread;
> Whilst with confirmed success, his crown
>   shall flourish on his head.

And, to add another insult to the Mathers and their friends, the ceremony closed with singing the *Gloria Patri*.

A somewhat emasculated version of this ceremony was used at the inauguration of President Conant in October, 1933, in the Faculty Room of University Hall. The keys, charter, and seal — the same charter and the same seal —

were presented to him by Mr. George Agassiz, who succeeds a long line of Governors as President of the Board of Overseers; but he did not deliver a Latin oration. We sang the traditional Commencement Psalm, the Seventy-eighth, instead of the One-hundred and thirty-second; nor did we conclude with the *Gloria Patri*. What we really missed, however, was the Leverett inauguration feast, which was certainly sufficient to make all Sion's Saints shout for joy. The Steward's accounts show what victuals and drink were consumed by the Corporation and their fifty-odd guests on that festive occasion: 146 pounds of beef, pork, and mutton; 14 fowls, 4 turkeys, 19 apple and mince pies, and 16 gallons of wine; 4 dozen churchwarden pipes and two pounds of tobacco were provided to top off the repast. Judge Sewall concluded his account of the ceremony, 'Got home very well. *Laus Deo*.'

Leverett's first care was to look after long-neglected college properties. The English rents assigned to the College for Indian students and missionaries were secured, but only one Indian, Benjamin Larnel, could be induced to enter Harvard; and he, after falling into 'dreadful Snares of Sin,' died. The General Court was induced to disgorge Anne Radcliffe's scholarship fund, with interest; and the important Hopkins legacy was finally secured from the executors of Governor Edward Hopkins, who had died half a century before. It is by no means clear whether Governor Hopkins had intended to leave this to Harvard, or to the college at New Haven which was being talked of even in his lifetime; and Jeremiah Dummer (A.B. Harvard 1699) was retained by Yale to put in her plea for it before the Court of Chancery. But Jeremy wisely concluded that a Harvard-Yale game in Chancery would soon consume the entire legacy of £500, and refused to contest, later attempting to make amends to Yale by soliciting for her a share of Thomas Hollis's bounty. Naturally, Mr. Dummer was considered a traitor by both colleges, who were not surprised to hear that he was living scandalously with a bevy of 'nymphs.' The Court established a special corporation in Boston to administer the Hopkins legacy for the benefit of divinity students and the Cambridge Latin School; and the 'Honorable and Reverend the Trustees of the Hopkins Charity Fund' still perform these duties.

No important changes were made by Leverett in the curriculum, and the ancient custom of having students translate the Scriptures from one sacred tongue to another at morning and evening prayers was revived. The Commencement theses show that mathematics was very little studied, and even in President Wadsworth's time the senior sophisters had to review arithmetic before they took up geometry. It is probable that students were allowed to take private lessons in French, which by this time was part of a 'gentleman's education,' from a private tutor, a Scot named Thomas Blair, whose 'Short and Easy Rules' for pronouncing the language (Boston, 1720) are dedicated to the President, and mention his aid in obtaining pupils. An innovation that the students did not relish was the engagement of Judah Monis, an Italian Jew who had come to Boston by way of Jamaica and New York. Educated in the Jewish academies of Leghorn and Amsterdam, he attracted the attention of Benjamin Colman, and was admitted to the Master's degree at Harvard in 1720.[1] The same year he presented the manuscript of 'an essay to facilitate the Instruction of Youth in the Hebrew Language' to the Corporation, and in 1722 he was formally converted to Christianity at an impressive public ceremony in the college hall. Within a month, Monis was chosen 'Instructor of the Hebrew Language' in Harvard College for a year, with an annual salary of

[1] At Oxford and Cambridge at this time, and in most of the universities of Christendom, no Jew could be admitted to a degree, on account of the religious tests and oaths that went with it.

£50. The three upper classes were required to attend his instruction four days a week, and each member to own a Hebrew psalter and lexicon, and after Monis had published a Hebrew grammar, to purchase that too. The Corporation soon had occasion to invite Mr. Monis to revise his teaching methods, which were 'thought so tedious as to be discouraging,' but he had no better success than the tutors who preceded him, or the professors who followed, in making Hebrew interesting to the average undergraduate. Judah Monis's appointment was annually renewed, and his salary frequently raised, until his resignation in 1760; but by 1755 the study of Hebrew had become an elective, and the few earnest souls who chose it occupied Mr. Monis's time only one afternoon a week.

Although each of the four tutors took entire charge of a class, one of them, Thomas Robie (1708), specialized in Science, and induced the Corporation to acquire so much 'philosophical apparatus' that a special chamber was assigned to it in Massachusetts, the roof of which was used as an informal astronomical observatory. An eight-foot telescope, installed in 1712, was replaced in 1722 by a magnificent twenty-four-foot instrument donated by Thomas Hollis, with a quadrant which was 'the very same Dr. Halley used at St. Helena.' Robie corresponded with the Reverend William Derham, F.R.S., who had printed in the Philosophical Transactions several of his observations of lunar and solar eclipses, of the 'Light that strikes up toward the Pleiades,' and of Jupiter's satellites, as well as meteorological data and curious occurrences such as the effect of a spider bite on Nathaniel Ware of Needham, and 'Alcalious Salt produced by burning rotten Wood.' The President and Fellows showed their appreciation of Robie by voting him a bonus of £24 'for his Mathematicall Observations Communicated to the Learned Abroad'; and Leverett, at his resignation, recorded 'that Mr. Robie was no small honour to Harvard

College, by his Mathematical performances and by his Corrispondence thereupon with Dr. Derham and other Learned persons in those studys abroad.' When we reflect how slowly and reluctantly the continental universities took to scientific research, these efforts toward the advancement of learning by a small colonial college are memorable.

The Treaty of Utrecht, in 1713, inaugurated an era of peace, prosperity, and expansion in New England. Classes rose rapidly to eighteen, twenty-three, and even thirty-seven members in 1721. In November, 1718, there were a hundred and twenty-four students in residence, including *domini* studying for the M.A. and other resident graduates; but Old Harvard and Stoughton College accommodated no more than seventy-five. The Overseers, declaring in Biblical language that 'the Numbers of the Sons of the Prophets are now so increas'd, that the Place where they were wont to dwell is become so Streight,' petitioned the General Court for a new residential hall; and Massachusetts, now our oldest building, was erected at the public charge, and completed in 1720 at a cost of £3500, leaving a balance of £116, which was presented to the Committee by the Court in joyful surprise at their not exceeding the appropriation. From that time to 1763, when Hollis was built, the group of 'colleges' (except for the addition of Holden Chapel in 1744) was exactly as portrayed in the famous Burgis 'Prospect' of 1726. Old Harvard, Massachusetts, and Stoughton College, which almost closed the gap between their eastern ends, formed an open quadrangle, or 'court' as Tutor Flynt called it in the faculty records. North of Old Harvard, the Spencer Orchard, purchased in 1697, had been set aside in 1712 as a 'play-place' or recreation ground for the students. South of Massachusetts was the college brew-house, and east of Stoughton the 'fellows' barn,' where presumably the hay cut in the Yard was stored. The fence between the Yard and President Leverett's own property ran north and south, just in front of the site of University. The increase in registration after 1713, small enough from our quantitative standards, nevertheless recalls the 1920's, when the whole country seemed to be 'going collegiate.' The increase came largely from the seaports, which reaped the first harvests from land speculation and West India commerce, and the rum business; and where the influence of court manners was most quickly felt. The new crop of young men came to be made gentlemen, not to study. President Leverett had always differed from those who regarded Harvard merely as a seminary for orthodox Congregational divines. Former presidents liked to refer to Harvard men in commencement orations and the like by the Old Testament phrase *filii prophetarum*, or 'Sons of the Prophets.' Leverett called the alumni *Harvardinates*, or 'Sons of Harvard.' At Commencement, 1711, he gloried in the fact that Harvard graduated not only learned ministers, but scholars (*beaux-clercs*), judges, physicians (*Filii Æsculapii Apollonisque Nepotes*), soldiers dedicated *tam Marti quam Mercurio*, merchants (wise ones, '*not* comparable to apes, peacocks, and parrots'), and simple farmers 'whom academic culture serves but to soften and polish rustic manners.' He was well prepared to deal with the inevitable follies of youth; but the unfortunate thing about these post-war extravagances was the fact that they gave Leverett's administration unfavorable notice from the public just at the moment when Harvard needed friends. As every college dependent on public funds knows, legislators expect college students to stick to their books (or, nowadays, to their football), and balk at granting money to an institution whose members are represented by the newspapers as living in riot and luxury. And for the first time Harvard attracted the unfavorable attention of the press. The Franklins, whose *New England Courant* introduced sprightliness and personalities into

Boston journalism, attacked Harvard from the lower end of the social scale, while the Mathers were marshalling their forces from the other. 'Silence Dogood,' who was none other than sixteen-year-old Ben Franklin, declared in the *Courant* for May 14, 1722, that the Temple of Learning was veiled by Idleness and Ignorance, and reflected on the

extreme folly of those Parents, who, blind to their Children's Dulness, and insensible of the Solidarity of their Skulls, because they think their Purses can afford it, will needs send them to the Temple of Learning, where, for want of a suitable Genius, they learn little more than how to carry themselves handsomely, and enter a Room genteely (which might as well be acquired at a Dancing-School), and from whence they return, after abundance of trouble and Charges, as great Blockheads as ever, only more proud and self-conceited.

'John Harvard' defended his college in the conservative *Gazette*, but Franklin retorted in the *Courant* with a long poem, concluding:

Long have the weaker Sons of Harvard strove
To move our Rev'rence and command our Love,
By Means, how sordid, 'tis not hard to say,
When all their Merit lies in M. and A.
The knowing Sons of Harvard we revere,
And in there just Defense will still appear;
But every idle Fop who there commences,
Shall never claim Dominion o'er our Senses.
We judge not of their Knowledge by their Air,
Nor think the wisest Heads have curled Hair.

Leverett's Diary shows that the Faculty was having plenty of trouble with 'profane swearing,' 'riotous Actions,' and 'bringing Cards into the College' in 1717; and an undergraduate diary of the time shows that students were frequently slipping off to Boston for horse races, pirate hangings, and other diversions. The first college clubs were founded not by these 'rakes and blades,' but by the pious students, in self-defense. An unnamed 'Society of Young Students' was formed in 1719 'to meet together for the worship of God' on 'Saturday and Sabbath-Day Evenings'; fifteen of the twenty-six members became clergymen. And the Philomusarian Club, 'concerted' in 1728, declared in its preamble that whereas 'Conversation, which is The Basis of Friendship The fundamental Principle of Society . . . Is Now att A Very Low Ebb . . . Vice and folly Are In Their Zenith and Meridian and Gild the Hemisphere of The Muses with Meteors Whose false Glare is By Many Mistaken for the Refulgent Stars of Wisdom and Virtue.' And whereas 'Vice is Now Become Alamode and Rant Riot and Excess is Accounted The Heigth of Good Breeding and Learning — In Order Therefore to Stem That Monstrous Tide of Impiety and Ignorance,' the Philomusarian Club is formed, to meet at one another's chambers thrice weekly, read members' poems, and indulge in learned conversation, pipes, tobacco, and beer. Club proceedings are to be devoid of 'Railing Curses Imprecations, vile Appellations, obsceness,' and are to be strictly secret. Seven of the ten organizers became ministers.

Leverett's administration also saw the birth of the first college periodical, 'The Telltale,' in 1721. It is secular in tone, consisting largely of essays in the Spectator manner, with amusing references to the game of 'push pinn,' apparently a form of student gambling, and to two persons resembling pickled cucumbers, 'chattering upon themes of Predestination and Foreknowledge' that they did not understand. A letter in Number 11 states that the writer has 'found out several Clubbs in Colledge,' including 'The Mock club' founded in 1719, composed of 'Persons Rawbon'd humpback'd and Monophthalmic.' After a few numbers had been circulated in manuscript, the editors of 'The Telltale' appear to have organized themselves and their friends into the Spy Club, at which the members read lectures in turn and discussed, not only religious subjects, but such questions as 'Whether there

THE GREAT LEVERETT   63

be any Standard of Truth,' and 'Whether it be Fornication to lye with ones Sweetheart (after Contraction) before marraige.' Nearly all the members of this club, too,
became ministers; four members from the 'learned class'
of 1721 were Charles Chauncy, the liberal theologian,
Ebenezer Pemberton, one of the founders of Princeton,
Isaac Greenwood, our first mathematics professor, and
John, first of the Harvard Lowells. The only feature common to these early societies and to twentieth-century
college clubs is the elaborate constitution and by-laws
that were drawn up, adopted, and promptly forgotten.

These 'exorbitant practises' of the post-war generation
gave a handle to the enemies of Leverett and liberalism,
who had been biding their time since his inauguration;
and from 1717 he was in almost continual hot water. The
controversies of his administration are readily under-
standable if we translate the religious conservatism or
orthodoxy of his day into the 'patriotic society' brand of
'Americanism' that has been causing our colleges no
little vexation in the last few years. As today, the inevitable concessions of college authorities to the needs and
tastes of post-war youth were made the occasion for a
general attack on enlightenment. In 1720, important elements of New England society were, in imagination, still
living in the puritan century, just as today numerous very
worthy people believe in the economic and social theories
of the last century, and resent the fact that it is no longer
possible to live by those formulae. Then, as now, the fundamentalist elements looked with extreme disfavor on
educational institutions which endeavored to prepare
their alumni for the age in which they were to live, and
which sought to advance knowledge rather than to embalm it. In both eras the enemies of enlightenment were
led by good men of the ruling class who were genuinely
concerned for the integrity of a form of society that they
believed to be divinely ordained, and were supported by

half-educated masses who enjoyed disturbing men of learning whose serenity they resented. In Leverett's day, the higher element was represented in the Provincial Council, and among the ministers who with the Council constituted the Harvard Board of Overseers; the lower element was represented in the lower house of the Massachusetts General Court. Councillors like Samuel Sewall and Isaac Addington, and ministers like the Mathers, believed it to be Harvard's mission to send forth young men with the same ideas as theirs; in other words, they wished the College to be definitely sectarian. That is why a central point of attack was the use of liberal Anglican divines by President Leverett in his divinity instruction, instead of the orthodox puritan writers of the previous century. President Leverett's 'Tory' leanings, his friendship with royal governors and reputed sympathy with Episcopalians, stirred the vague fears of the New England people that the prelacy from which their grandfathers had fled was being subtly promoted by the senior college of New England.

Leverett's caution, tact, dignity, and innate conservatism might have quenched these unjustified fears but for the malignant opposition of Cotton Mather, whose pride had been wounded beyond cure by his father's being dropped from the presidency in 1701 and by his own claims to that office being passed over in 1708. Increase maintained a dignified aloofness from college affairs, never attending a meeting of the Board of Overseers, and Cotton endeavored to ape the parental attitude, but curiosity once got the better of consistency, when he attended in order to view the delicious spectacle of President Leverett's falling out with the Dudley tribe. That breach, which bedevilled Leverett for the rest of his administration, occurred in 1714, when the Corporation declined to appoint the Governor's son William to the vacant college treasurership, a post of trust and honor for which they considered him wholly unfit. And finally, the President aroused opposition in his own house, which was improved by his enemies outside.

Fortunately for the College, before anything happened Governor Dudley had been replaced by Governor Samuel Shute, who found in Leverett a man after his own heart. Things broke at Commencement, 1718, when Ebenezer Pierpont of Roxbury, son of one of the Dudleys' neighbors, was denied his second degree by the Corporation for 'contemning, reproaching and insulting the Government of the College.' This action was immediately reported to the Overseers, 'upon which the Governour said Well, there is an end of it.' But it was not the end. Pierpont violated university custom and precedent by entering a suit for libel against Mr. Tutor Sever, whereupon the Corporation, disliking to wash dirty college linen in the courts, petitioned the Governor for a special meeting of the Overseers. Two meetings were held, at which Paul Dudley, the former Governor's son, supported Pierpont to such purpose that the Overseers, instead of sustaining the Corporation, washed their hands of the whole affair. Fortunately the Middlesex County Court quashed Pierpont's complaints. Leverett hints that if the case had come to trial the whole Corporation would have resigned.

Cotton Mather's contribution to this controversy was a letter to Governor Shute endeavoring to persuade him that the College Charter was waste parchment and Leverett a 'pretended President'; hence his Excellency could and should order the 'abused and oppressed Pierpont' to be granted his degree, and the pretended Corporation must obey.

While the case of Pierpont *vs.* Sever was still pending, a meeting of the Overseers was called at the Council Chamber in the Old State House on the question of the size and cost of the future Massachusetts Hall. At a pause in the discussion, Chief Justice Sewall arose to say that he desired to be informed on more vital matters — how the worship of God was being conducted, and whether it was true that Leverett no longer observed the time-honored custom of making weekly expositions of Scripture in college hall. Leverett tried to avoid being drawn into a discussion, and Governor Shute rebuked the Chief Justice for a motion so 'very improper and Altogether out of Course'; but with Paul Dudley's aid, Sewall managed to start a discussion about the religious state of the College before the business at hand was attended to. This incident taught Leverett what to expect.

If Leverett and liberalism won these two bouts, the honors in the next were divided. The object of this contention was our first endowed professorial chair, the Hollis Professorship of Divinity. Thomas Hollis (1659–1731), eldest of six members of a family to whom Harvard owes more than to any other benefactors outside her own alumni, was a merchant of London, and a Baptist. A correspondent of Colman, he was persuaded that the liberal administration of Leverett made Harvard College, despite her strong ties with the Congregational churches that had persecuted his New England brethren, a proper object of his benevolence. A parcel of books for the College Library, and about £300 for poor scholars, as earnest of his bounty, came over in 1719. In 1720 Mr. Hollis sent about £700 more for scholarships for students in divinity. Leverett and Colman, in thanking him, observed that the College had no divinity professorship; would not Mr. Hollis care to endow one? Promptly Maecenas took the hint, ordered that out of the moneys he had given, and would give, £40 per annum be paid to a Professor of Divinity appointed by the President and Fellows, providing 'that none be refused on account of his belief and practice of adult baptism,' and reserving the right to dictate statutes for the chair. The Corporation promptly accepted the gift on these terms, and on June 28, 1721, appointed to the Hollis chair Edward Wigglesworth (A.B. 1710), a talented young cleric whose deafness had prevented his obtaining a parish. The story of how the Overseers, with the more or less reluctant consent of the Corporation, perverted this gift to sectarian purposes is a sad one. In the proposed statutes for the chair which he caused to be drafted by some of his learned friends, Baptist and others, Hollis proposed that Baptist communicants of the Presbyterian and Congregational churches be eligible for the professorship, and that it be 'recommended to the electors' (the Harvard Corporation) that they prefer a man 'of sound and orthodox principles,' who would declare his belief that 'the Bible is the only and most perfect rule of faith and practice.' What Hollis meant by orthodoxy is questionable; but there can be no doubt that the Overseers, in altering their recommendation to a positive qualification, meant 'orthodox' to be taken in the strict New England Congregational sense, and to exclude a member of any other denomination from the chair. Judge Sewall was quite frank in declaring that he preferred to lose the donation if this exclusion could not be inserted; Mr. Hollis could not bribe *him* to say that infant baptism didn't matter! Hollis, if he noticed the alteration, generously overlooked it; and President and Fellows not only accepted it, but consented to consider the former election of Wigglesworth null, and to present his name to the Overseers only after he had declared his faith in Ames's *Medulla Theologiæ*, the Westminster Assembly catechism, the Thirty-nine Articles (to which the New England puritans always asserted their faithfulness), the doctrine of the Trinity, the divinity of Jesus, Predestination, 'special efficacious grace,' and 'the divine right of infant baptism'! Thus satisfied, the Overseers confirmed Wigglesworth, and he was solemnly installed Hollis Professor of Divinity in the college hall on October 23, 1722, with one of those lengthy academic ceremonies that Leverett loved.

As Quincy wrote a century ago, 'These proceedings can hardly be reconciled with good faith to Mr. Hollis'; and of the inquisition into Professor Wigglesworth's beliefs, let us hope that Hollis was never apprised. Yet President Leverett's acquiescence in this deceit was the policy of an academic statesman. By letting the orthodox have the shell, the liberals got the oyster for Harvard; stoutly standing on principle would have lost to the College both the chair and Edward Wigglesworth. Future generations would take care of 'orthodoxy,' [1] and the professor was worth a little pious deceit to secure.

Edward Wigglesworth had given his adhesion to the high points of Calvinism, but his career once more proved the vanity of academic oaths and tests. One of the first theologians in New England who dared publicly to challenge the 'five points of Calvinism,' he employed the deadly method of doubt and inquiry, rather than direct attack. A true gentleman and ripe scholar, Wigglesworth was a prime favorite with Harvard students, and he and his son Edward, who succeeded him, had a very great influence on New England theology. It was the Wigglesworths who trained the pioneers of liberal Christianity in New England — the ministers who led the way out of the lush but fearsome jungles of Calvinism, into the thin, clear light of Unitarianism.

In the matter of allotting the ten Hollis scholarships of £10 each, the Corporation were not hindered by the

[1] There have been seven Hollis Professors of Divinity. The two Edward Wigglesworths (1722–91) and David Tappan (1792–1803) were in a formal sense Calvinist Congregationalists; Henry Ware (1805–40) was a Unitarian Congregationalist; David G. Lyon (1882–1910) was a Baptist; James Hardy Ropes (1910–33) was a Trinitarian Congregationalist; the present incumbent, Dr. Henry J. Cadbury, is a Friend. From 1840 to 1882 the chair was in abeyance, as the income from the Hollis endowment had dwindled away almost to nothing.

Overseers from carrying out Mr. Hollis's liberal intentions. One of the first Hollis scholars was John Callender, a nephew of the Harvard-trained minister of the First Baptist Church in Boston; Callender became the Baptist minister of Newport, and historian of Rhode Island.

Before the Hollis professorship was settled, Leverett and the College had become involved in the severest controversy of his administration, involving the composition and rights of the Corporation.

After the revival of the Charter of 1650 in 1707, President Leverett and the Fellows continued for a time the practice of the previous century, electing every college tutor, after a short period of probation, a Fellow of Harvard College. But in 1716 the Corporation began a new policy toward tutors. A rule was adopted that their terms henceforth should be three years, instead of during good behavior. And in 1716–17, when three deaths created as many vacancies on the Corporation, that body, instead of following precedent by electing the two tutors to its fellowship, chose three settled ministers: Joseph Stevens (A.B. 1703), a former tutor; Benjamin Colman,. of the Brattle Street Church, Boston; and Nathaniel Appleton (A.B. 1712), pastor of Cambridge. This left but one tutor, Flynt, on the Corporation, and two, Thomas Robie and Nicholas Sever, outside.

Sever, the first to be appointed under the three-year rule, found this position humiliating. Unlike almost every other tutor of the period, he was a man of some age and experience, a former minister, thirty-six years old, who had resigned his pulpit because of an impediment in speech. His salary was but £50, less than half what President Leverett had had as a tutor, and in depreciated currency. Tutor Flynt, by being a Fellow of the Corporation, had much more authority over the students than the tutors who were not Fellows, even though these last were called Fellows of the House. Sever complained that President Leverett treated him not as a colleague but as an employé. 'In the case of Parker, when for a bold insult upon me I gave him a box on the Ear Mr. President upon his complaint countenanced him by saying "What! did he box you?"' And in the case of Wolcott, similarly boxed, Leverett called Sever to account: '"What!" said he, "do you think it A light matter to box a Schollar?" and reprimanded me, with Extream heat and passion.' In 1720, Sever, Flynt, and Robie began one of the most famous controversies in Harvard history by addressing to the Board of Overseers a memorial demanding as of right fellowship in the Corporation.

For the next three years memorials and counter-memorials, protests and counter-protests, flew back and forth. Sever may, as Quincy insinuates, have timed his opening shot to coincide with the Hollis professorship controversy, but he cannot be dismissed as a mere trouble-maker. If we approach the main question, 'when is a Fellow not a Fellow?' in the spirit of a modern constitutional lawyer, and examine only the text of the Charter of 1650, and the practice since, Sever had no case. There was nothing in the Charter to prevent the Corporation co-opting any resident of Massachusetts they chose; and in several instances in the seventeenth century they had gone outside the tutorial staff. But, as we have seen, President Dunster and the General Court of 1650 undoubtedly intended the fellowships to be reserved for teachers or resident scholars, as in the English colleges; and it was now for the first time practicable to do this. The College in 1720 was large enough to require a professor and four tutors, and rich enough to support them; under those circumstances it was hard on Sever and Robie that they should be excluded from fellowships, and treated as mere short-term employés of the Corporation.

What was best for the College is a different question. If Sever won his point, the College would be controlled, as the Oxford and Cambridge colleges still are, by the resident scholars who did the actual teaching; but this democratic system had been grossly abused by the fellows of English colleges since the Restoration, and continued to be abused until Parliament reformed the universities in the 1850's. On the other hand, if Leverett won, it meant that Harvard would be controlled by the President, assisted by a board of non-resident and usually subservient trustees. This form of college government by President and external trustees (for which the short-lived Harvard Charter of 1692 and the Yale Charter of 1701 were the precedents) has become the standard American method of university government, and, though a happy government for Harvard, it has elsewhere been as fruitful in abuses as the English system.

From the time that Sever's memorial was presented, there began a contest which somewhat resembles a bitterly solemn game of chess. The Board of Overseers, in which the sectarian party had a majority, took Sever's part. For, if his claim were allowed, Colman and Appleton, the two noted liberals on the Corporation, must go. Overseers recommended that one of the college tutors be elected to the Corporation in place of Joseph Stevens, who had just died. Corporation countered by electing neither Sever nor Tutor Welsteed, who had joined him, but Robie, who had backed out of the Sever party. Overseers declined the gambit. Corporation refused to renew Sever's appointment as tutor. Overseers insisted that he was still a tutor, since they had never ratified the three-year law. Corporation presented Robie's name a second time. Overseers now move their king and queen — they appeal to the General Court to enlarge the number of the Corporation, so that it will accommodate all the tutors, as well as the three non-resident fellows.

Now transferred to a purely political arena, the issue was befogged by personalities, fears of the 'dangerous tendencies' of Leverett and Colman, rumors of 'extravagances and disorders' among the students, and a desire to tease Leverett's friend, the Royal Governor. A joint committee of both houses reported that all the tutors of the College, not exceeding five in number, had a charter right to be Fellows of the Corporation; that no Fellows should be at the same time Overseers; and that the Corporation could not fix salaries without the Overseers' consent. This report was embodied in a resolve by both houses, and sent up to Governor Shute for the required approbation. His Excellency, with tongue in cheek, gave his consent with this proviso — that 'the Rev. Mr. Benjamin Wadsworth, and the Rev. Mr. Benjamin Colman, and the Rev. Mr. Appleton are not removed by said orders, but still remain Fellows of the Corporation.'

That let the cat out of the bag. The House of Representatives (where the sectarian interest was strongly entrenched) declared that his Excellency's proviso 'entirely defeated the design and purpose of those votes,' and requested him to withdraw it, which the Governor not only declined to do, but gave notice before leaving for England that if any resolve of like tenor got by his successor he would see that it was disallowed by the King.

In the early months of 1723, before Sever and his politico-religious allies launched their final effort, Leverett played with the idea of soliciting a royal charter from King George I. He had had some correspondence on the subject with Henry Newman, who first suggested it, but later advised that it would be impossible to obtain such a charter without Anglican supervision, which would probably send all candidates for the Congregational ministry to Yale. In Leverett's papers is a draft charter in his own hand; but it was never even presented to the Corporation, so far as the records show.

In August, 1723, Sever and Welsteed wrote another

memorial, and the House again proposed to pass the resolutions rejected by Governor Shute. This effort was synchronized with an investigation of the College by a committee of the Overseers. Cotton Mather, working as usual from ambush, tried to stir up this committee by insinuations (based on tales told by his pious son Samuel, who had recently graduated with the aid of a Hollis scholarship) to the effect that the students read privately books such as 'plays, novels, empty and vicious pieces of poetry, and even Ovid's Epistles, which have a vile tendency to corrupt good manners,' that the tutors recommended works on Theology 'that have rank poison in them,' and that really good young men had to forget all they learned in college before they could become 'excellent young ministers.' But the Overseers' visiting committee was headed by Judge Sewall, an honest man. His committee found nothing worse to report than promiscuous reading of popular Anglican divines such as Dean Sherlock and Archbishop Tillotson; 'several immoralities' such as 'too frequent use of strong drink'; too much time spent in 'visiting one another rather than praying Saturday evenings'; and 'going into town, on Sabbath mornings, to provide breakfasts.'

The Overseers appear to have felt that a general revision of the College Laws, which had remained unchanged since the last century, was the proper way to meet these deficiencies and 'immoralities.' But before anything had been done, President Leverett died. The contentions of the last four years had not improved his health, and he had financial worries as well. Devotion to the College had forced him to neglect his landed interests in Maine, New Hampshire, and Rhode Island, where sundry squatters had relieved him of a large part of his private means. The General Court, in an era of rising costs and depreciated currency, had given him a maximum salary of £200 and a minimum of £150, which had a purchasing value hardly equal to the £55 that President Dunster received — the consequence being that he ran in debt about £1500. For two years he had been troubled with a swelling of the limbs. He tried the Lynn mineral springs and sea bathing to little effect; and on May 3, 1724, died quietly in his bed.

Leverett left behind him no published works (for which Cotton Mather referred to him posthumously as the 'infamous drone'); but his manuscript 'Discourses' in the College Archives testify to his wealth of classical learning, an elegant Latinity, and a broad and liberal approach to Theology. Samuel Sewall, who had consistently opposed Leverett's policy, justly admitted that he was 'full of sweetness and candor, displayed in the government of the College, tempered by a convenient severity.' To all who studied under him he was the 'great Leverett'; no other Harvard President between Chauncy and Kirkland was so warmly remembered. Thirteen years later, Tutor Flynt paused in the midst of a funeral oration on President Wadsworth to make a glowing eulogy on President Leverett, *ille vir amplissimus et doctissimus*. We should inscribe on his monument, said Flynt, those words which Aristotle long ago would have carved on the tomb of his master Plato: 'Here lies a man whom it is neither seemly nor permissible for the irreverent or the ignorant to praise.'

Leverett took the presidency when Harvard was weak and disorganized, after a generation of charter-mongering and of non-resident presidents. He put her finances on a firm basis, and obtained her first endowed chair. But his service to the College and the country lies more in the principles that he maintained and the precedents that he established, than in positive accomplishments. In an era of political and sectarian strife, he was steadfast in preserving the College from the devastating control of a provincial orthodoxy. He kept it a house of learning under the spirit of religion, not, as the Mathers and their kind would have had it, the divinity school of a particular sect. Leverett, in a word, founded the liberal tradition of Harvard University.

V

WADSWORTH TO LANGDON

AFTER the death of Leverett, Cotton Mather confidently expected to be the next President. Sixty-one years old, and with over 350 imprints to his credit, a D.D. from Glasgow and a fellowship in the Royal Society of London, he did not imagine that the Corporation would have the effrontery to pass him over a third time. An historian cannot help regretting that the Corporation did not take Mather at his own valuation. With only four years to live, he could not have done the College much harm; and what fun his presidency would have been to write about! For Mather 'knew it all,' and dreamed of the impossible: to modernize the curriculum, yet restore the pious atmosphere of Chauncy's 'School of the Prophets'; to improve higher education, yet force the young 'blades' of 1725 into the mould of 1630. We cannot blame the Fellows for feeling that anyone was preferable to Dr. Mather as President of Harvard College; they had had sufficient experience with his arrogance, omniscience, and meanness to those who differed with him. As the situation seemed to demand a conservative, they elected Joseph Sewall (A.B. 1707), son of Judge Sewall and minister of the Old South Church in Boston.

'The Corporation of the College mett, and . . . chose a modest young Man, of whose Piety (and little else) every one gives a laudable Character,' sneered Mather in his Diary. But the probability is that Dr. Sewall did not want the presidency, for his church declined to release him.

The Corporation then swung to the opposite extreme and elected the Reverend Benjamin Colman of Brattle

Street Church, foremost of the liberal Congregational party. 'The Corporation of our miserable Colledge do again . . . treat me with their accustomed Indignity,' noted Mather. Colman would have made an admirable President; but after sounding out the General Court he found himself so obnoxious to the conservatives that his election would threaten the best interests of the College, and magnanimously he declined.

The way was now open for a compromise candidate; and on June 8, 1725, the Corporation chose one of their number, Benjamin Wadsworth (A.B. 1690), fifty-eight years old, and for thirty years past minister of the First Church in Boston. A kindly, intelligent, and sufficiently learned gentleman, curiously wanting in courage for a son of the hero of Sudbury fight, Wadsworth had succeeded in pleasing both liberals and conservatives. He was not eager for the office, but accepted out of a sense of duty. The Overseers promptly gave their consent, and the General Court as promptly voted Wadsworth a salary of £150. Before the end of the year he received a bonus of £70, together with the accumulated six years' net study rents of Massachusetts Hall, £180, which Leverett had asked for but not been allowed to touch; and the Court appropriated £1000 for a presidential dwelling in the Yard.

President Wadsworth was formally installed on Commencement day, July 7, 1725, but sixteen months elapsed before he could move into the new house, which served as presidential mansion for over a century, through President Everett's administration. Until the widenings of Massachusetts Avenue shortly after, Wadsworth House had a pleasant front garden; and a portion of the College Yard was fenced off for a President's Orchard, which was fertilized from the 'south privy,' the contents of which were voted by the Corporation to 'be at the Presidents Disposal.' A stable was provided, where President Wadsworth kept his horse until it reached the mature age of twenty-three, when he turned it in with £25 to boot for a 'dull and wapish' eight-year-old; and the old Bradish lot across the street (the site of Holyoke House) was a presidential perquisite, to grow hay, or what he would. One of the unpaid duties of freshmen was to make the President's hay. Massachusetts Avenue east of Harvard Square was a mere lane in the eighteenth century, called 'The Way to the Parsonage'—i.e., the parsonage built in 1670 on the edge of the present Yard, about opposite Plympton Street. The Charlestown Road (Kirkland Street) and Wood (Boylston) Street were the main roads into Cambridge. Travellers from the west came up the present Brattle Street as far as Craigie, and debouched into the Common near the site of Radcliffe.

Wadsworth's presidency of a little more than ten years re-established cordial relations between the two Governing Boards and with the provincial administration. As a final gesture of reconciliation, Nicholas Sever was elected to the Corporation in 1725, and on his marriage (and consequent resignation as tutor) he was succeeded by Tutor Prince. But it was an era of internal turbulence: for Wadsworth was no disciplinarian, and the young men resented a puritan restraint that was fast becoming obsolete. The faculty records, which begin with Wadsworth's administration, are full of 'drinking frolicks,' poultry-stealing, profane cursing and swearing, card-playing, live snakes in tutors' chambers, bringing 'Rhum' into college rooms, and 'shamefull and scandalous Routs and Noises for sundry nights in the College Yard.'

President Wadsworth was faithful, devoted, and methodical. He combed the records for evidence of college property, and did his best to recover lands alienated through the neglect of college officers or the enterprise of squatters. An Overseers' committee reported in 1732 that the annual free income of the College from investments was £728 7s per annum. A new code of college laws in eight chapters and ninety articles, the first since 1692, was drawn up by the Governing Boards after enough meetings to draft a state constitution, and promulgated in 1734. Improvements were made in the curriculum. Thomas Hollis, never wearying in well-doing although 'jeered and sneered at by many' for lavishing his property on the little college overseas, founded the Hollis Professorship of Mathematics and Natural Philosophy in 1727, with an endowment of £1200, and apparatus such as telescopes to go with it. He had intended to leave the money for this foundation by will; but Isaac Greenwood (A.B. 1721), a pupil of Thomas Robie's who visited London and studied science, persuaded Hollis to establish the chair at once, and to designate him as the first incumbent. Hollis carried out the promise, but lost confidence in his candidate when Greenwood departed from London £300 in debt. 'Perhaps, now he is free from his rakish company, and confined for weeks on shipboard, he may bethink himself,' wrote our truly charitable benefactor to the Harvard Corporation.

Greenwood not only bethought himself, but did much for science in New England by giving a course of popular lectures with demonstrations of 'the discoveries of the incomparable Sir Isaac Newton,' offering private lessons in higher mathematics, and undertaking (at Cotton Mather's suggestion) to be responsible for communicating meteorological observations to the Royal Society. He also published in Boston, shortly after his arrival in 1726, an excellent 'Experimental Course in Mechanical Philosophy.' The Corporation were still watchfully observing his personal habits when Thomas Hollis alarmed them by proposing to send over a Baptist as the first Hollis Professor. Knowing that such an appointment would renew the unhappy sectarian controversy with the Overseers and the public, they begged him 'not to nominate a Baptist

Professor' and hurriedly elected Greenwood. Mr. Hollis had a right, under the statutes of the chair, to veto the election; although sorely grieved by this unkind reflection on his faith, he accepted Greenwood, and sent the College a few more microscopes and quadrants.

Isaac Greenwood was installed the first Hollis Professor of Mathematics and Natural Philosophy on February 13, 1728. For several years he was an ornament to the College, and a great stimulus to science in the colonies. He was not kept outside the tutorial scheme of instruction, as professors are at Oxford, for the two upper classes were required to attend his 'publick[1] and private Lectures and Instructions and the Course of Experimental Philosophy.' Greenwood's appointment did much to bring the College in tune with the age, and to arrest the trend of practically inclined young men to private schools and to business. His 'Arithmetick, Vulgar and Decimal' (Boston, 1729) was the second arithmetic to be published in the English colonies, and the first by a native American. His several published papers in the Philosophical Transactions of the Royal Society, on meteorology, mine-damp, the Aurora Borealis, and Dighton Rock, show him a true child of the 'century of enlightenment'; and he urged the Society to undertake that for which the world had to await Matthew F. Maury — a systematic observation of meteorological phenomena at sea as a means of compiling a 'History of the Winds, and Weather in most parts of the Ocean.' But these publications and communications ceased after 1730. We may guess the reason from a vote of the Corporation in 1737, to the effect that 'the Mathematical Professor notwithstanding repeated warnings and Admonitions given him by the Corporation and the Honourable and Reverend the Overseers, hath been lately

---

[1] Public lectures in colonial Harvard, and until 1870, meant lectures open to the entire University, as distinct from private lectures to selected classes.

guilty of Various Acts of gross Intemperance, by excessive drinking, to the dishonour of God and the great hurt and Reproach of this Society.' After a public admonition and confession in hall, before the students, he was given another chance, but slipped twice in the next two weeks. The Corporation then voted his removal (December 7, 1737), but the Overseers, in view of the 'humble confession of his past Miscariages,' gave the Professor another six months to reform. He 'relapsed into his former crime of intemperance,' and was permanently separated from his alma mater in July, 1738. Under his pupil and successor, John Winthrop, Hollis Professor from 1738 to 1779, the chair gathered reputation without reproach.

President Wadsworth continued Leverett's policy of allowing Harvard students to take French lessons of an authorized outside instructor. Monsieur Louis Hector Piot de l'Angloiserie, son of a chevalier de Saint-Louis who emigrated to Canada, came to Boston as a tutor in the family of Governor Burnet. After the death of his patron, in 1729, 'Mr. Longlazaree' (as President Wadsworth called him) opened a French school in Boston, and in 1733 began spending three days a week in Cambridge, where the Harvard Faculty licensed him to give private lessons to college students, if their parents permitted. Within two years, however, Langloiserie began to experience strange visions and receive divine inspirations; and when Mr. Tutor Rogers and some of the students 'began to be favoured with *Visions* too,' the Overseers investigated, and declared M. Langloiserie's license void. Yet there was so much demand for the language of *la Grande Nation* that Nathaniel Gardner (A.B. 1739), a resident graduate, was allowed to give French lessons — President Holyoke's son was reading *Télémaque* with him in 1748. For the next forty years there was a succession of these licensed French teachers, one of them being a young gentleman named Albert Gallatin, lately arrived from Geneva. The first salaried instructor in French or in any modern language was Joseph Nancrede, appointed in 1787.

President Wadsworth died in office, on March 16, 1737, and after a decent interval of a month the two Governing Boards proceeded to an election with as much solemnity as if they had been a conclave of cardinals at Rome. On May 4 they spent the entire forenoon in the College Library 'in prayer to God for his gracious direction in the Important affair of Chusing a President.' Jehovah apparently was not quite ready to intervene in this matter of great moment. The Corporation spent the afternoon deadlocked, three to three, between the liberal Mr. Holyoke (A.B. 1705) of Marblehead and the conservative Mr. Gee (A.B. 1717), Mather's successor in the Second Church in Boston. After a long wait in the college hall for the divine afflatus to descend, the Overseers lost patience, desired the Corporation's presence, and informed the Fellows through Governor Belcher that they could have three weeks (with God's assistance) to decide, when they might communicate their choice to the senior Governing Board at the Council Chamber in the State House. William Cooper (A.B. 1712), Colman's colleague at the Brattle Street Church, was elected as a compromise candidate, but declined. What looked to be another prolonged contest for the presidency was apparently settled at Governor Belcher's dinner table. A conservative guest challenged the soundness of Holyoke's religious principles, but his colleague John Barnard declared him to be 'as orthodox a Calvinist as any man,' yet 'too much of a gentleman, and of too catholic a temper, to cram his principles down another man's throat.' 'Then he must be the man!' said the Governor, whose expert political ability was employed to such good purpose that Holyoke was unanimously elected, approved, and granted a salary of £200, plus the rents of Massachusetts Hall, by the legislature. A bonus of £140, to Marblehead, voted by the General Court, dried the tears of Mr. Holyoke's church.

President Holyoke's inauguration in the college hall on September 28, 1737, was the first occasion noted in our records when Psalm 78, 'Give ear my Children,' the traditional Commencement psalm, was sung. That evening, the Boston press informs us, 'the Windows of the Three Colleges were finely illuminated, while the Chambers rang with melodious Joy and Singing.'

Edward Holyoke's presidency of thirty-two years, the longest in our history save Eliot's, was one of prosperity and progress for the College. President Stiles of Yale describes Holyoke as a 'polite Gentleman, of a noble commanding presence'; he was forty-eight years old at the time of his election. In character and talents he much resembled Leverett: a man of sufficient learning to direct a society of scholars, and of requisite worldliness to deal with royal governors and members of the provincial legislature; no orator or author, but a gentleman of innate dignity and sense of justice, who understood young men and liked them. The students nicknamed him 'Guts,' of which he certainly had a-plenty. His native vigor and determination stand out in Copley's excellent portrait, in which he is shown seated in the ancient Tudor chair, the presidential throne that was presented to the College in his day. Holyoke felt that, after the cautious administration of Wadsworth, it was time to return to the relatively aggressive liberalism of Leverett's day; and it is probably more than a coincidence that so many of the New Englanders who took a leading part in the American Revolution had their education under him.

Just what did this Harvard liberalism of the eighteenth century amount to? Not very much, according to our modern lights; there was just enough notion of academic freedom to give Harvard a bad name among strict Calvinists. In Holyoke's time the Overseers asserted their 'right to examine into the principles of all those that are employed in the instruction of the students of the College, upon any just suspicion of their holding dangerous tenets,' and insisted on quizzing every new tutor on religion before confirming the appointment. When three M.A. candidates at Commencement, 1739, proposed to take the negative of Calvinist tenets such as 'Whether Three Persons in the Godhead are revealed by the Old Testament,' the Overseers insisted on the printed Quaestiones being altered with pen and ink to the affirmative. Many other items may be culled from our records to indicate that Harvard was then what we should now call a denominational college; but it is significant that such acts as we have quoted were generally done by the Overseers who represented Church and State, rather than by the President and Fellows of the College.

Despite inspectorial vigilance, both Harvard College and the Congregational Church were broadening down from primitive Calvinism to eighteenth-century Deism or Unitarianism. This peaceful process was rudely interrupted by an evangelical revival known as the Great Awakening. The preliminary rumblings of that movement in the Connecticut Valley did not disturb Cambridge; but in September, 1740, the whirlwind revivalist George Whitefield arrived in Boston, addressed fifteen thousand people on Boston Common, and on the twenty-fourth preached to students and townspeople in Cambridge meetinghouse. Harvard men were divided in opinion as to the wisdom and value of this first of modern revivals. Many who feared that religion was in a declining state welcomed an evangelist who packed the churches and made shoals of converts; conservatives who deplored the liberal tendencies of the age were delighted at the straight hell-and-damnation Calvinism that Whitefield preached; but 'enthusiasm' in general and Whitefield's pulpit antics in particular offended the good taste

and settled traditions of New England Congregationalism, whilst the rabble-rousing tactics of certain Whitefield disciples alarmed the propertied classes. College-
trained ministers who refused to lend countenance to the
revival were denounced by Whitefield, and the exhorters
who followed in his wake, as 'unconverted heathen,'
'Priests of Baal,' and the like; churches were split, families
rent, and the harvest of converts was followed by an after-
math of uncharitableness, backbiting, and the most offensive holier-than-thou attitude toward sceptics and opponents.

Whitefield was entertained by President Holyoke, and
listened to with eager attention by the students; but he
found little to praise at Harvard, where, so his supporters
told him, the state of 'piety and true godliness' was not
much better than at Oxford and Cambridge. 'Tutors
neglect to pray with, and examine the hearts of, their
pupils,' who read 'bad books' such as the works of Tillotson and Clarke, Whitefield observed. A bit of repartee
from Tutor Flynt was highly relished by the Harvard
community. Whitefield remarked, 'It is my opinion that
Dr. Tillotson is in hell for his heresy,' to which Flynt replied, 'It is my opinion that you will not meet him there!'
The same wise and level-headed old tutor, then beginning
his forty-second year of teaching youth, recorded in his
diary the effect of Whitefield's visit, and that of his disciple Gilbert Tennent, on the undergraduates: 'Many
Schollars appeared to be in great concern as to their souls.
. . . They prayed together sung Psalms and discoursed
together 2 or 3 at a time and read good books.' They
told eagerly of their visions, convictions, assurances, and
consolations. One 'pretended to see the divil in shape of
a bear coming to his bedside'; some were 'under great
terrors'; others 'had a succession of clouds and Comforts';
some talked of 'the free grace of God in Election and of the
decrees.' 'I told him that the Almightys decrees were

above them and they should not much trouble themselves about them at present.' President Holyoke and the other fellows and tutors were, or came to be, of the same opinion; but the Overseers, as usual, took the other side. On the ground that Whitefield had made 'extraordinary and happy impressions of a religious nature' on the students, to the good of college order and discipline, the Overseers appointed a public day of thanksgiving, which, one gathers, was considered rather a joke by most of the students. The faculty records certainly show no signs of improvement in undergraduate conduct. In 1740 Guy Fawkes Day was illegally celebrated as usual with firecrackers and squibs, and there were so many rum parties in the Yard as to suggest a spiritous rather than a spiritual cause of the ursine apparition at the student's bedside.

A typical effect of the Great Awakening on its converts was shown in the conduct of a Harvard student named Bird. This young man was complained of to the Faculty by his pastor, an Overseer of the College, for gross discourtesy, such as refusing to stand or uncover in his presence, and calling him a 'dumb dog that cannot bark.' The young man admitted the charge, and defended himself on the ground that this reverend gentleman was unqualified for the ministry because 'when he preached against sinners it comes to no more than against open and scandalous sinners, and never preaches the Doctrines of original sin, Election, Justification of Faith and Regeneration.' As Bird refused to apologize and declared he wanted no college degree, he was taken at his word and expelled. But the young fanatic soon found his want of a degree a bar to the settled ministry, and almost drove the college authorities frantic by his persistent demands that the once despised A.B. be conferred on him out of course.

On Whitefield's next visit to New England he was not invited to preach at Cambridge, and both he and his fellow-exhorters began to denounce Harvard from the pulpit as a house of impiety and sin. In view of his large popular following, this was a serious matter. The Faculty, after much cogitation, published 'The Testimony Of the President, Professors, Tutors and Hebrew Instructor of Harvard College, Cambridge, Against the Reverend Mr. George Whitefield, And his Conduct' (Boston, 1744), describing him as a person who by his 'furious zeal . . . had so fired the passions of the people' as, in many places, to have 'burnt up the very vitals of religion,' and denouncing his reproachful reflections on the College as rash, arrogant, slanderous, and 'a most wicked and libellous falsehood.' Whitefield replied in a pamphlet sufficiently betraying the hearsay nature of his knowledge of Harvard, but persisting in his opinions. Professor Wigglesworth answered the reply, others joined in, and for a year or more the pamphlet warfare continued. Twenty years later, when the Harvard Library was burned, Whitefield was so magnanimous as to give both money and books, and to procure 'large benefactions from several benevolent and respectable gentlemen,' for which the College gave thanks, and procured the evangelist's portrait for her gallery. But the impression of 'godless Harvard' that Whitefield created among New Englanders whose piety was only equalled by their ignorance, persisted until the Unitarian controversy offered something new in Cambridge to rail at in the name of religion.

Coolness and firmness against the menace of fanaticism paid the College in the end, but depressed its enrolment for many years. An oath bill, designed to impose Calvinism on Harvard, was talked of in 1747, but came to nothing. Yale, which had also frowned on the revival, though from an extreme conservative rather than a liberal repugnance, was less fortunate. As a result of clerical and political pressure, the Yale Corporation voted that 'the students should be established in the principles of religion, according to the [Westminster] Assembly's Catechism.

Dr. Ames's "Medulla" and "Cases of Conscience,"' and none other; and that every officer of the College must publicly subscribe to the Westminster Confession of Faith and the Saybrook Platform of the Congregational churches of Connecticut before entering upon his duties. Thus the second college in New England became definitely sectarian, just as sectarian control of Harvard was breaking down; and it must be admitted that Yale took the popular side. Shortly after this test was imposed, her enrolment pulled ahead of Harvard's. When Christ Church, the first Episcopal church in Cambridge, was built in 1760, the Harvard Faculty allowed students to attend service there, instead of at the Congregational meeting, if their parents permitted; but Yale forbade her students to attend Episcopal service in New Haven, well into the next century. And while Yale stoutly upheld the revivified Calvinism of the great Edwards, Professor Wigglesworth at Harvard invited his divinity pupils to examine both sides, declined Edwards's own request to take part in a joint offensive against Arminianism, and helped to educate such harbingers of liberal Christianity as Jonathan Mayhew (A.B. 1744).

This distinct difference in religious temperature between the two colleges was determined very largely by their respective communities: New Haven was a small place, and Connecticut a rural colony, curiously isolated from the outside world, at a time when Massachusetts was a royal province with a miniature viceregal court, and Boston a trading metropolis that aped the manners and reflected the fashions of England. On the whole, Harvard succeeded in keeping as far ahead of popular religious prejudice, and so far independent of sectarian control, as the times and circumstances made wise or possible. Too abrupt a change in religious matters would have isolated Harvard in the New England community, diminished her usefulness, and, at the time of the Revolution, endangered her existence. There are still those who believe that, by keeping the Calvinist machine running, Yale and Princeton conserved certain values that were dissipated at Cambridge in the exhaust of Unitarianism; but it is difficult nowadays to imagine a Harvard linked up with fundamentalism. It was not inevitable that Harvard College should become a great university; the wisdom and devotion of countless people have furthered the process; but for the indispensable preliminary of clearing the religious air, we may well give credit to Leverett, Colman, Holyoke, and Wigglesworth.

The curriculum was much in need of overhauling when Holyoke became President. Tutor Prince complained that Aristotelian texts were still being used in Logic, Physics, and Metaphysics; even the newspapers complained of bad Harvard Latin. Over a period of twenty-five years so many obsolete books were replaced by new works that the undergraduate course at the end of Holyoke's régime had little in common with that of Leverett's day. Professors Greenwood and Winthrop modernized the scientific instruction, and in 1743 Watts's Astronomy, Gordon's Geographical Grammar, and an excellent digest of Natural Philosophy by Newton's Dutch disciple 's Gravesande, were adopted. Fordyce's Elements of Moral Philosophy and Locke's Essay on the Human Understanding became the textbooks of Ethics and Metaphysics. In 1755 further improvements in methods as well as materials were initiated by the Board of Overseers, which by that time included a number of unusually intelligent and cultivated gentlemen, such as Thomas Hutchinson, Jonathan Mayhew, Andrew Eliot, Charles Chauncy, Mather Byles, Isaac Royall, and Benjamin Lynde. In order to improve English oratory, an important consideration in that age of budding lawyer-politicians, the system of Exhibitions, which lasted over a century, was introduced in 1756. Twice a year, in spring and fall, selected students of the two upper classes gave a Public Exhibition, as it was called, of debates, dialogues, and orations, mostly in the English language. For the first time in the college history prizes were offered for scholarship; and the books provided by the Hopkins Trustees, formerly awarded to needy students, were now given for merit, as the bookplate with the college arms and the legend *Detur Digniori* ('to the more worthy let it be given') proclaimed. Freshmen were ordered to begin Caesar's Commentaries after finishing William Brattle's Compendium of the Port Royal Logic; and 'Horace shall be earlier enterd upon, than of late hath been practis'd.'

The most essential reform of Holyoke's administration was doing away with the ancient system of each tutor's taking a class through all subjects in the curriculum. The four tutors became specialists in January, 1767; to one was assigned all instruction in Latin; to another, Greek; to a third, Logic, Metaphysics, and Ethics; to a fourth, Natural Philosophy, Mathematics, Geography, and Astronomy; and all four taught Rhetoric, Elocution, and English composition, in accordance with the excellent principle that everyone should teach English, no matter what other subject he taught. The Hollis Professor of Divinity took charge of religious instruction, and Professor Winthrop continued to deliver his 'experimental lectures' in Natural Science until the hegira to Concord separated him from the 'philosophical apparatus.'

Commencement Theses and Quaestiones showed progressive tendencies, and even included subjects in political theory, with particular reference to the disputes that were beginning with the home government. For instance:

1729. Is unlimited obedience to rulers taught by Christ and His Apostles? Joseph Green argues the negative.

1733. Is the Voice of the People the Voice of God? Nathanael Whittaker argues the affirmative.

1743.   Is it Lawful to resist the Supreme Magistrate, if the Commonwealth cannot otherwise be preserved? Samuel Adams argues the affirmative.

1743, 1747, 1751, 1761, 1762.   Does Civil Government originate from Compact? Samuel Downe, Thomas Cushing, Charles Chauncy, Thomas Wentworth and Nathan Goodale argue the affirmative.

1758.   Is Civil Government absolutely necessary for Men? John Adams argues the affirmative.

1759.   Is an Absolute and Arbitrary Monarchy contrary to Right Reason? Joseph Sluman argues the affirmative.

1765.   Can the new Prohibitary Duties, which make it useless for the People to engage in Commerce, be evaded by them as Faithful Subjects? Elbridge Gerry argues the affirmative.

1769.   Is a Just Government the only stable foundation of Public Peace? William Pepperrell argues the affirmative.

1769.   Are the People the sole Judges of their Rights and Liberties? John Hunt argues the affirmative.

1770.   Is a Government tyrannical in which the Rulers consult their own interest more than that of their Subjects? Thomas Bernard argues the affirmative.

1770.   Is a Government despotic in which the People have no check on the Legislative Power? Increase Sumner argues the affirmative.

How prophetic are the quaestiones of the 'brace of Adamses' of their future careers! And Gerry's of the finespun distinctions with which he was wont to justify his political tergiversations! But William Pepperrell, grandson of the hero of Louisburg, became a Tory; and Thomas Bernard, son of the Royal Governor, followed his father to England. Joe Green, at the head of the list, may be suspected of arguing with his tongue in his cheek; for he became a leading wit, poetaster, and member of that Fire Club the name of which pious Bostonians prefixed with 'Hell.'

As early as 1758 we find evidence of plays being performed by the undergraduates in college hall: Addison's *Cato* and *The Roman Father*; *The Recruiting Officer*; *The*

Orphan; a scene from Terence before the Overseers' Visiting Committee (1762); and, in 1765, 'Scholars punished at College for acting over the great and last day in a very shocking manner, personating the Devil, etc.'

President Holyoke was particularly interested in what Stiles called 'mathematical-mechanic Philosophy,' and he gave every aid and encouragement to the Hollis Professor of Mathematics and Natural Philosophy. John Winthrop, who was appointed at the age of twenty-four to the chair vacated by his master Greenwood, was the first important scientist or productive scholar on the teaching staff of Harvard College. He had prepared himself with general reading and observations of natural phenomena; he mastered Newton's *Principia*; and with the excellent apparatus presented by Thomas Hollis and others, devoted himself to teaching the mathematical and physical sciences, and to research. In that happy century when the frontiers of science were so close that a man might range the entire length, Winthrop's versatility equalled that of Benjamin Franklin, whose lifelong friend he became; [1] and with the time and means at his disposal, he was able to carry investigation deeper than Franklin on many subjects. As early as 1746 Winthrop delivered experimental lectures on electricity. He made the first scientific observations on sun-spots in America. Well aware of the importance of transit observations, his report on the transit of Mercury over the sun in 1740 was printed with two others by the Royal Society of London, and he induced the General Court of Massachusetts to co-operate with the College in fitting out the first American astronomical expedition, to Newfoundland, in order to observe the transit of Venus of 1761. In his 'apparatus chamber' in Massachusetts Hall, later transferred

---

[1] Harvard and Yale gave Franklin his first honorary degrees the same year, 1753; and Franklin was assiduous in procuring at London books for the Harvard College Library and apparatus for Professor Winthrop.

to the west end of Old Harvard, and re-established in the upper east chamber of the present Harvard Hall in 1765, Winthrop ruled over the first laboratory of experimental physics in this country. He may also claim the title of seismologist for his two lectures in Holden Chapel on earthquakes, following the famous Lisbon quake of 1755. In proving that earthquakes were purely natural phenomena, and not manifestations of divine wrath, he attracted the unpleasant attention of some of the clergy, and demonstrated to the laity the value of experimental research, untrammelled by theological considerations. Thus academic freedom was established in at least one department of knowledge. His observations on Halley's comet, first read as a lecture to Harvard students and later to the Royal Society by Dr. Franklin, carried on the work begun at Harvard by Thomas Brattle; and the results of other investigations by Winthrop were of practical value to geographers, navigators, and meteorologists. Equally skilled as a teacher, Winthrop had the privilege of introducing four decades of undergraduates to the scientific point of view, and of imparting the first impulse to at least one greater American scientist than himself — Benjamin Thompson (Count Rumford), who described him as 'an excellent and happy teacher.'

One of the smaller telescopes that Professor Winthrop used, the orrery with which he demonstrated the solar system to the students, and several other specimens of his 'philosophical apparatus' are still owned by the College, gathering dust in a storage basement. It would be a graceful gesture, and one of great importance to the history of science, if the old 'Philosophy Chamber' in Harvard Hall, where the future Count Rumford sat at the feet of this 'happy teacher,' could be restored as an eighteenth-century laboratory, and our ancient scientific instruments there displayed.

Holyoke's administration saw the first addition to the

group of three college buildings shown in the well-known Burgis view of 1726. Thomas Hutchinson (A.B. 1727), future royal governor, was responsible for obtaining in 1741, from Jane, widow of Samuel Holden of London, Governor of the Russia Company and a director of the Bank of England, £400 to build a college chapel. Holden Chapel, a little gem of Georgian architecture, with Mrs. Holden's arms magnificently achieved on the east pediment, was completed in 1744. It was originally entered from the western end, and the pews were arranged longitudinally as in an English college chapel. Holden was used as a chapel for but twenty years, and then only for daily prayers, as the College continued to attend the Sabbath meetings of the Congregational Church in Harvard Square. When Harvard Hall was built, the western room on the ground floor became the 'new chapel,' and Holden was used successively as a lecture room, barracks for the Continental army, college lumber room and fire-engine house, medical lecture hall and anatomical museum, medical museum and chemical lecture room, and practice hall and lecture room for the departments of Philosophy, Music, and Public Speaking. Although some of the unsightly partitions and other 'improvements' were removed fifty years ago, the complete restoration of Holden Chapel to its original decency and beauty remains to be done.

By 1761 the College was so crowded that over ninety students were compelled to lodge in town, and the Governing Boards petitioned the Province to provide them with a new residential building. The General Court generously appropriated £2500, and appointed a joint committee to oversee the construction; the College had no more to do with it than to furnish the ground and stake out the site. On January 13, 1764, the building was dedicated, and by Governor Bernard named Hollis Hall, after the English family that had sent a steady stream of benefactions to Harvard for almost half a century. Like all the older buildings of the Yard, Hollis was designed to face westward, as may be seen by the particular attention paid to the now closed doors on that façade. Originally two passages, one for each entry, went straight through the ground floor; but the apparently blocked-up doors in the centre were false from the beginning, inserted presumably in order to fulfil a provincial interpretation of Palladian symmetry. Hollis and its later and less distinguished companion Stoughton (1805) were the last Harvard buildings to have the medieval chamber-and-study arrangement. Most of the corner studies were thrown into the chambers in 1869–70; but a few remain, as in Hollis 7, 11, and 15, between the chimney breast and the inner partition.

A few days after the opening of Hollis, on the night of January 24, 1764, occurred the worst disaster in the history of the College — the burning of Old Harvard Hall. It was winter vacation, and the building was being used for sessions of the General Court during a smallpox epidemic in Boston. A fire left burning overnight in the library got into the floor-beams, and before anything was suspected the whole building was in flames A northeast snowstorm was raging at the time. President Holyoke (aged seventy-five) and Governor Bernard personally directed the townspeople and members of the General Court in the work of rescue. The unknown author of *Harvardinum Restauratum* describes how 'Our senators, By fell contagion, from the Capital Driv'n out,'

> . . . Rush'd forth amid huge banks of snow,
> With resolution arm'd; each active hand,
> Obedient to the heart, in learning's cause
> Engag'd, was full employ'd, with force to oppose
> The stanch devourer, but alas! in vain!
> Down rush precipitate, with thund'ring crash,
> The roofs, the walls, and in one ruinous heap,
> The ancient dome, and all it's treasures lie!

The most they could do with heavy snow on the ground, and only well-water in buckets available for an extinguisher, was to save Hollis. The entire library of five thousand volumes, excepting some two hundred that were lent out at the time, was consumed; the whole philosophical apparatus, the portraits of presidents, benefactors, Duns Scotus, and Keckermann, were burnt up; the stuffed animals and birds, model of the *Boston* man-of-war, piece of tanned negro's hide, 'Skull of a Famous Indian Warrior,' and in fact the entire 'Repositerry of Curiosities,' were seen no more.

This disaster was the occasion of a wonderful outpouring of generosity to the College. The General Court, taking the responsibility for our loss,

> Command another edifice t' ascend,
> From the same spot where ancient Harvard stood;
> But O! how diff'rent, from that antique pile!
> In room of Gothic structure, erst the taste
> Of Britain's sons, now Grecian elegance
> And Roman Grandeur rising to the view,
> Here strike the modern eye. . . .

The students were indemnified for the loss of their personal belongings; the Province of New Hampshire, presided over by Governor Benning Wentworth (A.B. 1715), appropriated a sum of money to restore the library; Thomas Hollis (third benefactor of that name) sent over a remarkable collection of well-bound books on political theory stamped with his peculiar devices; and graduates emptied their bookshelves to replace the volumes destroyed. It seems to have been realized then, as today, that a library is the heart of a university, the first necessity of a society of scholars. And in the new Harvard Hall, completed in June, 1766, from designs by Governor Bernard,

> The splendid tomes, throughout the spacious room,
> Like orient sol diffuse their beamy glories!

The new library was installed in the upper west chamber of Harvard Hall, arranged in ten alcoves, with the names of the principal benefactors emblazoned in blue and gold, as in Duke Humphrey's Library at the Bodleian. Across the entry a passage led to the Philosophy School (later called Philosophy Chamber), which was Professor Winthrop's lecture room and laboratory; and on either side of the passage was a small lecture room 15 by 17½ feet; the southern one was the 'Hebrew School,' and the other, in 1769, was allotted to the new 'Musaeum.' These were the first rooms ever built specially for lectures or recitations at Harvard College, and Harvard Hall was the first of our buildings that included no chambers and studies. The ground floor was divided by the traditional throughpassage into two finely proportioned rooms, 36 by 45 feet; that on the east end was the college hall. Originally it had no windows in the eastern end where the dais was; in the centre was the hall fireplace, and on either side a niche where portraits of George III and Queen Charlotte hung — but not for long. Even after commons were removed to University Hall in 1815, and until Memorial was built in 1874, this hall remained *the* college hall, and was used for commencement dinners and class day dances.[1] The room on the west end was the 'New Chapel,' replacing Holden, which was given over to various baser uses. The college kitchen in the eastern end of the basement continued, like the old kitchen, to be one of the sights of Cambridge; the buttery, for want of proper accommodation in new Harvard, was transferred to the ground floor of Massachusetts.

Indirectly, the fire of 1764 provided a new college sport, described in a song of the last century as running

---

[1] In 1841-42 the hall was made to embrace the whole lower story; in 1869-70 the proportions were ruined by an addition to the south side of the building, and numerous partitions within. Since that date the three rooms on the lower floor have been used for physical laboratory, historical reading room, recitations, and lectures.

'with the old ma-chine.' In 1764 the General Court presented a 'water engine' worth £100, which the students were delighted to operate, in rivalry with the Cambridge apparatus. Sam Chandler describes how, on May 29, 1773,

... by reason of their seeing the Fire first also ours being locked up, the Town Engine got their before ours but by the Activity of the Scholars our Engine got placed (although they had to go over and break down several Fences to git in a proper place) filled, played upon the House extinguished the Fire and got away from it before the Town's had got filled and rady to play. this is not the first time that the Scholars have had the Prefirence.

In the matter of buildings, the College obtained in the eighteenth century the best that provincial architects could devise, and master builders erect. Hollis, Holden, Harvard, and Massachusetts are justly considered models of Georgian architecture; and Old Harvard, had it lasted, would be one of the curiosities of the country. But the College Yard, which in colonial days extended only as far east as a line roughly parallel to the front of University, was an unseemly clutter of outhouses. It appears to have been almost treeless, except for the elm shown in the Burgis Prospect of 1726, the 'sacred, venerable Elm' referred to in 'The Lamentation of Harvard' (1764), and the 'Liberty' or 'Rebellion Tree' on the east side of Hollis. The well-known Class Day Tree of the last century showed only 127 annual rings when it was cut down in 1911, but there was a small tree on the site in 1790.

President Holyoke held his office to a greater age than any of his predecessors or successors. He died after a long illness on June 1, 1769, shortly before his eightieth birthday. Boston was then occupied by British troops, and the House of Representatives refused to assemble 'with cannon, pointed at the very door of the State House,' as inconsistent with their dignity. Governor Bernard cynically adjourned the legislature to Cambridge, where they held their sessions first in Holden Chapel and subsequently in the 'new chapel' on the ground floor of Harvard Hall. Professor Winthrop, who presided at the following Commencement, was offered the presidency of the College, but declined on account of his age. After one or two others had refused, the Corporation elected a thirty-five-year-old country clergyman, the Reverend Samuel Locke (A.B. 1755) of Sherborn. He had been a good scholar in college, and, like many such, had spent the intervening years since his graduation buried in a country parish. President Stiles of Yale considered President Locke a man of strength, penetration, and judgment, superior to Holyoke in everything except classical learning and personal dignity. But for the unfortunate weakness that undid him, Locke might have been a great President.

President Locke's 'Installment,' on March 21, 1770, was the first inauguration ceremony in the meetinghouse in the Square, and the last of the colonial era. A procession, led by the students and concluded by 'The honorable House of Representatives,' 'The Reverend Clergy,' and 'A considerable number of respectable Gentlemen,' marched from Harvard Hall to the meetinghouse, where Lieutenant-Governor Hutchinson went through the usual ceremony of presentation, 'and the Solemnity was concluded with an Hymn and an anthem performed by the young Gentlemen of the College.' The procession then returned in reverse order to Harvard Hall, where Governing Boards, Representatives, 'and the other Gentlemen who had honored the solemnity with their presence,' were entertained at dinner.

President Holyoke remarked on his deathbed, 'If any man wishes to be humbled and mortified, let him become President of Harvard College.' Poor Mr. Locke soon had reason to subscribe to this statement. The College was full of brawls and politics, symptoms of the approaching war. Mr. Ezekiel Hersey (A.B. 1728), the venerable physician of Hingham, left the College £1000 'towards founding a professorship of Physic in Harvard College, an institution which has been long wanted in this Society'; but the time was past when the interest on that sum would keep a full professor. A lottery was started to provide a new building, but proved a failure. And on the first of December, 1773, it was announced to an astonished public that Mr. Locke had resigned his exalted position. No Harvard President had done such a thing for almost a century. No reason was given, and the Corporation, with a discretion quite unusual in that body, kept it a close secret. Not until the present century did it come to light, in the published Diary of President Ezra Stiles of Yale. A maidservant in the house of President Locke was great with child. Mr. Locke took the blame, retired to the country, and was promptly forgotten. His successor, the Reverend Samuel Langdon (A.B. 1740) of Portsmouth, New Hampshire, a man little qualified for the presidency either in learning or sense of government, happened to be a classmate of Samuel Adams, a friend of John Hancock, and an ardent patriot, which were considered more important qualifications for the presidency at that juncture of affairs than character or literary reputation. 'When President Langdon took the chair [October 14, 1774] it gave great delight to the sons of liberty,' but no particular gratification to the Sons of Harvard, who got rid of him as soon as they dared.

But before that day came, a great war had been fought almost to a finish, and the College had moved from its ancient seat to Concord and back.

VI

GOOD OLD COLONY TIMES

1710–1775

In the good old colony times,
  When we lived under the king,
Each Saturday night, we used to get tight,
A-pouring down gin-sling.

And Hollis used to roar,
  And Stoughton used to sing,
When the rollicking rabble lay under the table,
A-pouring down gin-sling.

THE only fault with this song (a popular one at Harvard in the eighteen-sixties) is the gin-sling. Rum, straight, diluted, or compounded in punch, was the popular colonial beverage in the eighteenth century; Madeira, the aristocratic wine; flip, negus, and other compounds were concocted in the College Yard and adjacent taverns; but gin-sling belongs to the degenerate era of saloons. It took the American Revolution to awaken Yankee distillers to the possibilities inherent in their native juniper berries and their garden mint, which, added to gin, sugar, and water, made the sling. As the residuary legatee of a tradition passed down from some five or six generations, from a series of grandfathers to grandsons, uncles to nephews, and fathers to sons, to the effect that 'there was far more drinking when *I* was in college than there is *now*' — a pronouncement always received with a certain incredulity — I am unprepared to believe that the year 1759, so studded with glorious victories to celebrate (Quebec, Ticonderoga, Quiberon

Bay, Minden) — *annus mirabilis* 1759 — marks the all-time high of student potation. For it was this year — on April 24, to be exact — that the Honorable and Reverend the Board of Overseers formally recommended to President and Fellows the repeal of 'the Law prohibiting the drinking of Punch,' and that the Corporation permitted a Commencer to 'entertain any of the Guests at his Chamber, with Punch.' Two years later, with even more victories to celebrate, the Overseers brought the Corporation to concur in a joint vote that 'it shall be deemed no offence, if the scholars, shall in a sober manner entertain one another and strangers with punch (which as it is now usually made, is no intoxicating liquor).' Good old colony times, indeed!

Even then, there was more to the College than drinking. Harvard in the eighteenth century was conducted very much as it had been during the century of foundation. Numbers increased; but the largest graduating class before the Revolution, that of 1771, numbered but sixty-three; and it was not until 1810 that another reached that figure. The median age of entering freshmen rose from a low of little over fifteen years in 1741 to seventeen years in 1769, and stayed at about that point during the rest of the century. A very large proportion of the students came from eastern Massachusetts and New Hampshire. The Harvard men who settled in Connecticut or in the central valley of Massachusetts mostly sent their sons to Yale, although occasionally one of these became dissatisfied and transferred to Harvard. Not a single New Yorker entered between 1737 and 1790. The largest 'foreign' clientele came from the Carolinas and the West Indies; about one student every two years from 1737 on. Socially, the College was fairly representative of the upper layers of New England. Merchants, magistrates, and ministers furnished the larger number, but there were a good many sons of plain farmers and artisans, as the town and country parsons made it their business to shape up poor but promising lads for 'university learning'; and there were now plenty of scholarships and exhibitions to pay all or part of a student's expense. President Leverett wrote to Thomas Hollis in 1720 that £20 a year would cover the board and lodging of a poor scholar; but the cost of doing it comfortably was of course much higher. One father testified that his son's Harvard education in the Class of 1769 cost £213 6s 8d lawful money of New England, in specie.

The eighteenth century saw an increase in comfort and convenience in household furnishings that was reflected in the students' rooms. The lists submitted by the students burned out in 1764 show tables, chairs, and feather-beds; pictures and looking-glasses; Spectators, Tatlers, Gentleman's Magazines, and books of plays; pipes and tobacco, rum and other spirits (prohibited by the college laws), corkscrews, glasses, beakers, punch bowls, chafing-dishes, and tea sets; clothing, wigs, and crisping irons; and one Bible.

Admission requirements remained much as they always had been: the College Laws of 1734 stated them as ability 'ex tempore to read, construe and parse Tully, Virgil, or Such like common Classical Latin Authors; and to write true Latin in Prose, and to be Skill'd in making Latin verse, or at Least in the rules of Prosodia; and to read, construe and parse ordinary Greek, as in the New Testament, Isocrates, or such like, and decline the Paradigms of Greek Nouns, and Verbs.' Entrance examinations were conducted by the President and tutors, and held shortly before Commencement, the date being announced in the newspapers. The examinations were oral, except that the student was usually required to write a Latin essay, to test his skill in 'making' Latin. If the President was satisfied, the candidate procured a copy of the College Laws and presented it to him to have his *admittatur* signed. The freshman then went home for the six weeks' summer vacation. When the fall term began, about the middle of August, the class was 'placed' in temporary seniority by the College Steward; and in the following spring the Faculty went through the solemn business of settling the permanent seniority. The principles of this important rite still remain pretty much of a mystery. As late as 1712 we have evidence that it was done on the basis of scholastic merit, except that the head of the class, who by custom had to give a dinner for his classmates, was generally a member of the colonial aristocracy: son of the Royal Governor, or of a Councillor, or of one of the great mercantile families. Fellow-commoners were always placed ahead of anyone else, but very few parents cared to pay the double tuition and present the piece of plate that bought this privilege for their sons; the last Harvard fellow-commoner was George Ball of the Class of 1734. Students who entered after the official 'placing,' or who were transferred from one class to another, were placed at the foot of the class; and degradation of one or more places, sometimes to the very foot, was a common punishment for misconduct. The culprit generally made his humble confession, and was restored to his original place, before graduation.

It is clear that by 1749 the entire class were placed in the order of the presumed official or social rank of their parents; but there was no exact slide-rule for this, and a good many apparent discrepancies are found. As the classes became larger, this process became more and more complicated, and the task of placating provincial pomposity more difficult. Finally in 1769, after a proud father (Samuel Phillips) had complained that his son was placed in the Class of 1772 below a boy whose father had not been a Justice of the Peace as long as he, the Overseers voted that the arrangement in future should be alphabetical. Yale had so decided the year before. There is no evidence that democratic feeling had anything to do with the change; social pretensions became progressively difficult to rate as classes increased, and the existing system caused too much vexation and jealousy. After the change, as before, students marched in the frequent academic processions, and took seats in commons, at prayers, and in the meetinghouse, according to their order of seniority.

One of the first rites of the college year was for the sophomores to take the freshmen into the 'Long Chamber' over the Library in Old Harvard, read them the 'College Customs,' and threaten them with all manner of dreadful punishments if they did not strictly obey. These College Customs were not written down (so far as we have record) before 1735; but there is reason to believe that most of them went back to the earliest days of the College. They had reference chiefly to a system of freshman servitude similar to the fagging in the English public schools, and so called at Harvard. As a sign of his inferiority, a freshman must not wear his hat in the Yard or at meals, 'except it rains, snows, or hails, or he be on horse back or haith both hands full,' and outside the Yard he must uncover to his seniors — i.e., to a sophomore or upperclassman. He may not halloa up or down the corridors, toss a ball in the Yard, 'mingo' against the college wall, or enter the fellows' 'cuzjohn.' He must stand upright, not 'lean,' at prayers. He must run errands for any of his seniors who requires his services, and not consider himself dismissed until his temporary master says 'It is well' — the eighteenth-century equivalent of 'O.K.' But his errands must have been much interrupted, for a member of any of the seven classes in the college hierarchy could 'take' a freshman away from anyone of the class next but one below his. For instance, a senior sophister could take a freshman from a sophomore, and send him on a different errand; a Bachelor of Arts could take from a junior sophister, a Master of Arts from a

senior sophister, and a tutor from anybody. Apparently
the youngsters were kept very busy taking wigs to be
curled and clothes to be washed or pressed, fetching food
and drink from taverns, and carrying notes from one
building to another; for the Cambridge shopkeepers of
the time maintained no delivery or 'valeteria' service,
and Harvard employed no 'scouts.' In a textbook, for
instance, we find the inscription:

> Call for a Tankard
> My Cloths at pollards
> Get some Pisado: Clarett
> buy a grater.   Some Lime-juice

— which was probably a message for some errand-run-
ning freshman; and on the flyleaf of another book is
written this genial message:

> Davenport: Sir these are to entreat you to step up to Swans study
> and drink a glass of ale
> > So I rest yours to serve
> > > JOHN PHILLIPS

The wise freshman attached himself to a definite senior
sophister, who protected him from the importunities of
juniors and sophomores, and allowed him to study in his
chamber, in order to be handy for personal errands.

The general use of academic gowns came in during
this century. A graduate in 1712 offered to outfit the
members of the College with gowns, but apparently
nothing was done about it at the time. Burgis's 'Prospect
of the Colledges' of 1726 shows figures stalking about the
Yard in loose, trailing gowns; but he may merely have
been copying Loggan's pictures of Oxford and Cambridge colleges. President Holyoke, in a letter of 1766,
refers to 'some years since, viz when the Scholars first
wore Gowns' (he was then thinking of having one himself); and the following curious certificate seems to indi-

cate that there was a ritual about acquiring gowns in 1747:

H: C: September the: 23 1747.

This may certify all, whom it may concern that Oliver Prescott Student at Harvard-College has paid sufficient Beverage for a new Gown one Side of which is red Russel and the other Plad.

As Witness our Hands. —

ARTEMAS WARD
JACOB CUSHING
TIMOTHY POND —

Prescott was a sophomore, Artemas Ward (the future Major-General) and Cushing were senior sophisters, and Pond a junior. I infer that sophomores were allowed to procure themselves gowns after treating the upperclassmen to drinks, and that the gowns might be of any bright color, like those of eighteenth-century Oxonians. In 1773, on the occasion of a classmate's funeral at Boston, the freshmen were allowed to wear 'Black Gowns and Square Hats'; and 'seemed very grand' as they 'walked about the Town with their Black Gowns on, the Inhabitants not knowing what it ment nor who they were.'

Above the four undergraduate classes were the junior bachelors, middle bachelors, and senior bachelors, studying for their Master's degree; most of them candidates for the ministry. A curious duty of junior bachelors was to wait on table at the Commencement dinner; one year, when there were only twelve in this class, two resident Masters had to help, or provide substitutes. Masters of Arts might engage a college chamber and remain members of the academic society indefinitely, and a considerable number did so, while waiting for jobs. Some of them were difficult to get rid of. In 1734, for instance, Mr. Thomas Pierpont (A.B. 1721), for cutting prayers and saying the college laws were 'not fit for a dog,' was given a month to clear out; but on confessing his fault and submitting that he had nowhere to go, he was allowed another month's grace. The next year he was still there. Two years later he was found to be lodging with various undergraduates, and was only pried loose from the College by the Faculty's forbidding the students under severe penalties to feed or lodge him

In this closely regulated college society, the President was a great and awful personage. One had to uncover or stand in his presence, and pay him every mark of deference known to a courteous age. He generally conducted morning and evening prayers in hall or chapel, and moderated the disputations of the bachelors, but took no part in the instruction unless a tutor was ill or absent. The President and the two Hollis professors, the Hebrew instructor, and the Hancock Professor of Hebrew (instituted in 1764) lived in their own houses, in or near the Yard; but the four tutors, who were not allowed to marry, lived in College, and took their meals in hall. The Steward, an important permanent official, lived outside, but the butler generally, and the librarian always, was a resident Bachelor or Master of Arts.

There was a considerable turnover in tutors, as in the seventeenth century; but the active teaching staff was academically inbred. Except for the French instructors, Harvard did not have a single professor or teacher not a Harvard graduate, before the nineteenth century. The only tutors who remained more than a few years were Belcher Hancock (A.B. 1727), a stupid fellow nicknamed 'the Bowl,' who remained a quarter-century; Nathan Prince, a gifted man who had to be expelled for repeated intemperance in 1742 after nineteen years' service; and the perennial Henry Flynt (A.B. 1693), tutor from 1699 to 1754. 'Father' Flynt was the great college character of the century. Presidents came and went, but Henry Flynt was always on hand when the first bell rang for prayers at the end of summer vacation. We have seen his cool and sceptical attitude toward the Great Awakening; when

Whitefield attacked the manners and morals of Harvard, Flynt's pupils rushed into print to testify that he had taught them to fear God and obey his commandments. The young 'blades,' as the sporting students were called early in the century, played wicked tricks on him: hid his wig, drank his wine behind his back (but he had a mirror, and caught them), cropped his mare, put snakes in his chamber; but he was always the one to plead for offenders in faculty meeting, saying that 'wild colts often make good horses.' David Sewall (A.B. 1755) has left a charming account of a chaise journey with the old gentleman from Cambridge to Portsmouth, New Hampshire. His speech was still of the puritan century, and he enjoyed his pipe and his morning glass of flip, and his evening bowl of punch. Every few miles along the road was the house of a former pupil eager to entertain him. One of the hostesses bespoke his charity for a young parson and his wife, who had lately been brought to bed with twins. Mr. Flynt observed that this event was not his fault, but consented to present a silver Spanish dollar. Madam remarked that she hoped this was simply a first instalment of his generosity, upon which Father Flynt said, 'Insatiable woman, I am almost sorry I have given you any thing!'

It was the custom for every graduating class to present their tutor with a tankard, or chafing-dish, or some such piece of silver plate. A number of these, by the best colonial silversmiths, have come into possession of the College, and are displayed in the Fogg Museum. Tutor Flynt accumulated so many of these tokens that one of his later classes, at a loss for something new, had made for him a solid silver chamber-pot, inscribed

Mingere cum bombis
Res est saluberrima lumbis,

and bore it to him in solemn procession on Commencement morning.

The students had somewhat more freedom than in the puritan century. The college day still began at six, with morning prayer in hall, followed by breakfast, which might be taken in hall or in one's chamber; and the custom grew up of giving breakfast parties, especially Sunday mornings, with food and drink brought in from town taverns. From eight to twelve there were lectures or recitations; then dinner, and recreation until two; from that time until supper the students were supposed to keep to their chambers and study. The former Spencer orchard, the lot on which Holden Chapel and Phillips Brooks House stand, was set apart as a 'play-place' in 1712, and later enlarged by the whole north end of the Yard; but the only hint of what games the students played therein is found in the 'college custom' that 'Freshmen are to find the rest of the scholars with bats, balls, and footballs.' Besides the summer vacation of six weeks, a winter vacation of five weeks, beginning the first Wednesday in January, was introduced in 1749, in order to allow poor scholars to keep school; one such student schoolmaster was allowed a six weeks' extension on the plea of his selectmen employers that they could find no substitute. In addition, students might go home four days every month, if they lived within ten miles of Cambridge, or, if they lived further away, take twenty-one days' absence twice a year. Requests for leave to go home early, and unauthorized tardy returns, were as common then as now; George Mountfort of New London was allowed to go home three weeks early in 1763, 'having Opportunity to ride back an horse that wou'd otherwise go home empty.' Eighteenth-century Harvard was quite 'horsey.' Five students went on an expedition in January, 1748, recalling the classic drive in Owen Wister's 'Philosophy 4.' They hired a 'Slay,' drove into Boston, then to the Greyhound Tavern in Roxbury, where they had supper and consumed drinks until ten or eleven, and returned to College about midnight, with much 'hollowing' and scampering behind buildings to elude the tutors. Sam Chandler, on a Wednesday in February, 'got Lieve of El[i]ot [his tutor] to go out of Town and went to Boston, upon a Frolick did not return till Thursday in the time of Commons.' In 1765 horse-races by students on the Common in study hours and after ten-thirty in the evening, 'being the Occasion of a great Riot,' had to be broken up by the Faculty.

Although the regulations left no apparent time for it, the students managed to get off for long rambles in the country in summer, or in winter to skate all the way to Boston on the rare occasions when the entire river was frozen. A poem that first appeared in the *New England Weekly Journal* in 1731, and has been reprinted in Mr. Aubin's 'Harvard Heroics' (1934), sings the charms of Fresh Pond in the true pastoral tradition:

> Of ancient Streams presume no more to tell,
> The fam'd Castalian or Pierian Well.
> Fresh-pond Superior, must those rills confess
> As much as *Cambridge* yields to *Rome* or *Greece*:
> More limpid Water can no Fountain show
> A fairer bottom or a smoother brow. . . .
> The throng of *Harvard* know thy pleasures well,
> Joys too Extravagant perhaps to tell;
> Hither oftimes the Learned Tribe repair,
> When Sol returning warms the growing Year.
> Some take the Fish with a delusive Bait,
> Or for the Fowl beneath the Arbours wait. . . .
> But some more humane seek the shady gloom,
> Taste Natures bounty and admire her bloom,
> In pensive tho't revolve long vanish'd toil,
> Or in soft Song the pleasing Hours beguile.

The usual punishments were pecuniary fines, or mulcts. The following list extracted from the College Laws of 1734 is arranged in a rising scale of heinousness, the fines in each instance being the maximum; which was seldom exacted.

Tardiness to prayers or lectures 2*d*

Absence from prayers or lectures 4*d*

Tarrying after vacation, per day 8*d*

Tarrying after chamber in study hours; going outside the Yard without coat or gown; entering meetinghouse before the bell (and so, probably, starting a rough-house) 2*s*

Absence from divine worship on the Sabbath; failure to repeat sermons; keeping a gun or pistol; going gunning, fishing, or 'scating over deep waters' without leave 3*s*

Fighting; lying; drunkenness; neglecting declamations; cutting classes; frequenting forbidden houses in Cambridge; gambling for money; swapping books or clothing; 'Tumultuous and Indecent Noises'; using or sending for distilled spirits, punch, or flip; going on roof of Old Harvard, or cutting lead from same 5*s*

Profane cursing and swearing; playing cards or dice; neglecting analysis of Scripture; walking or other diversion on the Sabbath; firing gun or pistol in Yard 10*s*

Breaking open doors or picking locks 20*s*

Blasphemy, fornication, robbery, forgery, 'or any other very atrocious crime' .... expulsion.

Expulsion was not a mere matter of telling the culprit to pack up his things and leave; it was a very solemn business, like breaking an army officer. The entire College was assembled in hall; the President announced the crime and the Corporation's sentence, and delivered a solemn warning to the students; the butler then brought in the buttery table, the bulletin board on which the names of all members of the College were posted in order of seniority, and cut out the expelled member's name.

Often that was not the end of it. The Faculty consistently maintained the Christian principle of forgiving any offense, however grave, if the culprit made a public confession and satisfied them that he repented of his sins. There are several instances of students' being expelled for

fornication or other 'atrocious' crimes who were readmitted after a year or so, graduated with their class, and
became useful and respected citizens, even ministers of
the gospel. Tutor Flynt was right: wild colts often did
make good horses.

Besides these formal punishments, President, professors, and tutors were permitted by college law and custom 'to punish Undergraduates by Boxing, when they
shall Judge the Nature or circumstances of the Offence
call for It.' Boxing consisted in making the culprit kneel,
and smacking him sharply with the hand on the ear. It
succeeded the flogging of the puritan century, the last instance of which that has come to my notice having occurred in 1718. The angry father of the victim wrote to
President Leverett complaining of this 'Horse disciplin.'
'I rather haue my Son abused as a man, then a beast. . . .
The rod on my Sons back, is a great rod on my Sper-
itt. . . .' In a postscript the President was reminded that
his grandfather the Governor once condemned *his* son,
President Leverett's father, to lie in jail from Saturday to
Monday!

President and tutors were especially vigilant lest their
prerogative of boxing be usurped by the upperclassmen.
One of the first measures of Leverett's administration was
to punish several sophomores for boxing freshmen; but,
wrote one of the culprits, 'the Gentlemen Freshmen in-
terceeded for us' by petitioning the Corporation to let
them off; and forgiven they were.

As a summary punishment, boxing was liable to abuse
even by those authorized to administer it, and the rising
notions of human dignity finally ruled it out. Samuel
Jordan (A.B. 1750) 'behaved himself with great Insolence
in resisting one of the Tutors attempting to box him for
singing in his Chamber in Studying time.' Five years
later the boxing law was suspended, and in the recodifi-
cation of the College Laws in 1767 it no longer appeared.

Nothing that any college faculty has ever devised has been completely successful in restraining the natural ebullience of youth. At Harvard the most frequent disturbances of the peace, judging from the faculty records, were 'indecent tumultous noises' and 'hollowing' or 'Huzzas' in the Yard late at night, sometimes followed by throwing brickbats through tutors' windows. President Wadsworth notes in his diary for Commencement, 1727:

> Sir Saltonstall, who had been appointed the first *Respondent* for the approaching Commencement, having been a Ringleader in revelling, and making great rackets and hollowings and tumultuous, confus'd noises in the College yard, was put by from being *Respondent*.

Saltonstall made a public confession in hall the next day; 'But, such a disorderly spirit at that time prevail'd, that there was not one undergraduate in the Hall besides Saltonstall, and three Freshmen. . . .' Two days later the Corporation met and considered the case of Saltonstall and his fellow-ringleader in the late uproar, appropriately named Howlett. Both were allowed to take their degree, but Saltonstall was degraded from head of his class to a place halfway down, and Howlett from the middle to the foot.

Late in the century there must have been a bowling alley in Cambridge, for Samuel Chandler (A.B. 1775) notes in his diary for that year bowling against his classmates for cakes and ale; he 'lost only one Bottle.' This was on an April afternoon, after prayers; and the next day Chandler slipped off to Boston to see the Cadets drill on King Street to the sound of a 'band of Musick which has lately come over.' The next day he missed morning prayers because 'at Morses to git my Heir dressed,' and was ordered by his tutor to keep his chamber until further notice. 'I am very tired after my Towr and almost resolved not to go to boston any more publeck Days.'

The Fifth of November was an anniversary that the

students never failed to remember, despite annual admonition from the Faculty to the effect that there should be no bonfires, firing off crackers in the Yard, or destruction of fences on Guy Fawkes' day, and that everyone must be in his chamber by nine o'clock. Jedediah Foster (A.B. 1744), future Judge of the Supreme Judicial Court, was one of those concerned in 'contriving and abetting the Firing of Squibs in the College Yard,' and degraded four places and fined 5s 'for most obstinately and impudently persisting' in lying about it. But the students were allowed to have a bonfire and fireworks to celebrate the coronation of George III, which the College officially observed by printing *Pietas et Gratulatio*, a collection of complimentary verses in Latin and English by graduates and students. A copy was formally presented to the popular young monarch, but he deigned not even to acknowledge it: a notable instance of his bad manners which, as Barrett Wendell used to declare, did much to alienate the colonists' loyalty to the British monarchy.

Another frequent undergraduate offense was sending out for rum, making punch, and holding a 'Drinking Frolick,' sometimes in company with a town character. President Wadsworth's slave Titus, who hung about Cambridge long after his master's death, was a frequent guest and entertainer on these festive occasions. Finally he was forbidden to enter the Yard; and the famous John Hancock and Samuel Quincy (A.B. 1754) were degraded 'for being most remarkably active in making drunk' another sable son of Cambridge 'to Such a Degree as greatly indanger'd his Life.'

In President Wadsworth's time some of the most daring college criminals used to cut divine worship on the Sabbath in order to go through the students' cellar bins with false keys and obtain liquor. Josiah Langdon (1741), a sophomore, varied this exploit by opening a resident graduate's bottle-case with a 'Picklock' and obtaining rum which he handed around to fellow-students at church, thus profaning 'of the public Worship of God.' He was degraded to the freshman class and rusticated for six months, and five others who shared in this unseemly refreshment were publicly admonished in hall.

Until well on in the nineteenth century, college students had no opportunity to visit or dance with young girls, except in vacation. Consequently, true to the medieval tradition, the older and less restrained among them resorted to wenching. There are several complaints in the records of a tavern on the road to Charlestown, just over the present Somerville line, where students made rendezvous with ladies of easy virtue, whom the Charlestown selectmen were requested to warn out of town. And in 1770 '2 women of ill Fame' were discovered to have spent the night in a certain college chamber.

A minor variety of college crime was stimulated by the poor quality and want of variety in commons. An effort was made to improve the amenities of hall in 1734, when the new code of college laws required the Steward to furnish the tables with pewter plates instead of the greasy old wooden trenchers, to supply 'clean linnen cloaths,' to be changed twice weekly, and to sweep the hall once a day and wash it down at least four times a year. Beer and cider remained the standard beverages for all meals, although free beer for supper was suspended on the ground that molasses, owing to the Seven Years' War with France, had reached the inordinate price of 3d per gallon; the connection is hard to discern. At the close of this war the cost of commons was 5s 10¾d per week. There was certainly no decline in beer consumption, since a new brick brewhouse, 24 by 25 feet, was built in the Yard in 1762; but milk was provided for those weaklings who preferred it, and a considerable variety of beverages is found in the commons regulations of 1765. Breakfast consisted of bread and butter with a bowl of coffee, tea, chocolate, or milk, or a 'cue' (half-pint) of beer. Until 1764, when breakfast began to be served in hall, the students had to procure it at the buttery hatch and consume it in their chambers, or in the Yard; in the breakfast rush the liquids were often spilled and the 'sizings' trodden under foot. Twelve o'clock dinner was a dish of meat boiled or roasted, excepting salt fish on Saturday, topped off with pudding and washed down with beer; and supper was usually concocted of the remains of the meat incorporated in a pie, with bread and milk. One student was excused from commons 'because he could by no means eat Pyes,' and another, who declared his stomach refused mutton, was promised a substitute of 'Apple or Cranberry Pye' at supper 'when the Pyes are Meat, and made with Mutton.' 'The Provisions were badly cooked,' remembered an old graduate; 'the Soups were dreadful we frequently had Puddings made of flower and Water and boiled so hard as not to bee eatable we frequently threw them out and kicked them about.' As fowl never appeared at commons, a favorite sport of the students was to steal poultry in town and roast it at night over their chamber fires. This was an old college custom — as long ago as 1672 there was trouble over turkey-stealing — and in the eighteenth century the favorite bird was goose. Peter Oliver (A.B. 1730), the future Chief Justice of the Province, as a junior was admonished and degraded for 'being concernd in stealing the Geese lately taken on the Common; and also for stealing a Turkey.' Harrison Gray Otis (A.B. 1783) remembered 'our old College practice' of driving furiously by a flock of geese, wrapping the whip-lash weighted by a bullet around the neck of the nearest bird, and jerking it into the chaise. Goose or gander, tender or tough, the bird must then be roasted and eaten.

The earliest recorded College rebellion occurred in the spring of 1766 over bad butter at commons. The Reverend Joseph Thaxter (A.B. 1768), reminiscing in 1820, declared that the trouble lay in New England colonial economy. Little butter was produced in winter; hence the merchants imported Irish butter in the fall, and by the spring it was 'bad very bad.' On this butter rebellion there is a contemporary satire written in Biblical style, according to which Asa Dunbar (A.B. 1767, grandfather of Henry Thoreau) complained to Tutor Hancock: 'Behold our Butter stinketh!' He received no satisfaction; and on his return to commons with the bad news, the scholars hissed and clapped. For this demonstration Dunbar was condemned by the Faculty to confess the sin of insubordination, and be degraded in seniority. The students then met in Holden Chapel and passed resolutions, in pursuance of which they walked out of hall at the next breakfast, before 'giving thanks,' gave three cheers in the Yard, and breakfasted in town. A committee of the Faculty examined the Steward's stock of butter, condemned six firkins absolutely, and allowed four 'for Sauce only'; but the conduct of the students was regarded as equivalent to a treasonable combination against the Sovereign. Corporation met; Overseers met, presided over by his Excellency Governor Bernard; and both insisted that the offending students must sign a humble confession, or leave College. The students, led by the Governor's son, and including a future Senator of the United States (George Cabot), drew up a formal brief in the style of patriots protesting against unconstitutional oppression. An equivocal confession was offered the Governing Board and rejected. And finally, 155 students signed a confession of 'irregular and unconstitutional' proceedings, with a 'Promise of future good Conduct.' It is clear that the Governing Boards would stand for almost any individual misconduct, but that a concerted effort must be vigorously suppressed lest the students suppose that 'in union there is strength.'

All other days of college life were pallid in comparison with the great festival of Commencement. Preparations were made long before. In September the senior sophisters held a class meeting (which was apt to be accompanied by 'drinking prohibited Liquors') to choose class officers, who appear to have been two Valedictorians, and four Collectors of Theses, who drafted the thesis sheet. According to an ancient custom of the College, senior sophisters' recitations ended March 10, when the Class presented their tutor with one or more pieces of plate; Tutor Robie, for instance, received in 1721 two chafing-dishes, a server, a porringer, and four spoons, with a presentation speech by Foster Hutchinson. The day after, the seniors held a meeting in hall, attended by President and Fellows 'with their Hats on' (notes President Wadsworth), at which the valedictorians performed, alluding in as witty Latin as they could muster to the events of college life, and freely predicting the future. After March 10 the senior sophisters (who were now entitled to the baccalaureate 'Sir') were supposed to put in their time preparing for 'sitting solstices,' as the final oral examinations were still called in 1717, in May and June; and as many as conveniently could went home to read and review. After the examinations, the seniors 'treated the fellows' and the fellows 'treated the senior sophisters,' on different days. Not long after the Hollis professorships had been established, seniors were required to reside and attend courses of public lectures on Divinity and Natural Philosophy during the two or three months between the end of recitations and sitting solstices. Consequently, as there seemed no point in saying farewell to classmates whom you would see every day for another term, valedictories were postponed from March to June; and there they remained until 'Seniors' Valedictory' became Class Day, a century later.

As early as President Leverett's day, we find that the

head of the freshman class, when placed, was expected to give his classmates a dinner; and by mid-century the senior head entertained his classmates at the valedictory. One spring morning in 1773, after prayers, the unfortunate President Locke 'red over a heap of new Laws such as to prevent any publick Entertainment' at the valedictory, recorded Samuel Chandler of the sophomore class. On June 18 he heard the senior valedictorian deliver 'a very fine Oration' in 'the Chappel Something full' — and after dinner in hall some persons became full as well. 'The afternoon I spend the Time chiefly in drinking till my Company goes away,' writes Chandler. 'The College have been chiefly in company a drinking to Day and at Night they seem to all be drunkedness and confusion this seems to be the Effect of their depriving one Scholar — the Valedictory Orator — to make an Entertainment for the Senior Class which has always before been customary.' This ceremony was the rudimentary beginning, not only of Harvard Class Day, but of senior rejoicings in all the colleges and universities of the United States, as distinct from the official ceremonies connected with Commencement.

Commencement came on the first Wednesday in July from 1684 to 1726, and on the first, second, or third Wednesday from 1736 to 1801, with few exceptions. As early as President Oakes's administration, the college authorities were becoming alarmed at the excessive hospitality, the drunkenness and disorder, at Commencement, and Presidents Mather and Leverett adopted severe prohibitions against commencers' providing 'Plumb-Cake' and 'mix'd drink made with distill'd Spirits' in their chambers, under penalty of losing their degree; nor were they 'to evade it by Plain Cake.' But the crowds increased, and with them the disorder; for the New England people were allowed very few holidays, and the concourse of so many people, coincident with the loosening of collegiate discipline, naturally brought together all the cheap-jacks, Indian medicine men, acrobats and public entertainers, that New England afforded. This brought money as well as excitement to placid Cambridge, and created a sort of vested interest in the non-academic features. In 1718, about the time that Cotton Mather wrote to a friend at New Haven that he hoped the Sons of Eli would improve their Commencement with religious conversation, and not indulge in idle and vicious pastimes as at Cambridge, the following 'Satyrical Description of Commencement' is said to have been printed: [1]

> . . . Early, long before the Sun's
> Bright Beams illuminate the Horizon,
> Vast Numbers from far distant Places are
> Seen to'ards the Place of Concourse to repair:
> (As if by some Magnetick Virtue they
> Are drawn, they all direct their Course one Way)
> All Sizes, and each Sex, the Ways do throng,
> Both Black and White ride Jig-by-jole along!
> Others on Foot (half roasted by the Sun)
> Can scarce arrive before the Day is done:
> Or if the Clouds propitious Showers dispense,
> (As oft they do, when our learn'd Youths Commence)
> See! how the dripping Throngs trip o'er the Plains,
> The Nut-brown Country Nymphs and rural Swains
> From diff'rent Roads, the diff'rent Squadrons join,
> To form the gen'ral Congress, all combine.
> Tag, Rag, and Bob-Tail, in their best Array,
> Appear there on this celebrated Day:
> Thus till near Night they flock; and in a Word,
> The Town's a Cage fill'd with each kind of Bird!

---

[1] *A Satyrical Description of Commencement. Calculated to the Meridian of Cambridge in New-England* (first printed in the year 1718. Boston; the Heart and Crown, n.d.). The unique copy is in the Chapin Library at Williams College, which kindly furnished me with a photostat. From the language, I doubt whether this masterpiece was composed before 1760.

But who is able fully to display,
The various kind of Things which on this Day
Transacted are?   To Taverns some repair;
And who can tell what Pranks are acted there.
Some spend the Time at Pins (that toilsome Play)
Others at Cards (more silent) pass the Day.
In Rings some Wrestle till they're mad out-right,
And then with their Antagonists they fight.
For Fighting is the Effect of Wrestling, as
Men draw Conclusion from the Premises.
All kind of horrid Noises fill the Street,
While distant Woods their Eccho's back repeat.
On Horses some to ride full Tilt along
Are seen; while on each Side a numerous Throng
Do gaze. . . .
While some intoxicated are with Wine,
Others (as brutish) propagate their Kind:
Where amorous Lads to shady Groves resort,
And under Venus with their Misses sport.
Some sing, some dance, some lay the Ground upon,
Whatever fails, the IRON-WORK goes on.
Our Rustick Sparks (to Taverns glew'd) they stay,
And scarce can blunder Home by break of Day.
Some lie in open Fields; others there are,
Who to their Homes half Boozy do repair;
Others go Home half starv'd: Some in the Way
Get Fox'd, and then in Barns are forc'd to lay;
So end the Actions of this famous Day.
But not the Revel!
                    Each successive Day,
Venus and *Bacchus* bear alternate sway.
The raking Tribe their lawless Games repeat,
Nor can three Days their Bacchanals compleat.
To close recess, the Sons of Vice retire,
And cool their raging Thirst, or quench their wanton Fire
Thus the loose Croud forbidden Pleasures seek,
Drink HARVARD dry, and so conclude the Week.

The fun became so fast and furious in President Wadsworth's day that the Corporation tried to keep the date a
secret until a week or two before, and transferred Commencement to Friday, so that the rest of the week would

not be consumed in Saturnalia. This was held an intolerable grievance, not only by the public, but by the country clergy, for whom a Friday Commencement gave insufficient time to sober up and get home for the Sabbath. Even so, 'the Meeting House was so prodigiously crowded' in 1735 'that the Galleries were in danger of falling; and several Persons . . . jumped out at the Windows.' In 1736 the date was once more announced as the first Wednesday in July, and thenceforth the glories of Commencement were in crescendo until the American Revolution.

A colonial Commencement has never been better described than by John Holmes (A.B. 1832), the Autocrat's brother, in 'The Harvard Book' of 1875:[1]

The Commencement tents beginning here [outside the Johnston Gate] extended somewhat beyond the northerly line of the College grounds, and this was the central point of the holiday, considered apart from the College exercises. These tents were open on the western side, and having opposite them various stands and shows, made a street, which by nightfall was paved with watermelon rinds, peachstones, and various débris, on a ground of straw, — all flavored with rum and tobacco smoke. The atmosphere thus created in the interests of literature was to the true devotee of Commencement what the flavor of the holocaust was to the pious ancient. One or two large tents stood somewhere within the lower half of the largest common enclosure. These probably demanded comparative retirement, for the enjoyment of 'papaw' or 'props,' a popular form of gambling, and of dancing. . . .

The tents were framed with joists set in the ground and connected by the strips of board, and were covered with old sails, adding a slight marine flavor to all the others that accompanied the festival. They were furnished with tables and seats extemporized from pine boards, and rude counters for their array of liquors. Where dancing was intended, a floor of planed boards was laid. . . . In the last century, before the building of West Boston Bridge, they must have reached

---

[1] I have substituted present names of streets and buildings for those of 1874, when Mr. Holmes wrote his sketch. He was born in the parsonage on Holmes Place in 1812, lived all his life in Cambridge, and served as repository of many stories and traditions of colonial days.

well down Kirkland Street, to meet the bulk of the travel, which came in that direction. . . . History does not give us the name of the first sober colonist who, wending his way to the annual solemnity, and arriving at these wells of (strong) water in the wilderness, lingered in delicious repose until the College performances were over, nor tell us how he accounted for the day to his family. Whoever he might be, his example was extensively followed in after times. . . .

In the village of Cambridge this day was the ideal and the realization of perfect festivity. The notice given from the pulpit to pew-holders, to remove their simple furniture from the dangers of the expected crowd, shot inexpressible delight across the solemnity of Sunday to juveniles and adolescents, — possibly shared by the elders. A day or two beforehand the agent charged with that duty measured the spaces on the Common allotted by the town, for a consideration, to the occupants of tents, and scored the number of each in the sod. Grave citizens watched the numerals; children circulated their reports with increase. The popular test of Commencement was the number of tents erected. When the work of construction began, fathers led out little children that they might themselves without reproach, loiter near the delightful tumult. Selectmen are said to have hovered around the spot in a semi-official attitude. The inhabitants of the town, alive to their responsibility, prepared, and tradition says worthily, to bestow their hospitalities. And truly it was time to be up and doing. A man might pass the whole year, until Commencement, without knowing the number and value of his friends. Then everybody and everything turned up. A prodigal son, supposed on a voyage up the Straits, arrived on Monday by coaster from Chappequiddick, to eat the fatted calf. In the afternoon an unappreciated relative, presumed to have perished in the late war, appeared with an appetite improved by open-air residence among the Indians. The more remote affinities at this period revealed their strength. On Tuesday, after the nearer relatives had arrived, there might drop in at evening a third cousin of a wife's half-brother from Agawam, or an uncle of a brother-in-law's step-sister from Contoocook, to re-knit the family ties. The runaway apprentice, who was ready to condone offences and accept hospitality, was referred to the barn, as well as the Indian from Mr. Wheelock's Seminary, whose equipment was an Indian catechism and a bow and arrow, with which latter he expected to turn a fugitive penny by shooting at a mark on the morrow. The wayward boy over whose watery grave Mr. Sam. Stedman had so many times fired his long ducking-gun (cannon being scarce in those days), returned from a truant visit to his uncle on the 'New Hampshire Grants.' The College sloop, that shadowy craft which floats in time indefinitely, always arrived in time for the flood-tide on Tuesday. The Watertown lighter was uniformly driven ashore on Tuesday evening by the perils of the seas, that is, by the strong current that prevailed in the river about Commencement. The captain and crew, like judicious men, made it a point to improve their minds while detained, and always attended literary exercises on the Common. Old graduates who had been boarders were willing in some cases to banish mercenary considerations, and spend Commencement as guests.

On the great roads the regular beggars of the day were making their best speed toward Commencement. The chronic cripples were among the foremost. Blind men were pressing on to see the sights, dumb men to sing convivial songs, and the lame to join in the dance. Paupers, 'let out' by their towns to the lowest bidder, were let out by him to live for a term on the public. Others escaped from almshouses, and, unaccountably, were not pursued. Poverty, however, is seldom chased by its benefactors. Poor lunatics mingled amongst this crowd of travellers, instinctively seeking the centre of excitement. Cambridge Common was the paradise toward which these directed their steps. They were mostly such as had rather be door-keepers in the tents of the wicked than dwell anywhere else. The careless charities, drunken treats, and small pilferings of such an occasion were to supplement what they had begged on their way.

At Bradish's tavern (on the west side of the present Boylston Street, now a grocery), on Tuesday, the arrivals of dusty one-horse chaises, and horsemen with fat saddle-bags, became more frequent till late in the evening, when the goodly tavern overflowed with guests, and its barn and sheds with horses and vehicles. Miss Sarah Chadbourne's house, opposite 'Bradish's,' with gable to the street, little court-yard before the door, and a lusty young buttonwood-tree therein, also overran with returning graduates who had formerly lodged there: their applications, with the claims of her regular guests, obliged her at last, in naval phrase, 'to repel boarders.'

Toward evening arrivals thickened. Occasionally a heavy coach, which had worked its way by slow stages from Portsmouth, Salem, or Providence, deposited the family of some provincial grandee at Bradish's tavern, whence they were likely to be soon enticed by the hospitality of the few Cambridge magnates. As evening came, the small crowd which had speculated and guessed on every newcomer adjourned to Bradish's low but ample bar-room. There, after all the standing questions had been disputed with zeal, — such as the amount of the run of alewives at Fresh Pond Brook, of marsh hay cut that season, of the respective takes of 'sea-perch' at Brighton Bridge, by those (always numerous in Cambridge) who laudably strove to harmonize industry and amusement, — the whole company decided unanimously that to-morrow was going to be the greatest Commencement yet known. . . .

During the sultry night at Bradish's the crowded lodgers in his great room below, in bed, on the floor, on three chairs, and on the table, all were miserable, and all envied one another some fancied advantage. All animated nature was wide awake in Cambridge during Commencement. The mosquitoes particularly, who are shrewd fellows, had their headquarters at Bradish's and its neighborhood on that occasion. . . .

The night, we may be sure, was a lively one for the scholars. Tutors listened despairingly to those horrid endless choruses which conviviality engenders. President Holyoke's dreams even, at the remote 'Wadsworth House,' were invaded by jovial fancies which he would have dispelled, officially, had sleep allowed him. These terrible choruses were ambulatory, now in front of Hollis, now back of Stoughton, and more formidable from the narrow limits of the then College Yard.

The morning dawned fair and hot. So far as we have evidence, it never rained on Commencement Day. The labors, maraudings, and revels of the night had bestowed a late but deep slumber on the denizens of the Common, who began to stir themselves and take that condensed refreshment which needs no cooking. To describe the state of the popular mind at finding the long anticipation converted into reality is beyond our power. It was as near celestial as the terrene character of the day admitted.

All were early astir. The Commencers of the day, whose life for four years had been 'war to the knife' (and fork) with the butler, appeared, meditative, at the buttery hatch, and asked amiably for their sizings and their cue. They shook hands with their old adversary, and said pleasant things of his fare. Taken thus in an unexpected quarter, he, when he had served them, retired into the interior, and 'shed some natural tears.' A cue of beer restored him; but he looked coldly on the provision he had so warmly defended hitherto.

The task of dressing for the day now occupied all energies. When we consider the multiplied fopperies of the time, this was a very responsible matter. The ruffles, the cue, the silk stockings, the buckles, — stock, knee, and shoe, — the wigged or powdered head, make the dress of today appear barbarously simple.

The Commencers worked hard, declaiming their theses and dressing alternately, and consulting the glass, if the excessively simple furnishing of the College room of the day included that article. Some of them had sat up all night to keep the work of the hair-dresser unimpaired. . . . Even Fellows and Tutors felt the importance of preparing for this occasion. They surveyed with solemn satisfaction new and voluminous coats, vast silver shoe-buckles, and silk stockings of hue delicate, impressive, or overpowering, according to the animus of the wearer. When the business of dressing was completed, the robust man contemplated with satisfaction a well-turned leg; the more spiritual admired the leaden lustre of his shoes. . . .

The roads from Boston, by the Charlestown Ferry and through Brookline, were alive with passengers in various stages of progress. The greatest throng was by the former; the vehicles came mostly by the latter. Here were seen the aristocratic chariot and pair; the heavy family coach; the C-spring chaise, indicating easy circumstances, possibly wealth; and the wooden-springed chaise, representing comfort and thrift. Eager pedestrians accompanied the train, and socially partook of the dust it raised.

Down the Menotomy Road (from Arlington and North Cambridge) a goodly throng, but more scattered, came on; among them, as elsewhere, the country ministers within easy reach of Cambridge, with many a sudden pull on one rein as their nags viewed the questionable wonders of the Common. All residents of the village and visitors were early on the way to secure the seats open to ladies only and their squires in the galleries. The Market-Place (Harvard Square) was tumultuous, and the energies of the various beaux were in demand to secure passage for their convoys. . . .

It was now half past nine o'clock, and the Faculty, the scholars, and 'the rest of the gentlemen' were assembled near Holden Chapel, to await the Governor and his escort. The crowd on the Common held itself also in readiness to meet him, whether he came, as was sometimes the case, through Watertown, or by the more obvious way of Little Cambridge (Brighton). A sort of telegraphic hint from 'down in town,' and flight of quick-sighted boys in that direction, announced his approach by the latter way. The Market-Place and parts adjacent were filled. Little children with their peculium of savings fled as from instant massacre at the hands of the horsemen, and the Governor and his escort with abundant tumult, but probably without cheers, made their slow way, assisted by the 'constable with six men,' to the place of gathering. Then followed a ceremonial of which we have no record. We are contented with the assurance that the Governor's cocked hat and the President's square cap described all the curves proper to the occasion.

The procession set forth silent and slow. No music gave a martial tone and port to its advance. The meeting-house bell tolled its thin and solemn notes as for public worship. The order of procession, as would appear by reference to a former occasion, was as follows: 'The Bachelors of Art walked first, two in a rank, and then the Masters, all bareheaded. Then followed Mr. Holyoke, alone, as President. Next the Corporation and Tutors, two in a rank, then the Honorable Governor Bernard and Council, and next to them the rest of the gentlemen.'

The sober academic colors were relieved by occasional gold-laced hats and coats, by a sprinkling of his Majesty's uniform, and by the scores of silver shoe-buckles which glistened in the sun at every footstep, to the delight of the public and of the wearers of them. The crowd flowed back with the procession to the meeting-house, disturbing the small wayside traffic, and when it had entered, protected by two specials at the door, a portion filled all the spare room in the meeting-house; the rest, content with the honor they had paid to literature, returned to the Common. . . . The President occupied the pulpit, and the Governor the great chair in front; the rest, with mutual congees, self-sacrificing offers, and deprecatory acceptances of seats, distributed themselves on the stage [especially erected for the occasion]. The cocked hats were hung on the brass-headed nails which lined the beams projecting from the wall between the pulpit and the galleries. The very few of the audience who were seated rose when the venerable President began his prayer. . . . Let us look around us. And first at those brown-handed ministers from the country, men who can preach, or lay stone-wall, or hoe corn, as the occasion calls, and who on a scanty salary send a boy or two to Harvard, and live respectably. . . . Well placed in the south gallery, numerous, and conspicuous, in the latest-arrived fashions from 'home,' are the fairest maidens of what might be termed the court circle. . . . They blend prettily the courtly elegance which they emulate, with the simplicity of manner that is their provincial birthright. Their holiday life is to be a short one. . . . Not many years hence those soft eyes will look westward through exiles' tears to the home that is to know them no more. . . .

The familiar 'Expectatur Oratio,' etc., is heard, the Salutatory orator gallantly mounts the stage, and makes all the requisite reverences. He addresses the Honorandi, the Venerabiles, and the Spectatissimi. In what ingenious manner he contrives to evade the prohibition to address the *puellae* we cannot say; but a reluctant smile passes along the grave faces on the stage, which broadens at some new hit, and spreads among the audience by infection, as few understand what is said. The old Louisburg chaplain, with whom military boots have become constitutional since the siege, actually brings one of them down on the stage. The fans which have paused awhile, go furiously, — they always know when there is anything in the wind. The Salutatory goes off brilliantly, that is to say, nobody seems depressed by it, and the audience chats in a lively manner. A Latin thesis is called for, which goes rather heavily. . . . Another Latin thesis is helped off by a row at the west door of the church, at the sound of which young James Winthrop slips out and witnesses the victory of the 'constable and six men' over two drunken English sailors. . . .

The 'Oratio in lingua vernacula' was called, and Huntington appeared. This was a novelty, and was listened to with profound attention. We do not know his subject. We are quite sure that if he used the words 'the loyal subjects of the best of monarchs,' the 'prerogative man' in the audience smiled approvingly, and at the words, 'the sacred rights and liberties bequeathed us by our pious fathers,' the approval passed over to other faces. The line of cleavage between the parties was obvious enough, but the wedge was not yet inserted.

The exercises closed with this oration, and it was time. The legs which had been complacently extended on the stage were drawn up, and those that had been shyly withdrawn were extended. The punctual colonial appetite told of noon long past. The graduating class ascended the stage in successive parties of four, and received from the President, with a short Latin formula, the document [1] which made them Bachelors of Arts. It was their clearance on 'the voyage of life,' so often mentioned at the graduating period; but before they quitted their moorings, they were to entertain their friends, at their chamber or elsewhere. The President made a short prayer; and when he had pronounced the benediction, the crowded house broke up like a river in a thaw.

The procession was formed and marched back to Harvard Hall, attended by a numerous crowd, some of whom would have taken pleasure in assisting at the academic dinner, but were repulsed by the constable and his men, who, according to the provision of 1733, were watching and walking in the entry of the hall at dinner-time. If the commencers and undergraduates were expected to go back with the procession, it is reasonable to suppose there were many vacancies. The commencers had their friends to entertain 'in a sober manner' with punch at their chambers or elsewhere; the undergraduates had acquaintances in the village or among the visitors, whom they felt it a pleasant duty to escort on such a day to their places of destination, whether in the immediate village or to Milk Porridge Lane, up the

---

[1] This is not correct; diplomas were not presented at Commencement before 1813, and it was the vote of the Governing Boards that made the seniors Bachelors of Arts. Thus early was the diploma confounded with the degree!

road toward Menotomy or to the rather distant Milk Row. We see them gallantly making way for their convoy through the crowd by the present College House, causing the pigs and bears in the children's pockets to squeak as they pass the toy-stands. At the Stimson House, just beyond Church Street, a canvas painted in the grand style, with its inscription, invites them to visit the Great Russian Bear. Another, to inspect 'the Mermaid, which the same was taken by two mariners belonging to the sloop Verity in Shalure Bay, and is certified by three settled ministers of those parts.'

At the northeast corner of the burial-ground they find the nucleus of a crowd, which somewhat later in the day is to become almost permanent, enclosing two combatants who are forced to a truce by the pressure of the spectators, until the constable comes and plucks the offenders forth and carries them to some unknown bourne. Whatever the tumult, the law is characteristically submitted to. It is true that occasionally the village Samsons may volunteer as amateurs, to assist, but, generally speaking, the respect for law in its corrective form is strikingly visible. . . .

Some little interval occurred between the end of the exercises and the dinner at Harvard Hall, during which old graduates musingly traversed the College yard and its immediate neighborhood; those who had been long absent peered inquiringly around them. Old men leaned on their canes or pointed with them to this and that window in the different buildings. One said, 'There's where I lived in my Freshman year; Sir Foxcroft was my Senior.' Another, 'There's the room where Bilson found the toast in his boots.' Another, quite advanced in years, 'Look up there! don't you see a sort of notch? There's where Tutor Flynt caught me cutting off lead on the top of the College. . . . It cost me three shillings, — money was money, too, in those days.'

A group at the Buttery-hatch, at the north end of Harvard, recalled with clamor and laughter their frugal rations, delivered by a functionary whose mind was graduated to pints, quarts, and sizings, and who recognized man, only in his relation to those measures. At the Playground (somewhere near the present Holworthy, — no road then intersecting), from old time the scene of wrestling-matches, slight withered men fired up with vague remembrance of their exploits. . . .

The College bell, with familiar voice, yet with a certain vindictive twang in its tones, to men who had paid so many fines for neglecting them, called to dinner. The guests, speedily arranged in due order, entered, and seated themselves after a blessing had been asked. The President, with the Governor, occupied the middle of the table extending along the north side of the Hall, with dignitaries and ministers on either hand. At the tables along the ends of the Hall the residue of 'the rest of the gentlemen' were seated. . . .

Among 'the rest of the gentlemen' at the other tables, were some commencers who found it convenient to dine at the Hall. These young men had improved the interval before dinner by drinking punch 'in a sober manner,' according to the ordinance, but, notwithstanding their repeated acts of sobriety, were somewhat elevated. One asked to be helped to some Medulla (Ames's Medulla); another said, 'College has done well by us' (Wollebius); another, 'This here board is better than common' (Hereboord's Meletemata). These evidences of mental debility were received with excessive laughter. . . . The President shortly after arose and returned thanks and announced the hymn. . . .

The afternoon audience, we may suppose, was largely composed of those who attend everything on principle. All reasonable people were now in a blissful state. The excellent Dr. Appleton, the minister of the parish, walking in the afternoon procession, smiled unconsciously on the collective license of the crowd. The rough village doctor, though witnessing the abominable breach of hygienic law everywhere, felt the cheering influence of the day, and his old mare with perplexity missed half her usual allowance of cowhide. The dry, sceptical village lawyer, returned from his dinner at Miss Chadbourne's to his dusty office in his best mood, prepared to deny everything, advanced by anybody, and demand proof. On the Common, the Natick Indians having made large gain by their bows and arrows, proceeded to a retired spot, and silently and successfully achieved the process of inebriation.

Mr. Holmes makes no mention of Commencement dances; but they must have been common, as the Corporation in 1760 forbids dancing in Commencement week 'either in the College-Hall or Chapel.'

To conclude the day, we may now cut back to a contemporary mock-heroic, 'The Sequal of Commencement,' which appeared in *The New-England Weekly Journal* for July 3, 1727.

> The scatt'ring Croud, now like the ebbing Tide,
> Prepares in diff'rent Channels to divide:
> Some by the Smiles of kind propitious Stars,
> On Horses bound, or whirle in rattling Cars; . . .

Here simpering Damsels string from side to side,
There swarthy Swains with jocund Aspects stride,
Swelt'ring in Dust and Drought, some by the Way
With naucious Tiff, their burning Thirst allay;
Where, to compleat their Sports, they'll frisk and Rant,
As to the Viols screeking Sound they Chant.
Here gravely march our solemn Senators,
There loit'ring Youth indulge their wanton Airs.
One shall his Feats and vile Adventures boast,
Another mourn his Pence and Labours lost.
Some with sweet Tales of Love relieve their Toil,
Others with nobler Themes, the tedious Steps beguile.

Thus in promiscuous Throngs their Way they force,
And down to *Charlestown* bend their boisterous Course.
'Till near the Boats the gathering Squadrons blend,
And late at Night, keep thickning on the Strand. . . .

The Charlestown ferry, unable to cope with holiday crowds, takes hours to get everyone across to the Boston side, where all the Boston girls not invited to Commencement turn out to greet the returning revellers:

A radiant Ridge of Females, deck'd with skill,
Blazons the Brow of *Cop's* aspiring Hill.
From their fair Forms such lively lustres play,
As kindly lengthens out the dying Day. . . .

Colonial Commencements are said to have reached their acme in 1772, when Judge Inman gave a lavish entertainment for hundreds of guests at his mansion near the present Inman Square, in honor of his son George, who graduated that day. Three years later, the Inmans were Tory refugees, and during the war years Commencement was a mere shadow of its former self. There was a renaissance after the war; but as the Fourth of July became more generally celebrated, it drew to itself the popular features of Commencement, which once more became a purely academic festival, lubricated only by the buckets of rum provided by celebrating classes of old graduates.

VII

THROUGH CHANGE AND THROUGH STORM

1768-1781

THIS 'was a Time when Liberty was the universal Cry,' remembered a student of that era. In 1768 we first hear of a 'liberty tree' or 'rebellion elm' in the Yard, opposite the middle of Hollis, where the students assembled to pass resolutions and organize resistance against an imaginary act of oppression by Tutor Willard. The moving spirit of this rebellion was future Brigadier-General James M. Varnum, who finished his education at Brown. The senior sophisters threatened, if their 'rights' were not respected, to go to Yale; but this desperate measure could not be carried out for want of a recommendation to New Haven from President Holyoke. The Corporation overrode their President and readmitted the ringleaders on the ground that suitable penance had been performed, and many 'friends and benefactors' of the College had 'condescended to intercede in their behalf.'

Liberty was in the air. In 1768 the seniors voted to refrain from tea; the senior sophisters determined ' to take their degrees in the manufactures of this country,' and their Theses bore the legend 'In Papyrum *Miltoni* in *Nov-Anglia* confectam.' This practice continued until the Townshend duties were repealed; and whenever the tainted breeze of tyranny was snuffed in the Yard, there was trouble. In 1769 there appeared a mock-heroic poem entitled 'A True Description of A Number of ty-

rannical Pedagogues, A Poem. Dedicated to the Sons of
H*****D.' It opens with a tribute to ancient times when
tutors

> Nobly disdaining (what the tyrant craves)
> To fix a distance as of Lords to slaves:
> But shew'd their pupils all that they could shew,
> And gladly taught them every thing they knew.
>
> Sure tutors were then as they ought to be,
> Facile in teaching, and in converse free,
> Humane and gen'rous, affable and kind,
> Polite and easy, and of open mind.
> Was H*****d bless'd with governors like these,
> Her sons would join in unity to please.

And then describe the manners and methods of the
actual tutors:

> The Roman uses supercilious airs;
> From whom e'en magick of the keenest guile,
> Could ne'er extort the shadow of a smile,
>
> Before his pupils he will swell and flout,
> And with importance turn his chair about,
> There strut and then display a lofty crest,
> To strike a terror into ev'ry breast.
>
> The stiff logician wipes his greasy face,
> Then spits his venom in sarcastick wit,
> And grins in laughter at the object hit;
>
> A frown comes tumbling from the Grecian brow
> Soon as you enter his imperial dome,
> Or dare approach the monarch on his throne.

And the author concludes:

> I would advise the sons of H*****d then,
> To let them know, that they are sons of men;
> Not brutes, as they would to the world display,
> By their ill usage and unmanly way:
> Then cast contempt upon the demi-gods,
> Their frowns, their mulcts, their favors and their nods.

Apparently the tutors bowed to the spirit of the times, if an incident related by Sam Chandler in his diary for 1774 is typical. It appears that Tutor Eliot, to whom his class should have recited Greek in the winter quarter, went on a preaching tour, and Tutor Hall was substituted. The juniors declined to accept the substitution, and voted *nem. con.* to absent themselves from the recitations, for 'wee don't chuse to spend any more of our time in the study of Greek then wee should be willing to throw away. that it would be more agreeable to study Latin.' Tutor Hall, however, appealed to their loyalty by pointing out that further absence would simply get him in trouble with the Corporation. 'Thus arguing with all mildness . . . he has gaind the Class not by tyranicle Authority but by calm and mild Arguments,' records Chandler. Take notice, King George!

Discipline appears to have been very slack under President Locke. Chandler cuts chapel morning after morning, often stays in bed until dinner, and visits Boston whenever so inclined. A loyalist lady wrote, 'Here is a Colledge indeed, but the Independancy and Liberty with which the Youths are brought up, and indulged, makes too many of 'em proficients in Vice.'

Governor Hutchinson, in his 'History of Massachusetts Bay,' intimates that Harvard was already heart and soul for the popular cause when President Holyoke died, and points out the influence of two Fellows of the Corporation, Professor Winthrop and the Reverend Samuel Cooper, in the patriot party. College men in general, and Harvard men in particular, bore such an important part in bringing on and carrying through the American Revolution that some direct connection between patriotism and the curriculum has been suggested. Burlamaqui's 'Principles of Natural Law,' the only book on political science in the curriculum, provided a good basis for Whiggish doctrine and American constitutional law; but it was the classics that made Harvard men of that day effective in politics and statesmanship. In Plutarch's Lives, the orations of Cicero and Demosthenes, and ancient history, young men saw a mirror of their times; in Plato's Dialogues and Aristotle's Politics they learned the wisdom to deal with men and events. The classical pseudonyms with which our Harvard signers to the great Declaration [1] signed their early communications to the press were not mere pen-names chosen by chance, but represented a very definite point of view that every educated man recognized. American revolutionary leaders, both North and South, Madison, Wythe, and Jefferson, the Rutledges and Pinckneys, as well as Hamilton, Jay, and the Adamses and Trumbulls, could never have rendered their distinguished services to the young republic without that classical learning which is denied to most Americans today. The Marquis de Chastellux well said of Samuel Adams that he began 'by the Greeks and Romans, to get at the Whigs and Tories.' Thus Harvard rendered her sons fit to serve their country, not by 'practical courses' on politics and government, but by a study of antique culture that broadened their mental vision, stressed *virtus* and promoted ἀρετή, the character appropriate to a republican.

A circumstance that did much to quicken the patriotic ardor of the collegians was the convocation of the General Court at Cambridge, in order to escape mob influence in Boston. Cambridge was the place alluded to in the Declaration of Independence as 'uncomfortable, and distant from the depository of their public records,' where tyrant George 'called together legislative bodies . . . for the sole purpose of fatiguing them into compliance with his measures.' Nor were the Corporation pleased at hav-

[1] The two Adamses, John Hancock, Elbridge Gerry, and Robert Treat Paine of Massachusetts, William Ellery of Rhode Island, William Williams of Connecticut, and William Hooper of North Carolina.

ing to provide the 'new chapel' (on the ground floor of Harvard Hall) for sessions of the House, and the Library for the Council; but the Cambridge innkeepers were pleased, and the student body highly delighted at this thrilling interruption to the academic routine. For three years, from March, 1770, to March, 1773, the General Court held all its sessions in Cambridge. At the first of them, a few days after the Boston Massacre, James Otis (A.B. 1743) addressed the House before proceeding to business. According to his biographer William Tudor (A.B. 1796),

. . . the students were attracted by the novelty, as well as by a sympathy, that was felt with all the ardour of youth for a patriotic legislature, placed under a kind of proscription and driven from their own halls. These youths were clustered round the walls in listening groups, to witness the opening of their deliberations. He spoke of the indignity that had been offered them, on the sad situation of the capital, oppressed by a military force, on their rights and duties, and the necessity of persevering in their principles to obtain redress for all these wrongs, which the vile calumnies and misrepresentations of treacherous individuals had brought upon them. He harangued them with the resistless energy and glowing enthusiasm that he could command at will; and in the course of his speech took the liberty, justified by his successful use of it, as well as by the peculiarity of the occasion, to apostrophize the ingenuous young men, who were then spectators of their persecution. He told them the times were dark and trying, that they might be soon called upon in turn, to act or suffer — he made some rapid, vivid allusions to the classic models of ancient patriotism, which it now formed their duty to study, as it would be hereafter to imitate. Their country might one day look to them for support, and they would recollect that the first and noblest of all duties, was to serve that country, and if necessary, to devote their lives in her cause. *Dulce et decorum est pro patria mori.* They listened with breathless eagerness, every eye filled with tears, and their souls raised with such high emotion, that they might have been led at once, to wrest from their enemies the cannon, which had been pointed against the legislature.

About the same time, the Reverend Andrew Eliot (A.B. 1737) of the Corporation wrote to Thomas Hollis (who as a 'Republican' was doubtless pleased):

The young gentlemen are already taken up with politics. They have caught the spirit of the times. Their declamations and forensic disputes breathe the spirit of liberty. This has always been encouraged, but they have sometimes been wrought up to such a pitch of enthusiasm, that it has been difficult for their Tutors to keep them within due bounds; but their Tutors are fearful of giving too great a check to a disposition, which may, hereafter, fill the country with patriots; and choose to leave it to age and experience to check their ardor.

The earliest college club that has in some form continued to the present day was founded as a direct result of this feast of patriotic oratory. A number of senior sophisters, led by Samuel Phillips, future lieutenant-governor and founder of Phillips Academy, Andover, alleging a 'cold indifference to the practice of Oratory' on the part of the Corporation (which had done its best to encourage oratory for several years!), formed on September 11, 1770, the Speaking Club; and about the same time a group of underclassmen, led by Fisher Ames (A.B. 1774), formed the Mercurian Club; both for the purpose of practising public speaking. There was also, in 1774, a Clitonian Club for the same object. All three were secret societies; even mention of their names was penalized by expulsion, and graduates referred to them in letters by their initials only.

Members of the Speaking Club were serious fellows; a majority of members in the classes of 1771 and 1772, which were the last two classes to be placed in social order, belonged to the second half. Of Phillips, the founder, it is told that, when a young graduate, he was so busy reading in the College Library on the day of Bunker Hill that he did not even hear the guns! The Club hired a room in the house (the later Holmes mansion) of Steward Hastings, whose son was a member. Out of the initiation fees (three shillings) there were provided six tin candlesticks, and a two-by-four 'rostrum,' whence every member in turn declaimed fortnightly before a highly critical audience of his fellows. Only a minority of the 'pieces' were on political subjects; passages from Pope, Shakspere (Othello, Julius Caesar, Coriolanus, and Hamlet), and Addison's Cato were favorites. Some of the others, noted by title in the excellent Club records, are:

1770

October	9	Joshua Thomas '72: The Pernicious Practice of Drinking Tea
November	6	Joseph Avery '71: Oppression and Tyranny

1771

March	4	Israel Keith '71: Humphry Gubbins' Introduction to his romantic Cousin
March	18	Thomas Burnham '72: Extract from Churchill's Gotham
July	2	John Shaw '72: Colonel Barré's Speech in Parliament at the Commitment of the Lord Mayor
September	3	Abner Morgan '73: Speech of Junius Brutus occasion'd by the Suicide of Lucretia
November	5	Nathaniel W. Appleton '73: Speech of Titus Quintius from Livy.
December	2	Nathan Bond '72: Letter IX of Mrs. Rowe

1772

March	17	Joshua Thomas '72: A poetical Essay on a certain Provincial Governor
July	7	Nahum Cutler '73: Extracts from Demosthenes' Harangue for Chersonesus
August	19	Abner Morgan '73: Speech of Appius Claudius
November	10	Samuel Fales '73: Declamation upon *Nulla est Sincera Voluptas*

1773

March	16	Abel Fiske '74: Extract from Dr. Warren's Oration on the Massacre
March	23	Moses Taft '74: Rise and Progress of the Arts and Sciences
April	6	Oliver Peabody '73: Nicias' Speech to the Athenians
May	11	John Haven '76: The Story of Dionysius and Damocles
July	13	Fisher Ames '74: An Address to the People of England

As we approach the Revolution, the Speaking Club becomes more and more classic. Publius Valerius, Hannibal, Pericles, Cicero, Callicrates, and Appius Claudius occupy the rostrum and candlelight, occasionally pushed by Mr. Erskine, the Bishop of St. Asaph, and Dr. Warren; but not (strangely enough) by Burke or Fox. Around 1777 the taste begins to change;

> The throes and swellings of a Roman soul,
> Cato's bold flights, th' extravagance of Virtue

make way for 'Characters,' Hervey's Meditations, Milton, Mr. Pope, Tristram Shandy, Thomson's Seasons, and Young's Night Thoughts, with an occasional Prophecy of the Future Glory of America.

One is not surprised to find that the Overseers' visiting committee commented with pleasure in 1773 on the improved quality of elocution at the annual exhibition, predicting that 'those literary accomplishments' would render the students 'ornaments to the College and Blessings to their Country,' whilst cultivating the 'Art of Speaking . . . will greatly add to the Reputation this seat of Learning hath already obtained.' They little suspected that this was the work of secret societies. A forensic dispute 'On the Legality of Enslaving the Africans' held at Commencement, 1773, was thought good enough to be printed.

Speaking Club and Mercurians amalgamated in 1773; and for a time enthusiasm ran so high that there were weekly meetings at 'Mr S—— H——gs.' Just before the war broke out there was a decline in interest, but the 'S——g C——' was 'revived upon its primitive Foundation' — in deepest secrecy — by several members of the classes of 1776 and 1777, including two future senators, Christopher Gore and Rufus King. Throughout the Revolution, even when the College was at Concord, the Club continued to meet, declaim, 'sound' candidates, and elect members. After two changes of name, and the absorption of sundry rival organizations, the Speaking Club became 'The American Institute of 1770' in 1825, and continued a flourishing though not exactly literary existence under a portion of that name until absorbed in turn by the Hasty Pudding Club over a century later.

Another manifestation of the spirit of liberty was the formation, in 1769 or 1770, of the first college military company, called from its motto (*Tam Marti quam Mercurio*) the Marti-Mercurian Band. The members drilled in long blue coats faced with white, nankeen breeches, white stockings, black gaiters, and three-cornered cocked hats; after each drill three or four buckets of rum toddy were passed around. In April, 1771, the House of Representatives desired Governor Hutchinson to place a hundred stand of arms at the disposal of 'such Students of Harvard College as may be disposed to acquaint themselves with the Art Military'; and a record of the company election that fall shows that it had sixty-one members, including a captain, two lieutenants, an ensign, four sergeants, two corporals, and a clerk; the Captain was William Eustis (A.B. 1772), future Secretary of War and Governor of Massachusetts; both he and several other officers became surgeons in the Revolution, and physicians in private life. This swagger company never saw service as a unit, although many of its graduates did; about the year 1787 it ceased to exist.

In the spring of 1771, Harvard held the last great ceremony of the old régime. Thomas Hutchinson (A.B. 1727), who had been acting governor since the departure of Sir Francis Bernard, received a royal commission as Captain General and Governor in Chief of the Province of Massachusetts Bay, and took the oaths of office on March 14, 1771. In accordance with ancient custom, he should be formally received at the College; but would precedent be observed? Nobody could deny that the Governor was the most distinguished Harvardian, although as a high Tory and upholder of the absolute sovereignty of Parliament he was the most hated man in the Province. To at least half the Corporation, and to most of the students who had been listening to patriotic oratory, the Governor was *persona ingratissima*; and for the inconvenience of the court's meeting at Cambridge he was generally blamed. But there was now a comparative lull in the political storm, and the Corporation decided to go through with the reception and make it a memorable one. President Locke and the Fellows 'waited upon his Excellency' on March 28 with a complimentary address, declaring that the King's appointment reflected honor on the College, and trusting that his Excellency's 'thorough acquaintance with the advantages of literature' and the 'affectionate regard' he had expressed 'for this seat of learning' afforded the 'pleasing prospect' that they would find in him 'a patron and a friend, ever ready to protect the rights and promote the interests of a society, founded by our fathers on the most catholic plan and upon which the welfare of the community greatly depends.'

We may pause a moment to ponder the significance of that phrase 'founded by our fathers on the most catholic plan.' Obviously, the liberal tradition had already entered its second phase; liberalism was now supposed to have been the original purpose of the College. At the death in 1766 of the Reverend Jonathan Mayhew (A.B. 1744) of Boston, a prominent Overseer and herald of liberal Congregationalism, all four Boston papers printed an obituary in which it was stated that the deceased 'was a sincere Friend to that Freedom of Education which is essentially necessary to the well being of any Academy designed for the Education of Youth and the Benefit of Mankind.'

On April 4, 1771, his Excellency 'was pleased to visit the College.' The cavalcade left the Province House at an early hour: Governor Hutchinson and Lieutenant-Governor Andrew Oliver (A.B. 1724) in their carriages, escorted by the troop of Horse Guards. From this picturesque rather than efficient organization are descended the Lancers who escort his present Excellency to Commencement. In an age when men's dress was becoming neat and dapper, the Horse Guards appeared like one of Marshal Saxe's old squadrons, with their old-fashioned full wigs and large club of hair bobbing up and down behind, great three-cornered hats bound with yellow braid, blue uniform coats with broad red lapels, red waistcoat and breeches, gorgeous saddles and caparisons, gold-edged royal standard, and trumpets with festoons of gold braid. The cavalcade was met at the county line by the Sheriff of Middlesex, the 'principal gentlemen of the town of Cambridge in their carriages,' and hordes of small boys with the cry 'Milk ho! Milk!' a delicate allusion to the supposed occupation of the troopers when not caracoling about his Excellency. We may continue in the words of the Corporation records:

At the steps of Harvard Hall, his Excellency was received and congratulated by the President, Fellows, Professors and Tutors in their habits. In the Philosophy Chamber he was met and welcomed by the Honorable and Reverend Overseers.

The Chapel not being large enough to accommodate the gentlemen who were present on this occasion, and the members of the society; his Excellency, with the Lieutenant Governor, the Overseers, Corporation, Officers of the College, and the other gentlemen, went in procession from Harvard Hall to the Meeting House, preceded by the Students of the College, Graduates and Undergraduates.

The General Court being then setting in the College, a Committee of the Corporation waited on the Honorable House of Representatives to ask their attendance on the exercises of the day. Which invitation they were pleased to accept off (*sic*).

The public exercises began with a handsome gratulatory Oration in Latin pronounced by William Wetmore, A.B. To this his Excellency made an elegant reply in the same language, testifying his affection to the seminary in which he had his education, and his regard to the interests of literature.

Then followed an Anthem, composed, set to music and performed by some of the Students.

The words of the Anthem.

We have heard with our ears, O Lord, and our fathers have told us of thy might! Thy wonders which thou didst of old; how thou didst drive out the Heathen from among them! For they got not their land by their own sword; but it was thy right hand and thine arm, and the light of thy countenance. . . . Lo! thus shall the man be blessed that fears the Lord.

Thus saith the Lord, from henceforth, behold all nations shall call thee blessed; for thy Rulers shall be of thine own kindred; your *Nobles* shall be of yourselves, and thy Governor shall proceed from the midst of thee.

Awake! awake! put on thy strength, O Zion, — break forth into joy with Hallelujah! for the Lord hath redeemed his people.

Blessing and glory, salvation and wisdom, thanksgiving and honor and power and might, be unto the Lord God Almighty, who sitteth on the throne and unto the Lamb forever and ever, Amen.

Praise the Lord.

When the Exercises were over, the Procession returned to the Hall, where a genteel entertainment was provided for his Excellency, the Honorable and Reverend Overseers, the Honorable House of Representatives, and the other gentlemen. The whole was conducted with greatest decorum and elegance.

Unfortunately, the music of this anthem has not been preserved; but, if the words may be considered a guide, the student composers were considerably indebted to Handel's Messiah.

Only a month or two after this outpouring of loyalty the senior sophisters created a sensation by taking the printing of their commencement theses from the Tory *Boston News-Letter*, which had done the job for over half a century, and assigning it to the patriotic *Massachusetts Spy*; by the one side they were lauded for their patriotism, and by the other scolded for supporting 'faction.' The year 1772 was comparatively calm; in the summer of 1773 the political uproar again reached a high pitch when the

House of Representatives printed in garbled form the letters of Governor Hutchinson that Franklin had procured in England. Shortly after, the Harvard Corporation appointed John Hancock (A.B. 1754) Treasurer of Harvard College.

Politics, and a desire to secure for the College a part of the fortune of which John was being rapidly relieved by his political friends, doubtless account for this appointment. John, nephew and legatee of Thomas Hancock, who had founded the Hancock Professorship of Hebrew, was the wealthiest young merchant in the Province. He had given sundry books and subscribed £500 sterling toward the restoration of the Library, carpeted the second floor of Harvard Hall and richly papered the Philosophy Chamber, and presented 'a curious Coralline on its natural bed' to the new Museum. In consequence of these 'repeated demonstrations of his affectionate regards to Harvard College' he had already been 'invited to dine in the Hall' and 'sit with the Governors of the College' at every 'public entertainment,' and requested to sit for his portrait at the College's expense, for which Mr. Copley rendered a bill of forty guineas, together with eight guineas for 'a large frame for ditto.' And although it never paid the bill, the Corporation found this venture extremely costly, whether weighed in the political or the financial scale.

On June 1, 1774, the Boston Port Act and the other coercive acts passed by Parliament as punishment for the famous tea-party went into effect, and Boston was occupied by British regulars. The College Corporation, 'considering the present dark aspect of our public Affairs Voted that there be no public Commencement this Year'; nor was there another until 1781. On June 17, 1774, the General Court was dissolved; and during that summer the people broke up the courts, held county conventions, and prepared for resistance. The British troops in Boston struck back in early September by seizing munitions which local patriots had collected in the powder-house at Somerville, and carried off two field-pieces from Cambridge. Thousands of armed rustics poured into Cambridge, surrounded the court house on Harvard Square and forced the aged Judge Samuel Danforth (A.B. 1715), appointed Councillor by royal mandamus, to resign his commission. A mob of four thousand welled out from Boston, surrounded the mansion house (the later 'Elmwood') of Lieutenant-Governor Thomas Oliver (A.B. 1753), and compelled him to resign as Mandamus Councillor. One by one the great ones on 'Tory Row' (Brattle Street), the Vassalls and Brattles, Lechmeres and Sewalls, closed the splendid Georgian mansions where they had been wont to make 'merry with music and the dance,' tumbled into their coaches, and rolled into Boston to be under the protection of the British army. Few of them ever returned.

In the midst of all this excitement, President Langdon was privately inaugurated on October 14, 1774, in order to avoid deciding the question whether or not to recognize the mandamus councillors as Overseers. During the winter, both sides prepared; but the 'first blood of the Revolution' narrowly escaped being shed in Harvard Hall on March 1, 1775, over the 'detest'd plant' tea brought in by a group of Tory students. Thereupon the Faculty solemnly resolved that

Since the carrying India Teas into the Hall is found to be a Source of uneasiness and grief to many of the Students, and as the use of it is disagreable to the People of this Country in general; and as those who have carried Tea into the Hall declare that the drinking of it in the Hall is a matter of trifling consequence with them; that they be advised not to carry it in for the future, and in this way that they, as well as the other Students in all ways, discover a disposition to promote harmony, mutual affection, and confidence, so well becoming Members of the same Society: that so peace and happiness may be preserved within the Walls of the College whatever convulsions may unhappily distract the State abroad.

If any Tories remained in College after that, they kept very quiet; but many loyal graduates bore an active and honorable part on the losing side of this first civil war in America.[1] And of them it is pleasant to record that even in exile they remembered Alma Mater. Among the graduates, Major William Erving (A.B. 1753), who fought on the British side, endowed our third medical professorship by will in 1791; and the Rumford Professorship on the Application of Science to the Useful Arts was endowed by another loyalist, the famous Benjamin Thompson, Count Rumford, who had attended Dr. Winthrop's scientific lectures just before the Revolution.

On April 19, 1775, the tide of war rolled into Cambridge. Six 'scholars' marched off with the minutemen. Lord Percy with his reinforcing columns came by the long route over Roxbury Neck and through Brookline and Brighton, crossed the 'great bridge' that connected the College with the south side of the Charles, and met his first check on Cambridge Common, not knowing which of the numerous tracks led to Lexington. Students and townspeople, on being questioned, pled ignorance, but Tutor Isaac Smith (A.B. 1767) thought he 'could not tell a lie' and directed Lord Percy on his way. The General Court that fall recommended the Governing Boards to 'dismiss those who by their past or present Conduct appear to be unfriendly to the Liberties and Privileges of the Colonies.' Tutor Smith, finding the attitude of his pupils and neighbors unpleasant, had already sailed for England, whence he returned some eleven years later to become College Librarian. Percy's column met the retreating British just short of Lexington Common, and

[1] A careful check-up of Harvard graduates living on January 1, 1776, from the lists of loyalists in Sabine and a manuscript list compiled by the late Benjamin Rand, yields the following result: total living graduates, 1224; total loyalists, 196, or 16 per cent. Included in this list are passive loyalists or Tory sympathizers, such as Judge Edmund Trowbridge of Cambridge, who were neither exiled nor molested during the war.

covered their disastrous retreat, fighting minutemen most of the way; in a skirmish near Porter's Station were killed Major Isaac Gardner of Brookline (A.B. 1747), the first Harvard man to fall in the war, and John Hicks of Cambridge, whose ancient dwelling is now the library of Kirkland House. Fortunately for Lord Percy and the College, he retreated to Boston by the shortest route, through Charlestown; otherwise he would have met a hot reception in Cambridge from farmers embattled in the College buildings, and there would have been a Battle of the Harvard Yard to chronicle.

Comparatively few undergraduates left College to 'enter the army'; and some of them petitioned to be let back before the siege of Boston was over. Major-General Artemas Ward (A.B. 1748), whom Washington succeeded in high command, was Harvard's most distinguished soldier. The College rendered her proper service to the country in council, through the constructive labors of such men as John Adams and James Bowdoin, rather than in the field or at sea. But it is pleasant to relate that, among those who had stirred up the young men of Massachusetts, many acted on their own precept, *dulce et decorum est pro patria mori.* One of these was Dr. Joseph Warren (A.B. 1759), the flaming Son of Liberty, who fell at Bunker Hill. Thomas Allen (A.B. 1762), the fighting parson of Pittsfield, accompanied the men of his flock to Bennington, himself fired the first shot in the battle, and lived to play a decisive part in the events that led to the framing of the State Constitution of 1780.

Cambridge was the natural headquarters for the patriot besiegers of Boston; and 'the colleges' were wanted for military purposes. Committee of Safety gave the students a premature summer vacation on May 1, 1775; and shortly after the Provincial Congress commandeered the buildings, ordering library and philosophical apparatus to be transported to Andover, out of harm's way.

Professor Winthrop, aided, it is said, by the future Count Rumford, spent two days 'packing apparatus and library.' When and where the College should reassemble long remained undecided. The respective merits of Andover, Haverhill, Worcester, Concord, and Northampton were discussed. On September 7 the *New-England Chronicle or Essex Gazette*, then printed in Stoughton College, carried an advertisement to the effect that 'the Town of Concord . . . is pitched upon by the Honorable and Reverend Corporation and Overseers of said College, as a proper place for convening the Members of the said public Seminary of Learning.' The students were notified that by October 4 they were expected to reassemble at Concord, 'where all necessary Provision is made for their Reception, and they will have Boarding and Chamber Furniture at a reasonable Rate.' And for eight months in 1775–76 Harvard endured a not unpleasant Babylonian Captivity at the future shrine of New England letters.

Although the Corporation reported that Concord could accommodate a hundred and twenty-five students, it is unlikely that even a hundred went there; many withdrew from College, a few joined the army, and only twenty-four freshmen entered in October. Concord meetinghouse, court house, and schoolhouse were placed at the disposition of the College for prayers and recitations; President Langdon and the professors hired houses — Professor Sewall, the 'bullet-hole house' opposite the Old Manse; Professor Winthrop, a house on the site of Hawthorne's 'Wayside.' The two remaining tutors and the students boarded in taverns, which displeased the Faculty, or in private houses, which delighted the Concord maidens; their favorite walk with student lovers, a secluded lane, is still called the College Road. A temporary College Library was arranged in Humphrey Barrett's house, midway between Professor Sewall's and the

Square. Anticipating a long stay, the Corporation voted to bring on the college clock, museum, and fire-engine to Concord, and some extra sets of the indispensable Burlamaqui and 's Gravesande were placed at the students' disposition; but Professor Winthrop complained of insufficient apparatus to conduct his experimental lectures.

In March, 1776, the British were forced to evacuate Boston; and on April 3 the Corporation and a handful of Overseers, meeting at Watertown, voted to confer on that *Vir illustrissimus Georgius Washington, Armiger, Exercitus Coloniarum in America Foederatarum Imperator praeclarus*, the honorary degree of *Doctor Utriusque Juris, tum Naturae et Gentium, tum Civilis*. They waited on his Excellency the same day, presumably at his Cambridge headquarters in the Craigie House, and conferred the degree and presented the diploma. On April 4 Dr. Washington left Cambridge for New York; his adopted alma mater did not see him again until 1789, when he was President of the United States.

Concord was pleasant enough, but the College was eager to return to Cambridge by this time. Provincial Congress granted permission to reoccupy the college buildings on June 11. The next day the Faculty passed a vote of thanks to the Town of Concord, hoping that the scholars had not committed 'any incivilities or indecencies of behaviour,' and concluding with a prayer to which we may all subscribe:

> May God reward you with all his blessings, grant us a quiet resettlement in our ancient seat to which we are now returning, preserve America from slavery, and establish and continue religion, learning, liberty, peace, and the happiest government in these American colonies to the end of the world.

On June 21, 1776, the College reassembled at her 'ancient seat,' where she has since remained for a greater length of time than had elapsed between her foundation and the year 1775.

Considering that 640 soldiers had been quartered in the 32 chambers of Massachusetts Hall, a like number in Hollis, 240 in Stoughton (in addition to a printing office), and 160 in little Holden, it is surprising how little damage was done. Much of the interior woodwork and most of the brass door-knobs and box locks on the studies had disappeared from the older buildings, and half a ton of lead from the roof of Harvard had been moulded into bullets to speed the British from Boston. But the total loss was valued by the College at less than £450, which the State assumed. Stoughton College, which had been in a bad condition before the war, was never reoccupied; it stood for several years vacant and dilapidated, until, in 1781, Deacon Aaron Hill was allowed to take it down for the materials. The carved Latin inscription and achievement of Stoughton arms on the façade were ordered to be carefully saved, but by the time the new Stoughton Hall was built, in 1805, they had disappeared; and so passed all trace of our last seventeenth-century building.

Throughout the rest of the war, the College labored under great difficulties. Students fell off in numbers; an average class of thirty graduated from 1778 through 1783, as compared with forty-six between 1771 and 1777. Although the din of war never again disturbed 'Harvard's classic shades,' trade and transport were so dislocated that it was often difficult to procure supplies for the college community of less than a hundred and fifty people. Sylvanus Bourne wrote home in 1777 that the Steward never knew one day if he would have food for commons the next. The shortage of textbooks became so acute that in 1778 President and Fellows petitioned the State for license to plunder the sequestered Tory libraries, and this indulgence yielded sundry classical texts, Guthries, 's Gravesandes, Lockes, and Burlamaquis that were of no further use to the loyalist sons of Harvard. In the winter of 1777–78 another dispersal of the College was threatened, to accommodate Burgoyne's surrendered army. General Heath, who had to find quarters somewhere for the prisoners, made every effort to procure the college buildings, and went so far as to order the students and their effects removed. On recommendation of the Overseers, the students were sent home in late November, but the Corporation got its back up and refused to hand over anything but a wooden dwelling to the army. In the end, barracks were found for the British troops; 'Gentleman Jack' Burgoyne and his staff occupied Apthorp House, and the other officers were quartered in private houses. So the net result was a three months' winter vacation for the students.

British officers and gentlemen of Burgoyne's army must have been high social lights in Cambridge, compared with the sorry student body of war years. Very few members of the war classes attained distinction, and the number of misfits and downright rascals was considerable. Ephraim Eliot, who in after life became an apothecary, has left for us a mordant account of his own Class of 1780, thirty strong at graduation. One, a transfer from Yale to the senior class, was 'a good scholar and respectable'; a second, a transfer from Dartmouth, was 'a decent scholar, and rather more than a quack doctor'; and there were also three or four 'respectable characters' who had not been to other colleges. But there was a sad example of the over-bright freshman, who, with too much time on his hands, fell in with gamblers and 'became a dissipated sot,' along with a classmate who turned out an 'expert gamester.' One of an old Bay Colony family 'never had an idea in his life, except to grease his hair and clean his buckles.' A descendant of a long line of ministers 'was spoilt by a residence in Virginia, where he became dissipated'; two others became drunkards without faring so far. One committed suicide shortly after graduation, two went insane, a fourth was 'burnt to death by foolish sport after election day playing with squibs,' and a fifth was murdered! Equally startling is the tolerance of the college authorities toward irregularities in residence. Students slipped off to the army for a year or more, and returned to their old standing without examination or 'make up' of any sort, provided they paid the college fees for the period of their absence. One student, who in after life was 'a contemptible lawyer — very immoral and despised,' showed up at Cambridge for the first time on July 18, 1780, passed oral examinations in seven subjects, paid $300 for tuition that he had never received, and obtained his Bachelor's degree the following day.

There was reason for this undignified attitude; the College was in desperate financial straits, owing to war, currency inflation, and John Hancock. Never a great hand at business, John became so completely engrossed in politics within a year of his appointment as Treasurer, that the Corporation could get no word from him, much less an accounting. The first reply that they received to repeated letters begging him to make an accounting was on April 11, 1775, to the effect that he very seriously resented their importunity, but 'if the Gentlemen Chuse to make a public Choice of a Gentleman to the Displacing him, they will please to Act their pleasure.' That, in view of Hancock's power and influence, they dared not do as yet; but they authorized President Langdon to receive rents, legacies, and donations. This eased the situation somewhat, and Hancock's accounts show that he received no money on behalf of the College after November, 1774, nor made any payments after March, 1775, except in the year 1778, when the Corporation was so hard up that it induced him to pay certain salaries out of his unaccounted balance. Still, certain creditors made lack of a Treasurer's receipt an excuse for postponing payments, while the currency depreciated month after month.

Almost a year passed, and the Treasurer was not heard from. In March, and again in April, 1776, when Hancock was at Philadelphia, the President wrote to him in language of humble supplication; in May, the Treasurer condescended to reply that he had sent off a messenger in a light wagon, with orders to bring all the College account books and papers across country to Philadelphia. This at a time when New York, part of the Jerseys, and half the valley of the Hudson were in enemy hands! The President replied, expressing his concern at this untimely removal of valuable papers, and hinting that Mr. Hancock's resignation would be acceptable. Mr. Hancock neither took the hint nor made an accounting.

The Board of Overseers then tried a hand; but no word could be obtained from Mr. Hancock. Tutor Stephen Hall was despatched to Philadelphia, or 'wherever Mr. Hancock may be,' to procure the records. He left Cambridge in December, overtook the Continental Congress at Baltimore, started home on February 16, 1777, and arrived on March 6 with the essential documents in his saddlebags, together with a letter from the Treasurer expressing his resentment at the Overseers' 'severe and unmerited censure' on his dilatoriness. On March 12, 1777, Hancock's attorney delivered up to the Corporation bonds, notes, mortgages, etc., to the nominal value of over £16,000; but his accounts were not settled, nor was the balance in his hands known to him, or anyone else. A few days later the Overseers advised the Corporation 'to choose a treasurer that shall constantly reside in the State.' It took the Corporation some time to screw up their courage to do this; but on July 16, 1777, Ebenezer Storer (A.B. 1747), merchant of Boston, was chosen Treasurer of Harvard College.

Hancock chose to interpret this as a personal insult and political slight — an unforgivable offense to him, as to other vain men in politics. A tactful vote of the Corporation to pay for the Copley portrait, and a request that the distinguished subject, who had retained it, would permit his effigy to be 'conveyed to the College, and placed in the Philosophy Chamber, by that of his late honorable uncle,' failed to move the former Treasurer to square his accounts; but he did turn over additional notes which he had forgotten, to the face value of £624. A motion to put in suit his treasurer's bond was made in the Overseers, but lost. A fulsome address to him in 1780, when first elected Governor of the Commonwealth, coupled with a renewed request for a settlement, was received in silence. A committee of the Overseers reported at a meeting in February, 1783, at which Hancock presided, that 'it is not known what sums the late Treasurer had received and paid'; and Dr. Gordon moved that the Corporation be advised to put the treasurer's bond in suit, but no one dared second the nomination. His Excellency considered this an 'indignity,' but made no other reply than to absent himself from the next Overseers' meeting, and to transfer two boys for whose education he was paying from Harvard to Yale. On October 20, 1783, Hancock made a curious offer to President Willard. In spite of the 'illiberal . . . Treatment' he had met 'from some of the former and present Governors of the College,' wrote the Governor, he wished to provide the College Yard with a 'Respectable Fence' to take the place of the one torn down for firewood by the soldiers in 1775–76. The President would please to give orders to the college carpenters accordingly, and send his Excellency the bill, which would 'meet with immediate payment.' John Hancock's meaning of 'immediate' when applied to 'payment' being well known, the Corporation sent the college carpenters 'to wait upon' his Excellency, who was asked to give them his orders, and 'direct every thing' agreeably to his 'own taste,' which would be that 'of every judge of architecture.' Our failure to hear the result of this interesting interview creates the suspicion that the college carpenters demanded cash down; the new and ornate wooden fence on the west side of the Yard, which appears in views from 1790 on, was provided by the College itself. A fresh occasion of offense was taken by Governor Hancock in October, 1784, when Harvard conferred upon General Lafayette an honorary LL.D. At the dinner given by the Corporation in Harvard Hall, the President sat at the head of high table, with the Marquis at his right, facing down the hall, and the Governor opposite, with his back to the assembly. Hancock thought that he should have had Lafayette's place. Nevertheless, on or about February 10, 1785, and before President Willard had had a chance to explain the rules of precedence observed at college dinners, Hancock condescended to render his eight years' overdue accounts, and acknowledged a balance due of £1054.

The Corporation's expectation of promptly receiving this sum was soon dashed. Year after year passed, and Mr. Hancock still postponed payment, although living in a style of extravagant luxury and giving lavish entertainments. On December 3, Hancock sent a verbal message to Treasurer Storer that he would pay the debt on January 1, if apprised of the amount. Storer sent him a bill for £1495 14s 2d, which included a small fund of Dummer Academy in the College Treasurer's hands. But Hancock died on October 8, 1793, before paying a penny. Finally, in 1795, his heirs paid simple interest on the debt, and arranged to pay the principal within seven years. Treasurer Storer's laconic statement, 'The heirs of Mr. Hancock refused to pay compound interest, whereby the College loses upwards of $526,' concludes the protracted negotiations between the great patriot and his alma mater. That was a low fee for the lesson very thoroughly learned by the Harvard Corporation, to keep politics out of the College Treasury.

Ebenezer Storer faithfully and intelligently managed the college property through the troubled years 1777–89, and for eight years longer. His efforts were ably seconded by the 'solid men of Boston' whom the Corporation began to elect to vacancies in 1779. For about half a century previous to the Revolution, the Corporation, reversing President Leverett's policy, had filled its vacancies almost exclusively with professors and tutors. Probably it was a sense of their own inadequacy in dealing with the bewildering changes of the seventeen-seventies, and with a man like Hancock, that induced the clerical and pedagogical fellows, after the death of Professor Winthrop in 1779, to elect James Bowdoin (A.B. 1745) to his place. Bowdoin was an eminent patriot, President of the Council that governed Massachusetts after the breach with England, a wealthy merchant, and a patron of learning and letters. He resigned from the Corporation in 1785 when his election as Governor of Massachusetts made him *ex officio* President of the senior Governing Board.

According to President Stiles of Yale, who knew much of the affairs of other colleges besides his own, Harvard College had a total income of £1550 (lawful money of New England) in 1774, made up by £900 income from its own property and funds, £450 from the Province, and £200 from ferry, tuition fees, and study rents. The face value of the mortgages and interest-bearing personal bonds and notes received by Treasurer Storer from Treasurer Hancock in July, 1777, amounted to £16,443 11s 10d, representing over two hundred different items. Within four months the premium on specie had reached 175 per cent; the Corporation authorized the Treasurer to invest all currency received as income or principal, and which had to be accepted at its face value, in continental loan certificates or state treasury notes, both securities bearing six per cent interest; and by September 1, 1779, the College owned £15,000 in the former and £600 in the latter. Fortunately the bulk of the private and state notes were paid off before continental currency touched bottom. The College further protected itself against depreciation by raising rents on its real estate whenever a lease expired, and on college rooms; over £18,000 in 'study and cellar rents' was collected in 1781, as against £341 in 1778, and the 'assessments' on students rose in the same period from £1250 to £52,000, in round numbers. Massachusetts made a new emission in 1780 at the rate of 1 to 40, but, as there was not enough of it, specie began to reappear; so for a time Treasurer Storer had to run two accounts in currency and one in specie. By 1782 the College was entirely on a specie basis, and as Congress issued no new loans, and the old ones were scaled down to the specie value of the notes when subscribed, Treasurer Storer began to make more investments in state treasury notes, which could usually be had at a discount, and in the heavily discounted certificates that Congress issued for interest and supplies. Public securities which the College had taken in an earlier stage of the war because it had no choice were now deliberately selected for investment at very attractive prices.

Financial assistance also came from the State. During the Revolution, and for the years 1784–85–86, the Commonwealth continued to pay the President's salary, and to make additional grants for the three professors; the annual average grant for these purposes in ten years was $1475, in specie value. It became more and more difficult to obtain these grants. Experience of the unreliability of financial promises made by political bodies, and of wayward individuals like Governor Hancock, made the Corporation wish heartily for the day when the College might live on her own estate. Possibly this worthy ambition was the reason for electing as Fellow of Harvard College in 1784 a second 'solid man of Boston,' John Lowell (A.B. 1760). Judge Lowell's judgment and integrity did much to bring the College through the hard times that followed the peace of 1783. Moreover, he founded a veritable dynasty that has been constant in devotion to the University, the Commonwealth, and the cause of learning.[1] Gradually the Corporation became filled with men of the Bowdoin and Lowell stamp — public-spirited lawyers and business men of Greater Boston — with an occasional clergyman or man of letters. No more tutors were appointed Fellows of Harvard College after the resignation of Caleb Gannett in 1780; or professors, after that of Eliphalet Pearson, in 1806.[2] Thus, the critical

[1] The 'Lowell Dynasty': —

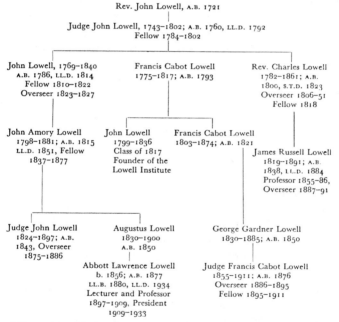

Rev. John Lowell, A.B. 1721

Judge John Lowell, 1743–1802; A.B. 1760, LL.D. 1792
Fellow 1784–1802

John Lowell, 1769–1840
A.B. 1786, LL.D. 1814
Fellow 1810–1822
Overseer 1823–1827

Francis Cabot Lowell
1775–1817; A.B. 1793

Rev. Charles Lowell
1782–1861; A.B.
1800, S.T.D. 1823
Overseer 1806–51
Fellow 1818

John Amory Lowell
1798–1881; A.B. 1815
LL.D. 1851, Fellow
1837–1877

John Lowell
1799–1836
Class of 1817
Founder of the
Lowell Institute

Francis Cabot Lowell
1803–1874; A.B. 1821

James Russell Lowell
1819–1891; A.B.
1838, LL.D. 1884
Professor 1855–86,
Overseer 1887–91

Judge John Lowell
1824–1897; A.B.
1843, Overseer
1875–1886

Augustus Lowell
1830–1900
A.B. 1850

George Gardner Lowell
1830–1885; A.B. 1850

Abbott Lawrence Lowell
b. 1856; A.B. 1877
LL.B. 1880, LL.D. 1934
Lecturer and Professor
1897–1909, President
1909–1933

Judge Francis Cabot Lowell
1855–1911; A.B. 1876
Overseer 1886–1895
Fellow 1895–1911

[2] Excepting that Ephraim W. Gurney was elected Fellow in 1884, when still professor of history. At least two Fellows, Joseph Story in 1829, and James Walker in 1838, were appointed to professorial chairs, and continued to hold their fellowships.

decade 1779–89 saw what proved to be the final stage in the evolution of the Harvard Corporation from a group of teaching fellows on an English collegiate model to a board of external trustees, connected with the living organism of the University only through the President.

In the meantime, Treasurer Storer and Judge Lowell were quietly working toward making the College financially independent. By 1789 the college investment in public securities had risen to over £30,000 in specie value, not including £8000 in overdue interest. Shortly after, the Treasurer converted his accounts from pounds into dollars at the standard exchange, $3.33. Hamiltonian finance was a great help to Harvard, by paying at par the national debt and assuming state debts, in both of which the College was deeply interested. In 1793 Treasurer Storer reported that the whole personal estate of the College amounted to over $182,000, of which $100,000 was not tied to specific objects. In comparison with the $55,000 estate of 1777, this was a very notable achievement.

Any anxiety that the College may have had as to its future status under a republican government was removed in 1780. The Massachusetts constitutional convention, which assembled in the meetinghouse of the First Church in Cambridge on September 1, 1779, was led by sons of Harvard who treated Alma Mater handsomely. John Adams, in drafting the Constitution, gave an entire chapter to the 'University at Cambridge,' which thereby was first officially designated as a university. The 'President and Fellows of Harvard-College, in their corporate capacity, and their successors in that capacity, their officers and servants,' were confirmed in all their ancient 'powers, authorities, rights, liberties, privileges, immunities and franchises . . . forever,' as well as all 'gifts, grants, devises of houses, lands, tenements, goods, chattles, legacies and conveyances, heretofore made, either to Harvard-

College in Cambridge, in New-England, or to the President and Fellows of Harvard-College, or to the said College, by some other description.' John Adams thought of everything! The Board of Overseers was declared to consist henceforth of the Governor, Lieutenant-Governor, Council, and Senate of the Commonwealth, and the ministers of the Congregational churches in Cambridge, Watertown, Charlestown, Boston, Roxbury, and Dorchester.

Although the town meetings, which debated and voted on this Constitution before it was returned to the convention for ratification, showed a highly critical and even captious spirit about some of its provisions, very little adverse notice was taken of the chapter on Harvard College. Two towns where Baptists were strong demanded that ministers other than Congregational be eligible as Overseers (this was finally adopted in 1843); Bellingham proposed that the College Treasurer should be required to publish an annual financial statement (which would have been embarrassing to Governor Hancock); and Petersham, where the Harvard Forest is now located, thought it

too much to give the Corporation of the University at Cambridge a Section of our Constitution. We are of the mind that it might with safety be left to the care of the Legislature and that it may be possible that the Legislature may find it necessary to Curtail that Rich and Growing Corporation lest it should Endanger the Liberties of the Commonwealth.

Apparently the College had won golden opinions for the services of her sons in war and peace; and there was no serious objection to her ancient rights and privileges being confirmed by the new régime.

As soon as Harvard's position was secure in the new Constitution, she turned out President Langdon. As in the case of President Hoar, it is now impossible to get to the bottom of the matter. Langdon had been elected largely for political reasons, and his patriotic election sermon of 1775, and parting prayer to the army on the eve of Bunker Hill, did much to ingratiate the College with the Revolutionary party. President Stiles of Yale declared that Langdon's 'literary character was similar to President Holyoke's'; that is, he was rather good at mathematics and science, 'yet was not of great erudition' in anything else. According to the letters of John Eliot (A.B. 1772), who studied in College for his M.A. and soon thereafter became an Overseer, the real fault lay in the President's personality. He stepped off on the wrong foot, in 1774, by giving expositions of Scripture (the ancient puritan rite) lasting ninety minutes, and by 'abolishing Sunday evening singing, to give more time for his harangue.' In 1775 he became 'rather more popular'; but as the spirit of '76 declined, his popularity waned. 'So disgusting hath he been in his whole deportment,' even in his manner of 'addressing the Deity' at prayers, that detestation was 'absorbed in meer thorough contempt.' In the summer of 1780 the students drafted a petition to the Corporation for his removal. A committee of them had the boldness to inform the President what they proposed to do, and the insolence to address him in these words: 'As a man of genius and knowledge we respect you; as a man of piety and virtue we venerate you; as a President we despise you.' Whereupon poor Langdon admitted 'his incapacity for the office, imputing it to the week state of his nerves, and gave them a promise that he would resign.' That he promptly did; and his resignation, after a hot protest by one of the Overseers, was accepted on August 30. The students were so sorry for the poor man that they sped his departure with a complimentary address and a subscription of money. Shortly after he obtained the pulpit of Hampton Falls, New Hampshire, played a prominent part in the New Hampshire ratifying convention of 1788, and died at the ripe age of seventy-four, greatly beloved by his parish and famous throughout the State.

Langdon was a good example (along with three or four others in Harvard history) of a man, exemplary in private life, sufficient in learning, and eminent in his profession, who was a complete failure as a college President for want of that divine spark which has made otherwise ordinary men great leaders in education.

VIII

FEDERALISTS AND UNITARIANS

AFTER the usual difficulty in obtaining a suitable candidate for the presidency, the Reverend Joseph Willard (A.B. 1765) was chosen to that office on September 20, 1781, and inaugurated three months later. Governor Hancock, who presided, 'in an elegant Latin Speech, congratulated the University . . . which he considered in some sense, the Parent as well as the Nurse of the late Happy Revolution, in this Commonwealth.' Mr. Willard, being invested with seal, charter, keys, and records, delivered his inaugural address in Latin; and the Governor made a short reply. The President then ascended the pulpit, and announced that the University had conferred the degree of LL.D. on the Chevalier de la Luzerne, minister of Louis XVI to the United States, the Honorable Arthur Lee, Esq., and his Excellency John Adams, Esq.[1] Elijah Paine (A.B. 1781) pronounced a Latin oration, the Reverend Mr. Howard prayed, 'and the solemnity was closed by an anthem, well performed by the young gentlemen of the University.' The 'Colleges' were illuminated that evening, the lights disposed 'in a variety of figures' which 'exhibited a very pleasing and brilliant appearance.'

Joseph Willard, if not a great President, must be accounted a success. Born at Biddeford, Maine, in 1738 to

[1] John Adams was much pleased at this attention. He wrote the President, 'The System of Education at your University is so excellent that I should not wish to see it essentially changed, much less conformed to the Models in Europe, where there is much less Attention to the Morals and Studies of the Youth'; and his son J. Q., whom he took out of the University of Leyden and sent to Harvard, wrote to him (April 2, 1786) '. . . . take it all in all, I am strongly confirmed in your opinion, that this university is upon a much better plan that any I have seen in Europe.'

the Reverend Samuel Willard (A.B. 1723), grandson of the Vice-President of that name, Joseph lost his father at the age of two, and was reared in poverty, his mother having married for second husband the ill-paid minister of Scarborough. Joseph early showed a genius for mathematics, learned navigation, and made several coasting voyages, in preparation for a seafaring life; at the age of twenty-one he decided to take up medicine, but was balked by his ignorance of Latin. Samuel Moody (A.B. 1746), the famous schoolmaster of York, Maine, prepared him gratis for Harvard — and, some thirty years later, had the satisfaction of visiting the College, where the President and all three professors were his old pupils. Graduating from College at the advanced age of twenty-seven, Willard was persuaded by Professor Wigglesworth to enter the ministry. An appointment as college butler allowed him to remain after his graduation until the tutorship in Greek fell vacant in 1766; after four years of that the First Parish of Beverly called him to their pulpit.

Beverly was then the residence of several active and public-spirited merchants (Cabots, Danes, Lees, and Thorndikes), whose love for Parson Willard followed him to Cambridge, and enriched the College; whilst within a short radius were several ministers of liberal views and tastes, such as Menasseh Cutler of Northwest Territory and botanical fame, and John Prince, theologian and amateur maker of mathematical instruments. Willard, too, kept up his interest in science, and prepared a paper on 'A Method of finding the Altitude and Longitude of the Nonagesimal Degree of the Ecliptic.' On the famous 'dark day' of May 19, 1780, when the sun's light was almost completely obscured by dense clouds of smoke from northern forest fires, and the common people thought the end of the world was at hand, the people of Beverly were somewhat reassured by their parson's cool manner as he set up his instruments on the Common, to make observations. An alarmist came running from the shore, exclaiming in terror, 'The tide has done flowing!' 'So it has,' said Willard, drawing out his watch, 'so it has, for it is just high water!'

Clerical interest in science may astonish those brought up on the 'warfare between Science and Theology' thesis; but it has always been common among Harvard-trained parsons. Those of Willard's generation, were determined to improve the American Revolution for spiritual, scientific, and educational ends. In contrast to the Civil War and the World War, which left both victors and vanquished intellectually maimed and spiritually gelded, the War of Independence liberated intellectual energies from the bog of colonialism. Immediately following the peace new schools and colleges sprang up in both Southern and Northern States. The little group of Essex County intelligentsia to which Willard belonged even gained knowledge from privateering! A Salem corsair brought into harbor the library of Dr. Richard Kirwan, the eminent Irish scientist; Willard and his friends bought it in at the prize auction and placed it in the Salem library, where they, and many others, including a poor young lad named Nat Bowditch, browsed upon scientific literature and the transactions of learned societies. And in 1780 there were already enough *virtuosi* in Massachusetts to form the American Academy of Arts and Sciences, of which Willard was elected the first corresponding secretary.

The formation of this Academy gave great delight to the European liberals like Turgot, who regarded America as the 'hope of the world'; especially to those, like Dr. Richard Price, who were elected corresponding fellows of the American Academy. Even before the war was over, Willard began corresponding with Price, an old friend of Franklin's; with Joseph Priestley and with Thomas Brand Hollis, last of a notable family of English liberals and patrons of American learning. Hollis writes in 1785: 'I have this day *4 July*, ever to be celebrated and had in remembrance, made up a Box of Books various and mixed, but all I hope will have their use. The larger Number is for the Library of Harvard University, a small Number for the American Academy of Arts and sciences.' And in 1788, after praising the new federal constitution and expressing his gratitude at receiving an LL.D. from 'so illustrious a University' as Harvard, he writes: 'Our papers mention that there is an intention of having the Olympic Games revived in America. All her friends wish it and say they are capable of it, and having acted on Greek principles should have Greek exercises.'

Harvard had been recognized as a university by the state constitution which went into effect on October 25, 1780, a year before President Willard took office. Before another year elapsed Harvard College became a university indeed, by providing instruction in Medicine. This step, anticipated as far back as President Dunster's day, was long overdue. The Medical Schools of the University of Pennsylvania and Columbia University were founded respectively in 1765 and 1767; but physicians in New England continued to depend for instruction on apprenticeships to existing practitioners.

A few years before the war, a group of Harvard students of the classes 1770–1772, including John Warren, Samuel Adams, Jr., and William Eustis, formed an 'Anatomical Society,' which met for secret dissection of cats and dogs. At the outbreak of hostilities these and many other Harvard graduates who were learning or practising medicine became military surgeons and won distinction, in contrast to certain 'very great rascals,' as Washington called the unlettered bone-setters and ignorant horse-leeches with which the Army Medical Department abounded. Common experience in hospital and field gave these young military surgeons a corps consciousness that the profession lacked in New England; and in May, 1780, a number of them, led by Warren, head of the army hospital in Boston, formed the Massachusetts Medical Society. A young and energetic practitioner, Warren saw that, even more than standards, the profession needed systematic instruction and clinical experience. Already he had been giving anatomical demonstrations to his staff; and in 1781 he induced the new Medical Society to provide a course of medical lectures and demonstrations at the military hospital, on the site of the present Massachusetts General. These were attended by fellows of the new Academy, President Willard, and several senior sophisters from Harvard. The next step, a natural one, was for the College to take Warren and medical instruction under her wing, using the Hersey legacy of 1772 and whatever other moneys she could lay her hands on.

The Harvard Medical School was founded on September 19, 1782, when the Corporation adopted an elaborate plan, drafted by President Willard and Professor Wigglesworth, that looked to enriching 'the library of the University' with medical and chemical books, acquiring 'a complete anatomical and surgical apparatus,' founding three professorships as soon as funds could be obtained, and organizing lectures, *accompanied always by clinical instructions and observations.* These would be open to upperclassmen, college graduates, or non-collegians twenty-one years old; and such students, when found qualified to practise by a public examination held before the Massachusetts Medical Society and the 'Governors of the University,' would receive a certificate to that effect.

This was two months before the war was over, several years before John Hancock disgorged his balance, at a time when the total budget of the University was perhaps $15,000, and when the only fund for medical instruction was Mr. Hersey's bequest of £1000, which had not 'improved' much in the last ten years. But the Corporation went straight ahead; medical professors could be supported by fees (as all the existing Harvard professors then were, in part) if in no other way. On November 22, 1782, John Warren, aged twenty-nine, was chosen Professor of Anatomy and Surgery. For the chair of Theory and Practice of Physic there was available Dr. Benjamin Waterhouse of Newport, who during the war had studied medicine at Edinburgh, at Leyden (where he commenced M.D. in 1781), and at London, where he assisted his great-uncle Dr. John Fothergill. The Professor of Chemistry and Materia Medica, Aaron Dexter, was elected on May 22, 1783, at the mature age of thirty-three. A grad-. uate of the College in the Class of 1776, he had served as ship's surgeon during the war, and studied under Samuel Danforth (A.B. 1758), a practising chemist and physician of Boston.

Commencement in 1783, the first since the peace, was particularly brilliant. Honorary degrees were conferred on James Bowdoin, President of the American Academy and donor of the Bowdoin Prizes, and on Edward Augustus Holyoke, President Holyoke's son, and a famous practitioner of Salem, who thereby became Harvard's first M.D. Harrison Gray Otis, 'the first scholar of the first class of a new nation,' delivered the English oration, indulging 'the impulse of a sanguine temperament in building what doubtless seemed . . . castles in the air,' but which as he looked back on them from the bicentennial in 1836 appeared moderate expectations in comparison with the reality that came to be. And Ephraim Eliot (A.B. 1780), for his Master's degree, delivered an Oration on the Art of Medicine, in which he eagerly looked 'forward to the time, when the University of Harvard shall be ranked with that of Edenburgh, now the seat of medical sages; when her sons shall be registered in the same catalogue with a Whytt, a Munro, and a Cutter. . . . May peace be spread throughout the world, and "Health, without whose cheerful active energy, no rapture swells the breast," be universally diffused through every land.' The 'Medical Institution of Harvard University,' as it was originally called, was formally opened on October 7, 1783, with a solemn inauguration of the professors in Cambridge meetinghouse. All the proceedings were in Latin, except the 'declaration and promise' of each professor, which was amusingly lengthy and complicated, reflecting no doubt a lurking clerical belief in the medieval proverb, *ubi tres medici, ibi duo athei*. Medicos were supposed to be wild fellows, given to body-snatching and other impious or abominable practices! Each professor had to declare himself to be a Protestant Christian, and promise to discharge his trust with fidelity and diligence, to 'consult' the 'prosperity' of other University departments as well, and 'to promote the interests of virtue and piety' by his 'own example and encouragement.' He promised, further, to demean himself 'as a good citizen of the United States of America,' to support their union and promote their happiness, and in particular to support 'the present constitution of the Commonwealth of Massachusetts,' and obey its 'wholesome laws.' But he was not subjected to the indignity of being forced to take an oath to these declarations.

For this new Medical Department, Holden Chapel, which had served as college lumber-room since the siege of Boston, was promptly appropriated. Exactly when the medical lectures began is not certain. Warren seems to have opened his course in Anatomy immediately, but Waterhouse and Aaron Dexter probably did not get going until 1785, since the first two medical graduates did not receive their degrees until 1788, after a three years' course. These degrees, in accordance with ancient university precedent, were Baccalaureates in Medicine; the Doctor's degree was offered to practising M.B.'s of at least seven years' standing, after public examination and a Latin and an English respondency. Between 1788 and 1810, inclusive, the M.B. was conferred on fifty students, of whom four-fifths were graduates of Harvard and other New England colleges, and five of these fifty M.B.'s, including the famous James Jackson (A.B. 1796), proceeded M.D. in course. Upon a representation of the professors in 1811 that other medical schools in this country and abroad conferred the M.D. after two or three years' study of Medicine, the Doctorate was offered on the same terms as the M.B., which was then abolished, and all Harvard Bachelors of Medicine were allowed to proceed Doctor if they so desired.

Conducting the Medical School at Cambridge was difficult for want of clinical facilities, and plenty of professional jealousy. In 1784 the College Corporation tried to induce the General Court to establish a public infirmary in Cambridge, or to let the professors and their pupils practise in the Boston almshouse; these proposals were defeated by a peppery memorial of the Massachusetts Medical Society, charged with animus against Warren. Dr. Waterhouse resented the popularity of Dr. Warren, and developed an unexpected though valuable interest in Natural History at the expense of his lectures on health and disease. He took charge of a cabinet of mineralogical specimens sent by the French Government in 1784, and accumulated a collection of stuffed birds, preserved fishes, and the like, in the Philosophy Chamber of Harvard Hall, greatly to the disgust of the Hollis Professor, who had a prior claim to that room. But Dr. Waterhouse kept up his English correspondence, and had the courage to inaugurate vaccination for smallpox in the United States. In 1799 he reported in print on Jenner's discovery, announced the year before; in 1800 he obtained some vaccine from England, and vaccinated his four children in succession. The Boston Board of Health took the matter up two years later, and in 1802, 'after three unsuccessful attempts,' Waterhouse 'succeeded in getting some infected threads to Monticello, where President Jefferson vaccinated all his immediate family and servants.' Dr. Jenner sent Dr. Waterhouse a snuffbox and set of lancets, after which he became quite insufferable. But we must also credit him with the first lectures on Natural History at Harvard, promoting the Botanical Garden, and providing the first formal tree-planting in the Yard.

This was a line of Lombardy poplars just inside the new fence along the west (the Common) frontage. In the early nineteenth century it was a sign of unterrified democracy in New England to plant Lombardy poplars, because that short-lived tree had been introduced by Thomas Jefferson. Federalists admitted their value for quick effect, but pointed out that their soft, pulpy wood and attraction for worms resembled the brain of the gentleman who introduced them. Dr. Waterhouse must have had many a chuckle over Federalist Harvard's adopting this dendrological badge of Jeffersonian Republicanism.

Holden Chapel was divided up in 1801 according to a plan that gave ample accommodation for the three medical professors and their not very numerous students.

In 1809 Professor Warren's son, John Collins Warren (A.B. 1797), who had had his medical education in Europe, was appointed Adjunct Professor of Anatomy and Surgery, and John Gorham (A.B. 1801; M.B. 1804) Adjunct Professor of Chemistry and Materia Medica. Yet the conduct of a Medical School in Cambridge became increasingly difficult. All the professors except Waterhouse lived and practised medicine in Boston; and even the new West Boston Bridge (opened on Thanksgiving Day, 1793) did not make the constant coming and going easy. Clinical facilities, short of Boston and Charlestown, there were none; and the Massachusetts Medical Society threatened to start a new medical school in Boston. The consequence was that the 'Medical Institution of

Harvard University' moved to Boston in 1810, and there, through many removals and vicissitudes, it finally fulfilled the sanguine prediction of young Ephraim Eliot to rival even the famous medical school of Edinburgh. Massachusetts and Hollis Halls had been sufficient to house the student body in the war period; but as the classes rose again to forty or fifty students it became necessary to replace Stoughton College by another residential hall. A small college lottery in 1788, for the purpose of purchasing Joseph Pope's orrery (price £450) for the College, was so successful that in 1793 the Governing Boards petitioned the General Court for the right to hold a lottery to provide a new building. There was some opposition, on the ground that the virtuous National Convention of France, on motion of Citizen Barlow, had abolished lotteries 'forever'; but Harvard obtained her desired privilege, appointing a highly respectable board of managers including George Richards Minot (A.B. 1778) the historian, who received five per cent on the tickets they sold. Three 'classes' of 25,000 tickets at $5 each, 8358 of them 'in the money,' and a grand prize of $10,000, went off very well; but a fourth class of $10 tickets and double prizes sold very slowly, in spite of appeals to 'lovers of literature and the college to aid the cause,' and ended in an unseemly squabble between the winner of the grand prize, the managers who were unable to pay it, and the Corporation. The total cash received by the College by 1796 was a little over $11,000. This sum, together with eight years' interest and about $5000 from the general funds, completed Stoughton Hall in 1805. By that time the College needed still more room, and a new lottery was launched. Although this method of raising funds was very popular in the early nineteenth century among towns, churches, and public bodies generally, it was wasteful, inefficient, and damaging to the good name of the College, which only realized about 2.3

per cent of the amount paid by the public for their chances of growing rich.

A few days before Willard's inauguration, the Overseers adopted a resolution that gave him his sailing orders, and reflected severely on the retired captain:

> That it be recommended to the Reverend Mr Willard, that when he shall be inducted into the office of President, he take due care to support the honor of the Chair, by exercising that power and authority respecting both government and instruction with which the Constitution invests the President; and which his Predecessors in that office before the war, have exercised for the good order and benefit of the University.

President Willard's notion of maintaining authority was quasi-military. One thinks of him as young Washington Allston caricatured him in 1798: strong, rugged features peering out from an enormous white wig; black small-clothes and black gown. Every student's or tutor's hat must come off when the President entered the Yard, or woe betide! To delinquents his attitude was austere and forbidding. 'Stiff and unbending,' he 'feared to treat his most exemplary pupils with the least familiarity lest it should engender contempt.' Undergraduates who entered his study were greeted with 'Well, child, what do you wish?' In 1786, partly to enforce authority and partly to lessen competition in expensive dress, the Corporation forbade students to wear silk and prescribed a uniform coat of blue-gray, with waistcoat and breeches of the same, or nankeen, olive, or black, and distinctions to mark the different classes: plain buttonholes and no buttons on cuffs for freshmen; buttons on cuffs for sophomores; 'cheap frogs to the button holes' *except* those on the cuffs for juniors; frogs all over for seniors. Juniors and seniors might wear black academic gowns, and were urged to 'appear in them on all public occasions.' Gold and silver lace, cord, and edging were forbidden. The students loathed this livery, and evaded it as far as they dared; after efforts to enforce it by dreadful penalties, the class distinctions were abandoned for a time; but the blue-gray tailed coats, cut much like dress coats of today, and scholar's gown, remained *de rigeur* for some years. Around 1822 an Oxford gray coat with 'skirts reaching to the bend of the knee' and a great-coat 'with not more than two capes, were required.' 'Nightgowns' or 'banyans' — what we should call dressing-gowns — could always be worn in the Yard, as they were the gentleman's undress of the time; but no scholar might appear in shirt-sleeves at any time.

The more 'buckish' sort of students affected to despise Harvard College. Harrison Gray Otis wrote his Albany classmate Stephen Van Rensselaer in 1782 that he hoped soon to 'bid adieu to the sophisticated Jargon of a superstitious Synod of pension'd Bigots and ramble in the fields of liberal science.' College Logic repelled an exquisite young fop, Joseph Dennie (A.B. 1790, of later *Port Folio* fame), who refers to it as 'that nonsensical syllogistical mode of reasoning which the united *wisdom* of the President and Tutors prescribes.'

Coincident with the ratification of the Federal Constitution, a fresh epidemic of disorder broke out; 'a spirit of buckism was very prevalent,' remembered John T. Kirkland (A.B. 1789), the next President but one. Eliphalet Pearson, Hancock Professor of Hebrew, even kept a 'Journal of Disorders' in 1788–89, of which these are some of the items:

Dec 9, 1788. Disorders coming out of chapel. Also in the hall at breakfast the same morning. *Bisket, tea cups, saucers*, and a KNIFE thrown at the tutors. At evening prayers the *Lights* were all extinguished by powder and lead, except 2 or 3. Upon this a general *laugh* among the juniors. — From this day to 13 December disorders continued in hall and chapel, such as *scraping, whispering*, etc. . . .

December 15. More disorders at my public lecture, than I ever knew before. The bible, cloth, candles, and branches, I found laid in confusion upon the seat of the desk. During lecture several pebbles were snapped, certain gutteral sounds were made on each side the chapel, beside some whistling.

December 16. Still greater disorders at Doctor Wigglesworth's public lecture. As he was passing up the alley, two vollies of stones, one from each side, were thrown at him, or just before him. . . .

January 1 [1789]. In the evening Mr. *Smith* prayed. Several coppers were thrown at him, while in prayer, as was supposed by juniors on the north side of the chapel. . . .

February 24. . . . Mr. *James* found . . . *Mackey* was drunk in bed, and *Dennie* and *Trapier* were also highly intoxicated. Mr. *James* saw the room cleared. . . .

April 2. On Tuesday morning of this week, the Front door of Harvard was barred, the inner kitchen door tied to the buttery door, the chapel and hall doors braced too by a bench, the bell rope cut off, and the scuttel door fastened down by a board laid over it across the balcony.

On the morning of the second of this month another dog was found in *Mrs. Marsh's* well.

May 29. In the evening *Russell, Adams* 1, Blake first and second, *Sparhawk*, and *Ellery*, went to Bradish's, and there supped with one *Green*, an Englishman. The expense was mutual. About 3 o'clock next morning the company left the house, and on their way to College grossly insulted the *President* by shouts and yells, challenges, curses, threats of laying siege to, undermining, and burning his house, by throwing clubs and stones. In College yard *Mr. Abbot* found *Green* and *Sparhawk* conducting *Russell*, naked, to his chamber.

Naked Russell, who did not graduate, was the son of a wealthy merchant; his chum in the Class of 1789 was Isaac Adams, a poor farmer's son. One dark winter's night they stole the sign of Porter's tavern in the Square; but while celebrating their success, a student came running to inform them that Porter had already discovered his loss, and informed the President, and that a visit from a tutor might be expected shortly. The young monkeys then split up the sign with a hatchet, and started feeding it into the fire, while a friend prayed loudly, sitting on a chair with his back against the chamber door. At this juncture the tutor came up the stairs, but, hearing a prayer-meeting going on, waited politely until the sign was consumed, and the prayer was brought to an end with 'a wicked and adulterous generation seeketh after a sign, and no sign shall be given unto it, but the sign of the Prophet Jonas.'

The crest of this wave of disorder came in 1791, when a new college law, that the three upper classes be publicly examined by a joint committee of the Governing Boards, first went into effect. This was an innovation in college history (since 1655, at least) for any but senior sophisters. As the 'College Bible' explained it, the purpose was 'to animate the Students in the pursuit of literary . . . fame, and to excite in their breasts a noble spirit of emulation'; but the spirit it excited was altogether different, and some Yard lawyer gave the lead in declaring the law *ex post facto* for all but freshmen, *ergo* unconstitutional. On the morning of the examination some students, when the cook's back was turned, threw a large dose of tartar emetic into the copper boiler that contained all the water used for breakfast. The result may better be imagined than described. The examination of pale and retching undergraduates grimly proceeded, under college officers who had not breakfasted in hall, and 'was closely pursued, three days till after sun-down every day.'

Rustication was the common method of dealing with young men whose high spirits interfered with their own and their classmates' studies. This meant exile to a country parsonage, where the young man's studies continued under the minister's supervision; for until 1850 or thereabouts it could be safely assumed that any intelligent graduate was capable of tutoring a young man through his college course. Francis Cabot Lowell (A.B. 1793), son of the eminent judge, was rusticated to Bridgewater for five months, after building a bonfire in the Yard. Joseph Dennie was apparently highly delighted at his rustication to Groton, in 1789. His sleigh journey was pleasantly interrupted by a call at Concord on a certain 'rural charmer,' when he 'enjoyed the luxury of her lips' and 'received a lesson on the celestial globes.' His Groton host, the Reverend Daniel Chaplin (A.B. 1772), was 'a sensible priest, one who has read Rabelais, as well as Cruden's Concordance, and who is as expert at a jest as at a sermon.' To a classmate Dennie writes:

In this delicious hamlet . . . have I at length found a tranquil asylum. Here are no interruptions, no *unseasonable* morning prayers, no Abbotts, and no damned fools. All is pleasant and cheerful. Here, I reduce the Chesterfieldian system of study to practice. The morning and forenoon I devote to dalliance with the Muses. The afternoon and evening, I spend with mere mortal females. A better, more royal social club of Lads cannot be found in America, College excepted, than at Groton. Most of them liberally educated, Sensible, liberal and spunkey.

After two years in this pleasant situation, Cambridge seemed unendurable to Dennie. The tutors 'who presumed to treat the scholars with insolence were invariably low born despicable rustics, lately emerged from the dunghill, who, conscious of their own want of genius, were determined to discountenance all, who possessed it.' Back he went to Groton, and so delightful were rambles over the hills, supper parties with the 'Lads,' and visits to the girls, that he declined to return to Cambridge and take his degree. 'Mamma' Dennie, who had something to say to that, appeared at Groton in a 'Hack' just before Commencement, 1790, and drove Joe to Cambridge; where, 'the cursed impertinence of a mock examination being over, a lying petition read, and the last acts of pigmy despotism exercised,' he took his degree with an admiring class, and then shook the dust of Cambridge from his shoes forever.

Dennie was exceptional; yet even such a superior genius as his might have benefited by college discipline. John Quincy Adams, three years Dennie's senior, wrote when still in College that the formal syllogistic disputations were detested, and, so far as possible, avoided; yet some of the college idlers 'merely from the horrors of syllogisms begin to study, acquire a fondness for it, and make a very pretty figure in college; and it is not uncommon to see young fellows, the most idle in a class the two first years, have the reputation of great students, and good scholars the two latter.'

How far did the tutors deserve the scorn of young gentlemen like Dennie? Early in Harvard history, when undergraduates chummed with tutors, the feeling between them was friendly and intimate; but in the eighteenth century tutors had their own chambers, and during the disorderly period of the Revolution, if not before, the undergraduates began to look upon them as their natural enemies. A lad who treated his tutor as a friend was looked down upon as a 'fisherman,' and the tutors regarded the undergraduates as inmates in a reformatory. By 1789 this had become a tradition; and about a century was required to change the pattern. Yet the tutors of Willard's and Webber's administrations were not bad fellows. Among the first forty-two appointed after 1781, covering the period 1783–1811, all but four had been undergraduate members of at least one student society; nineteen had belonged to two, and ten to three, clubs. Among their names one recognizes several college presidents, numerous professors, a few jurists, and many ministers. John Quincy Adams put his finger on the real trouble, in a letter to his father from Cambridge in 1786 — 'the tutors are so very young'; to which he might have added that they never stayed long enough to gather experience. Of these forty-two tutors whose records I have scanned, only eight were more than three years out of College when appointed; and only thirteen stayed more than three years. Harvard, like the Scottish universities, remained too long faithful to the medieval idea of the rotating regency; and for the same reason — economy.

If the college atmosphere seemed oppressive to young

scions of rich mercantile families, it was Elysium to boys
like the future Justice Story (A.B. 1798), who came up to
Cambridge from poor or provincial surroundings, after a
hard struggle to qualify:

> My college life was inexpressibly delightful to me. I awoke, as it
> were from a dream. I saw knowledge before me as by enchantment.
> I formed friendships which have endured to the present hour. I be-
> came enamored of learning, and have never ceased to love it cor-
> dially. I studied most intensely while in college, and reaped the fair
> rewards in collegiate honors.

Joseph Story also belonged to most of the college clubs
that there were — and for a college of less than two hundred students, there were a good many.

Although the Speaking Club goes back to 1770, the real
origin of the Harvard club system, and of all American
college fraternities, must be sought in the College of William and Mary. The leading student society of that ancient seat of learning was secret, and known to the unini-
tiated only by the initials F. H. C. In 1776 some young
men who were not elected to this club formed the rival
'S. P.' (Societas Philosophiae), better known by the initials of its Greek motto: Φ. B. K. Like the F. H. C., the
members sported a silver medal bearing the two sets of
initials and other emblems, suspended by ribbons of the
club colors. The Φ. B. K. of William and Mary died during the British invasion of Virginia; but in the meantime
sprigs of the plant had been carried North. Elisha Parmele, after graduating from Harvard in 1778, sojourned
at Williamsburg, where he was taken into the Φ. B. K.,
and thought so well of it that he obtained from his brethren a 'charter' to form a 'chapter' at Cambridge, in the
same manner that Masonic lodges were founded. Returning to Cambridge to take his M.A. at Commencement,
1781, Brother Parmele interested three junior sophisters in
his plan, and the Harvard chapter, 'Alpha of Massachusetts,' was formed on September 5, 1781, in 'Brother

Bartlett's room.' At the second meeting, five new members were nominated to be 'sounded,' and at the next, four brethren were requested to dispute on the question 'Whether Benedict Arnold can be considered a traitor.' At the same time silver medals were voted; the watch-key emblem originated with the Yale chapter around 1810, and it was not until the close of the nineteenth century that the Harvard brethren began to sport that umbilical adornment.

Phi Beta Kappa had an intricate and secret ritual of initiation, a secret grip, and a cipher for correspondence with other college chapters. The meetings were literary in character, like those of the Speaking Club. John Quincy Adams (A.B. 1787), who belonged to both, wrote: 'Of these societies friendship is the soul, and literary improvement the object; and consequently neither of them is numerous.' It was largely owing to his efforts in 1831 that the 'arcana' were exposed, and a curious world learned that the mystic letters meant nothing more than Φιλοσοφία Βιοὺ Κυβερνήτης: symbol of the Deism so fashionable in Virginia when the Society was founded. High rank in college studies quite early became the prime requisite for membership in Phi Beta Kappa; but membership was much sought after for the privilege of participating in the annual 'exhibition' and dinner, which remain the sole activities of the Harvard chapter at the present day.

Only a few years younger than the Phi Beta Kappa is the Porcellian, which began about the year 1791, with a group of choice spirits who met in each other's rooms, or at Moore's tavern, to dine on roast pig; Joseph McKean (A.B. 1794), the legendary initiator of these dinners, is the accepted founder. The 'Porcellian, or Pig Club' included the most lively and convivial lads in the College — 'The Bloods of Harvard' they were called even before 1800. Their Horatian motto *Dum vivimus vivamus* indicates that they made no pretense of cultivating literature or public speaking; their Greek motto, still known to the profane only in the abbreviated form 'Oμ. 'Ελ., doubtless had reference to the same genial view of life. A distinctive medal and ribbons were also adopted, and all subsequent Harvard clubs have followed suit; the club 'boards' for announcing meetings, crossed diagonally by club colors, came into use about 1815, when University Hall provided a place to post them up; the 'shingle,' or formal letter notifying one's election, began to be treasured and framed around 1850. For some years the P. C. was the largest college society; by 1800 it had become the most aristocratic, and the highest goal of undergraduate social ambition.

William Ellery Channing (A.B. 1798), though a quiet and studious youth, belonged to all the clubs and societies that we have mentioned, though he found the Porcellian 'too frankly epicurean and convivial,' and seldom attended its meetings. The one he enjoyed the most was the Hasty Pudding Club, founded in 1795 by some members of the junior class. This society has always been *sui generis*, although its character has completely changed in a hundred and forty years. At the start it was a rather jolly amalgam of literary, convivial, and patriotic elements. On 'Pudding' nights, when the bell tolled for the scanty evening commons, two members might be seen bearing on a pole an iron pot of steaming hasty-pudding from some near-by goodwife's kitchen to a member's room, where the brethren supped on that simple but filling fare, concluding their repast with 'sacred music,' which became less and less sacred as the years rolled by. On long summer evenings the brethren sometimes 're-tired to the play yard for a social game of bat and ball,' or 'paraded the streets of Cambridge till twelve o'clock with music in front.' The great annual event was a cele-bration of Washington's birthday, generally at Porter's tavern in the Square. Washington Allston (A.B. 1800) started the custom of keeping the records in rhyme, which has been the bane of all his successors. The Hasty Pudding's dues were less burdensome to the parental purse than those of the Porcellian, and after 1800, when debates 'on questions of literature, morality and politics' were organized to follow supper, it became the largest of the college societies. Debates were followed by mock trials, one of the perennial cases being Dido *vs*. Aeneas for breach of promise. Every generation or so the ' Pudding' invented some new initiation or tomfoolery; it sought out the wits of each class, regardless of gentility, and until late in the last century remained the principal college society to which any bright young man, regardless of social background or money, might expect to be elected.

The most short-lived club in Harvard history was a Society to Discourage the Perpetration of Crimes, formed in 1793. We know naught of this virtuous club except a hopefully enthusiastic resolve of the Corporation approving its formation; we fear that it was nothing more than a cruel hoax on that much harassed body.

Even at this early period a characteristic feature of the Harvard club system was in full vigor: anyone who belonged to one club was apt to be elected to some of the others. The Class of 1798, for instance, had forty-eight members who graduated. Of these, nineteen belonged to none of the four societies whose records are extant; thirteen belonged to but one (eight of them to the Porcellian); seven students belonged to two clubs; five were members of three societies; while William Ellery Channing, Artemas Sawyer, Richard Sullivan, and Stephen Longfellow (the poet's father) belonged to all four.

The median age of entering freshmen, which had been below seventeen in all but two of the pre-revolutionary classes, rose during the war, remained above seventeen until the Class of 1789, fluctuated between sixteen and a half and seventeen and a half until the Class of 1800, and then fell to a new low of fifteen and a half around 1810. From that point it slowly rose until, in 1845, the seventeen-year mark was again passed. Yet the students acted more maturely in Willard's and Kirkland's time than before. The Class of 1798 was the first not to be subjected to fagging. Tradition states that one stout fellow declined to doff his hat to a sophomore, who was so unpopular that his classmates refused to back him up; the sophomore complained to the Faculty, who were only too glad to see this ancient servitude challenged, and declined to interfere. For some years every senior had 'his' freshman, but only in an advisory capacity; and there was an idyllic interval for first-year men between the last of colonial fagging and the first of freshman hazing. The President, and for many years each member of the Faculty, also had 'his' freshman for clerical work and errands; such freshmen were excused from a part of their tuition fees, like the sizars of old Cambridge.

The examination crisis of 1791 had scarcely been passed when 'French infidelity' arose to bedevil the college authorities. There had been a good deal of Deism floating about since the seventeen-sixties; but the French Revolution, which was followed with breathless interest in America, gave a fillip to religious scepticism. As early as November, 1791, a writer in the Boston press accused Harvard of poisoning the minds of her students with Gibbon's Decline and Fall; to which President Willard felt obliged to reply that the *Éléments d'histoire* of the amiable Abbé Millot was the 'system taught,' and Gibbon never even thought of. Nathaniel Ames, after prematurely leaving College around 1812, recorded that Millot's was 'the most utterly worthless and contemptible work of that kind or any other extant.' He records a sample recitation on it. 'Did Cato die?' asked the tutor. Ames thought he was safe in answering, 'Yes, Sir!' But it seems he was wrong, 'for the profound and accurate tutor immediately replied, "No he did not, he killed himself!"'

Another book that was actually presented gratis to every student in order to counteract Tom Paine was Bishop Richard Watson's 'Apology for the Bible.' But for a few years the 'French mania' raged unchecked. The typical student of the early seventeen-nineties was an atheist in religion, an experimentalist in morals, a rebel to authority. Daniel Appleton White (A.B. 1797) records in his undergraduate diary the scene at morning prayers when a sophomore was ordered to stand forth in the aisle and receive a sentence of rustication. Seizing a large cane, the lad swung it around his head, shouting, 'It's a damned lie! You are a pack of devils, and I despise you!'

This phase did not last long. The ruling class of New England — the Congregational clergy, merchants, and village squires — began as early as 1794 to line up under Washington, Adams, and Hamilton in vigorous opposition to French Jacobinism and its American apologists. Boston supported Jay's Treaty and became the 'Headquarters of Good Principles.' Harvard in politics has always reflected the sentiments of the economic ruling class in Boston. A celebration of Washington's birthday, 1796, when 'upwards of 3700 lights, glittering at the same time, appeared the effect of enchantment,' was rightly interpreted as a demonstration of Federalism. 'Ye teachers of youth!' apostrophized the Federalist *Columbian Centinel*, 'learn from the conduct of these young men, the powerful effect of a great and brilliant example, and never cease to operate on their noblest feelings, if you wish to retain the Roman idea of *Education*.'

As resentment against France increased with the spoliations on our commerce, and the return of the 'X. Y. Z.' mission, Harvard students showed their colors unmistakably; every member of the College, it is said, except Dr. Waterhouse, wore the black cockade. A complimentary address, composed by young Channing and signed by one hundred and seventy students — almost the entire body — was sent to President Adams; 'Your youthful blood has boiled, and it ought to boil,' he replied. The Hasty Pudding Club celebrated Washington's birthday in 1798 with these toasts:

GEORGE WASHINGTON, a man brave without temerity, laborious without ambition, generous without prodigality, noble without pride, and virtuous without severity. *Three cheers in pantomime, for fear of disturbing the Tutor.*

JOHN ADAMS, President of the United States, the American *Terminus.* 3 cheers in pantomime, etc.

THOMAS JEFFERSON. May he exercise his elegant literary talents for the benefit of the world, in some retreat, secure from the troubles and dangers of political life.

THE constituted authorities of this UNIVERSITY. May the government of *our own choice*, never be assailed by *Jacobinism.*

And at Commencement that year a dialogue in French on Natural History was omitted from the programme, as it was feared that the sound of French would create disorder.[1] Harvard having gone Federalist, Cambridge naturally voted Republican; and this led to the students' trying to crowd into town meeting and jeer the local 'Jacobins' and break the windows of the town's Jeffersonian representative. The Corporation tried to keep the balance in 1799 by recommending two favorite sons of opposite camps, Timothy Pickering and Elbridge Gerry, for honorary degrees; but the Overseers dropped both names. That was just as well, for fiery Tim wrote that he would have sent back his diploma if the degree had been dishonored by being conferred on Gerry at the same time!

[1] French had been taught by a regularly appointed instructor since 1787. At this time it appears to have lapsed, but in 1806 the freshmen petitioned the Corporation to be allowed to study French instead of Hebrew.

After the death of President Willard, and the appointment of Chief Justice Parsons to the Corporation in 1806, the College became definitely partisan; with very few exceptions, none but a Federalist received an honorary degree from 1802 to the 'Era of Good Feelings.' William Bentley of Salem, one of the few Congregational clergymen who supported Jefferson, charged snobbery in the conferment of honorary degrees; but this was notably untrue in the case of his fellow-townsman, Nathaniel Bowditch. Still a practical navigator, Captain Bowditch brought his ship into Boston on the morning of Commencement Day, August 25, 1802. The custom-house was closed, and the consignees had gone to Cambridge; so the Captain followed the crowd, and at the close of the exercises, when President Willard was conferring degrees, made his way into the meetinghouse. It was an odd ceremony to this seasoned mariner — the President in his square cap and black gown, seated in the quaint presidential chair, and speaking in a dead language. But when the honorary degrees were conferred, he heard 'Nathanael Bowditch, Magister in Artibus,' and someone told him he was now an adopted son of Harvard. Considering that Bowditch knew nobody on either Governing Board, and that the first edition of his 'Practical Navigator' had appeared but two months before, so early a recognition of his genius is worthy of remark.

Harvard's going Federalist was of only temporary significance, but in the years 1804–06 occurred a college revolution that has influenced the University to this day: both the senior professorship and the presidency were captured by Unitarians.

David Tappan, the third Hollis Professor of Divinity, and a Calvinist, died on August 27, 1803. Election of a successor hung fire. The laymen on the Corporation desired a liberal Congregationalist such as the Reverend Henry Ware (A.B. 1785) of Hingham; but President

Willard declared he 'would sooner cut off his hand than lift it up for an Arminian Professor'; and Eliphalet Pearson (A.B. 1773), the Hancock Professor of Hebrew, was equally emphatic. Pearson, called 'The Elephant' by the students, as a pun on his name and a tribute to his bulk, was a dominant personality in the College. He pointed out that the statutes of the Hollis chair required that the Professor of Divinity be a 'man of solid learning in Divinity, of sound and orthodox principles.' But what did 'orthodox' mean? Calvinist, of course, said Pearson, and certainly not Arminian nor Unitarian; but the liberals pointed out that the late Professor insisted that 'orthodox' simply meant 'the general sentiments of the country' and no particular sect; that a similar insistence on first principles would void every ecclesiastical chair in Protestant Europe. Moreover, asked they, where among Harvard graduates could one find a learned minister, a gentleman qualified for the chair, who was orthodox in the 1720 sense? That stumped the conservatives; they knew whom they did not want, but could not decide whom they did want. President Willard died on September 25, 1804, before a successor to Tappan had been found.

The Corporation now chose Pearson acting president, and electioneering both for the professorship and the presidency began in earnest, with 'as much intrigue . . . as was ever practised in the Vatican,' wrote the Reverend John Eliot (A.B. 1772), junior fellow of the Corporation. On December 7, 'Megalony,' as Eliot in his diary called Pearson,

Made a more solemn speech — in which he told us how much he had prayed and thought upon this matter — that we were under a necessity of Electing a Calvinist, from the Records of the College, the public mind, the character of former professors, etc. He pleaded argued, scolded, discovered himself so much of the Jesuit as to bring about a wonderful revolution in my own mind! — not that a Calvinist should be chosen! — but that the sage professor had a part to act, and was destitute of that moral sentiment wh[ich] I had always supposed had an influence upon his mind. He was ill humoured, he is ever ill mannered. Upon this occasion he threw the foam of Billingsgate upon me, thinking he had a right to abuse me as I was a new member.

Shortly after, Pearson trotted out his candidate for Divinity Professor: the Reverend Jesse Appleton of Hampton, New Hampshire (a Dartmouth graduate, who later became President of Bowdoin); and trial voting for the next President of Harvard began. Eliot's diary, Pearson's manuscript account of the election from his side, and the little paper ballots among his papers, are so confused that I can make little of the details; but it is clear that Pearson was smoked out by someone who proposed Ware for President and Appleton for professor. Pearson wanted the presidency himself; and he might have had it, in return for voting for Ware for professor. In the end, Ware received enough votes for that office, despite Pearson's opposition.

Public interest in this election appeared when the Overseers met in the Council Chamber at the State House on February 15, 1805, to act on Ware's nomination. Of the Board of Overseers, as then constituted by the State Constitution, there were sixty-five members. Most meetings consisted of six to ten of the Reverends and two or three of the Honorables. But at this meeting, twelve Reverends and forty-five Honorables turned up. When the nomination was made, the Reverend Jedediah Morse, minister of John Harvard's old church at Charlestown, and a Yale graduate, 'dared to object in most open manner' because 'the Professor elect was not a Trinitarian, as the foundation required.' But 'after a long and patient discussion' the Overseers confirmed Ware; and there was nothing for Mr. Morse to do but write a pamphlet denouncing the election. Thus the theological department of New England's oldest university went Unitarian. Shade of Increase Mather!

Next came the presidency. 'Every minister and every man's friend in the Commonwealth' was proposed; the Boston papers were full of discussion. John Eliot was assailed on every side; flattered, abused, canvassed, lectured on the theme 'if so-and-so is not chosen, the University is sunk.' The first trial ballot showed two for the Reverend John T. Kirkland, and one each for Pearson, the Reverend Joseph McKean, Fisher Ames, and a certain Dr. Smith. On December 11, 1805, the Corporation elected Fisher Ames, the Federalist statesman who had recently turned Episcopalian. But Ames declined, on the ground of his 'feeble health' and 'advanced age' of forty-seven. The Corporation was determined not to choose Pearson; and on March 1, 1806, a letter from him was read, resigning both his chair and his fellowship. Two days later the Reverend Samuel Webber, Hollis Professor of Mathematics, a man 'without friends or enemies,' but with liberal religious views verging on Unitarianism, was chosen President. Almost fifty Overseers turned up at the next meeting of the senior Governing Board, on March 11; and Webber was confirmed, 35 to 14.

The Unitarian victory in this double trial of strength, a logical outcome of the liberal tradition that had been slowly gathering momentum since the days of Leverett and Brattle, was none the less momentous. It ranks with the election of Charles W. Eliot in 1869, and the tipping out of Increase Mather in 1701, as one of the most important decisions in the history of the University. Orthodox Calvinists of the true puritan tradition now became open enemies to Harvard. Eliphalet Pearson busied himself in founding the Andover Theological Seminary, which became the seed-ground of New England theology; pious families in the rural districts of New England, horror-stricken at Harvard's defection from the ancient faith, impelled their sons elsewhere. On the positive side, the effect was far-reaching. Unitarianism of the Boston stamp was not a fixed dogma, but a point of view that was receptive, searching, inquiring, and yet devout; a half-way house to the rationalistic and scientific point of view, yet a house built so reverently that the academic wayfarer could seldom forget that he had sojourned in a House of God.

THE AUGUSTAN AGE

1806-1845

PRESIDENTS

1806–1810   SAMUEL WEBBER
1810–1828   JOHN THORNTON KIRKLAND
1829–1845   JOSIAH QUINCY

IX

PRESIDENT KIRKLAND

THE Reverend Samuel Webber (A.B. 1784), a poor
boy from Byfield who had struggled for his education, was perhaps the most colorless President in
our history. 'He made himself safe by his prudence,'
wrote Bentley, 'but did not bless the University much by
his literary talents.' His great ambition was to establish
a Harvard Astronomical Observatory; but over thirty
years passed before that was realized. Dying after a short
term of office, on July 17, 1810, Webber was remembered
only by an 'erect declining sun-dial' that he constructed
for Massachusetts Hall.

The Reverend John Thornton Kirkland, Unitarian
and Federalist, succeeded without opposition. Kirkland
was a child of the frontier and of poverty, who early
stepped into the pleasant places of life. President Willard
never lost the rugged manner and weather-beaten look
acquired in his early struggles on the Maine Coast; but
Kirkland was named Agonewiska or Fair Face by the
Oneida Indians, and even as President his countenance
was that of a merry, rosy boy. A missionary's son, John
was raised on the New York and Berkshire frontiers, and
'fitted for college' at Phillips Academy, Andover. After
graduating from Harvard in 1789 he returned to the university that he loved, to study divinity and tutor in
Logic and Metaphysics. 'A complete gentleman in his
manners,' wrote one of his pupils, Mr. Kirkland 'aimed
to treat the students as gentlemen that, if possible, he
might make them so' — a revolutionary tutorial technique in 1792. The next year he became pastor of the
New South Church in Boston, where his personality won

back the younger generation from 'French infidelity' to the paths of virtue, and his sermons, logical, intelligent, and sugar-coated, led the parish into Unitarianism before they realized whither they were bound. His Phi Beta Kappa oration at Harvard in 1798 showed the students that wit and learning were no longer on the Jacobin side; and a sermon on the death of Washington earned him an honorary S.T.D. from his father's alma mater, the College of New Jersey.

A sociable bachelor and a high Federalist, Kirkland became intimate with the like-minded merchants, lawyers, and ministers of Boston. In 1806 he had been Boston's candidate for the presidency; in 1810 there was no rival. In a word, he embodied the Federalist ideal of a gentleman and scholar; the best of those 'old-fashioned New England divines softening down with Arminianism,' 'good, wholesome, sound-bodied, sane-minded, cheerful-spirited men,' whom Dr. Holmes remembered affectionately among the visitors to his father's parsonage.

Kirkland was one of the most remarkable presidents that Harvard has ever had, and the best beloved; and until the age of Eliot every successive régime was referred to his as standard. Perhaps the most impressive of the many tributes to his character and influence came from George Bancroft, in a letter that he wrote to President Eliot from the American legation in Berlin fifty-four years after he had received his Bachelor's diploma from Kirkland's hands.

During a long life, in which I have had the opportunity of seeing many men, in divers lands, famed for mind and accomplishments, I have seen few who were his equals, and no one who knew better than he how to deal with his fellow-men. His manners were marked by dignity and benignity; they invited confidence and repelled familiarity. . . . With severe reproofs of misconduct, he mingled so much humaneness and so easy and natural appeals to the better elements of character in those whom he was obliged to censure, that his reproof acted like a benediction, and they who received it left his presence

abashed, penitent, grateful, and attached. To those who showed apt-
ness for literary pursuits he was an unfailing friend. . . . There was
not in his nature a trace of anything that was mean or narrow. . . .
He opened the ways through which . . . [the University] has
passed onward to its present eminent condition, and his noble influence still survives to assist you, sir, in bringing time-honored Harvard still nearer to the excellence which the present age hopes for and
expects.

Although Kirkland wrote nothing of consequence himself, 'the magnetic charm of his conversation, the sweet
amenity of his manner, — the quaint and original suggestions of his fertile imagination,' were rated by George
Ripley, the critic, as among the influences that led to the
extraordinary burgeoning of literature and philosophy
among the Sons of Harvard in his day. 'The transparent
clearness of his mental perceptions, the fine and subtle
delicacy of his ethical instincts, his sympathy with whatever was rare and beautiful in literature, and the sagacity
and firmness of his common sense created around him an
atmosphere in the highest degree favorable to the cultivation of thought, freedom of research, and frankness of expression.' And this remarkable combination of qualities
was implemented by the love that he bore the University,
and every member of it. 'There lay the secret,' wrote
Samuel Eliot, 'and there lies still the glory of Kirkland's
success. He loved his work, he loved his students; they
were not merely students, but his students, his sons, and
as he loved them, so they loved him. For this the College
had been waiting almost two centuries.'

As Kirkland's fame, and the reputation of the University for liberalism, grew and spread, there came an
increasing number of students from the South, where presidential urbanity was appreciated, and religious liberalism, at that time, was fashionable.

The movement began as early as 1798, when Washington wrote of his step-grandson, who had not done well
at Princeton:

What is to be done with him, I know not. My opinion has always been that the University in Massachusetts would have been the most eligable (*sic*) seminary to have sent him to; First, because it is on a larger scale than any other, and second, because I believe that the habits of the youth there, whether from the discipline of the school, or from the greater attention of the people generally to morals, and a more regular course of life, are less prone to dissipation and debauchery than they are at the colleges south of it.

In 1804 the eminent Bishop Carroll of Baltimore wrote to President Willard proposing that John, son of Governor Thomas Sim Lee of Maryland, transfer to Harvard from Georgetown (where he had been studying several years), provided he could perform his religious duties at the Roman Catholic Church in Boston. It is not certain that young Lee entered Harvard; but two Carroll kinsmen of the Archbishop, and other Baltimore Catholics, certainly did, and all 'were allowed to attend the Catholic church in Boston, on Sundays, and on all other holydays . . . and they were excused from any attendance in College on those days.' The same privilege, in respect of the observances of his religion, was allowed to a Jew who entered Harvard about the same time. By 1810, eleven per cent of the entering class was from outside New England; after the war the proportion rose rapidly to eighteen per cent in 1816, and twenty-seven per cent in 1820, a proportion not again equalled until 1850 or surpassed until 1853.

These students from afar were a very important factor in the social life of the College. The Carolinians, in particular, were the *merveilleux* of that day, Dr. Holmes remembered. 'Their swallow-tail coats tapered to an arrow-point angle,' and 'their little delicate calfskin boots . . . were objects of great admiration.' They rubbed off the provinciality of the Yankee lads, themselves learned to respect the solid qualities of New Englanders, and contributed to the 'Era of Good Feelings' by the friends they made, which were legion. In the Porcellian Club for the classes 1822–1826, one finds a Carroll, a Calvert, and a Bonaparte from Maryland; a Tayloe from Washington; a Carter, a Marshall, and a Taliaferro from Virginia; an Elliott, a Yates, and two Manigaults from Charleston; a Cheves, a Fisher, and a Willing from Philadelphia; Larz Anderson of Louisville; and representatives of Savannah, St. Augustine, Mobile, New Orleans, Havana, Natchez, New York, Hartford, Vermont, Salem, and Boston.

These young bloods gave a certain tone to the College, and exposed it by their occasional indiscretions to reiterated charges of being a nursery of aristocracy; but they were not the 'typical Harvard men' of their period. The College was largely composed of boys from New England families of middling fortune, and the swells were outnumbered by horny-handed lads from the country districts, 'fitted for college' and provided with a scholarship through the efforts of the local minister. Out of countless examples of that sort of Harvard student, one may cite Jared Sparks (A.B. 1815), of obscure parentage in a backwoods Connecticut community, yet a leader in his class, admired and respected by all; William Person (Class of 1820), a lad who knew neither father nor mother, whose wants in College were supplied in the most delicate manner, through a subscription taken up by one of the Charleston aristocrats, and whose letters and poems were published by his classmates after his untimely death; or my own grandfather and three Morison great-uncles, left fatherless at an early age and forced to work on farms and in factories, yet earning their way through Exeter and Harvard to useful careers in divinity, education, and medicine. Boys of that stamp are more likely to feel lonely and lost in our bloated colleges of today than were their fellows in the small Harvard classes of the Augustan age. 'Classmate' in those days meant something more than brother; Holmes's poems to the 'Boys of '29' were something more than a sentimental abstraction. Before a class graduated, the members wrote their 'class lives,' often with most interesting details on their struggles for an education, in an album, which the class secretary carried off with him, and kept up to date; the Class of 1822 was the first to print a report. Periodical class reunions at Commencement began about this time; and classmates who lived in or near Boston dined frequently at some member's house, and drank their own Madeira, with the class numerals blown into every bottle.

As undergraduate life showed little change from 1810 to 1846, we may consider the social history of the College in Kirkland's and Quincy's administrations as a unit.

'The expense of a college life at Cambridge is very great . . . near three hundred dollars a year,' wrote a freshman in 1816; to do it in fashionable style must have cost nearer four hundred. And a little earlier, the Hon. John Rutledge of Charleston wrote to the friend in Boston who paid his son's bills, 'With a due regard to economy (which I hope he will observe) Six hundred Dollars a year will be a sufficient allowance during his residence at Cambridge.' These expenses did not include the Commencement spread, for which fashionable or socially ambitious parents spared no expense. For instance, Stephen Salisbury (A.B. 1817), of Worcester, whose average quarter-bills were less than $40, had a dinner for one hundred guests under a tent on the lawn of a Cambridge caterer that cost his parents $780. The wine bill alone was $79, ice cream cost $2 a quart, and the traditional Commencement 'plumb cakes,' $9 each. President Kirkland, in order to encourage poor scholars, created a number of petty offices besides that of the President's Freshman (who lived under the President's office in University — Emerson had the post for the Class of 1821): tutors' freshmen, monitors, and bell-ringers, whose stipends were met by various assessments, such as that for 'care of lecture halls,'

on the paying students. Besides the annual state grant of
$2500 for free tuition, there were scholarship funds upon
which the President might draw at discretion to cancel
term bills of worthy students. Moreover, the winter vacations were so arranged, until 1825, that a poor scholar
(like the Dartmouth lad in Whittier's 'Snow-bound')
could, with two weeks' extra leave, get in a whole term
teaching district school — an experience more valuable
in character-building than lucrative. The Corporation
claimed that, in spite of the annual tuition being raised
from twenty dollars in 1807 to fifty-five dollars in 1825,
there were more opportunities for free education at Harvard than elsewhere. Be that as it may, Harvard was
more expensive for the paying student than any other
American college, except possibly the University of Virginia, because it had never abandoned the English tradition that a university student should be both a gentleman
and a scholar. It could not compete for economy with
colleges like Dartmouth and Amherst, which in their
early days made a virtue of 'the lean and sallow absti-
nence.'

A larger proportion of Harvard graduates of this period
became distinguished than at any previous or subsequent
era; yet at no era did the students enjoy themselves more.
The curricular requirements were not exacting, so that
boys like Emerson and Thoreau had ample time to
browse and dream, whilst the livelier spirits found abundant occasion to play and frolic. Music became increasingly popular; as early as 1793 'the singing club, accompanied by the band, performed Williams's "Friendship"'
at the senior valedictory. In 1808 a student orchestra, the
Pierian Sodality, was organized; in 1819 it combined with
the otherwise unrecorded 'Anacreontics' to serenade
President Kirkland; within a few years the Sodality had
spawned a Glee Club. When a new chapel (the present
faculty room) was built in University Hall, in 1814, the

College gave up Sabbath-day worship in Cambridge meetinghouse; a college church was organized, and a college choir was trained by William H. Eliot (A.B. 1815) after his return from the grand tour, to sing German and English chorales. College journalism began in 1810 with the *Harvard Lyceum*, a painfully literary fortnightly, which lasted less than a year; and there was *Harvardiana*, in one of whose numbers Henry Thoreau first preached education from Nature. Every few years some literary enthusiast organized another periodical; but all before 1866 met the same premature death.

Clubs fairly pullulated. The Speaking Club was now a freshman society, the first sixteen elected at the end of the first term; in 1825 it combined with two rivals, the Hermetic Society (originally a science club) and the Ἀκριβολογούμενοι, as the Institute of 1770; but its character was unchanged: lectures and debates at fortnightly meetings. The witty lecture on 'The Puritans' by Francis Parkman (A.B. 1844), who already 'showed symptoms of Injuns on the brain,' was long remembered. In 1848 the Institute absorbed another club of like nature, the I. O. H., and with it a library. The Hasty Pudding and Porcellian early began to collect books; these club libraries were kept in the undergraduate librarian's rooms, and afforded the brethren an opportunity of general reading, for which the College Library was then ill equipped. Emerson, who did not belong to Hasty Pudding, organized an undergraduate book club which took in periodicals and popular novels; he was also secretary of a short-lived literary society called the Pythologian; and there was a Chit-Chat Club, of which Francis Parkman was the founder and leading spirit. The Porcellian, too, had her rivals: the Δειπνοφάγοι, who held a bacchanalian symposium about once a month, whilst the more modest Porcellian 'had a regular built strait blowout only once a year'; sundry informal 'blowing clubs'; the Conventicle, whose officers were 'archbishops' and 'bishops,' and to which Emerson belonged his senior year; the Knights of the Square Table, who amalgamated with the Porcellian in 1831, and added their plumed helmet and crossed swords to the boar's head on the elder society's medal. This union brought together in the same club five young Boston aristocrats, Tom Appleton, Lothrop Motley, Charles Sumner, Edmund Quincy, and Wendell Phillips, who were not destined to remain together long.

In the eighteen-twenties the Greek-letter fraternity epidemic, after half a century's isolation in Φ B K, broke out in colleges and universities all over the country. At Harvard, a chapter of A Δ Φ, from which the A. D. stems and the Fly claims to, was founded in 1836. In order to escape faculty condemnation of 'secret and unauthorized combinations of students,' the Harvard Alpha Delts were fain to exist for some years under the humiliating pretense of being honorary members of the Yale chapter, although they hired rooms and began a library; in 1846 they were 'recognized' by the Faculty.

It is difficult to see how any student of this period, unless invincibly unsocial in temperament and tastes, could have been wholly unclubbed. Lack of money or of social background was no bar. John Weiss (A.B. 1837), the future Transcendentalist, son of a Jewish barber of Worcester, belonged in College to the Institute of 1770, the Phi Beta Kappa, and the Hasty Pudding, of which he was secretary and poet. His classmate Henry Thoreau, on the other hand, belonged only to the Natural History Society, which was organized by his class; they hired the lower northeastern chamber of Massachusetts, which was soon filled with cases of specimens — fauna, flora, and minerals — collected in afternoon rambles, and they cultivated a small botanical garden on the site of the University Museum. For forty years this Society was very active, and among its members and officers were several distinguished naturalists, such as Francis Parkman, Edward Tuckerman, and Alexander Agassiz. A Humphry Davy Society for amateur chemists flourished for several years; and even the students of evangelical tastes had their club, to show that Harvard was liberal enough to include orthodoxy. The Saturday Evening Religious Society in Harvard College, formed under the aegis of Eliphalet Pearson in 1802 to check French infidelity, united with a Wednesday Evening Society in 1821 to become the Society of Christian Brethren, which was open only to fundamentalists 'impressed with a sense of the infinite importance of vital piety.' These weekly meetings were always religious in character, and during the revivalist era of 1841–42 the brethren met daily for prayer; in 1874 they were still going strong, with over fifty members.

Two societies that have had no successors or imitators were the Navy Club and the Med. Fac. The former consisted of all seniors who failed to receive parts at the last 'exhibition' of the class before Commencement. The 'Lord High Admiral,' jolliest of all 'jolly blades' in the class, organized his staff, consisting of the Vice-Admiral (the poorest scholar), the Rear-Admiral (the laziest), the Chaplain (the most profane), the Boatswain (the most obscene), and so on down to powder monkeys. There was always a procession in burlesque naval uniforms: the Lord High mounted, Rear-Admiral reclining on a triumphal car, 'privates' marching two-by-two, and the place of least honor occupied by the 'digs,' wearing academic caps and gowns and carrying spades. There was usually a 'cruise' down the harbor, and a mammoth chowder on one of the islands. One such picnic was held on Cape Cod and required three days; and a tradition not to be meticulously inquired into records that in 1814 the Club's chartered flagship was captured by a British man-of-war blockading Boston, and released after the members had been reduced by their enemy hosts to a blissful state of intoxication. In the spring of 1815 a large marquee labelled 'The Good Ship Harvard' was moored in the woods near the site of Conant Hall and the floor fitted up like the deck of a man-of-war. There, for several weeks, the mariners of the Harvard Navy spliced the main brace every evening.

The Med. Fac., organized about 1818, was a roaring burlesque upon learned bodies in general and the College government in particular. It had regular meetings, at which a pseudo professor delivered a fake medical lecture; neophytes were given elaborate fake diplomas; and every few years a fake Latin triennial catalogue was issued. The officers included Professores Obstetricologiae, de Multifariousness et Gout, Bugologiae, et Vitae et Mortis. Honorary members were elected and duly enrolled, with comic Latin distinctions, such as: —

ANDREAS JACKSON, Major General in bello ultimo Americano et *Nov. Orleans Heros* fortissimus; et *ergo* nunc [1824] Praesidis Rerumpub. foed. muneris *candidatus* et '*Old Hickory.*'

FRANCES WRIGHT, prænom. 'Miss,' sed vere neut. gen. prælector perfrictæ frontis, castitate stigmosa, quæ primum cum Owen patre, tum Owen filio vixit. Quæ Haytian cum Nigris adiit et ex rege nigro 100 'dollars' recipit.

ALEXANDER I. RUSS. Imp. Illust. et Sanct. Fœd. et Mass. Pac. Soc. Socius, qui per Legat. American. claro Med. Fac. '*curiositatem raram et archaicam,*' regie transmisit.

The last rubric records the Med. Fac.'s most successful hoax. They sent their 'honorary diploma' to the Emperor of Russia, who, thinking that he had actually been honored by the Medical Faculty of the University, returned his gracious thanks, together with some 'rare and ancient curiosity,' variously rumored to have been a medal, a surgical library, and a set of surgical instruments belonging to one of his imperial predecessors.

The Med. Fac. was supposedly suppressed in 1834 for the first time; but revival and suppression were a part of its feline existence. In the eighteen-eighties it had basement rooms on North (now Massachusetts) Avenue, where deep potations were drunk from silver vessels apparently shaped for baser uses. At that time, the essential qualification for membership was some act that if discovered would have resulted in expulsion from the University. The 'final' suppression is said to have taken place in 1905, after a now highly respectable financier had been caught stealing the bust of Phillips Brooks from Brooks House. But the records and regalia are still somewhere in existence; and at every major prank of today one is sure to hear it whispered, 'The Med. Fac. has come to life!'

There were other amusements than societies. Early in the century the primitive game of football was played informally in the 'play-place,' which, after Holworthy was built, was transferred to the Delta, a triangular lot just west of Memorial Hall, and which had been separated from the Yard by the new Cambridge Street. By 1820 there was class football, for which every red-blooded freshman turned out the first evening of the college year, to maintain the prowess of his class against the sophomores; and for weeks the battle continued, the ball being put in play at the noon hour, and kept very much in play until the commons bell tolled at twelve-thirty.

> The Freshmen's wrath, to Sophs the direful spring
> Of shins unnumbered bruised, great goddess sing!

invokes the unknown author of 'The Battle of the Delta' in the *Harvard Register* for 1827. The 'Freshman Hector' of this mock-heroic is one 'Peter of Stonington,' who contends with Jotham, 'A Soph of stature, and of glory too.'

Cricket and 'bat and ball,' the primitive ancestor of baseball, were played informally in the spring; a few took fencing lessons; at high tide in summer there was bathing in the river; a 'new bath' is mentioned in the college records for 1810, and by 1841 there were bathing houses on the college wharf, where the wood-sloops from Maine landed their cargoes. But 'there is want of some system for bodily exercises,' admitted the Faculty in 1825 — hence the frequent riots and occasional rebellions. It was largely in the hope of working the devil out of the students that the Governing Boards authorized Dr. John Collins Warren and Charles Follen, the new German instructor, to establish a college gymnasium in the spring of 1826. A set of parallel and horizontal bars, trapezes and flying rings, was set up in the Delta —

> . . . the Gymnasium mast, erected high,
> Which oft has made the country people pause,
> Or wonder, as they pass at slower speed,
> What can a college of a gallows need?

Elaborate rules were drawn up, and monitors appointed to exercise the 'gymnasts' in accordance with the best German principles. The 'south inner dining-hall' in University was fitted up with some simple apparatus for winter exercise. But for some reason, possibly because there was too much of the drill-master element, the students soon tired of gymnastics; and it was not until the 'old Gym' (the circular brick building on the site of the fire station) was built in 1860 that gymnastics became a usual student activity. Follen led the first cross-country run, 'all college at his heels,' point-to-point across fields and over stone walls; but before these pioneer Harvard harriers attained their destination at Prospect Hill, Somerville, an irate farmer stopped them.

The ordinary run of students were content for exercise to walk in the then lovely country about Cambridge. The picturesque woodland 'Sweet Auburn' had an irresistible attraction for romantic youth, even after it had become Mount Auburn Cemetery. A walk to it down Brattle Street (sometimes prolonged to Fresh Pond, where there was a country hotel with bar and nine-pin alley, and boats to let) was a common afternoon excursion. And for those who could afford them, there was a stable of sorry nags, 'most commonly worn out by continual exercise,' on hire at a livery stable. It is difficult to understand how the students found time for these jaunts. Recitations were held at every other hour during the day, from immediately after six o'clock chapel to four, in order to keep them from straying. Saturday mornings, after chapel, and perhaps one short recitation, and entering their names in the President's Freshman's book as about to visit real or fictitious relatives, almost the entire College walked to Boston over the West Boston toll bridge; for the sole means of public transportation until 1840 was a stagecoach with eleven places, which left Harvard Square for Boston twice or thrice daily, Morse the jolly coachman driving through the Yard and winding his tin horn. You were supposed to be back in time to enter your name at eight p.m., and pass the puritan Sabbath eve quietly in your room. A dancing school was licensed by 1815, but the Boston theatre was out of bounds for many years after. As early as 1809 a long-suffering Southern father protests, 'John writes to me of the brilliance of Mrs. Apthorpes Ball, Mrs. Otis's Parties, etc. This is all wrong, and these Boys must not be permitted to have any engagements but with their Books.'

University Hall contained four halls on the ground floor for college commons, one for each class. The large round oriels between the partitions on the ground floor were designed to give a certain unity to the Commencement dinner, which took up the entire ground floor; in the meantime, they offered tempting openings through which insults and bread could be hurled from one class to another. One Sunday night in 1818, according to the mock-heroic 'Rebelliad' that was written in honor of the event,

> . . . Nathan threw a piece of bread.
> And hit Abijah on the head.

> The wrathful Freshman, in a trice,
> Sent back another bigger slice;
> Which, being butter'd pretty well,
> Made greasy work where'er it fell.
> And thus arose a fearful battle;
> The coffee-cups and saucers rattle;
> The bread-bowls fly at woful rate,
> And break many a learned pate. . . .

The fight continued until most of the crockery was broken, and many heads as well. 'Old Pop' (Dr. Popkin, Professor of Greek), who was supposed to keep order, hastened to President Kirkland,

> . . . and looking sagely droll,
> Let out the anguish of his soul:
> ' Λινότατε, most rev'rend Sir!
> Μὴ ἔρχομαι your breast to stir;
> 'Αλλ' κλῦθι μεῦ the business state,
> Which brought me here so very late.
> Νῦν ἐγὼ ἔχω in this scroll
> Τοὺς ἥρωας of Commons Hall;
> Ὤ κακοί, who just now did wage
> Τὸν πόλεμον with woful rage.
> Τὸ δεῖπνὸν μου, (my evening diet,)
> I lost — and went to quell the riot;
> Καὶ μοι μὲν αἰνὸν ἄχος ἦν
> 'Οφθαλμοῖς εἴδειν such a scene.
> Τὸ θάμβος, as we say in Greek,
> Would scarcely let a fellow speak;
> Till βαρυστενάχων within,
> I cried Ὤ πόποι, how much sin!'

Four sophomores, including 'Nathan' (Robert W. Barnwell, the future President of South Carolina College), were rusticated; but their classmates (including Emerson) voted this tyranny, and, led by youths bearing names that had once made George III tremble, the class rallied round the Rebellion Tree. Each swore to stick to his comrades, and plucked a twig from the tree as a sign. 'Lord Bibo' (President Kirkland) summoned the leaders to his presence, and forbade them to return to the tree; George Washington Adams returned with this announcement, which the sophomores thought worthy of Patrick Henry or an ancient Roman: 'Gentlemen, we have been commanded, at our peril, not to return to the Rebellion Tree: *at our peril we do return!*' Old John Adams thought that flogging should be revived; but softer counsels prevailed, and after 'a new crop of rustications and suspensions' (which gave young Emerson a few weeks to dream away at home), 'this burlesque of patriots struggling with tyrants gradually played itself out, and came to an end.'

One might easily write a volume on the student life of the Augustan age, so rich and abundant is the material; but we must return to the University, and its relation to the community.

The gods smiled when Kirkland became President of Harvard, and bade him govern. The demon of party politics might rage without and at the College, but all was calm within the Yard. His Corporation, who trusted him, were busy men, and let him and the Faculty run the College, granting him larger powers than any Harvard President since Dunster had enjoyed; and the Corporation changed little from 1810 to 1826. John Davis, formerly a fellow, became Treasurer in 1810. Two fellowships were held by a succession of clergymen, Boston liberals all, and including the great Channing. The other three seats were occupied by Federalist lawyers and statesmen: John Lowell (A.B. 1786) was succeeded by H. G. Otis in 1823; Chief Justice Parsons by Christopher Gore (A.B. 1776) and William Prescott, Otis's classmate and colleague; John Phillips (A.B. 1788), schoolmate and college-mate of Kirkland, followed his cousin Judge Wendell; Mr. Justice Story, Channing's classmate, followed Phillips. Nor has the Harvard Corporation greatly changed since. President Eliot, at a dinner to

Prince Henry of Prussia in 1902, remarked that the Fellows of Harvard College who had welcomed him that morning [1] belonged to families who had served College and Commonwealth for at least seven generations. To an economic determinist, as to the Calvinists and Jeffersonians and Adamses of Kirkland's day, this set-up must seem very sinister — an ill-disguised attempt to take the College into camp, and make it a breeding-ground for little religious liberals and political conservatives. Actually, the age of Kirkland proved to be one of the great eras of Harvard University. The Law and Theological Schools and fifteen new professorships were founded; the undergraduate curriculum was reformed; the first European-trained scholars were appointed to the Faculty; and the College bred young men who became great men in letters, statesmanship, reform, and the Church, long after the Federal party was dead and buried. And this came about largely because the Federalists and Unitarians who governed the College cared little for sectarian or political triumphs, but a great deal for excellence.

During the first few years of Kirkland's presidency, it must have seemed doubtful whether the alliance with Federalists was wise, although an incident of Webber's administration made it seem necessary. In 1805 there had been another 'Bread and Butter Rebellion,' a walk-out of students as a protest against bad commons. The college authorities, as in 1766, suspended half the College, and demanded unconditional surrender; the students were too spirited to submit. A committee of the Overseers, led by Lieutenant-Governor Levi Lincoln (A.B. 1772), a Republican, reported in favor of reforming commons, and pardoning the offenders. This led to a prolonged debate

[1] Henry Pickering Walcott, Henry Lee Higginson, Samuel Hoar, Francis Cabot Lowell, Arthur Tracy Cabot, and Charles Francis Adams. All save (I think) the last were direct or collateral descendants of members of Kirkland's Corporation.

in the Overseers on strict party lines, the Federalists insisting on upholding authority, and the Republicans on students' rights. The Lincoln report was rejected by the narrow margin of twenty-nine votes to twenty-six.

The prospect of a 'Jacobinical' Board of Overseers overriding a Federalist Corporation was so unpleasant that early in 1810, when the Federalists had (thanks to Jefferson's embargo) recovered control of the state government, they pushed through a law altering the constitution of the Board of Overseers. By eliminating the State Senate, the *ex officio* members were reduced to eleven, and the clerical members were limited to fifteen, keeping existing ministers (all 'men of correct principles') in office until death or removal; fifteen new laymen were to be elected by the Board itself; and the new Board, thus constituted, would fill future vacancies by co-option. The first lay members elected by the Board were all Federalists, of the same type as the Fellows — indeed it would seem that one purpose of this Act was to make the Overseers a sort of 'waiting club' for the Corporation.

Wise Kirkland predicted ' the *example of change* will do more hurt than the nature of it will do good.' What one General Court could do, the next could undo; better have rested on the Constitution. At the spring election in 1810 the Republicans came back in all branches of the state government but the Senate, and Elbridge Gerry (A.B. 1762) was elected Governor. He came out to Commencement and received the LL.D. in a huddle of Federalists — President Dwight of Yale, President Smith of Princeton, Chancellor Kent, and Senator Pickering. At the next state election (May, 1811) the Republicans won all three branches of the state government, and a jolly year of spoils and gerrymandering ensued. The next Thanksgiving Day proclamation made some pointed references to Federalist pulpit politics, which when read in Cambridge meetinghouse were greeted by Harvard students with 'a most indecent shuffling of their feet, so that the minister could scarcely be heard'; Dr. Holmes declined to continue until the 'scraping of the scholars' had ceased. When apology was demanded for this 'indecent transaction,' the students made matters worse by explaining that they meant not to insult the parson, only to express their disapproval of the Governor. This affair, wrote Bentley, convinced 'the Governor's friends' that Harvard must be rescued from the new Board of Overseers; it was bad enough to have the Corporation in Federalist hands. On February 29, 1812, the Act of 1810 was repealed, making the now thoroughly gerrymandered State Senate the makeweight on the Board. This Act of 1812 did not (like that of 1810, and all other acts of the Commonwealth respecting the College) provide for its own suspension until and unless accepted by the Governing Boards. The Corporation, therefore, denied its validity, and the ousted Overseers proposed to bring it before the courts, but, thinking better of it (since the spring election of 1812 went Federalist), forbore to press the point, and relinquished their records to the 'Jacobin' Board.

The Federalists, learning wisdom from defeat, now discarded the Unitarian and aristocratic Gore and nominated for Governor Caleb Strong (A.B. 1764) of Northampton. A Calvinist both in a religious and a Coolidgian sense, Strong defeated Gerry for Governor in 1812; and two years later, after the Federalists had obtained control of the Senate and killed the gerrymander, they repealed the Act of 1812 and restored the Board of Overseers as of 1810, but with the unfortunate addition of the State Senate to the *ex officio* members. This Act of February 28, 1814, which was promptly accepted by both Governing Boards of the University, remained the organic act of the Overseers for almost forty years. In the same month the legislature celebrated its restoration to 'good principles' by an Act 'for the encouragement of Literature, Piety,

Morality, and the useful Arts and Sciences,' appropriating to Harvard, Bowdoin, and Williams for ten years the proceeds of a tax on the Massachusetts Bank, in the proportion 10:3:3.   Harvard's share amounted to ten thousand dollars a year — a most welcome addition to the College income. One-fourth of it, by terms of the Act, was earmarked for scholarships; out of the rest, University Hall and the 'Massachusetts Medical College' on Mason Street, Boston, were built.

Harvard men played little part in the War of 1812,[1] the general sentiment of New England being strongly against it; and the honorary degrees conferred at Commencement, 1814, told the world that the Governing Boards were in full sympathy with the states' rights movement. John Lowell, the leading New England secessionist, Harrison Gray Otis, who was planning the Hartford Convention, Judge Isaac Parker, one of the three Massachusetts justices who had advised Governor Strong to disregard the President's order to call out the militia, and Chief Justice Tilghman of Pennsylvania, who had upheld the rights of his State against the Supreme Court of the United States, became LL.D.'s of Harvard. But the college students were more patriotic. In 1811 they resurrected the old Marti-Mercurian banner, and organized the Harvard Washington Corps: a swagger company that paraded in blue coat, white vest, trousers and gaiters, black hat for the privates, and chapeau for the officers. President Kirkland appealed to Governor Gerry for sixty stand of state arms and accoutrements; his Excellency generously sent enough for a hundred scholars in arms. They drilled twice weekly, and paraded on Cambridge Common at least four times a year; in the summer of 1812, and again in 1814, when a British attack was expected, the H. W. C.

---

[1] One of the exceptions was Samuel L. Dana (A.B. 1813), who served throughout the war, subsequently took a medical degree, and won distinction as an industrial and agricultural chemist.

'performed a great variety of evolutions' on Boston Common and State Street, amid the 'repeated and enthusiastic huzzas' of the citizenry. This student corps survived
the war by twenty years, and at full strength mustered
one hundred and twenty officers and men. To be elected
Captain of the Harvard Washington Corps was one of
the most coveted college honors, for it was conferred by
the ballots of the entire undergraduate body. One of the
picturesque features of college life was the spring parade
of the Corps through the Yard to drill on the Common.
At one time it took part in the annual militia muster
and 'Cornwallis'; but the Corps was not much liked by
the citizen soldiery, who on one occasion pursued the
slender Washingtonians at point of bayonet to the Yard
gate, when, like regicide Goffe at Hadley, suddenly appeared the gray-haired Professor of Greek, Dr. Popkin,
shouting, 'Now, my lads, stand your ground, you're in
the right now! Don't let one of them set foot within the
College grounds!' And Mercury vanquished Mars.

   The physical appearance of the University was im-
mensely improved in the early part of Kirkland's administration. Holworthy Hall, completed in 1812 from the
proceeds of a second successful lottery, was the first residential hall to abandon the medieval chamber-and-study
system; each unit contained two small bedrooms on the
north side, and a pleasant sitting-room or study facing
the Yard. It became at once the most desirable place for
undergraduates to room, and so remained for over fifty
years; its popularity returned around 1906, and has endured to the present day. University Hall, completed in
1814–15, relieved Harvard Hall of commons and recitations; the Library took over the entire second floor
of Harvard, and the 'philosophical apparatus' moved
downstairs.
   Although the main frontage of the buildings on the

Common had been pretty well cleaned up in Willard's time, Kirkland found the interior of the Yard an 'unkempt sheep-commons,' almost treeless, provided with no regular paths, and cluttered up with a brewhouse, the college woodyard, and sundry privies. The University now went out of the brewing business; and to replace the 'houses of office' a long, low structure, discreetly screened by a grove of pines (some of which still survive) was constructed on the east side of University Hall. The late Dr. Walcott's father remembered Kirkland's pointing to it with pride from the window of the presidential office and saying, 'You can see how we have improved matters!' This structure was promptly named by the undergraduates 'University Minor,' which gave rise to a word in Harvard slang that endured until the World War. A neighboring nuisance was the college pig-pen, where the Corporation's own porkers fought with rats for the commons garbage; for years the hideous clamor of a pig-killing was wont to disturb recitations in University. In the Yard proper, once cleared of unsightly and offensive objects, the elms were planted that reached their full beauty and maturity around 1910, when the elm-tree beetle attacked and killed them. Regular paths were laid out, and the mangy turf was teased into becoming a proper lawn.

Before Kirkland's accession, the movement to replace tutorial instruction in the College by that of professors on endowed chairs had begun. The Boylston Professorship of Rhetoric and Oratory, after short tenures by John Quincy Adams and Joseph McKean, was given in 1819 to Edward Tyrrel Channing, who held it for thirty-two years. Channing and Edward Everett may be said to have created the classic New England diction — the measured, dignified speech, careful enunciation, precise choice of words, and well-modulated voice that (for men of my age at least) will ever be associated with President

Eliot. Without waiting for special foundations, University professorships of Latin and Greek were created in 1811.[1] In natural science, a subscription of $31,000 raised in 1805 founded the Botanic Garden (1807) and the short-lived Massachusetts Professorship of Natural History. At the death of the first incumbent of that chair, William Dandridge Peck, in 1822, the fund was no longer sufficient for both objects, and henceforth was devoted to the Garden, of which the roving naturalist Thomas Nuttall was appointed curator in 1822. It was during his ten years' tenure of the post that he wrote his popular Manual of Ornithology, and wrote several papers on Mineralogy and Geology, as well as lecturing to Harvard juniors and seniors on Botany and Zoölogy. He was the first scholar to whom the University gave an appointment with the permission to devote most of his time to research. Nuttall, though accorded but six lines in Quincy's History, was easily the first man of science in Augustan Harvard.

Postponing to the next chapter a consideration of the new intellectual influence from Germany, and the important reforms associated with George Ticknor, we may here consider the events that led to the resignation of our academic Augustus.

From 1814 to 1824, Harvard basked in the 'Indian Summer of Federalism.' Year after year the conservative party of Hamilton and Ames won all branches of the state government. A series of bitter attacks on the College for its supposed aristocracy and atheism, in the *New England Patriot* of 1819, were intended to undermine the University in the Constitutional Convention of 1820; but Harvard passed through that ordeal unscathed. Daniel Webster (M.A. Dartmouth and *ad eundem* Harvard 1804) wrote the report of a committee that gave the University

---

[1] A University professorship at Harvard means a professorship supported from the general funds of the University, rather than from a definite endowment.

a clean bill of health, and recommended that her rights and privileges be maintained, but that ministers of all denominations be made eligible to the Board of Overseers. The Convention accordingly adopted an amendment to that effect, and in recommending it to the people declared that the powers conferred on that University 'have always been exercised, and that the duties required of it, have always been performed, with a sincere, and ardent desire, to promote the diffusion of useful knowledge; and to establish and preserve an honorable reputation in literature and morals, in this community.' The amendment was rejected by the people, and it was not until 1843 that a legislative act threw open the clerical positions on the Board of Overseers to ministers of all denominations.

In 1823 Governor Brooks refused to run again, and the popular but vulnerable Harrison Gray Otis was nominated as his successor; Dr. William Eustis (A.B. 1772) was the Republican nominee. At this juncture the new Amherst College which had been promoted by orthodox Calvinists of the Connecticut Valley, with the avowed object (as Noah Webster wrote) 'to check the progress of errors which are propagated from Cambridge,' was struggling to obtain a state charter. Harvard, as a body, made no objection. No vote was passed by the Governing Boards against the chartering of a rival Massachusetts college, as had been done in the case of the proposed Queen's College at Hadley in 1762. Indeed, Harvard had viewed the rise of two rivals, Williams and Bowdoin, with equanimity, and had cultivated friendly relations with the Calvinist Theological Seminary at Andover. In this instance, the religious liberals in the General Court believed that a second centre of orthodoxy was not wanted, most of the western members wanted no rival to Williams, and the Brown graduates in the legislature were also unfriendly. There is no ground for the statement, repeated by every historian of Amherst College, that Harvard influence was

responsible for the delay. A Harvard man, Daniel Davis
(A.M. 1797), made an 'eloquent plea' for the Amherst
Charter, and the principal opponent of it in the legislature was a Yale graduate; moreover, the first large donation came from a Harvard graduate, David Sears (A.B.
1807). But the friends of Amherst decided that their only
hope in 1823 was to defeat the Federalists; and so, after
extracting a promise from William Eustis, the Republican
candidate, that he would promote the charter, the Reverend Austin Dickinson of Amherst directed a menda-
cious but successful campaign against H. G. Otis, on the
ground that he was an 'immoral character,' a profane
swearer, Sabbath-breaker, and 'connected with a Harvard College aristocracy.' A parallel attack on Harvard
was waged by the Calvinist *Recorder* of Boston: out of
three hundred and two undergraduates, there were alleged to be but a dozen 'professors of religion'; the
College had never staged a religious revival; there was
no missionary society as at Williams; and no private
prayer-meetings were held by the students. 'Can the
pious parent . . . be willing to send a beloved son to a
college where he will be exposed to the snare of those
fatal errors?' As a result, central Massachusetts went Republican for the first time in history, and the long-
thwarted Jeffersonians captured all three branches of the
state government.

Amherst obtained her charter; but Harvard and Williams lost their state subsidy. The grant of $10,000 a year
which the University had enjoyed since 1814 was not
renewed; nor did the State again contribute to Harvard
University. This loss of revenue created a financial embarrassment with which the liberal and easy-going President and the elderly and unbusinesslike Treasurer Davis
were unable to cope. The University now had a total
estimated income short of $45,000, of which students' fees
and rents accounted for almost half; and student enrol-

ment, as a result of an intensive 'Don't send your son to Harvard' campaign waged by the Calvinists, was declining. There was a deficit of $4000, and unappropriated funds were being used as income. Nathaniel Bowditch was elected to the Corporation in 1826. A self-made man, not educated in college, fearless, tactless, and inflexible, he forced a financial investigation, and discovered that the accounts of Treasurer Davis and Steward Higginson were in hopeless confusion. Both men were induced to resign, and a severe programme of retrenchment was adopted by the Corporation. President Kirkland's salary of $2550 was docked, and he was deprived of a student secretary; professors' salaries were reduced from $1700 to $1500, and they were put on a hard-and-fast schedule of so many teaching hours per diem. The college sloop *Harvard*, whose periodical arrivals with firewood from the college lots 'down East' gave a maritime flavor to Cambridge, was sold, and wood purchased in the open market, at a great saving in expense. The Corporation even made the students pay for their sacramental wine in chapel, and presented the college choir's bass viol to the Pierian Sodality, in order to save the expense of repairing that instrument!

President Kirkland accepted these economies with apparent grace, but infuriated the Practical Navigator by ignoring them in practice, so far as he could. And in 1827 the President had a paralytic stroke. Finally, at a Corporation meeting on March 27, 1828, Mr. Bowditch delivered a violent tirade against the President, who surprised them all by handing in his resignation the next day. It was accepted by the Corporation with alacrity, received by the students with stupefaction and indignation. A farewell address presented to Kirkland by the senior class is the most generous and eloquent tribute ever penned by Harvard students to one of their presidents.

We thank you for the honors which your award has made more sweet, and we thank you for the reproof, which has been tempered with love. We thank you for the benignity of manners which engaged our confidence, for the charities which secured our hearts. We thank you, sir, for all the little, nameless, unremembered acts of your kindness and authority. We are deeply in your debt, but the obligation is not irksome; it is a debt of gratitude we are well pleased to owe.

We should have been happy, had your connexion with the University, at least, subsisted until we had been dismissed from its walls. . . . But it has been ordered otherwise, and we can only now assure you, sir, that though you have ceased to stand to us in the relation of President, there are other tender relations between you and us, which will terminate but with life, and it is our prayer to God, that your years may be very long protracted amid pleasant recollections and troops of friends. . . .

The prayer of these affectionate sons was answered. Dr. Kirkland had lately married a lady of independent means. He made a triumphal tour through the country, entertained at one Harvard household after another, and enjoyed many years of quiet life. But in losing Kirkland the College lost something more than a personality. It broke definitely with the old paternal tradition of the Harvard presidency.

X

EXPANSION AND REFORM

POLITICS almost strangled the Harvard Medical
School shortly after it moved to Boston. A group of
Republican physicians in and near Boston petitioned the General Court in 1811 to give them a charter
as the Massachusetts College of Physicians. It was well
understood that this was an entering wedge for a rival
medical school; yet Professor Waterhouse added his name
to the petition, and Governor Gerry announced omi-
nously that educational monopoly was a bad thing, excluding 'men of the most enlarged, liberal, and informed
minds,' and providing 'an opiate to genius.' Harvard
Corporation and Massachusetts Medical Society protested, vitriolic articles appeared in the newspapers,
pamphlets flew about, and in the end the petition for a
College of Physicians was defeated by a narrow vote in
the House.

Professor Waterhouse, the only Republican on either
Harvard faculty, had followed the Medical School to
Boston with very ill grace. He had a Cambridge practice
and a snug house facing the Common; but in 1809, four
years after the Massachusetts Professorship of Natural
History was founded, the Corporation took from Waterhouse the mineralogical cabinet and the natural history
lectures which (so he wrote to President Kirkland) had
kept him in wood, hay, and cider. The proponents of the
rival medical school had undoubtedly offered Waterhouse
a chair in that institution, in return for support which he
lent in a not very tactful manner. He inserted in a Boston
newspaper an anonymous squib about the town's wanting

a new fire-engine and being opposed by 'Captain Squirt' of the old fire company, who declared that the new one would reduce the efficiency of the old; and that even if he grew too old to run to fires, his son 'young Squirt' would carry on. Lest anyone miss the point of this satire, Dr. Waterhouse rang Dr. Warren's doorbell on Park Street with the paper in his hand the morning it appeared. Dr. Warren appeared at the door long enough to remark, 'You damned rascal, get off my steps, or I'll throw you off!' Dr. Waterhouse then walked down State Street, stopping every acquaintance he met to point out the article, relate what Dr. Warren had said, and exclaim, 'Now, *what* do you suppose Dr. Warren meant by *that*?'

Dr. Warren meant just what he said, and before the year was out Old Squirt, Young Squirt, and Professor Jackson petitioned the Corporation to remove Dr. Waterhouse from his chair. The Corporation seems to have examined the case with great care, and Dr. Waterhouse had ample opportunity to defend himself; but finally the Corporation decided that his usefulness to the University was at an end, and shortly after the state election of 1812 removed him from office. In 1809 the Doctor had been dismissed from the staff of the United States Marine Hospital at Charlestown for taking supplies home to his family, but Vice-President Gerry now procured him a new job at the local Military Hospital, whence he was removed by President Monroe for another irregularity of a nepotistic nature. For almost thirty years longer the Doctor and his wife lived in their house facing Cambridge Common (6 Waterhouse Street), raising a considerable part of their food in the five-acre garden in the rear. James Russell Lowell remembered the brisk, dapper little figure, with slender, tapering queue 'held out horizontally by the high collar of his shepherd's-gray overcoat, whose style was the latest when he studied at Leyden in his hot youth.'

Out of the proceeds of the state subsidy that began in 1814, the University built the 'Massachusetts Medical College' on Mason Street, Boston, for the Medical School. In thirty years' time this was outgrown, and a new 'Medical College' was erected on Fruit Street at the foot of Grove, adjoining the grounds of the Massachusetts General Hospital. During this period the Medical School was held to the University only by the tenuous thread of degrees. Medical students merely attended lectures or clinical demonstrations, for which they bought tickets at so much a course; the final examinations were oral and scandalously easy. It was only the distinction of the faculty — men such as the Warrens and Jacksons, the elder George Cheyne Shattuck, Walter Channing, Jacob Bigelow, and George Hayward — that enabled the Harvard Medical School to enjoy considerable reputation and standing in the profession.

Harvard was now approaching her bicentennial; yet, with the exception of the first three presidents, the first Hollis Professor of Mathematics, and two of the medical professors, not a single scholar with English or European training had been appointed to the teaching faculties. Tutors and professors alike had been home-bred, and inbred. It had never occurred to college authorities, it seems, to import European scholars; nor did the result of Thomas Jefferson's efforts, a little later, to obtain such men for the University of Virginia suggest that they could have been secured. The next best thing was to send young Harvard scholars abroad for their training.

The first opportunity of this sort arose in 1814, when Samuel Eliot, merchant of Boston, and grandfather of President Eliot,[1] founded a Professorship of Greek Literature with the then very generous endowment of $20,000. The chair was offered to the most brilliant young gradu-

[1] See page 225 for note.

ate of recent years, the Reverend Edward Everett (A.B. 1811); and the offer was coupled with a vote of the Corporation, the wisdom of which was then unprecedented, and even nowadays would be unusual, that he might study abroad two years on the full salary of $1200 before assuming his active duties. Everett was inaugurated professor in the new chapel of University Hall on April 12, 1815, the day after his twenty-first birthday; four days later he sailed for England, in company with George Ticknor, a young Dartmouth M.A. admitted *ad eundem* at Harvard the previous Commencement. As soon as the Hundred Days were over, the two young scholars proceeded to the University of Göttingen. There they were

¹ The 'Eliot Dynasty': —

Andrew Eliot, 1683-1749; cordwainer of Beverly, subsequently merchant of Boston

Andrew Eliot, 1718-78; A.B. 1737, Fellow 1765-78, Secretary Board of Overseers 1758-78		Samuel Eliot, 1713-45; Boston bookseller

Andrew Eliot, 1743-1805; A.B. 1762, Librarian, Tutor, and Fellow 1763-74, minister of Fairfield.	John Eliot, 1754-1813; A.B. 1772, Fellow 1804-13	Samuel Eliot, 1739-1820; merchant, founder of Eliot Professorship of Greek

William Havard Eliot, 1795-1831; A.B.1815	Samuel Atkins Eliot, 1798-1862; A.B. 1817, Treasurer 1842-53	Catharine, m. Andrews Norton, A.B. 1804, Tutor, Librarian, and Dexter Professor 1811-30	Anna, m. Geo. Ticknor, A.M. 1814, Smith Professor 1817-35

Samuel Eliot, 1821-98; A.B. 1839, Overseer 1866-72, President of Trinity College, Hartford	Charles William Eliot, 1834-1926; A.B. 1853, Tutor and Asst. Prof. 1854-63, President 1869-1909, Overseer 1868-69, 1910-16	Charles Eliot Norton, 1827-1908; A.B. 1846, Lecturer and Professor 1874-98, Overseer 1899-1905?

joined shortly after by Joseph G. Cogswell (A.B. 1806), lately tutor of Latin; and, in 1818, by George Bancroft (A.B. 1817), who was on one of President Kirkland's informal and elastic scholarships. At Göttingen a new world of scholarship opened up before the delighted gaze of these four young men. The German universities were in the first bloom of their renaissance, leading the western world in almost every branch of learning. The Americans knew not what impressed them most: the boundless erudition, critical acumen, and 'unwearied and universal diligence' of the professors; pious pilgrimages to Weimar to meet Goethe (who, out of regard for Cogswell especially, presented a set of his works to the Harvard Library in 1819); the *Lernfreiheit* which permitted even state-supported professors of Theology to question divine revelation; flexible university organization, devoid of classes and fixed curricula, which permitted a student to choose his own course and set his own pace; manners and customs of German undergraduates, which made those of rowdy Harvard seem ladylike in comparison. 'If truth is to be attained by freedom of inquiry,' Ticknor wrote to Thomas Jefferson, 'the German professors and literati are certainly in the high road.'

Everett took his Ph.D. in 1817, and, obtaining another two years' leave, passed a winter in Paris, meeting literary lions like Benjamin Constant and Madame de Staël, reading in the Bibliothèque Royale, and conversing at the Institute with Alexander von Humboldt. Thence he proceeded to Cambridge, where his 'eyes filled with tears' as he thought of what Harvard might be and what it was; to Scotland, where Sir Walter received him at Abbotsford; then on to Rome, where he met Ticknor and Cogswell, and had the poor taste to prefer the family circle of Lucien Bonaparte to the company of his sister, the Princess Borghese; then on foot through Greece, marvelling at the country and the ruins, reading the inscriptions, and imbibing the beauty (but not, alas! the spirit) of Hellas. After these adventures, it was difficult to settle down in Cambridge; and after five years of it, Everett decided to mount the political ladder. But in those five years there came under his instruction young men such as William H. Furness, Frederic H. Hedge, Robert C. Winthrop, Cornelius C. Felton (his successor), and, above all, Emerson, who recorded that Everett's influence in Cambridge was 'comparable to that of Pericles in Athens'; 'the rudest undergraduate found a new morning opened to him in the lecture-room of Harvard Hall.' The 'radiant beauty' of Everett's person, his 'precise and perfect utterance,' affected even those unable to absorb the 'new learning' which he communicated with 'ingenious felicity,' a learning which 'instantly took the highest place to our imagination in our unoccupied American Parnassus.' The Pierian spring, having run a little thin and sour through almost two centuries of New England winters, was renewed by Everett into its pristine purity and strength; his successors have never allowed it to run dry.

Cogswell returned a year later than Everett, bringing as trophy the rich Ebeling collection of Americana to begin that department of the College Library, and feed the later labors of Sparks, Hart, and Channing. Cogswell served a few years as College Librarian (rearranging the Library 'on the same plan with that at Göttingen'), and as Professor of Mineralogy and Geology. Bancroft, returning in 1822 to a humble tutorship in Greek, stepped off on the wrong foot by saluting Professor Andrews Norton with a kiss on both cheeks. He became 'the laughing butt of all College' by his foreign affectations, and aroused the students' wrath by dividing his classes into sections according to proficiency, insisting that the better students read more than their fellows. After a year's sojourn in this 'sickening and wearisome place,' as

Bancroft described Cambridge, he joined Cogswell in founding the Round Hill School at Northampton.

It was a delicate matter to reform Harvard; one that required tact and patience as much as enthusiasm and learning. Cogswell and Bancroft, exasperated with President Kirkland because he did not back them to the limit, lived to admit that Kirkland was probably right. The President wanted reform, and he was determined to resist the popular American demand for a cheap and practical rather than a sound and liberal education. Like Jefferson he believed it his patriotic duty to produce from democratic materials an educated élite who would guide the Republic in paths of wisdom and virtue. On the other hand, he knew that Harvard was too old and sturdy to be pulled up by the roots and replaced by a fresh crop of plants grown from German seed. Fortunately, one of the scholars returning from Germany had the patience and persistence to accomplish something permanent.

George Ticknor was at Göttingen, and in his twenty-fifth year, when he received news of his appointment to the new professorship of the French and Spanish languages and of Belles Lettres founded by Abiel Smith (A.B. 1764); and that he might prolong his stay in Europe to prepare himself for the new post. Like Everett he concluded his studies at Göttingen, passed several months at Paris, proceeded to Venice, where he acquired the friendship of Byron, and to Rome, where he made a lifelong friend of Bunsen. Then on to Spain, where he spent six months in travel, studying Spanish literature, and meeting all manner of social, literary, and ecclesiastical grandees. Ticknor took up his new post at Harvard in August, 1819, with the same enthusiasm as Everett, a similar preparation, and a far greater perseverance; for Ticknor was primarily interested in education and scholarship, and Everett chiefly in his personal career.

Permitted by the Corporation to reside in Boston,

LECTURES.

Term I.

By the Professor of Divinity, six a week for six and a half weeks, at morning study bell, to *Seniors*.

"   Astronomy, first three days, at XI., to *Seniors*.

Term II.

By the Professor of Hebrew, six a week for six weeks, at morning study bell, to *Juniors*.

"   Mathematicks and Experimental Philosophy, five first days in the week (except every second Thursday), at XI., to *Seniors* and *Juniors*.

"   French and Spanish Literature, till April 1, five first days of the week (except every second Thursday), at IV. P. M. From April 1, Monday, Tuesday, and Thursday, at morning study bell, to *Seniors*.

"   Greek Literature, till April 1, six a week, at morning study bell, to *Seniors*.

"   (Rumford), from April, Wednesday, Friday, and Saturday, at IX., to *Seniors*.

"   Anatomy and Surgery, or Chemistry, at V. P. M., five days of the week, to *Seniors*.

"   Natural History and Mineralogy, at times to be announced in this and the succeeding term.

Term III.

By the Professor of Chemistry, five first days of the week, at V. P. M

"   Law (Royall), four days in the week, at X.

"   (Rumford), Wednesday, Friday, and Saturday, at IX.

"   French and Spanish Literature, five first days of the week, at XI.

"   Greek Literature, Monday, Tuesday, and Thursday, at morning study bell,

} to *Seniors*.

"   Rhetorick and Oratory, Monday and Wednesday, at morning study bell, and Friday at X., to *Juniors*.

Subjects of the Bowdoin Prize Dissertations for 1824.

1. The importance of the study of the learned languages as a branch of education.

2. The antiquity, extent, cultivation, and present state of the empire of China.

One first premium, being a gold medal of forty dollars; and two second premiums, of twenty dollars each, in books, are offered.

The candidates will mention their standing, as Graduates or Undergraduates, and if Undergraduates, of what class, and deliver their performances by the middle of June.

Ticknor soon became the centre of a cultivated circle which gave Boston the name of 'the Athens of America.' At Harvard he began an ambitious course of lectures on the literature of France and Spain; lectures which were a body of consecutive and historical criticism, the first of that kind that Harvard had ever known. His 84-page Syllabus of the Spanish Literature Course (Cambridge, 1823) is a remarkable production, considering that the subject had never been covered systematically in any language; and it adumbrated his great History of Spanish Literature, one of the worthiest monuments of New England scholarship. But it did not take him long to discover that the German lecture system, superimposed on class recitations in prescribed books, was a mere luxury in which few students could afford to indulge, and from which a still smaller number could benefit. Unless he could break down the recitation system, he might as well retire. In 1821 Ticknor got the ear of the Governing Boards, and induced the Corporation to direct a questionnaire to the Faculty on improvements in teaching; their replies were discouraging. To a committee of the Overseers Ticknor wrote: 'We are neither an University — which we call ourselves — nor a respectable high school, — which we ought to be, — and . . . with *Christo et Ecclesiae* for our motto, the morals of great numbers of the young men who come to us are corrupted.'

Reform appeared to be hopeless when the Harvard students, by another 'Great Rebellion,' convinced the authorities that something was radically wrong with discipline and instruction. The Class of 1823 was uncommonly rowdy. A class history kept by a member chronicles class meetings and forbidden dinners, battles in commons, bonfires and explosions in the Yard, cannonballs dropped from upper windows, choruses of 'scraping' that drowned tutors' voices in classroom and chapel, and plots that resulted in drenching their persons with buckets of ink-and-water. A schism developed between the 'high fellows' of the class and the obedient 'blacks,' who, curiously enough, included in their ranks George Ripley the radical reformer and Thomas Wilson Dorr of rebel fame. The climax came in the spring of senior year when a 'black' played informer against a 'high fellow' who was expelled; and the rebels swore an oath under the Rebellion Tree that they would leave College until the departed hero was reinstated and the informer deprived of his Commencement part. The Faculty, determined to rule, expelled forty-three students out of a class of seventy, almost on Commencement eve; and although John Quincy Adams, the parent of a rebel, protested vigorously, President and Fellows were inflexible. Twenty-five of those expelled (including John Adams, forty-seven years after the death of his protesting father, and thirty-nine after his own) were afterwards admitted A.B. 'as of' 1823; the rest, including Ellis G. Loring, the anti-slavery leader, and Robert T. Dunbar, the wealthy planter of Natchez, never again appeared on the printed roll of the Sons of Harvard.

This 'Great Rebellion' convinced Governing Boards and the public that something was radically wrong. Professors Ticknor, Ware, and Norton started things moving by private discussions with a few Overseers, in July, 1823. At their instance the cumbrous wheels of College government began slowly to revolve in the reluctant motion of reform. Committee of Overseers; Committee of Corporation; Joint Committee of Overseers and Corporation, Mr. Justice Story chairman, and long report; new Committee of Overseers, John Lowell, Esq., chairman, thirty-one questions addressed to the Immediate Government; Committee of Immediate Government instructed to prepare reply; reply reported, with proposed changes in the College laws, discussed, amended, and adopted (fifty-eight pages, giving an immense amount of information about the College and conjectures about the students); colossal report from Mr. Lowell's committee, including the above, dated January 6, 1825, and printed; Mr. Lowell's report found insufficient by the Overseers; the same together with Mr. Justice Story's report discussed by the Overseers, with the result that the latter, the more radical of the two, prevailed; Mr. Justice Story's report sent down to the Corporation, with instructions to draft on that basis (not neglecting the promising features of Mr. Lowell's report) a new code of College statutes; new code sent up by Corporation and confirmed by Overseers; and in June, 1825, appeared the new 'Statutes and Laws of the University in Cambridge, Massachusetts' — one hundred and fifty-three laws in thirteen chapters.

The principal reforms in this portentous code were a rearrangement of vacations on the theory that warm weather produced rioting; a requirement that the President submit an annual report to the Overseers; the abolition of fines as a method of punishment; a stricter supervision of students; reorganization of the Immediate Government — now for the first time called the Faculty — into six departments; a slight concession to the elective principle for upperclassmen; and in Law 61, a revolutionary division of classes:

The Students shall be formed, for the purpose of instruction, into as many divisions as shall be found practicable, and conducive to their improvement; the divisions shall be made with reference to their proficiency and capacity, and each division shall be encouraged to proceed as rapidly as may be found consistent with a thorough knowledge of the subjects of their studies.

Ticknor was frankly disappointed. He had hoped to discard the traditional four classes and reorganize the College vertically, by departments, within which a student might advance as fast as he liked, and take his degree after a departmental examination; and he wanted permission both for students and professors to 'rove.' There can be no doubt that if the Faculty and the New England public had been prepared for so radical a change in their beloved college system, Ticknor's reforms would have put Harvard College a generation ahead of her American rivals, made her equal to the smaller European universities, and offered a much sounder basis for introducing new subjects into the curriculum than the atomic subdivision subsequently adopted under Eliot. But conditions were not ripe, nor were Faculty or students prepared. Ticknor was sensible enough to realize that he was very fortunate to get so much. Law 61, he wrote, by encouraging able students to push ahead instead of chaining them to the droning pace of a fixed recitation, was 'a broad corner stone for beneficial changes in all our colleges.'

The Harvard Faculty, on the other hand, found Law 61 disturbing; and Ticknor soon discovered (what many academic reformers have since learned to their cost, and the regimenters and patrioteers have yet to learn) that a professor's power of passive resistance is immense and unpredictable. By the time the Code of 1825 went into effect, the other three German-trained teachers had left Harvard; and only the Hollis Professor of Divinity (Henry Ware the elder), who had little to do with undergraduates, was really on Ticknor's side. The Faculty were irritated at having Law 61 imposed on them from above, and disgruntled at the failure of a little rebellion of their own, in 1824.

The Corporation, as we have seen, had become, even before Kirkland's time, a body of external trustees. When a vacancy occurred in 1823, the Faculty decided to revive Nicholas Sever's rejected claim of exactly a century before, to a seat on that body. Obviously, if the teachers could get back on the Corporation, there would be an end to these bothersome inquiries and reforms. Everett, secure in his own popularity, had taken no interest in

Ticknor's reforms, but this question of prestige and constitutional right interested him keenly, and on behalf of his colleagues he composed an able memoir presenting their point of view. Ticknor regarded this movement as a red herring across the trail of reform. He pointed out that to combine the teaching, financial, and administrative functions in the same body would produce the same evils that had paralyzed the Oxford and Cambridge colleges in the eighteenth century. The Overseers decided against the Faculty, reaffirming the Corporation's right to co-opt whomsoever it chose. Everett, who in the meantime had orated himself into a seat in Congress, assuming that he could continue to profess Greek at Harvard by absent treatment, had the law against non-residence of professors invoked against him, and was informed by President Kirkland (March 8, 1825) that his chair was vacant.

Law 61, arranging class sections according to proficiency, was applied by some of the Faculty half-heartedly, and by others in a way that produced disorder among the students. President Kirkland then took the initiative in having the law modified so that its application was optional with the Faculty; and they allowed it to be continued in a given department only if that department desired it. The system was, accordingly, abandoned in all except Ticknor's department of Modern Languages. There, Ticknor had built up an excellent staff. To Francis Sales, the hearty French émigré whom he had found already installed as Instructor in French at Cambridge, he had induced the Corporation to add Charles Follen, a gifted young exile from the *Burschenshaft*, as Instructor in German; Charles Folsom (A.B. 1813), a former naval chaplain, as Instructor in Italian; and Peter Bachi, an exiled Sicilian, as Instructor in Italian, Spanish, and Portuguese. President and Faculty gave Ticknor a free hand in his own department, even making the important

COURSE OF INSTRUCTION.

	FRESHMEN.	SOPHOMORES.	JUNIORS.	SENIORS.
First Term.	1. Collectanea Græca Majora (4th Cambridge ed.) 2. Livy, 5 books. 3. Grotius de Veritate Religionis Christianæ. 4. Plane Geometry (Legendre's). 5. Adam's Roman Antiquities.	1. continued. 8. 9. finished. 11. Geometry of Planes and Solids (Legendre's). 12. History (Tytler's).	17. Logick (Dr. Hedge's). 18. Moral Philosophy (Paley's). 19. Hebrew, or a substitute.* 20. Chemistry.	26. Intellect'l Philosophy (Stewart & Brown). 27. Opticks (Camb. course of Nat. Phil.) 28. Astronomy. (Gumere's).
Second Term.	1. 5. continued. 2. 3. 4. finished. 6. Horace (Cambridge ed.) 7. Algebra (Lacroix's).	1. 12. continued. 13. Cicero de Oratore, or an equivalent in Latin 14. Analytick Geometry, including Trigonometry and Conic Sections. (Camb. course of Math.) 15. Blair's Lectures on Rhetorick. 2 vols.	16. continued; 21. Tacitus, or an equivalent in Latin. 22. Homer's Iliad (Robinson's), or other Greek. 23. Differential Calculus. (Camb. course Math.) 24. Mechanicks. (Camb. course of Nat. Phil.)	26. continued, or a substitute.‡ 27. continued. 29. Paley's Evidences. 30. Butler's Analogy. 31. Political Economy (J. B. Say's). 32. Chemistry, Mineralogy, and Geology, or a substitute.||
Third Term.	1. 5. continued. 6. 7. finished. 8. Greek Test. (Griesbach's). 9. Excerpta Latina (Wells' edition). 10. Lowth's Eng. Grammar.	1. 12. 13. continued. 16. Topography. (Camb. course of Math.)	24. finished. 25. Electricity and Magnetism. (Camb. course of Nat. Phil.)	31. 32. continued. 33. Philosophy of Natural History (Smellie's). [Composition and Speaking throughout the course.]

* Math., or Anc. Lang., or Mod. Lang.   † Mod. Lang.   ‡ Smellie's Phil. Nat. Hist. || Anc. or Mod. Lang.

concession of permitting freshmen to elect a modern language in place of half the prescribed work in Latin and Greek,[1] and reserving certain hours of the day for recitations and lectures in modern languages, so that there were no conflicts. And although the College Catalogue (to judge from the appended 'Course of Instruction' for 1825–26) treated modern languages as a shameful part of the curriculum, a mere footnote substitute for minds too soft for Hebrew, Chemistry, and Calculus; that mattered nothing to Ticknor so long as he was allowed to have students and to teach them languages as he and the instructors believed they should be taught: sound grammatical foundation, but plenty of reading at the earliest moment.

An abstract from the modern language part of the President's report on student progress for 1826–27 will give a good idea of Ticknor's organization. Out of thirty-six freshmen, thirty-two were taking French; after two months they were divided into proficiency sections of four, six, ten, and twelve students, respectively. Out of sixty-six sophomores, forty-nine in five sections were taking French. The books read were *Charles XII*, the *Henriade*, *Télémaque*, *Gil Blas*, the *Fables* of La Fontaine, and *Le Théâtre Classique*. One sophomore who already knows Italian grammar reads five cantos of the *Inferno*, a volume of Alfieri's *Vita*, and Botta; a beginners' class of seven study Bachi's Grammar, and read Soave and Goldoni. Three or four sections in Spanish get into Solis's *Conquista de Méjico* and *Don Quijote*. In junior year there are more beginners' classes in French, Italian, and Spanish, a beginners' class in German, and an advanced class of four students who read *Maria Stuart*, *Faust*, and Wallenstein's *Lager*. In the senior year, there are more beginners' sec-

---

[1] This vote, passed January 4, 1826 (Fac. Recs., x. 116), does not appear on the annexed tabular view, which was printed in the fall of 1825. I could find none for the following year; and the printed lecture list reproduced on p. 229 is for the fall term of 1823.

tions in French and Spanish, and advanced French classes in the *Théâtre Classique*, *Gonzalve*, and the *Henriade*. This was at the beginning of the new system, when the great demand was for beginners' courses. As it developed in the next few years, a Harvard undergraduate could begin French as a freshman, and follow it through; a sophomore or upperclassman could begin any of the other three languages, and go ahead as far as he was willing and capable. Sections were so small as to amount practically to a tutorial system. Portuguese was added to the curriculum in a few years; Bachi dedicated his Portuguese grammar to the members of the Class of 1832 who studied Camoëns with him. In Ticknor's department, over which he presided for ten years, great scholars of the next generation such as Lowell, Norton, and Child had their first training, and hundreds of young men like Motley and Thoreau carried away a reading knowledge of the Romance Languages and German as a part of their equipment for literature and life.

Another innovation that Ticknor got into the new Laws of 1825 was a provision for alumni of Harvard or other colleges to become 'Resident Graduates.' For a fee of five dollars they were allowed to attend any lectures they liked, and use the College Library and scientific collections. In the Catalogue for 1826–27 appear five 'Resident Graduates,' including 'Ralph W. Emerson, A.B.,' Edward Mellen from Brown, and Alexander Rives from Hampden-Sidney. Ticknor intended this provision to be an entering wedge for postgraduate instruction, but no such instruction was provided; and no degree was open to Resident Graduates unless they were Harvard A.B.'s, when they could take the A.M. in course. Hence the annual enrolment of this class of students never rose above fifteen, and usually was much less. But the opportunity to continue a scholarly life in academic surroundings was appreciated by a limited number until 1886, when the

Resident Graduate, so reminiscent of the scholarly leisure of the English universities, was finally abolished. The Graduate School of Arts and Sciences had already made a fresh start from a different basis.

For eighteen years Ticknor continued chairman of and sole professor in the Modern Language Department, giving his very life-blood to the College for a salary of $1000 (and after 1828, $600) a year. At the end of that time, feeling that the new system of instruction was firmly established in his own department, and despairing of extending it to the others, he resigned, happy in the news that Longfellow had been appointed to take his place; and to Longfellow succeeded James Russell Lowell. Thus for three-quarters of a century this premier American chair of Modern Languages was occupied by three distinguished men of letters. They demonstrated that academic duties were not incompatible with creative writing; and that the college lecture-hall was a sounding-board that carried a scholar's voice into all parts of the country.

At President Kirkland's accession the time was ripe to establish instruction in Law and to afford that profession, like Medicine, some better means of preparation than mere apprenticeship. Over thirty years elapsed after the death of Isaac Royall in 1781 before the University was able to obtain the proceeds of his legacy for a chair of Law. Finally, in 1815, the Royall Professorship was established, with an endowment of $7500. Isaac Parker (A.B. 1786), Chief Justice of Massachusetts, was that year elected the first Royall Professor of Law. Judge Parker, later described by Story as 'a good-natured, lazy boy when at College, a good-natured, lazy lawyer, and a good-natured, lazy judge,' was hardly the person for pioneer work; and for two years he simply lectured on The Law to anyone who cared to drop in. So in 1817 the University took another step: established a School of Law, provided for conferring the degree of Bachelor of Laws after three years' study, and appointed Asahel Stearns (A.B. 1797), a practising lawyer and politician, University Professor of Law. Three rooms on the ground floor of 'College House No. 2,' a gambrel-roofed brick house on the site of the well-known College House of the late nineteenth century, were assigned to the School; and the first class, six strong, graduated in 1820.

As conducted under Professors Parker and Stearns, the Harvard Law School still smacked of the old-time lawyer's office. The students, like lawyers' apprentices, spent much time at the apprentice work of copying pleadings, conveyances, and other legal documents. But from the start the School had a special law library, which grew from a few hundred volumes to over 3500 in 1834. Both professors lectured, and Stearns introduced the first moot court, ever a favorite method of learning law at Harvard. Next door to the Law School, on the site of the present Co-operative building, was the Middlesex County Courthouse; and Professor Stearns not only continued his private practice but served as district attorney of Middlesex until 1832. So the students had ample opportunity to observe law being administered and made.

For all that, the Harvard Law School offered so few advantages in comparison with apprenticeship to a leading member of the bar that the students dwindled away to but one or two a year. As neither professor was able to give full time to the institution, the resignation of each was requested, and given. In 1829, just when it was needed, a gift of $10,000 from Nathan Dane (A.B. 1778) was received; the Dane Professorship was founded, and accepted by Joseph Story, Associate Justice of the Supreme Court of the United States. John H. Ashmun (A.B. 1818) of Northampton succeeded Judge Parker in the Royall chair. Ten students who afterwards graduated, including George S. Hillard (A.B. 1828) and Benjamin R. Curtis

(A.B. 1829, the future Supreme Court Justice), entered that fall; and old College House No. 2 soon became over-crowded. At that juncture, the venerable Dane came forward with a gift and loan that gave the Law School its own building in the College Yard.[1] 'Yesterday, Dane Law College . . . a beautiful Grecian temple, with four Ionic pillars in front, — the most architectural and the best-built edifice belonging to the college, — was dedicated to the law,' wrote Charles Sumner to Charlemagne Tower on October 24, 1832. Dane Hall was the home of the Harvard Law School for more than fifty years.

Judge Story wished to make the School a purely graduate and professional school of law; but the penalty of two years' extra residence for students lacking the A.B. degree proved too drastic, and had to be dropped in 1834–35; however, three classes were organized the same year.

On the death of Ashmun in 1833, the Corporation made a fortunate choice for the Royall chair in Simon Greenleaf of Portland, a leader of the Maine bar, and one of the best legal scholars in New England. Story and Greenleaf, unlike in temperament and intellect, made a wonderful team. Story, with his perpetual high spirits and brilliant, flashing mind, impressed, amused, and stimulated the students; Greenleaf, deliberate and thorough, taught them how to work, and aroused an ambition for learning. Greenleaf continued his private practice, and Story was often absent in Washington; but young instructors (one of them Charles Sumner, A.B. 1830) were appointed to fill in the gaps. Story and Greenleaf founded the present Law School tradition of studying

[1] The present southwest corner of the Yard, the old Cambridge meetinghouse lot, was acquired in 1833, after the First Parish (Unitarian) had built the present church on the corner of Massachusetts Avenue and Church Street. Dane Hall, as originally built, occupied most of the space between the southern entries of Straus and Matthews Halls. In order to make room for Matthews, it was moved south, enlarged, and (after Austin was built) used for college offices until destroyed by fire in 1918.

jurisprudence as a science and a system of philosophy, the best groundwork for the sort of practice that would serve social ends rather than simply enrich the practitioner; they were rewarded by classes rising to sixty in number in 1846, and including numerous future professors of law, judges, members of Congress, and a President of the United States (Hayes, LL.B. 1845, who seems to have enjoyed hearing Professor Sparks lecture on Colonial History and Professor Longfellow on Goethe, quite as much as his law classes). Thus, the Augustan age of the Law School very nearly coincided with the Augustan age of the College.

The Harvard Divinity School (or Theological School, as it was renamed in 1922 after Andover Seminary had returned to the bosom of her errant mother) was the second professional school established in President Kirkland's administration; it is curious that it should not have come earlier. In the seventeenth century, and until about 1721, the clerical career was the favorite one for Harvard graduates. But, whilst fifty-two per cent of the graduates of the years 1642–1721 became 'settled ministers,' only twenty-seven per cent of the graduates of the next eight decades (1722–1801) did so; and in President Willard's administration, a little short of twenty per cent of the classes 1782–1804 followed a clerical career. From the earliest times graduates who intended to become ministers 'read' Divinity in College with the President and the Hollis Professor, or out of College, if they preferred, with a settled minister; Theology, like Medicine and Law, was in the 'prentice stage. Not until 1784 was any provision made for special instruction in Divinity for undergraduates who proposed to enter the Ministry, and not until the second year of Kirkland's administration was there any attempt at special classes in Divinity for graduate students. Kirkland's usual textbook was the Lectures of Philip Doddridge (1701–51), a favorite author with

English dissenters and low-church Anglicans; and a programme of reading for divinity students that Professor
Ware sent to Eliphalet Pearson at Andover contained
nothing to alarm that keen-eyed watchman on the ram-
parts of Calvinism. In 1813 Andrews Norton (A.B. 1804),
later known as the 'Unitarian Pope,' became Dexter
Lecturer on Biblical Literature. Possibly he was more
dogmatic; but it is clear that Kirkland and Ware, though
Unitarians, were trying to teach their pupils Theology,
rather than Unitarianism.

In 1815, as soon as the fear of 'French infidelity' was
finally conquered at Waterloo, the long-slumbering feud
between orthodox Calvinist and liberal Unitarian broke
out in the Congregational Church; and within a few
years a large minority of New England parishes had split.
The orthodox now had their own theological seminary at
Andover; Harvard was the natural place for training
Unitarian ministers. The Corporation issued an appeal
for funds in 1815, '*not* to inculcate the peculiarities of any
sect, but to place students of divinity under the most
favorable circumstances for inquiring for themselves into
the doctrines of revelation.' The distinction between a
Unitarian Divinity School and a school conducted by
Unitarians for 'impartial, and unbiassed investigation of
Christian truth,' resulting in well-trained candidates for
Unitarian pulpits, is too metaphysical for the present
writer to grasp; but the successive deans and professors of
the Harvard Divinity School always emphatically dis-
claimed any sectarian bias or intention. It is true that no
oaths, creeds, or tests were ever required, as at Andover
and other institutions; but, as the latest historian of the
Divinity School admits, 'none but Unitarians would
have been offered teaching positions' before 1870, 'and
nearly all the students were preparing for the Unitarian
ministry.' Even President Eliot considered that the

proper way to keep Harvard 'non-sectarian' was to appoint only Unitarians to fellowships and key positions.

Over $27,000 was raised in the first six months of 1816, and administered jointly by a Theological Education Society in conjunction with the Corporation; the constitutional relations between the two were constantly changing in the next few years. One may spare the reader a mass of detail by the dogmatic though somewhat inaccurate statement that the Divinity School began in 1819 as a Department of the University, under a Faculty of Theology consisting of the President and four professors. Six years later it acquired a building, Divinity Hall, then embedded in rustic woodlands, now almost stifled amid museums and laboratories.

Although no divinity degrees were granted until 1870, the Harvard school became the principal seminary for the New England Unitarian clergy, and for others as well; among the more distinguished graduates, before 1850, were Samuel K. Lothrop (1828), William Greenleaf Eliot (1834), the Unitarian pioneer in St. Louis and Chancellor of Washington University, Bishop Frederic D. Huntington (1842), and Thomas Wentworth Higginson (1847). In one class, that of 1836, were the great Theodore Parker (hon. A.M. 1840), George E. Ellis, Abiel A. Livermore, and John Sullivan Dwight, of greater musical than ministerial fame.

Emerson's address to the senior class on Sunday evening, July 15, 1838, was the most noteworthy event at the Divinity School in its early years. That masterpiece of revolutionary rhetoric seemed to float in from the New England countryside 'sweet with the breath of the pine, the balm of Gilead, and the new hay.' Presently the auditors realized that they were hearing a devastating criticism of all organized religion; at the end they were thrilled by the messianic hope of a 'new Teacher' who would 'see the world to be the mirror of the soul.' The reception of this address by the elders, especially the public criticism by Professor Andrews Norton, proved that Unitarianism had its metes and bounds beyond which one must not trespass; one respects it the more for declining Emerson's invitation to glide off in his mystical swan-boat. The unforgivable sin of the University was her failure to find Emerson the chair of Rhetoric that he craved, or to provide something to keep him in Cambridge, even if he did nothing more than play Socrates for half a morning hour at the Yard pump. As it was, Harvard asked no more of him for thirty years, when, his youthful fire quenched, she gave him an honorary degree and elected him Overseer.

The eighteen-twenties were the palmy days of Unitarianism, when Thomas Jefferson predicted that it would sweep the South, and when young Harvard missionaries of liberal Christianity preached in Southern legislative halls. Unitarianism seemed so simple and logical that its swift progress and early triumph were confidently anticipated. Faith in the divinity of human nature seemed the destined religion for a democracy, closely allied to confidence in the power of education to develop the reason, conscience, and character of man. But, alas for them, the Unitarians overlooked the emotional and aesthetic side of human nature; nor were the theological dogmas of the Protestant churches so obliging as to crumble at a touch of reason, like the wonderful one-hoss shay. The fundamentalist tide that had ebbed Southward flowed back; the transcendentalists floated off, and the Roman tide rolled in; but not before Harvard had become a fortress of the liberal outlook and faith. In that sense, but in no other, Unitarianism sealed Harvard with its spirit. We can never measure the relief, the stimulus, the exuberant joy, felt in the last century by thousands of young men who, after a stern upbringing in expectation of a hard struggle to escape eternal damnation, entered a college where hot-gospelling was poor form, hell was not mentioned, and venerable preachers treated the students, not as limbs of Satan, but as younger brothers of their Lord and Saviour.

XI

PRESIDENT QUINCY

TIBERIUS succeeded Augustus. Not that Josiah Quincy (A.B. 1790) was related to Kirkland save through common membership in the Federalist party and the Unitarian Church. He was a different type of man; a lawyer by profession, with long experience in Congress, in the state government, and as a reforming Mayor of Boston, energetic, straightforward, practical, eloquent in speech. He was forty-seven years old when his appointment was confirmed by the Overseers in January, 1829. Primarily an administrator, Quincy was not particularly interested in education as such; but he addressed himself to the task of building up the financial and material structure of the University, made excellent appointments, and did not greatly alter the pattern of the Augustan age.

President Quincy was brilliantly inaugurated in the old meetinghouse on June 2, 1829; it was the last occasion when the Governor of the Commonwealth and the President of the University addressed each other in Latin. Mrs. Quincy brought four unmarried daughters to live in Wadsworth House, still ample for a presidential household, though low-studded and old-fashioned. Never before or since have Harvard Commencements been such gala occasions, or such prolonged feats of endurance for all. Miss Maria Quincy described that of 1829 in her journal. The family were up early to roll the diplomas and tie them with blue ribbon.[1] At nine the girls joined the press around the doors of the meetinghouse; and when

[1] Harvard diplomas were always tied with blue ribbon; the students who attended the dedication of Bunker Hill Monument in 1843 wore blue

these were opened, what a scramble! Ladies running, and screaming as they ran; ladies vaulting over the backs of pews to secure good seats; distinguished strangers handed up to the stage. The students march in and fill the floor. At ten 'the President in full costume sailed up the aisle,' followed by Governor Lincoln and aides, 'and all the dignitaries, civil and ecclesiastical of the land.' Latin salutatory, followed by *fifteen* Commencement performances ('conferences' between three or four students, 'colloquial discussions' between two, poem by Oliver Wendell Holmes, forensic disputations — all in English now —, dissertations, essays), and the English oration by the first scholar of the Class, Charles S. Storrow. Ladies grow faint and have to be fanned, 'supported,' or even carried out. President Quincy takes his seat on the ancient chair, and confers degrees on Bachelors in batches of six and seven, handing to each his proper diploma. 'Delightful music from the band which had played at intervals during the morning.' Finally, the English Oration and Latin Valedictory by M.A. candidates. 'At four o'clock the Assembly broke up.' Family dinner at four-thirty, while the gentlemen hold their decorous Commencement dinner in University Hall, the Reverend Dr. Pierce setting St. Martin's on the old tuning-fork for the Seventy-eighth Psalm, as he had done since 1793, and would do until 1849. At five-thirty 'gentlemen and ladies began to pour in' to Wadsworth House; ladies in drawing-room, band in back parlor; Governor and aides, Admiral Sir Isaac Coffin and other distinguished foreigners, 'arriving and departing till half past seven, ice-creams and coffee circulating all the time.' Governor and staff escorted by the Lancers depart 'in a tempest of drums and dust.'

---

silk badges; and the decorations at the Bicentennial were blue and white. This was probably the survival of a medieval tradition that blue was the proper color of every faculty of Arts.

On the morrow, the same sort of thing recurred for the Phi Beta Kappa celebration. Boylston prize speaking by undergraduates for two hours, after which 'the Society entered,' two by two. On the stage, 'a striking assemblage of gentlemen of every age,' from Dr. John Prince (A.B. 1776), who had attended every Phi Beta Kappa for half a century, to the marshals of the day, Charlemagne Tower and Benjamin H. Andrews, 'two handsome young men who were very elegantly dressed and ornamented with their pink and blue ribbons and medals.' Oration by the Reverend Convers Francis begins shortly after noon and ends at a quarter past two; more ladies carried out fainting. Hour-long poem by Charles Sprague the 'banker poet,' 'full of humour and interest.' While the brethren dined in Commons Hall, President Quincy entertained a few gentlemen at home, including 'Judge Story, who talks all the time, and Dr. Popkin who never says a word'; the girls have 'a table spread in the little back parlour,' but rush into the dining-room at six-thirty to clean up the ice-cream and fruit. The presidential carriage and chaise are then ordered, and two Quincy sons and three daughters whisk off to a dance in Boston, while Mamma, Anna and Maria spend the evening 'in talking over the various events of the day, and the pleasure we had enjoyed during this week.'

It was not all frills and femininity on these occasions in 1837. The Reverend John Pierce, attending his thirty-fourth Phi Beta Kappa, noted in his diary, 'Rev. Ralph Waldo Emerson gave an oration, of $1\frac{1}{4}$ hour, on The American Scholar. It was to me in the misty, dreamy, unintelligible style of Swedenborg, Coleridge, and Carlyle. He professed to have method; but I could not trace it. . . . It was well spoken, and all seemed to attend . . . an apparently incoherent and unintelligible address.' This for age; now let youth speak through James Russell Lowell: 'an event without any former

parallel in our literary annals . . . for its picturesqueness
and its inspiration . . . crowded and breathless aisles . . .
enthusiasm of approval . . . grim silence of foregone
dissent.'

It seems probable that the presence of four unmarried
presidential daughters had something to do with the
transformation of the seniors' farewell into Class Day.
These formal valedictories began to be enlivened by a
class poem around 1795; and after 1802, when Commencement was shifted to the last Wednesday in August
(and so followed the summer vacation), the seniors made
more of their leave-taking in July. Friends and relatives
were invited to hear the class poem and oration in the
chapel — the 'poem by Emerson,' we are told by one of
his classmates of '21, 'was somewhat superior to the general expectation.' There was a printed programme called
'Valedictory Exercises of the Senior Class,' and the event
was by way of becoming a sort of minor Commencement, with this distinction: at the Valedictory Exercises or
Class Day, Faculty and public were guests of the Senior
Class; Commencement was conducted by the Governing
Boards. After the chapel ceremonies were over, the
seniors trooped into the President's house, where the
high-standing scholars received their deturs, and all were
entertained with cake and wine. The afternoon was spent
in the Yard, as described by James Russell Lowell:

So early certainly as 1834, the custom had begun of the Senior class
treating all comers to iced punch during the afternoon of Class Day.
This beverage was brought in buckets from Willard's Tavern (now
the Horse Railway Station) and served out in the shade on the northern side of Harvard Hall. As the weather was generally of the hottest
(the dog-days having been just loosed from their kennels), the *frigus
amabile* of this gelid liquor naturally prevailed with the thoughtless
over the unsophisticate lymph (*dulci digna mero*), which flowed from
the College pumps, albeit famous for its purity. Alas, it was this very
failure of foreign admixture that prevailed against it, and serious disorders resulted! The sub-freshman, initiated for the first time into the

mysteries of the higher education, found the streams which flowed from his Alma Mater's too liberal breasts of unexpected sweetness and dubious inspiration. Too soon he had occasion to cry with the god upon whose rites he had unwittingly intruded,

Quae gloria vestra est,
Si puerum juvenes, si multi fallitis unum?

In 1836 the College janitor, in vain protesting, yet not without hilarious collusion on his own part, was borne in wavering triumph on a door, the chance-selected symbol of his office. Nor was it an un-heard-of thing for bankrupt topers of the vicinage to circulate among the heedless crowd (like those revolving armies on the stage), assuming an air of strangeness at each return, thus repeatedly drenching their adust throats and blessing the one tap of all the year whose waste was not scored against them behind the door till it grew inexorable. Those were uncertain steps also with which many of the younger guests at these libations trod at evening the tangled pathway to their chambers, as if with two poor feet they were essaying to braid into one the com-bined *Trivium* and *Quadrivium* of the mediæval universities. Crowds gathered to witness these anarchic ceremonies. The windows which commanded the scene were bursting with heads, and in as much re-quest as formerly those which gave a near view of the ghastly tree at Tyburn. . . .

By 1838, Class Day (as it was already called) had be-come such an orgy that President Quincy warned the rowdy class about to graduate to abstain from punch and dancing, or they would lose their degrees. Faced by a pallid afternoon, the committee proposed that the lady guests be invited to remain, and spreads be provided. To this the Faculty agreed; and in the late afternoon, as the band was playing and young men and girls were strolling under the elms, Professor Webster inquired why they did not dance? On being told the reason, he hastened to Wadsworth House, and reappeared in a few minutes with 'Old Quin,' who, as soon as he saw the state of affairs, exclaimed, 'Music! Young men! Young ladies! No dancing! Take partners for a cotillion!' and Class Day was started. The dancing of course was square dancing, which in another thirty years' time was outmoded and replaced by waltzing in Harvard and Lyceum Halls.

It would be pleasant, but incorrect, to leave this impression of President Quincy in the reader's mind. His policy toward the students, an alternate cuffing and caressing, ended in making him the most unpopular President in Harvard history since Hoar. He was the first to address undergraduates as 'Mr.' So-and-so; even Kirkland had studiously withheld that title until the second degree was conferred; for 'Mr.' was originally 'Master.' But in his conferences with them he was abrupt and tactless, often committing the unpardonable sin of criticizing their dress, or the whiskers which (greatly to his disgust) began to sprout toward the end of his administration. He attempted to make commons more decent and orderly by replacing the base metal by silver stamped with the college seal, and the coarse crockery by Liverpool china with a college building on every piece; but he could not cope with the cheap-and-nasty tradition that bedevilled Harvard commons from Eaton's day until the Houses were built. Under the competition of Cambridge boarding-houses, commons shrunk into two of the four halls in University, then descended into the basement, and in 1849 were closed. As Mayor of Boston, Quincy had once quelled a riot by the mere force of his personality; and one thinks of him in College, his tall, martial figure clad in a blue camlet coat, leaping from his chaise, horsewhip in hand, taking command of a crowd of students who were offering fight to a mob of 'townies,' and driving them back to the Yard like a flock of sheep. But there are times, in dealing with students, when common sense is better than courage.

Quincy's 'heart's desire,' wrote his son, 'was to make the College a nursery of high-minded, high-principled, well-taught, well-conducted, well-bred gentlemen.' But there was too much hot blood and high spirits among the students to suit the President's high-toned standards; and his manner of dealing with student outbreaks showed a complete misunderstanding of youth. The Reverend David G. Haskins (A.B. 1837) remembered all his life the bad impression made on his Class when, after the first chapel their freshman year, President Quincy dismissed them with the minatory assurance that *if* they demeaned themselves as gentlemen, they would be treated as such. In the winter of that year, the freshman and sophomore classes began to feel their oats. There were bonfires in the Yard, made more interesting by billets of wood secretly loaded with gunpowder. According to one account, the Rebellion started with an altercation between a freshman and a callow young tutor in Greek; according to another, the freshmen and sophomores struck against Dr. Beck, the Latin Professor, when he compelled them to memorize Zumpft's Latin Grammar — a mere look into which is enough to give one a headache. The Faculty, as usual, attempted to 'make an example' of a few students; their classmates protested, at first by petition, and then, when that failed, by breaking the tutor's windows, destroying his furniture, and ringing the college bell in the middle of the night. On May 29, 1834, all the sophomores were dismissed for the year, and ordered to leave town at once; and as soon as they had gone, the President announced that, since the college authorities were unable to discover those who had done the window-breaking damage (estimated at $300), the power of the Commonwealth would be invoked, and the Grand Jury of Middlesex would root out the offenders and proceed against them by civil process.

Then, hell broke loose! Quincy had violated one of the oldest academic traditions: that the public authorities have no concern with what goes on inside a university, so long as the rights of outsiders are not infringed. The 'black flag of rebellion' was hung from the roof of Holworthy. Furniture and glass in the recitation rooms of University were smashed, and the fragments hurled out of the windows. The juniors, led by Ebenezer Rockwood Hoar, voted to wear crape on their arms, issued a handbill with an acute dissection of the President's character, and hanged his effigy to the Rebellion Tree. A terrific explosion took place in chapel; and when the smoke had cleared, 'A Bone for Old Quin to Pick' was seen written on the walls. A printed seniors' 'Circular,' signed by a committee who were promptly deprived of their degrees, gave their version of the Rebellion in language so cogent that the Overseers issued a forty-seven-page pamphlet by Quincy to counteract it. One student after another was sent to Concord to be quizzed by the grand jury sitting there; of course very little could be got out of them, and although two or three indictments were found, these were subsequently nol-prossed, and the whole business fizzled out. Quincy never recovered his popularity.

Besides the expulsions, which made the Class of 1836 the smallest that had graduated since 1809 (excepting the Rebellion class of 1823), the College lost many excellent students sent elsewhere as a result of so much washing of dirty linen in public. 'Numbers in a literary institution are by no means an unqualified blessing,' declared President Quincy; but numbers are taken by the American public as proof of progress, and it was not pleasing to Harvard men to find that their undergraduate enrolment was left far behind by Yale, Union, and Princeton, exceeded by Dartmouth, and pushed hard by Amherst and Middlebury.[1] The Rebellion was also the indirect cause of Harvard's losing one of her most gifted young teachers.

[1] The Albany *Journal* published a significant list of the number graduating A.B. from thirteen Northern colleges in 1836: Yale, 81; Union, 71; Princeton, 66; Dartmouth, 44; Harvard, 39; Amherst, 38; Middlebury, 32; Williams, 29; New York University, 26; Brown, 22; Bowdoin, 22; Rutgers, 21; Columbia, 20. The record Harvard Class of 1818, 81, was not exceeded until 1852.

Karl Follen, forced to flee from the University of Basel when the Prussian government complained that his republican ideas were poisoning German youth, came to America with his friend Karl Beck in 1824, and became German Instructor at Harvard under Ticknor. Full of warmth and fire, he was an effective teacher, and became somewhat of a lion in Boston, where he married one of the Cabots. The Corporation wished to promote him, but could not find the money; his father-in-law then came forward and provided his salary for five years as Professor of German Literature. At the end of the five years, in 1835, Mr. Cabot withdrew his support, and the Corporation failed to renew the appointment. Follen's friends let it be known that the reason for his being dropped was his ardent espousal of the anti-slavery cause and his ringing 'Address to the People of the United States' (1834) to get rid of the evil. It seems more likely that the real reason lay in the fact that Professor Follen opposed President Quincy's autocratic methods, and that Mrs. Follen, a rival queen to Mrs. Quincy, fomented the student Rebellion 'by her wit and talent.'

Quincy's hands are clean on the issue of academic freedom. The torch of *Lernfreiheit* was firmly planted at Harvard by the German exiles and students, and although it has burned higher and clearer at some times than others, the flame has never been extinguished. At Harvard, too, it developed a new aspect. By *Lernfreiheit* the Germans meant the freedom of a scholar in the subject on which he was a presumed expert; but never did they admit the freedom of a professor to be active in a political or social group of which the authorities disapproved. That freedom Harvard has uniformly maintained; doubtless exceptions could be found, but I have not discovered them. The Reverend Henry Ware (A.B. 1812) the younger, appointed Professor in the Divinity School in 1829, became an abolitionist at a time when the community that supported Harvard regarded the abolitionists much as communists are regarded by their descendants. He founded an Anti-Slavery society at Cambridge, and became its president. His brother writes that for espousing the cause of the slave Professor Ware was attacked in the Boston press, remonstrated with, told he would 'impair his usefulness,' 'damage the University,' and all that; but

he never recognized for a moment the right of the College, or of the friends of the College, to question him, or interfere with respect to the part he felt called on to take as to this or any other of the agitating topics of the times. It was reported, and believed by many, that the Government of the College had expressly made his silence in this matter a condition of his continuance in his office. He would not have held his office an hour on such terms; and I have the most direct authority for asserting, that such dictation was never dreamed of, and the supposition that it was possible, was repelled with indignation.

The authority to which he refers is a letter from President Quincy to Professor Ware's widow:

You ask me 'if at any time, during your husband's connection with the University, he was required by the Corporation to suppress the expression of his opinion upon the subject of slavery as a condition of holding his professorship'?

I am astonished at the question and wonder out of what stuff the calumny, which must have given rise to it could have been manufactured. I can only say unequivocally not only that no such requisition upon your husband was ever made but that I have no belief that any such proceeding was ever even discussed, or thought of by members of that Board.

In his History of Harvard University (1840), President Quincy made a measured declaration of the principles that had animated him, and on which, he believed, learning might prosper in the United States:

The labor of the last and the present age has been efficiently directed to soften the rigors and break the shackles of ancient discipline; to remove obstacles from the path of intellect, and to supply it with aids and encouragements. The principle of fear has been almost wholly banished from systems of education, and that of hope and reward substituted. The duty of considering science and learning as an independent interest of the community, begins to be very generally felt and acknowledged. Both in Europe and in America attempts are making to rescue the general mind from the vassalage in which it has been held by sects in the church, and by parties in the state; giving to that interest, as far as possible, a vitality of its own, having no precarious dependence for existence on subserviency to particular views in politics or religion; and, for this purpose, to place it like a fountain opened in regions far above those in which the passions of the day struggle for ascendency, — to which all may come to gain strength and be refreshed, but whose waters none shall be permitted to disturb by their disputes, or exclusively to preoccupy for purposes of ambition.

Almost a century has passed since Quincy penned that paragraph. The vassalage from which learning was emerging in his time has now returned, in the original home of *Lernfreiheit*. 'The duty of considering science and learning as an independent interest of the community' was repudiated by the legislature of Massachusetts in 1935. Fascism, Communism, and, in this country, the American Legion and Mr. Hearst, wish to treat teachers as an intellectual army in the service of the State or of party, rather than as priests of learning and guardians of truth. We must strip down to fundamentals again and inquire whether Quincy and the nineteenth century were right or wrong in maintaining academic freedom. For the future, no one may predict; but if experience can be our guide, there can be no doubt that the outstanding, effective reason why Harvard pulled ahead of the numerous field with which she contended in 1836, and reached her present eminence and stature, was her early and faithful adherence to that principle. Faith in academic freedom has often been tried, and it is well for us to remember that it is challenged not only by the ignorant, but by our own sons. Even in this tercentennial year, certain Harvard alumni have had the insolence to offer gifts on condition that we 'get rid of' this or that professor. Be that as it may, Quincy stands in the front rank of American leaders who have promoted the liberty of the scholar, along with Eliot and Lowell.

Religion rather than politics gave Quincy most of his trouble; the virulence of published attacks on the University for its 'treachery' to Calvinism, 'infidelity,' 'atheism,' and 'Unitarian Sectarianism' would surprise the present generation, which has happily forgotten what *odium theologicum* can be. In his first annual report, Quincy met this challenge with admirable boldness and directness. 'Conformable to the spirit of religious liberty which has, and it is to be hoped, ever will characterize this University,' he said, Harvard students might attend any religious service that they or their parents chose on Sunday. Daily morning and evening prayers continued in the College Chapel; but these were so brief and innocuous as to be inoffensive — and largely ineffective. Francis Calley Gray, of the Corporation, reported in a pamphlet of 1831 that, of fourteen members of the teaching and administrative force, six were Unitarians, three Roman Catholics, and one each Calvinist, Lutheran, Episcopalian, Quaker, and Sandemanian. This admission probably did not help Harvard to obtain recruits from the rural districts, where 'popery' was still a bugbear. What the New England democracy wanted in the period 1820–60, and even later, was not a liberal college, or a university, but a sectarian college, where sons would be reared in their fathers' beliefs, and obtain a Bachelor's degree in the shortest time, at the cheapest rate. It was extremely fortunate for Harvard that while the Board of Overseers was still largely political in composition Massachusetts was ruled by the Whig party, legatee of the Federalist combination of 'talent, learning, and virtue.'

Nevertheless, the Whigs were sometimes defeated; and one such occasion showed the danger that the University would always incur while the State Senate made up the majority on the Board of Overseers. In 1843 Massachusetts went Democratic. The local Democracy in those days was rustic Yankee and Calvinist. Thus it happened that in 1843–44 there were chosen to vacancies on the Board one Calvinist clergyman, one Calvinist layman, and George Bancroft, who had hitched his political wagon to Andrew Jackson's star and denounced Goethe in a religious periodical as dissolute, faithless, and insincere. Bancroft made a minority report of the Overseers' Committee of Visitation, highly damaging to the University, taunting it with diminished numbers, accusing it of decadence, excessive expense, and sectarianism. In 1845, the Commonwealth having gone Whig again, this minority report came up for debate, and President Quincy made a characteristically pungent and devastating reply to Mr. Bancroft, who was already slated for the Navy post in President Polk's cabinet.

Harvard College is represented as a society combined and laboring for the propagation of Unitarianism; as an association of infidels, without belief in the awful mystery of Christ's incarnation, placing no reliance on his propitiatory death, and deriving no assurance of a future state for his glorious resurrection and ascension; denying his divine mission, not acknowledging him either as Mediator or Redeemer, but resting all their hopes of a future life and happiness on their own merits; 'not mentioning Christ in their prayers,' and 'openly denying the Lord who bought them.' . . . Parents, who are found contemplating sending their sons to Harvard, are beset by the Calvinistic preachers or missionary in their neighbourhood, and entreated not to jeopardize their children's hopes, both as respects the present and the future life, by subjecting them to the temptations and dangers to which an education at Harvard College would inevitably expose both their bodies and souls. . . .

There is no question that systematic calumnies like these, circulated very openly and boldly, as I am informed, in the Middle, Southern, and Western States, have a powerful influence in turning young men from Harvard to other Colleges; and that they are the main cause of the diminished influx of students from those States, and from foreign countries, into Harvard, and of the comparative increase of their numbers in other Colleges. In Yale, Brown, Dartmouth, Williams, Amherst, and Harvard, there are *four hundred and fifty* students derived from these sources; of whom Yale has 201, the other four Colleges 146, and Harvard only 103. That such are the effects of representations like those above stated, assiduously made, circulated, and believed in those States, is notorious; and that these representations are utterly false is, in this vicinity, equally notorious.

It is now more than sixteen years since I accepted the office of President of Harvard College, and I here openly and unequivocally declare, that, so far from the influence of Harvard College being devoted to the propagation of Unitarianism, or the labors of its teachers being directed to this object, this has never, so far as I have seen, known, or believed, been made the chief or any special object of their thoughts or labors at all. For the purpose of avoiding, as much as possible, the communication of any peculiarities of religious opinion to the students, writings free from such an objection by the universal consent of all classes of Christians, such as 'Paley's Evidences,' and 'Butler's Analogy,' are selected as text-books. Episcopalian, Baptist, Calvinist, Unitarian, and every other denomination of Christians, have ever stood before the Corporation and Faculty in the same equal light, been treated with the same deference and respect, and have received an equal share of the College honors and beneficiary funds. . . .

Let the people of Massachusetts understand that the attempt now making by leading Calvinists in Boston and its vicinity is not merely to get Unitarianism out of Harvard College, but to put Calvinism into possession of it; that this has been their purpose and struggle for these forty years past; and unless their projects be counteracted and defeated by the vigilance and spirit of the community, they will ultimately be successful, though it cost a struggle of forty years more. The alliance recently, to all human appearance, entered into on the floor of the Senate-chamber of Massachusetts is a pregnant evidence of their aim and tact. The predominating influence of Calvinism is stamped, in characters not to be concealed or mistaken, on at least seven institutions for education in New England, — Yale, Williams, Amherst, Bowdoin, Dartmouth, Middlebury, and Burlington. There is also another highly endowed institution in Massachusetts, in which every article of the creed of this sect is riveted down for ever on the seminary by a subscription of faith required of the professors, to be renewed every five years. Yet with all this power they are not content. All this influence 'availeth them nothing, so long as' Harvard is not also in their possession. . . .

Brave 'old Quin'! He was none of your mealy-mouthed, apologetic liberals; he had definite beliefs, and was ready to defend them, whatever the consequences.

The good ship Harvard might lose her freight and the number of her mess; but the *Veritas* banner was nailed to the mast.

On the curriculum, President Quincy's influence was not good. The recitation system, which Ticknor had hoped to break down through the example of his department, was hardened by the adoption of a horrible 'Scale of Merit.' Marks had begun as a result of the reforms of 1825, and from these marks the first ten scholars were named in each class, beginning with that of 1826; but Quincy's Corporation required a daily mark on the scale of 8 for each recitation, subject to disciplinary deductions such as: absence from Sunday chapel, 16; cutting a required theme, forensic, or declamation, 32. Quincy had each instructor's and monitor's report sent up to him weekly, and himself totted up every student's credits. This system poisoned the already hostile relations between students and instructors, and made social intercourse between them impossible.

Almost every graduate of the period 1825–60 has left on record his detestation of the system of instruction at Harvard; and most of them agreed with James Freeman Clarke (A.B. 1829) that the root of the evil was the marking system. The Faculty were not there to teach, but to see that boys got their lessons; to explain difficulties or elucidate a text would have seemed improper. 'No attempt was made to interest us in our studies. We were expected to wade through Homer as though the Iliad were a bog, and it was our duty to get along at such a rate *per diem*. Nothing was said of the glory and grandeur, the tenderness and charm of this immortal epic. The melody of the hexameters was never suggested to us.' Quincy himself described the ideal college course as a 'thorough drilling'; and that is just what the Harvard course was.

It was this stupid method of teaching the ancient classics, not the classics themselves, that brought a revulsion against them in the second half of the century. And this when the young men in the modern language department, inspired by Ticknor and Longfellow, were doing everything in their power to make the study of French, German, Italian, and Spanish interesting and inspiring. John Farrar, the Hollis Professor of Mathematics, 'excited a living interest in physics, astronomy, mechanics, electricity, and the other sciences'; and by all accounts Edward Tyrrell ('Potty') Channing was a remarkably effective teacher of English. The Reverend Samuel Osgood (A.B. 1832) wrote:

I remember with especial pleasure our evenings with Chaucer and Spenser at Professor Edward T. Channing's study. How his genial face shone in the light of the winter's fire, and threw new meaning upon the rare gems of thought and humor and imagination of those kings of ancient song. Who of us does not bless him every day that we write an English sentence for his pure taste and admirable simplicity? I remember well also a little coterie who met to declaim choice pieces of prose and verse with the professor of elocution, our enthusiastic friend, Dr. Barber. . . .

By this time the ancient requirement that sophisters engage periodically in Latin disputations had been commuted into writing a certain number of English essays called 'forensics,' in which the pros and cons of a question were discussed. Underclassmen had to write 'themes,' which were simple essays. Henry Thoreau's themes and forensics, which have been preserved and printed, give one the uncomfortable reflection that student English has declined in the last century.

The saving grace of the old fixed curriculum was the comparatively slight demand that it made on time and effort. A bright student could quickly meet the bare requirements, leaving him time to educate himself in the College Library, or his club library. An essay of Thoreau's written his senior year shows that he was already dabbling in Persian and other modern Oriental literature. Of course this excessive attention to education got him into trouble; and when Emerson interceded for him with the President, Quincy answered that young Thoreau 'had . . . imbibed some notions concerning emulation and college rank, which had a natural tendency to diminish his zeal, if not his exertions.' Henry was fortunate in knowing exactly what he wanted in College, and seeing that he got it. Of the first ten scholars in his class of forty-seven, only one, Richard H. Dana (no. 5), became well known in the world, and Dana had spent two years of his course before the mast.

Quincy's administration, if reactionary in methods of instruction, made considerable progress toward allowing a choice in subjects, and would have gone still further had the funds permitted an expansion in the Faculty. As early as 1838–39 it was adopted in principle that students might abandon Latin, Greek, or mathematics after freshman year, in favor of History, Natural History, Chemistry, Geology, Geography, Astronomy, Modern Languages, or Modern Oriental Literature; but the task of providing instruction in all these subjects was too much for the Governing Boards. In 1841 a curriculum was adopted that offered, in theory, a very wide opportunity for choice after freshman year; but the taking of 'electives' was penalized by allowing for them but half the marks in the dreadful 'Scale of Merit' that could be obtained in prescribed studies. And in 1845, against Professor Longfellow's protests, no student was allowed to study more than one modern language. Regulations were excessively complicated, and constantly changing; my impression is that the sincere desire of President Quincy and several professors to give the students liberty of choice for about half their studies was thwarted by poverty, limited time, and the insistence on graded recitations. It took an exceptionally gifted and determined student to avail himself of the facilities that existed on paper. He must risk his chance of becoming one of the first ten scholars of his class, and insist on members of the Faculty supplying him with advanced instruction which they were either unwilling or too busy to offer voluntarily.

As an instance of how a bad system can blunt a fine instrument, take the case of Cornelius Conway Felton. Felton, reared in poverty at Newbury and Saugus, entered Harvard just in time to catch the sacred flame from Everett, made a host of friends, graduated high in the Class of 1827, and received his first Harvard appointment two years later. He was a true Hellenist, although not until late in life could he visit Greece; a warm, genial, sparkling spirit, whose favorite authors were Homer and Aristophanes; a sound scholar, one of the first Americans to edit Greek texts; exponent of Hellenism from Lyceum and Lowell Institute platforms; and one of those rare New Englanders whose aesthetic sense was as keenly developed as his intellect. Yet, look at Professor Felton's schedule! He was only a cog in the Quincy machine. He conducted recitations for at least twelve hours a week of the three upper classes, in alphabetical sections, and could not escape the requirement to hear and grade them on lessons from prescribed texts. It was not until the Class of 1852 entered College that the Greek department had sufficient staff to permit Professor Felton to lecture once a week for half the year.

If Felton's chair had not been in one of the prescribed subjects, the classical core of the curriculum, he might have had more leisure and been able to develop more flexible methods. Such was the happy privilege of the gentle Longfellow, who, succeeding Ticknor in 1836, after two years in Northern Europe, transcended all the tight traditions of the Harvard professoriat and used his chair to impart to a busy and unlearned people something of the beauty and culture of the Old World. His study in the Craigie House, where once the Tory Vassalls had caroused, became a temple of the Muses for his own pupils, and for outsiders as well. Men such as Elihu Burritt, the learned blacksmith, and (as Dr. Hale wrote) every tramp who could speak any of the dialects of Bohemia, appeared sooner or later at the Longfellow house; none were ever sent away empty. Nor could recitations cramp Benjamin Peirce (A.B. 1829), who as an undergraduate was noted by Bowditch as knowing more than the then Hollis Professor. In 1833, after a two years' apprenticeship as tutor, Peirce was appointed University Professor of Mathematics and Natural Philosophy, and he remained an active teacher until his death in 1880. And Jared Sparks (A.B. 1815), appointed to the new McLean Professorship of Ancient and Modern History in 1838, after a notable career as minister, editor, and historian, became like Longfellow a professor to the American public. He insisted on being allowed to instruct by lectures, assigned reading, and essays, rather than by set recitations, and in having eight months out of every twelve free for his researches in European and American archives. Sparks gave the first courses on American History in any university; and although his professorship proved to be a false dawn for modern history, it was none the less a portent.

Quincy was responsible for the first research unit, the Astronomical Observatory, being added to the University. Although Harvard had possessed one or more telescopes since 1672, and Professor Winthrop had made some notable observations in the provincial period, astronomy languished after the Revolutionary War. At one time or another efforts were made to establish an observatory, but nothing was done until President Quincy put his shoulder to the wheel in 1839. First he obtained the man: William Cranch Bond, observer to the famous Wilkes exploring expedition; then money was raised in Boston. By permission of the Federal Government, Mr. Bond transferred his whole apparatus to Cambridge, and it was mounted in or adjoining the 'large and commodious' house lately purchased with the Dana estate, in the southeast corner of the present College Yard,[1] 'Observations on meteorology and the elements of the magnetic power,' in co-operation with a plan elaborated by the Royal Society, promptly began. The Dana House proving insufficient for these awakened astronomical ambitions, a new subscription launched in the last year of Quincy's administration, provided both site and central building of the present Harvard Observatory. A splendid set of instruments was imported in 1846 (the ship cracking on all sail to escape the Walker tariff), and early in the new year the fifteen-inch telescope, of the same size as 'the largest refracting telescope in the world' at Pulkova, was mounted on granite piers under a thirty-foot dome on the new observatory grounds. Astonishing discoveries were promptly made by Mr. Bond. 'You will rejoice with me,' he wrote to President Everett on September 22, 1847, 'that the great nebula in Orion has yielded to the power of our incomparable telescope!' (Unfortunately it was a nebula, after all.) Quincy, by calling the attention of his kinsman Edmund Bromfield Phillips (A.B. 1845) to the University, was the means of obtaining his bequest of $100,000 in 1848, for the Director's salary and running expenses.

A letter that George Ticknor wrote from Göttingen in 1816, comparing the library of that university with ours, is a striking proof of his prescient genius; for it adumbrates a policy which, first adopted under Quincy, and almost steadily pursued ever since, has made the Harvard College Library a mighty force for scholarship.

---

[1] The wooden dwelling occupied successively in the last half-century by Professor Andrew P. Peabody, Professor George H. Palmer, and Mr. Richard M. Gummere.

. . . One very important and principal cause of the difference between our University and the one here is the different value we affix to a good library, and the different ideas we have of what a good library is. . . . We found new professorships and build new colleges in abundance, but we buy no books; and yet it is to me the most obvious thing in the world that it would promote the cause of learning and the reputation of the University ten times more to give six thousand dollars a year to the Library than to found three professorships, and that it would have been wiser to have spent the whole sum that the new chapel had cost on books than on a fine suite of halls. . . . I cannot better explain to you the difference between our University in Cambridge and the one here than by telling you that here I hardly say too much when I say that it *consists* in the Library, and that in Cambridge the Library is one of the last things thought and talked about, — that here they have forty professors and more than two hundred thousand volumes to instruct them, and in Cambridge twenty professors and less than twenty thousand volumes . . . we are mortified and exasperated because we have no learned men, and yet make it *physically* impossible for our scholars to become such, and that to escape from this reproach we appoint a multitude of professors, but give them a library from which hardly one and *not* one of them can qualify himself to execute the duties of his office. You will, perhaps, say that these professors do not complain. I can only answer that you find the blind are often as gay and happy as those who are blessed with sight. . . .

Both Ticknor and Everett made purchases in Europe on behalf of the Library; Cogswell not only brought home the Ebeling collection of over three thousand volumes and eleven thousand maps and charts, but became College Librarian in 1821. He soon left, discouraged at the lack of interest in new-modelling the Library; but a fresh start was made under Quincy, when Francis C. Gray (A.B. 1809), Fellow of the Corporation, scholar, and man of taste, became Ticknor's enthusiastic convert. At their instance, the Corporation in 1829 appropriated what critics of the College regarded as the monstrously extravagant sum of five thousand dollars for the purchase of books, some of which Gray selected in London from the Obadiah Rich collection of Americana. Already the Harvard College Library was the largest and most valuable collection of books and maps in the United States, and its works were in constant demand, for diplomatic and boundary negotiations, by the United States Government; but it was still wretchedly housed in Harvard Hall. President Quincy felt that a proper library building was the first need of the University. In 1833 the Corporation, seconded by the Trustees of the Theological Seminaries of Andover and of Newton, petitioned the legislature for a grant for that purpose, and were denied; but nothing could stop Quincy. Governor Christopher Gore had made the University his residuary legatee, 'for the promotion of virtue, science, and literature'; and the Corporation decided to devote the $100,000 that they realized from this bequest to the construction of a fireproof building. No models were at hand, and Gore Hall unfortunately was built of Quincy granite in the Gothic manner, the design being a simplified travesty of King's College Chapel, Cambridge. The cornerstone was laid in 1838; and in 1841 John L. Sibley moved the Harvard College Library of forty-one thousand volumes from Harvard Hall to Gore. It was expected to suffice for at least seventy-five years; but Librarian Sibley was so persistent and sturdy a beggar for books, and the Corporation, with one of the great donors, Samuel A. Eliot, was so comparatively liberal in its appropriations, that by 1863 Gore Hall was reported full. By a series of wings, stacks, and additional floors, it was made to do until 1912, when more than half a million books were moved out, pending the construction of the mammoth Widener Library on the same site.

As a symbol of his belief in the true function of a university, President Quincy was delighted when beginning research for the great History of Harvard University to find in the archives the first rough sketch for a College Arms, VERITAS on three books. The announcement was made at the bicentennial celebration; and in 1843, an ugly version of the design was formally adopted by the Corporation as their seal.

If our principles have little changed in a century, our manner of marking the passing of the centuries has. Quincy's account of the bicentennial suggests that latter-day Harvardians have a reduced capacity for meat, drink, and oratory. Invitations were sent to all alumni, and more than eleven hundred came; but no attempt was made to procure distinguished guests other than the presidents of other New England colleges, and only one accepted. At ten o'clock on September 8, the academic procession formed at University Hall.

When the Chief Marshal named the classes of the Alumni, it was deeply interesting to mark the result. The class of 1759 was called, but their only representative, and the eldest surviving Alumnus, Judge Wingate, of New Hampshire, being ninety-six years of age, was unable to attend. The classes from 1763 to 1773 were successively named, but solemn pauses succeeded; they had all joined the great company of the departed, or, sunk in the vale of years, were unable to attend the high festival of their Alma Mater. At length, when the class of 1774 was named, Mr. Samuel Emery came forward; a venerable old man, a native of Chatham, Barnstable County, Massachusetts, who, at the age of eighty-six, after an absence of sixty years from the Halls of Harvard, had come from his residence in Philadelphia to attend this celebration. The Rev. Dr. Ripley, of Concord, of the class of 1776, and the Rev. Dr. Homer, of Newton, of the class of 1777, were followed by the Rev. Dr. Bancroft, of Worcester, and the Rev. Mr. Willis, of Kingston, of the class of 1778; and, as modern times were approached, instead of solitary individuals, twenty or thirty members of a class appeared at the summons. . . .

The procession left the Yard by the gate between Massachusetts and Harvard, and, passing through two lines of undergraduates, entered the Unitarian Church, where the ladies had already taken possession of the galleries. After an invocation by Dr. Ripley, Samuel Gilman's ode 'Fair Harvard' was sung, for the first time, by a choir of professional singers. 'The touching allusions of this beautiful Ode excited a deep and solemn enthusiasm,' declares the official chronicler; 'and the Address of President Quincy commanded, during two hours, the attention of the audience.' It was this address which, expanded, became the President's great History of the University. A prayer, appropriately limited to seven minutes, was offered by the Reverend Jonathan Homer (A.B. 1777) of Newton, and then the whole congregation united their voices in the solemn strains of 'Old Hundred.'

Leaving the church, the procession streamed north through the Common until opposite Holworthy, then executed a turn, and marched south, so that the classes could pass one another, and the ladies (for whom there was no place in the subsequent exercises) might admire their menfolk to their hearts' content. Rounding the corner by Dane Hall, the alumni proceeded past Wadsworth House to a large pagoda-like pavilion, which had been erected on a natural amphitheatre in the College Yard, a part now covered by Widener. The tent poles were wreathed with evergreens and flowers, and pendants of blue and white radiated from the centre to the circumference. Aloft floated a white banner charged with a cartouche bearing the three books and *Veritas*, the first time that our earliest arms and motto were flung to the breeze. Thirteen hundred alumni and eighty invited guests, and two hundred undergraduates, found their places at the tables arranged like the tiers of a Greek theatre, and sat down at about half after one to a dinner that cost two dollars a cover, including what the Reverend John Pierce described as 'principally light wines.'

The Reverend the President of Amherst College asked a blessing. The dinner proceeded; 'the busy hum of many voices, the laugh, the joke, animated the scene.' Governor Everett, President of the Day, delivered himself of some five thousand words, and offered a toast to Alma Mater, with an appropriate Virgilian sentiment.

Toasts followed to the memory of John Harvard and the Founders, to President Quincy and to President Kirkland, who was received with tumultuous applause in this first public appearance since 1827. Kirkland made a warm plea for a new library and observatory, and offered a most happy toast:

Harvard University; may she hold in respect the precept of Bacon, viz. 'Take counsel of both times, of the antienter what is best, of the later time what is fittest; to reform without bravery or scandal of former times, yet to set it down to ourselves, as well to create good precedents as to follow them.'

Toast to the Divinity School; address by the Dean thereof (Dr. John G. Palfrey); toast to 'Learning and Religion . . . "whom God hath joined together, let not man put asunder."' Song to the tune of Auld Lang Syne, with words by Oliver Wendell Holmes. Toast to the memory of Nathan Dane, followed by speech by the Dane Professor, Mr. Justice Story. Toast to 'Our Ancient Mother, the University of Cambridge in old England.' Toast to the Medical School, and address by Dr. John C. Warren. Toast to the Supreme Bench, and address by Chief Justice Lemuel Shaw (A.B. 1800). Toasts to the ex-governors of the Commonwealth present, and brief remarks by Levi Lincoln (A.B. 1802) and John Davis (A.B. Yale 1812). The Hon. Hugh S. Legaré of Charleston offered toast no. 18, to the 'Fathers of New England.' Alanson Tucker, Jr. (A.B. 1832), then sang a comic interlude, *Carmen Seculare in Doodle Yankee cantandum*, by Dr. Jacob Bigelow (A.B. 1806), which delighted everyone with its chorus:

Nunc rite gratulandum est,
Nec abstinendum joco;
Peractis binis sæculis,
Desipitur in loco.

Toast by Dr. Ripley to the Union of Wise Education and Christian Principles. Toast to Religious and Civil Liberty, which, referring especially to Webster's efforts in the Senate, gave him the occasion for a speech which (one gathers) was not in his best vein. Near this point the company was relieved by a second, unannounced comic interlude: a song by Oliver Wendell Holmes, sung by the Autocrat himself to the tune of The Poacher's Song. Perhaps Quincy omitted it from his official record for the same reason that the present writer resents it:

> And who was on the Catalogue
> When college was begun?
> Two nephews of the President,
> And *the* Professor's son,

has obtained such vogue that most Harvard alumni believe it to have been literally true! Still, it was a jolly song, and a healthy sign that Harvard was already old enough to laugh at herself. And there were a number of modern glees and other songs led by a professional choir, sung between the toasts. Toast to 'Boston, the crowning City'; response by the Mayor. Toast to New York; response by Mr. Chancellor Jones. Toast to the State of New Hampshire, and speech by the Hon. William Plumer. Toast to Dartmouth College, 'the sister, not rival of Harvard.' Speeches by William Sullivan and Loammi Baldwin. Toast to Salem, and very long response by Mayor Saltonstall (A.B. 1802). Toasts nos. 28, 29, 30, 31. Speech by the Hon. Peleg Sprague (A.B. 1812), and toast to The Ladies. At this point the choir struck up an old bacchanalian ditty, 'Here's a health to all good lasses!'; Dr. John Pierce (A.B. 1793) and Dr. Charles Lowell (A.B. 1800), declaring it was 'time for old men and clergymen to retire,' led a small procession of the black-gowned alumni from the pavilion.

Alden Bradford (A.B. 1786), President of the Pilgrim Society, successfully quenched the amatory flame by offering a Greek toast to Φιλοσοφία ἀληθινή. Speech and toast by Franklin Dexter (A.B. 1812); speech and toast by

William H. Gardiner, first scholar of 1816, to Harrison Gray Otis, first scholar of 1783; toast by Daniel Webster to Paine Wingate, the oldest living graduate; toast to Daniel Webster; speech by the Chief Marshal, Robert C. Winthrop (A.B. 1828), and toast to the Founders; speech by William Elliott (A.B. 1809), the sportsman-poet of South Carolina; speech by Josiah Quincy, Jr. (A.B. 1821); and the concluding toast, no. 40:

> The flag that waves over us. May it a century hence see a more wise, a more virtuous, a more prosperous generation than the present. It will never float over Alumni who more justly honor the past, more gratefully acknowledge the present, or more confidently anticipate the future usefulness and glory of their *Alma Mater*.

It was now eight o'clock, darkness had descended on the pavilion, and numerous other alumni were all primed to offer volunteer toasts. So Josiah Quincy, Jr., hastily moved 'that this assembly of the Alumni be adjourned to meet at this place on the 8th of September, 1936.' Unanimously adopted.

Brilliant illumination in every window of the Yard by lamps arranged in patterns and mottoes by the students; glare of bonfires on neighboring hills; levee by President and Mrs. Quincy; and at ten o'clock the festivities 'concluded with a dignity and decorum worthy of the solemn festival of an ancient literary institution.'

THE AGE OF TRANSITION

1846–1869

PRESIDENTS AND ACTING PRESIDENTS

1846–1849   EDWARD EVERETT
1849–1853   JARED SPARKS
1853–1860   JAMES WALKER
1860–1862   CORNELIUS CONWAY FELTON
1862–1868   THOMAS HILL
1868–1869   ANDREW PRESTON PEABODY, *Acting President*

XII

MINOR PROPHETS

PRESIDENT QUINCY was so erect, so hale and hearty at the age of seventy-four, that the news of his resignation in the summer of 1845 took everyone by surprise. Mindful of Kirkland, he had always intended to retire before anyone could say that his faculties were impaired; and he chose this moment because Edward Everett had just returned from the London legation, and was available. It was time; as Emerson noted in a trenchant epitaph to the administration, 'Old Quincy, with all his worth and a sort of violent service he did the College, was a lubber and a grenadier among our clerks.' So, after a brilliant Commencement on August 27, 1845, Quincy retired to Boston, where he humorously complained that the 'unearthly quiet' kept him awake, after the nocturnal clamor of the Harvard Yard. He entered with his customary vigor into the activities common to old Boston gentlemen of literary tastes, and lived long enough to be photographed in a group with his four successors.

None of his five immediate successors (Everett, Sparks, Walker, Felton, and Hill) were successful presidents of Harvard, although each was a worthy gentleman and an excellent scholar. With the passing of Quincy, the presidency fell into a rut, from which it was only rescued when the genius of Eliot transformed a respectable university into a great one.

Edward Everett had been a favorite candidate for the Harvard presidency in 1828, when but thirty-four years old. Since that time he had completed ten years in Congress, served four annual terms as Governor of Massachusetts, and enjoyed the premier post in the diplomatic service. In each of these positions he had behaved with dignity, but, as Emerson wrote, had 'never done anything therein'; had been 'with whatever praises and titles and votes, a mere dangler and ornamental person.' Everyone now wished him to accept the Harvard presidency. Everett had a feeling that the post was below the dignity of an ex-governor and ex-minister to Great Britain, and he well knew that it was no 'eligible retreat for a man of literary tastes'; and a letter from Ticknor, declaring that Everett was wanted 'to defend the College against the united attacks of the Orthodox and the radicals,' made him feel like running away. But Daniel Webster told him that destiny called, and held forth the flattering prospect of the President lecturing on International Law and Diplomacy to the Law School. That would enable Everett to keep his oratorical talents in trim against the hoped-for day when the political lightning might strike once more. So he allowed himself to be swept along 'reluctantly, and with great misgivings,' into consenting 'to take charge of the University at Cambridge.' [1] On February 5, 1846, his election was unanimously confirmed at a full meeting of the Board of Overseers. A few weeks later began in Wadsworth House the three most wretched years of a life which, though crowded with honors, was singularly unhappy. For never did Edward Everett obtain the consideration to which he believed he was entitled by his dignity and parts.

The inauguration was brilliant and brittle: Emerson, who by this time saw through the idol of his youth, wrote a delicious description in his Journal of how Everett's

[1] Everett insisted on the term 'University at Cambridge' being used on all official publications during his administration. The name Harvard was completely disused, and on the way to being entirely forgotten when old Quincy in 1849 wrote a pamphlet 'A Plea for Harvard' which had the effect of restoring 'Harvard University' to the catalogues and pamphlets.

'political brothers,' Webster and Winthrop, 'came as if to bring him to the convent door, and to grace with a sort of bitter courtesy his taking of the cowl.' Compliments and Latin quotations flew about; all Boston was delighted at having a President 'so creditable, safe and prudent.' But the close of the inaugural address was 'chilling and melancholy. With a coolness indicating absolute scepticism and despair, he deliberately gave himself over to the corpse-cold Unitarianism and Immortality of Brattle Street and Boston.'

The students, with that uncanny second sight of youth, soon took their new President's measure, and proceeded to make his life a hell. Pranks increased both in number and ingenuity; and the dignified gentleman who had lately been the guest of Queen Victoria at Windsor Castle found himself debating with a worried faculty what should be done with students for wearing blue swallow-tailed coats to chapel, throwing chestnuts at Professor Ware in his lecture, upsetting the stove in University Hall, attending a cock-fight in young Mr. Bonaparte's room on Fast Day, and entertaining 'two females' in a college room at midnight. The tradition of Everett's complete ineptitude in dealing with undergraduates is well founded. William Watson Goodwin was summoned to the President's study, unconscious of sin. Everett, stern and dignified, confronted him with, 'Young man, I wish to know why, when I passed you on the street today, you did not take off your hat to me?' — 'I don't think that I saw you, sir.' — 'If I saw you, you must have seen me.' One morning at prayers many students showed evidence of having colds. Everett solemnly remarked, 'In England, gentlemen never blow their noses. They sometimes use their handkerchiefs.' Whereupon the entire College used their handkerchiefs in a most obstreperous manner. And another morning at prayers, after an unusually rough night in the Yard, Everett intoned from the pulpit:

'When I was asked to come to this university, I supposed I was to be at the head of the largest and most famous institution of learning in America. I have been disappointed. I find myself the sub-master of an ill-disciplined *school.*' Yet suddenly, in 1848, the students quieted down. There was only one expulsion in the entire year — or, as Everett characteristically reported it, 'On the part of individuals, one case only of immorality requiring separation from the seminary has come to the knowledge of the Faculty.' He did not know what to make of it, nor do we; for 1848 is not a year historically associated with peace and good order.

Among the young hooligans of the pre-1848 era was some of the finest scholarly and human material that ever passed through Harvard College. In the Class of 1846 were Charles Eliot Norton, at the threshold of his great career in scholarship and letters; Senator George F. Hoar; Fitzedward Hall, who was to teach Oriental Languages at Benares and London; two great Latinists, Charles Short and George Martin Lane; and, as first scholar, Francis J. Child. 'Stubby' Child, as he was known to Harvard men for half a century, was the son of a sailmaker, and had his first education on the Boston waterfront; the keen eye of Epes S. Dixwell, principal of the Boston Latin School, picked him out for a scholar and found him the money to go to Harvard. At graduation he was appointed a tutor, and as early as 1848 (quite unnoticed by Everett) he brought out his edition of 'Four Old Plays,' which began the tradition of sound scholarship in English language and literature so nobly carried forward by George Lyman Kittredge, John Livingston Lowes, and their peers. Studies in Chaucer, and the English and Scottish Ballads, were ahead for this choice young man, most beloved of teachers and ripest of scholars, of 'a moral delicacy and richness of heart' (so William James wrote to Henry) 'that I never saw and never expect to be equalled.' And in the next few years there graduated such men as the Reverend Edward Tuckerman, botanist of Amherst College; the Reverend Eugene A. Hoffman, long Dean of the General Theological Seminary; and Horace Davis, President of the University of California.

Everett conceived an intense dislike of everything that his predecessor had done, including the formal adoption of the *Veritas* arms and seal; and after a long wrangle with the Corporation, he plumed himself on having the Coney seal of 1693 restored, 'and this fantastical and anti-Christian Veritas seal removed to the forgotten corner of the records where it had slept undisturbed for two hundred years.' There it slept again until 1885, when, largely as the result of two vigorous sonnets by Dr. Holmes read before the Harvard Club of New York, *Veritas* was brought forth once more:

> Nurse of the future, daughter of the past,
>   That stern phylactery best becomes thee now:
>   Lift to the morning star thy marble brow!
> Cast thy brave truth on every warring blast!
>   Stretch thy white hand to that forbidden bough,
> And let thine earliest symbol be thy last!

Yet it was in Everett's short administration that Harvard thrust out another of those organs of learning in the evolution from the arts-college amoeba to the university primate. The Lawrence Scientific School was opened with an initial donation of fifty thousand dollars from Abbott Lawrence, merchant, manufacturer, and railroad builder, in 1847; and Lawrence Hall was ready in 1850. Mr. Lawrence had been inspired by Charles S. Storrow, who, after graduating first in the famous Class of '29, studied at the Ponts et Chaussées in Paris, and became chief engineer of the Boston and Lowell Railroad and of the Lawrence mills and waterworks. What he and the donor and the public wanted was an engineering school;

but the President and Corporation spoiled their plans by electing Louis Agassiz Professor of Zoölogy and Geology in 1847, a few months after his arrival in this country. Lieutenant Henry L. Eustis (A.B. 1838) of the United States Engineers' Corps was induced to open an Engineering Department in 1849; but in the meantime Louis Agassiz had 'stolen the show.' The first European-trained scientist on any Harvard faculty, and a man whose energy and knowledge performed an incalculable service in building up scientific collections, organizing research, and spreading scientific knowledge among the people, Agassiz made the Lawrence Scientific School an institution for individual study and research in Geology and Zoölogy.

The Class of 1851, the first to receive the S.B., was the most distinguished, consisting as it did of William L. Jones of Georgia, future Professor of Natural Science and Agriculture in the University of his native State; Joseph LeConte of South Carolina, who became one of the most eminent American naturalists; John D. Runkle, later President of the Massachusetts Institute of Technology; and David A. Wells the economist. But the opening of the Massachusetts Institute of Technology in 1862 gave the Engineering Department of the Lawrence Scientific School a rival with which it has been unable to compete.

President Everett was not consoled by this promise of better things for his 'ill-disciplined school.' As early as 1847 he proposed to resign, as the only means of restoring his health and prolonging his life; before the end of 1848 the letter of resignation was written, and early in the new year accepted, to the relief of all. The Whigs were back in power at Washington, and, after the death of Webster, President Fillmore appointed Edward Everett to the premier post in his cabinet.

Professor Jared Sparks, who was promptly chosen to the vacancy and confirmed by the Overseers without opposition on February 1, 1849, was of humble birth and rural origin. Like Everett, he had used the Unitarian ministry as a spring-board to literature; for over twenty years he had devoted the better part of his time to the writing and editing of American history and biography. Popular with the undergraduates, and a man of handsome presence and distinguished manners, his election to the presidency was hailed by the students as a return to the Augustan age of Kirkland. Yet Sparks made a singularly colorless President. The local tradition is that he was pushed into it by his second wife, the daughter of a merchant prince and United States Senator, who wished to queen it over Cambridge society. Certainly he was never happy in the office. At his instance the Corporation revived the office of Regent, to which Sparks delegated many of the clerical and parietal duties that had amused Quincy and exasperated Everett, and which are nowadays performed by a corps of secretaries and deans. New duties arose to take up the slack (which he had hoped to devote to historical work), and the office wearied him. Tradition records his exclaiming at a lengthy faculty meeting where the merits and demerits of undergraduates were being discussed, 'Oh, gentlemen, let the boys alone!' His reputation brought back to Harvard the stream of Southern students, which had begun to slow up in Quincy's day, until almost one-third of the undergraduates were from the South — a proportion never since attained. And his policy of 'salutary neglect' worked so well that the rowdyism of other days did not return. In his letter of October 30, 1852, resigning the office on the ground of 'a precarious state of health,' he declared with truth, 'Order and tranquillity prevail in all the departments; and I can say with entire satisfaction, that, during the four years in which I have superintended its administration, not a single occurrence has taken place, which has given me anxiety or uneasiness.' The resignation was accepted with great regret. Sparks consented to carry on until February 10, 1853, when the Corporation elevated one of its fellows, Professor James Walker, to the presidency of the University.

It was in the tranquil and gentlemanly administration of Sparks that occurred the gravest scandal in the history of the University.

In the old Latin triennial catalogues there are two entries close together, under the classes of 1809 and 1811, that have a perennial fascination:

Georgius Parkman, Mr., M.D. Aberd. 1813, M.M.S.S.   *1849
Johannes-White Webster, Mr., M.D. 1815, Chem. et Min. Prof. Erving., M.M.S. et A.A. et S.Geol. Lond. et S.Mineral. Petropol. Soc.   *1850

Those asterisks seem to stand out rubricated from the old yellowed pages; for Dr. Parkman was murdered in 1849, and Dr. Webster was hanged for the crime in 1850.

Dr. Parkman was a pioneer in the medical treatment of the insane. Inheritor of a considerable fortune, he was also given to good works, and the poorest people of Boston knew that they could rouse him from his Walnut Street mansion at the dead of night and lead him to an errand of mercy and healing without fear of rebuke, or apprehension of a bill. When the Harvard Medical School outgrew its Mason Street 'College' in 1846, Dr. Parkman gave the land for a new building at the foot of Grove Street in the West End, adjoining the grounds of the Massachusetts General Hospital on one side and the Charles River on the other. Shortly before two o'clock in the afternoon of Friday, November 23, 1849, his spare, lank figure, in a hurry as usual, dressed in black coat, purple vest, and top hat, was observed mounting the front steps of the new Medical School, whence it never emerged. A man of punctual and methodical habits, he was soon missed. A hue and cry was raised, but no trace of Dr. Parkman could be found.

Dr. John White Webster studied in England after taking his medical degree at Harvard; his signature can be seen on the register book of Guy's Hospital just above that of John Keats. For a quarter-century before 1849 he had taught Chemistry and Mineralogy at Harvard College and the Harvard Medical School. A pleasant though occasionally irascible man, with luxurious tastes far beyond his means, he borrowed money from Dr. Parkman, and as security gave him a mortgage on his personal property, including a fine private collection of minerals. In 1848 he borrowed an additional $1200 from Mr. Robert Gould Shaw, giving him a bill of sale for the same mineralogical cabinet. Dr. Parkman, hearing of this duplicity, became furious, pursued his debtor with unrelenting severity, dunning him repeatedly, and, when put off, taking a seat in the lecture-room and glaring at him when he was endeavoring to convey chemical instruction to the medical students. This lecture-room was on the left of the front entry to the Medical School on Grove Street; behind it was a back room or upper laboratory, and below it a second laboratory, to which there was access by a side door. Nobody but Dr. Webster and Littlefield the janitor had keys to these rooms.

On the Monday before Dr. Parkman disappeared, Littlefield was in the back room helping Dr. Webster make some chemical preparations. Dr. Parkman burst in and said, 'Dr. Webster, are you ready for me tonight?' — 'No, I am not ready tonight.' There was a short altercation, and Parkman left, saying, 'Doctor, something must be accomplished tomorrow.'

The next few days the creditor pursued his debtor in Cambridge and Boston without finding him; and in the meantime Dr. Webster made some significant inquiries of the janitor about the construction of brick vaults in the basement below his laboratories. On the fatal morning of Friday, November 23, Webster called at Parkman's residence and made an appointment to meet his demands that afternoon at the Medical School. It was the hour when the janitor was at his dinner and no other professors were about. Dr. Webster was ready that afternoon. The janitor had noticed a large sledge-hammer there that morning.

Most of the daytime during the week-end and the following Monday, Dr. Webster remained behind locked and bolted doors in the two laboratories, with the assay furnace, an ordinary furnace, and two stoves going full-blast, and the water tap running continuously. He explained to the excluded janitor that he was conducting important experiments, and did not wish to be disturbed. On Tuesday morning the Professor gave his usual chemical lecture, and conducted police officers in a perfunctory search of his rooms. Early Wednesday he was back at work behind bolted doors, although the Thanksgiving holidays had begun. Littlefield began to be suspicious. In the Professor's absence he forced a window and looked about, discovering something that might be bloodstains. On Thanksgiving Day he attacked a brick vault in the basement from the outside with a hatchet and cold chisel. By Friday, a week after the disappearance, he had excavated a hole in the brick wall large enough to introduce a light. A human thigh and pelvis were revealed. Professors and police officers were brought in, the laboratory was thoroughly searched, and, in one place after another, ghastly remains were uncovered. That night Professor Webster was arrested, and lodged in the near-by jail. A true bill was returned by the grand jury, and on March 17, 1850, his trial for murder opened before the Supreme Judicial Court, presided over by Chief Justice Lemuel Shaw, Fellow of Harvard College.

The trial was admirably conducted, and, despite the

mass of circumstantial evidence, lasted but eleven days. Counsel for the defense claimed that the Professor was the victim of a conspiracy. He knew nothing of how the human remains got there. He claimed to have paid his debts to Dr. Parkman on the day of his disappearance. The theory of the defense was that the Doctor had been murdered when collecting rents in one of the tenements that he owned near the College. President Sparks, and sundry colleagues, testified that Webster was a kind, peaceable, and humane man. Counsel for the defense appealed to the emotion of the jury: how could a man who had lived under the influences of cultivated, social, and domestic associations, 'a professor in a Christian University, whose motto is "To Christ and the Church,"' be capable of murder so foul? But Parkman's dentist, Dr. Nathan C. Keep, identified the false teeth in the calcined jaw as his work, and produced a cast that fitted the peculiar bones perfectly. The jury was out three hours, and returned a verdict of guilty of murder in the first degree.

After the usual petition for a writ of error had been dismissed, Webster confessed that he had struck Dr. Parkman with a stick of wood as a result of his creditor's abusiveness, and unexpectedly killed him, and described in horrible detail how he had tried to dispose of the body. On the ground that the murder was wholly unpremeditated and unintended, he appealed to Governor and Council for clemency. The authorities were inexorable, and on August 30, 1850, in the courtyard of the Leverett Street jail, John W. Webster of Cambridge in the County of Middlesex was hanged by the neck until he was dead. A subscription taken up for his wife and children was headed by the widow of Dr. Parkman.

I cannot trace any influence of this tragic murder on the fortunes of Harvard, or find that it was ever publicly mentioned in criticisms of the University. The story of it has been told here, in its chronological place, because the crime was fresh in the mind of everyone during the events I am about to describe.

The University was already on the defensive against a fresh political assault. We were then in the 'Young America' period, when age and respectability were cried down as 'old fogyism,' when most things were tested by utilitarian values, and strident democracy saw no use for colleges except in so far as they promoted holiness, or money-getting. Harvard was especially vulnerable for her age, wealth, and indifference to popular fads. Harvard, moreover, was the only New England college that published an annual report, from which newspaper scribes could extract juicy bits for the public taste. 'If,' wrote John Chipman Gray, 'the remark of Alexander Hamilton be correct, that jealousy is often the surest proof of strong attachment, Harvard College must be deeply seated in the affections of . . . our community. Its supposed merits and demerits stand in bold relief before the public, and are almost daily the subject of public or private discussion.' 'We work in a glass hive,' said President Quincy. President Wayland of Brown (the pioneer of the elective system) challenged all existing colleges in his 'Thoughts on the Present Collegiate System in the United States' (1842) — a tract probably productive of more mischief than any other in the history of American education — and gave the politicians a high-class stick with which to beat the colleges.

Since Quincy's bout with the Democrats, the Harvard Corporation (Chief Justice Shaw, the Reverend James Walker, John Amory Lowell, Charles Greely Loring, Benjamin R. Curtis, and Samuel A. Eliot, Unitarians all) had got along very well with the Whig administrations in Massachusetts. But the Calvinists were still hunting for Harvard's scalp, the Democrats regarded the College as the haven of a smug aristocracy, and the abolitionists and other reformers of the day were in a continual state of irritation because the University did not promote their pet theories.

Although Harvard graduates and professors such as Sumner, Adams, Dana, Lowell, Palfrey, Longfellow, and Beck were conspicuous among the organizers of the Free-Soil Party, in 1848, and although Wendell Phillips was the intellectual leader of the abolitionists, this radical minority failed to remove the popular impression that Harvard was reactionary, pro-slavery, and obstructing the 'Spirit of the Age.' 'The college fails to answer the just expectations of the people of the State,' declares a committee report of the General Court in 1850, because its organization and instruction are a quarter-century out of date. A college should be open to boys who 'seek specific learning for a specific purpose.' It should give the people the practical instruction that they want, and not a classical-literary course suitable only for an aristocracy. It should help young men to become 'better farmers, mechanics, or merchants.' Professors should be paid according to the number they attract. 'If a professor fail to draw students to his room, he should suffer pecuniarily. . . . The result would be, that those only would succeed who taught in departments, and in a manner acceptable to the public. That which was desired would be purchased, and that which was not, would be neglected.'

Here, in its crudest form, was a theory of higher education that has made a wide appeal in the United States since democracy came into her own. George S. Boutwell, the young Democratic leader who wrote this report, was simply expressing in his own way President Wayland's dangerously attractive formula, that 'every student might study what he chose, all that he chose, and nothing but what he chose,' in college. What most Americans wanted then of higher education, and want now, is a limited vocational training. For the last eighty years the universities of the United States have had to contend against that very thing; and many of the state universities have largely succumbed to it, as even a cursory inspection of their catalogues shows. Cornell University was founded by Ezra Cornell with that end in view, as his deed of gift proves; although the trustees very soon found that a university on that basis would not work. The demand was irresistible; in some form or other it had to be met. Eliot's greatest service to the country was to leap on the back of this wild mustang which Wayland had branded, and to break it into the civilized if somewhat jittery paces of the Harvard elective system. He managed to give the public a part of what it wanted, without completely sacrificing Thomas Jefferson's ideal of training an intellectual aristocracy to serve a political democracy.

The practical suggestions of the Boutwell committee were no less alarming than the theory. A bill was reported to increase the Harvard Corporation to fifteen fellows elected by the legislature for a six-year term. As an indication of the moving forces behind Boutwell, the orthodox religious press gave considerable space to attacks on Harvard; for the Democratic party in Massachusetts was still led by rural Calvinists, though supported in great measure by the urban Irish Catholic vote. For instance, the *Independent* declared that the public saw a great wrong 'in the tenure by which the dominant sect at Cambridge is holding this child of the Commonwealth in its suffocating grasp. Harvard College belongs to the people of Massachusetts and by the grace of God, the people . . . will yet have it and hold it, if not in one way, then in another.'

Fortunately for the poor suffocated child, Boutwell's report was postponed to the next General Court. By that time, there had been a political upheaval in Massachusetts. The Free-Soilers and Democrats formed the famous Coalition, which at the fall election in 1850 routed the old-time Whigs, elected Boutwell Governor, sent Charles Sumner to the United States Senate, made almost a clean sweep of Council and State Senate, and won control of the Lower House. The Harvard Corporation addressed a long memorial to the newly elected legislature early in 1851, written by President Sparks. They stoutly though tactfully defended the corporate rights of the University. They gave the recent history of the elective system, and reported that it was not a success.

This report fell into friendly hands. A new joint select committee headed by Giles H. Whitney, a classmate of Dana and Thoreau, gave the University a clean bill of health, advised against the proposed shake-up of the Corporation; but, wishing to infuse 'into the administration of the College, fresh blood, new ideas, movement, progress,' proposed a change in the composition of the Board of Overseers. The bill that they reported became the Act of May 22, 1851, which was promptly accepted with a gasp of relief by both Governing Boards of the University. This act was an important step in diminishing church and state representation on the Board of Overseers. It removed the clerical section altogether (though clergymen could still be elected on the same basis as others), and struck out the Council and State Senate, retaining only as *ex officio* members the Governor, Lieutenant-Governor, President of the Senate, Speaker of the House, Secretary of the Board of Education, and President and Treasurer of the University. Henceforth, the majority of the Board was to consist of thirty members, elected by joint ballot of House and Senate in annual classes of five each, each class to hold office for six years.

Favorable as this act proved to be, and excellent as were the elections made under it by the legislature,[1] Har-

[1] Among those elected Overseers in 1852-65 were John G. Palfrey, Robert C. Winthrop, Ezra Stiles Gannett, Samuel Hoar, David Sears,

vard in the meantime had been spanked in the person of one of her professors. The year 1850–51 was one of great excitement over the Compromise of 1850. Webster's famous Seventh of March speech, and his support of the Compromise, which are now generally regarded as the most disinterested and statesmanlike acts of his long career, were execrated by the liberal, radical, and democratic elements in Massachusetts. Harvard University, as a whole, saw eye-to-eye with Webster and the compromisers. Curiously enough, the students of that day had a better means of estimating the situation than the Massachusetts public; for there was a large delegation of Southern students both in College and Law School, most of them members of leading political families, who left no doubt in their classmates' minds that the alternative to compromise was immediate secession, and that the Fugitive Slave Law must be swallowed as the price of preserving the Union. Edward L. Pierce (LL.B. 1852), the biographer of Charles Sumner, relates that only six out of a hundred law students, in 1850, were Free-Soilers. Sumner, in his earlier canvass, had made a Free-Soil speech in Cambridge Lyceum Hall (on the site of the Harvard Co-operative) which his friend Longfellow compared to a Beethoven symphony played in a saw-mill, so beautiful was Sumner's language, and so harsh the shouts, hisses, and 'vulgar interruptions.' Horace Mann met a similar reception in 1851, and Emerson was 'hissed and hooted at by young law-students' when he attacked Webster in a lecture at Cambridge City Hall. Just at the right moment a victim was offered all bound and trussed for the political sacrifice, in the person of Professor Francis Bowen.

'Fanny' Bowen, as this quaint character was known to

Samuel M. Worcester, Abbott Lawrence, Emory Washburn, Stephen M. Weld, John G. Whittier, Nathaniel B. Shurtleff, and Richard H. Dana.

later generations of Harvard men, had tutored in Philosophy at Harvard for a few years subsequent to his graduation at the head of the Class of 1833. For seven years he had been editor of the *North American Review*, when, on May 25, 1850, he was chosen McLean Professor of Ancient and Modern History, the post lately vacated by Sparks. That fall he began lecturing on English Constitutional History and Modern European History to the upperclassmen, and on Greek History to the freshmen. As the by-laws of the Board of Overseers provided that no professorial appointment be submitted for confirmation unless the legislature were in session, Bowen's name did not come up until the annual meeting of the Board in January, after he had been teaching a term; and in the meantime he had been the object of lively attack in the press. Bowen believed that his real offense was an article that he wrote for the *North American Review* of July, 1850, warmly defending Webster and the Compromise. A friendly state senator told him that Stephen C. Phillips (A.B. 1819) of the Board of Overseers, lately Free-Soil candidate for Governor, was passing this article around the Senate as evidence of Bowen's depravity. But that was not the issue on which he was publicly attacked. His unforgivable offense, to judge from the daily press, was his unfriendliness to the Hungarian cause. He had published articles and delivered lectures showing up the humbuggery of Kossuth, and pointing out that Hungarian independence meant giving the Magyars free rein to oppress five million Southern Slavs, Slovaks, Roumanians, and German Transylvanians.

'Young America' at this time had forgotten the Monroe Doctrine; we were verbally crusading to free the downtrodden Hungarians, of whose subject races we were happily ignorant; it was as dangerous to doubt the complete virtue of the Magyars as, of late, to oppose Irish independence. Robert Carter, the fiery journalist who edited Boston's new Free-Soil organ, the *Commonwealth*, declared that the public 'have the right of demanding that the Professor of History . . . shall be a man imbued with American principles.' Mr. Bowen is a bigot of the 'fiercest and bitterest sort,' who 'would poison the ingenuous minds of the youth who should resort to him for instruction.' The *Christian Register* (Unitarian), on the contrary, declared that the real question was not the merits of Mr. Bowen's views on Hungary, but

whether a scholar and a teacher in a public institution, is to be at liberty to publish the results of his honest investigations of a complicated question of historical and political interest relating to a distant and comparatively unknown country, or whether he is to be assailed and ostracised, because his views formed from such materials as are within his reach, do not harmonise with ours?

On January 16, 1851, when Bowen's name came before the Overseers, Edward Everett presented a memorial of the junior and senior classes, praising Bowen's instruction and begging that he be confirmed. The memorial was tabled, and the question postponed to the next meeting. In the Boston *Atlas* of February 6, Bowen made a final rejoinder on the Hungarian question, with a humorous conclusion:

Gentlemen! Friends of the Magyars, and believers in their republicanism! Enlightened supporters of the unlimited freedom of the whole human race! I admit the patriotism of your intentions; I see as plainly as you do, the singleness of your motives; I respect your energy and activity, for I have been made to feel them. When the time comes for waging a grand war against all the despotic powers in Europe, I have no doubt you will all be found in the front rank, bravely contending for liberty or death. But will you be kind enough to reserve a portion of your courage and ardor for this great emergency, and not expend them all in crushing a poor book-worm. . . .

That afternoon, the axe fell. The Board of Overseers met; Mr. Bowen's confirmation was moved, and rejected, 33 votes to 39. Every Free-Soil and Democratic *ex officio* member voted against him; the Whigs and every elected member but Mr. Phillips, voted for him. His connection with the College was broken for the time being, and instruction in History (except for a few recitations to tutors) ceased; the McLean chair remained unfilled until 1853, when Bowen's classmate Henry W. Torrey, an amiable headmaster of a girls' school, received the appointment.

'Harvard College stands relieved of a precious incumbrance,' crowed the *Commonwealth* on February 7, 'and with a better chance of contributing its due share to the advancement of the state and the age.' This favor to the College, the State, and the Age was conferred by the Board of Overseers, it will be observed, a few months before it was stripped of most of its political members by the Act of 1851. Reading between the lines, it seems likely that the sacrifice of Bowen was the price that the University paid to oust the Council and State Senate from its senior Governing Board. Bowen was taken care of in 1853 by an appointment to the Alford Professorship of Natural Religion, Moral Philosophy, and Civil Polity; and his attenuated figure (which Lowell nicknamed 'Outlines of Pure Thought') was a familiar object in Cambridge over a period of thirty-six years. But his rejection, as part of the political manoeuvres of the last few years, taught the University a salutary lesson: that to protect academic freedom she must at the earliest opportunity free her government from political elements; and that, as a price of freedom, she must look to her own alumni and to the public, not to the Commonwealth, for support.

Professor James Walker, who succeeded Jared Sparks, was another good man and fair scholar who proved a presidential failure. At the time of his election, which was confirmed without opposition on February 10, 1853, Mr. Walker was in his fifty-ninth year. Born of respectable yeoman stock in Burlington, fitted for College at Lawrence Academy, Groton, he graduated in 1814, studied in the new Divinity School, and for nearly twenty-two years ministered to the Second or 'Harvard' Church in Charlestown. There, Dr. Walker became one of the leading protagonists of Unitarianism, or liberal Christianity, as he called it — and rightly so, for his motto was that of the Polish reformers, *We are not ashamed to improve.* 'It is the first boast of liberal Christianity,' he declared, 'that it does not make safety to depend on having found out all truth, but on being guided by the spirit of truth.' Dr. Walker was a famous preacher, cogent, meaty, sententious; it was largely the respect and attention with which his sermons were received by the students that marked him for the presidency.

President Walker's inaugural address was one of the most solid, sensible, and prophetic orations ever delivered on such an occasion. Particularly addressed to that 'spirit of the Age' which had bedevilled the University for the last ten years, it abounded in aphorisms, such as: —

Next to religion, there is no subject on which there is so much cant as education.

The boasted civilization of the nineteenth century is beginning to run out into follies and extravagances.

The radical difficulty in modern society may be expressed, as it seems to me, in two words, — *intellectual anarchy.*

Unfortunately, Dr. Walker was one of those wise persons, not uncommon in academic circles, who cannot get things done. He was too tired or indifferent to advance his own theories effectively.

Charles W. Eliot, who as Tutor in Mathematics used to prepare President Walker's docket for Corporation meetings, once disputed with Phillips Brooks, many years later, the date when Harvard reached its lowest ebb. Eliot said, 'I think the College struck bottom in 1853.' 'No,' said Brooks, 'in 1855.' These were the dates when they respectively graduated!

Considering that President Walker was stone deaf, and totally devoid of aesthetic sense, it is curious that the only new subject added to the curriculum in his presidency was Music. In the fall of 1856 the Faculty voted 'that an extra class in music be formed from members of the Junior and Sophomore Classes,' and the catalogue announced, 'The course will extend to the higher branches of part-singing.' Mr. Levi Parsons Homer, the choirmaster, was the instructor; the Glee Club revived in 1858, and in 1860, with the Pierian Sodality, was actually allowed to hire a hall and give a public concert, on condition that no tickets be sold. Thus modestly did the fourth subject in the Quadrivium enter the Harvard curriculum some two centuries after her sisters of the Seven Arts.

'Scholarships have only existed at Harvard since 1852.' On reading this astounding statement in President Eliot's Report for 1875–76, one immediately asks: What of the Lady Mowlson, the Hollis, the William Browne, the Madam Saltonstall, and other scholarships left by our early benefactors? The answer is, that these bequests (except for those like the Pennoyer and Governor Hopkins, which were administered by outside corporations) had long been treated as what we now call 'beneficiary funds,' and their identity lost. The President or Faculty, at his or their discretion, simply cancelled the term bills of worthy students up to a total annual sum determined largely by the Treasurer's method of book-keeping — a system not tempting to possible benefactors! There was also a loan fund, raised by subscription in 1838. The political discussions of the last few years showed that not only was more scholarship money needed, but also that the University should make more use of what she had. Accordingly, in 1852, the Harvard Alumni Association, at their tenth anniversary, recommended that each graduated class establish one or more scholarships, with a capital fund of $2000, the class to nominate the annual scholar, subject to faculty veto. This was promptly done by five or six classes, and individual benefactions for the purpose soon began to flow in. Dr. George C. Shattuck, a Dartmouth graduate who founded a Harvard medical dynasty, inaugurated a new series of specific scholarships with a bequest of $10,000 in 1854. These were kept distinct and separate; but Mr. John E. Thayer of Lancaster, evidently fearing a relapse into old ways, left his great scholarship fund of $50,000 in 1857 to a special board of trustees. Under President Eliot, the identity of the older foundations was restored, and accretions of capital from the general funds, as well as the amount and condition of each scholarship, were announced in the annual catalogues.

The close of commons (1849) and the discontinuance of evening prayers (1855) removed at least half the former occasions for student disorder. Appleton Chapel was completed in 1858, when services were transferred thither from University, where the old chapel was cut up into lecture-rooms. The Reverend Frederic D. Huntington, chosen Plummer Professor and Preacher to the University in 1855, after considerable discussion on account of his independence of denominational ties, introduced a certain ritual into the Sunday services of Appleton Chapel, reintroduced choral singing at morning prayers, and greatly improved the religious tone of the College during his brief term of office. In 1859 he announced to President Walker his impending resignation, owing to his conversion to Catholic theology and the Episcopal Church; and although President-elect Felton urged him to 'continue with us as our honored and beloved religious teacher and guide,' he felt that he could not do so, consistent with the public expectation at his appointment. Dr. Huntington was soon after ordained a priest of the Episcopal Church, and ended his life as Bishop of Central New York.

MINOR PROPHETS   297

Boylston Hall was built in 1857–58, out of the accumulated Ward Nicholas Boylston fund and private subscriptions, to house the college chemical laboratory and lecture-rooms, mineralogical cabinet, and the new Anatomical Museum that was being accumulated by Jeffries Wyman. The casts of the Discobolus, the Venus de Milo, and the Venus de Medici were there installed in quaint juxtaposition with the skeleton of the New Jersey mastodon, the bones of which had been assembled in comic disregard of pachydermic anatomy. Until the advent of the famous Blaschka Glass Flowers, these were Harvard's greatest attractions for tourists. Later the 'mammoth' was reassembled under the more expert direction of Jeffries Wyman, and took up his permanent abode in the new University Museum, or Museum of Comparative Zoölogy, as it is still officially called.

Agassiz had been working toward that building with his matchless zest and energy since accepting the new chair of Zoölogy and Geology in 1847. His opportunity came in 1858, when that tireless benefactor of the University, Francis Calley Gray, left fifty thousand dollars to establish a museum of natural history in connection with Harvard 'or any other institution.' Agassiz and his Boston backers, with the wisdom of the serpent, created a separate corporation, the Trustees of the Museum of Comparative Zoölogy, to administer this and other funds donated for the purpose; Agassiz promptly fascinated the General Court of Massachusetts into granting the Museum a hundred thousand dollars, at a time when they would not have given a penny to Harvard. The University gave the land, and in 1860 Agassiz was already installed with his collections and a corps of young naturalists no less enthusiastic than himself and destined to great careers — men such as Lyman, Hyatt, Morse, Putnam, Shaler, and Verrill. The Trustees, having served their purpose, were quietly swallowed up by the College Corporation in 1876.

The College Library was the subject of an interesting report by the Alumni Association in 1857, urging a subscription fund for book purchases. With 70,000 volumes (the second-largest collection in the country), the Library had but five hundred dollars a year for accessions, and some of the deficiencies reported by the professors were startling. No *Monumenta Germaniae Historica* or Henri Martin's *Histoire de France*; no Heine, Leopardi, or Gioberti; only half the *Annales* of Baronius, an early epitome of which had been given by Sir Kenelm Digby in 1655; few recent editions of the classics, and practically no books on economics. Although launched in the panic of 1857, the Alumni fund had produced an income of $2000 by 1867, when the Overseers declared it should be raised to $10,000, and a new library building built. In this, and in other ways, it is clear that the failure to obtain a state grant in 1849, and the subsequent political threats, had had a most salutary effect on the generosity of Harvard graduates; and the college treasury was so well managed that the University came through the panic of 1857 with little loss of revenue.

The eighteen-fifties at Harvard were marked by a second attempt at reform which, like the first in the eighteen-twenties, was initiated by a group of young scholars who had profited by post-graduate studies in Europe. George Martin Lane (A.B. 1846) succeeded Dr. Beck in 1851 as University Professor of Latin, after taking his Ph.D. at Göttingen, where he was fellow-student with Gildersleeve and his own classmate Child, who the same year succeeded Channing as Boylston Professor of Rhetoric. Josiah Parsons Cooke (A.B. 1848) returned from Paris in 1851 to take the Erving chair of Chemistry; William Watson Goodwin (A.B. 1851) took his Doctor's degree at Göttingen in 1855, became classical tutor at Harvard the next year, and succeeded Felton as Eliot Professor of Greek in 1860 — the year that his famous 'Greek Moods and Tenses' appeared.

These young scholars soon found themselves up against a more rigid system than Ticknor had encountered, since daily recitations, with the exhausting repetition involved when classes were approaching a hundred in number, had been reinforced by Quincy's deadly Scale of Merit. The first reform that they were able to effect was the result of a joint committee of Faculty and Overseers, of which the young Mathematics tutor Charles W. Eliot was secretary. The Faculty on March 9, 1857, adopted their recommendation that the annual examination of each class in each subject before a Visiting Committee of the Overseers be *in writing*, the papers to be set and marked by the instructor, apparently leaving the Overseers nothing to do but act as proctors. Here is the beginning of the now familiar blue-books and 'finals.' Professor Sophocles refused to have anything to do with the reform. He burned all the blue-books unread; for, said he, it wasn't fair to mark a man down if he had done well in recitations; and if his examination papers were a conspicuous improvement over daily marks, the student must have cheated!

Having adopted written papers for the Overseers' 'public' examination, which (with trifling exceptions) had been oral since 1642, it was an easy matter to procure the more important reform of allowing 'private' examinations by the instructor to be substituted for some of the daily recitation grades.[1] Professor Goodwin always regarded this change as the dawn of a new day, since it permitted instructors, if they chose, to devote many hours

---

[1] I have not found the exact date, but it was before July 6, 1858, when the Faculty adopted an elaborate scale of equivalents. For instance, in freshman Greek, Latin, and Mathematics an examination mark on the scale of 48 could be substituted for 6 daily recitation marks at 8 each, and a written exercise on the scale of 24 for 3 daily marks; but the total amount of recitation marks thus displaced must not exceed 528 (i.e., 66 recitations) per annum. We hear of 'private examinations' and 'written exercises' before 1857, but they did not 'count,' and hence were little used, and less regarded.

to actual teaching that would formerly have been consumed in ascertaining whether Smith and Jones had got
their lessons. Young Eliot and his friends had Quincy's
Scale of Merit by the tail; but the animal emitted such
bellows of rage, and inspired so much sympathy from old
graduates and lazy professors, that the boys required
thirty years to drive it out altogether.

Dr. Walker, like his immediate predecessors, found his
office irksome; he had arthritis, and disliked hobbling out
at night to fulfil the traditional presidential duty of quell-
ing every 'Rhinehart' in the Yard,[1] even though nocturnal disturbances were much less common than in the
roaring forties. 'A lady may now pass unattended, at any
hour, through the college grounds, secure from seeing or
hearing anything to alarm or offend her,' announced the
President in 1860, with an air of triumph. Walker's resignation, dated October 29, 1859, went into effect at the
end of the next February, when he was quietly succeeded
by Cornelius Conway Felton.

Professor Felton, with his ripe scholarship, well-
balanced mind, interest in education, and genial nature,
seemed to be admirably qualified for the presidency. 'He
counts among the most eminent scholars of this country,
and could occupy a no less distinguished position for
learning every where in Europe,' wrote Adam de Gu-
rowski, one of our foreign visitors; 'as to hospitality, his is
almost of the Homeric stamp.' He had served for many
years on the State Board of Education, as Regent of the
Smithsonian, and as president of a physical education

---

[1] 'Heads out!' was the cry in Walker's day; 'Oh, Rhinehart!' began
later, after a student of that name had repeatedly been shouted to by noisy
friends. In course of time it has become a sort of Harvard battle-cry, and
the word is now used to describe any Yard uproar, in which the calling of
Mr. R's undying name is an inevitable feature. The story is told that a
Harvard graduate, pestered by touts in the courtyard of Shepheard's
Hotel, Cairo, called 'Oh, Rhinehart!' and was presently answered in the
same kind from four or five windows, whose occupants then helped him to
disperse the beggars.

society in Boston; the new Harvard gymnasium was his pride. Although but fifty-three years old, heart trouble had already undermined Felton's health; and an effort to change his nature and become an austere, conscientious President killed him. Goodwin describes how, on one occasion, President Felton told him 'to run away for a day,' and then took all three of his sections on Aristophanes' 'Clouds,' and how, after it was over, he slapped the young professor's knee and said, 'Goodwin, there is no more comparison between the pleasure of being professor and president in this college than there is between heaven and hell.' Felton died on February 26, 1862. 'Harvard College,' wrote Goodwin forty-five years later, 'has never had in her society a man who was more affectionately loved, and whose company was more eagerly sought by all who knew him.'

XIII

WAR AND PEACE

1861–1869

THE dominant sentiment in the College in the critical winter of 1860–61 was for Union and conciliation. Seventy-four members of the Class of 1860 declared themselves at graduation to be Republicans, nine to be Democrats, and twenty-three to be Constitutional Unionists; but the last-named party held the only student torchlight procession during the presidential election. 'Bell and the Belles, 1860, Harvard,' read the marchers' badge. Most of the Southern students left in the winter vacation of 1860–61, never to return; and a volunteer company of undergraduates and instructors began drilling under a French officer; but few expected war until the firing on Fort Sumter. Flags then blossomed from college windows, and a transparency 'Harvard for War' appeared on Holworthy. A student company volunteered to guard the Cambridge arsenal (a survival of the siege of Boston) with its piles of cannon-balls and eighteenth-century ordnance, which were popularly supposed to be the destined objective of a dastardly attack by 'rebel' sympathizers. These intrepid defenders of the arsenal became the Harvard Cadets, who drilled in the old gymnasium on the Delta, for a time under the command of Professor Charles W. Eliot. By the fall of 1861 students began to leave College to enlist; but not many did so, and the first undergraduate to lose his life was Lieutenant Horace S. Dunn '63, who died of typhoid as a result of the Peninsular campaign.

It is difficult for anyone who knew Harvard in the years 1916–18 to understand the cool attitude of the College toward the Civil War. College life went on much as usual, and with scarcely diminished attendance. Public opinion in the North did not require students to take up arms, as in the World War; there was no mass movement into the army or navy, and draftees who hired a substitute were not despised. President Lincoln kept his son at Harvard until he graduated in 1864, and then gave him a safe staff appointment. The Harvard-Yale boat race was rowed at Worcester, before a large and enthusiastic crowd, on July 29, 1864, at a time when the Union was desperately in need of men; but not one of the twelve oarsmen enlisted. Among the graduates and undergraduates who did join the Union forces, the fatalities were proportionally three times greater than those suffered by the Harvard contingent in the World War; and of the 257 Harvard men who fought for the Southern Confederacy, one-quarter were killed or died in service.[1] No fear of being charged with cowardice, no public compulsion or worked-up propaganda, compelled these men to serve on either side. Those who died for the Union have their tablets in Memorial Hall. May not a place sometime be found at Harvard for the names of her sons who died for the Lost Cause? They too

> . . . come transfigured back,
> Secure from change in their high-hearted ways,
> Beautiful evermore, and with the rays
> Of morn on their white Shields of Expectation.

---

[1] Harvard men in the Civil War and the World War: —

	Total enlistments	Killed or died	Per cent
United States forces, 1861–65 . . .	1,311	138	10.5
Confederate forces, 1861–65	257	64	25.0
Allied and U. S. forces, 1914–18 . .	11,319	375	3.3

Many loved Truth, and lavished life's best oil
Amid the dust of books to find her,
Content at last, for guerdon of their toil,
With the cast mantle she hath left behind her.
Many in sad faith sought for her,
Many with crossed hands sighed for her;
But these, our brothers, fought for her,
At life's dear peril wrought for her,
So loved her that they died for her. . .

A disappointment of the last three administrations had been the failure of Presidents Sparks, Walker, and Felton to interest themselves in the professional schools and departments of the University. They had confined their attention to the College, and left the Medical, Law, Theological, and Scientific Schools to their several faculties, with the result that none of those departments except the last was much to boast of. In Harvard College, nothing had been done to solve the great question of modernizing the undergraduate curriculum; nobody had yet found any acceptable compromise between the literary and classical subjects, which everyone admitted were good, and the natural and social sciences which most people believed to merit more recognition.

When Felton died, the Corporation was dominated by John Amory Lowell, the senior fellow. The Reverend George Putnam was his pastor, Dr. George Hayward his kinsman, Francis B. Crowninshield his brother-in-law, and Treasurer Silsbee a relation of Crowninshield. Mr. Lowell decided that the University needed as President a clergyman to quiet the religious element, a Republican (or at least a strong Union man) to placate the politicians, an administrator to build up the professional schools, and a scientist to give new subjects their due place in the collegiate sun. The only man available who appeared to satisfy these requirements was the Reverend Thomas Hill (A.B. 1843), for many years Unitarian minister at Wal-

tham, an excellent mathematician and amateur natu-
ralist, and for the last three years President of Antioch
College, Ohio; he was what would nowadays be called
a 'progressive educator.' Louis Agassiz and Professor
Peirce (whose higher mathematical demonstrations Hill
was said to have been the only undergraduate of his generation to comprehend) electioneered vigorously for Mr.
Hill. Lack of funds forced him to give up his generous
plans for Antioch; and while weighing various calls to
Unitarian parishes in the West, he was elected President
of Harvard, on April 26, 1862, and confirmed by the
Overseers, after some opposition, on October 6, 1862.

President Hill had excellent ideas and the high ambition to make Harvard 'an American University in the
highest and best sense, — an institution offering opportunities to students and scholars, in every department of
knowledge, for attaining that amount of instruction and
aid which will enable them, however great their talents,
to take their true positions among the world's laborers in
science, art, and literature.' He wished to raise entrance
and age requirements (the median age of entering freshmen had been around seventeen and a half since 1847);
to raise standards, reform methods, and provide more
variety in undergraduate studies; to create a graduate
school of Arts and Sciences, reorganize the Lawrence
Scientific School, and improve the Divinity, Law, and
Medical Schools. All these things were needed, and
eventually were done; but it soon became clear that
President Hill was not the man to get them done. He
was too modest, easily balked by difficulty or opposition. With the air and appearance of a kindly, eccentric
country minister, he failed lamentably to match the traditional picture of a Harvard President, and shocked Cambridge folk by such lapses from clerical dignity as strip-
ping off his coat to plant ivy against Gore Hall. When the
University was attacked in the newspapers for a hazing

episode, the President scolded the press, with unfortunate consequences. He lost the respect of the Corporation, and his innate simplicity and childlike innocence
made him the sport of the students; for instance, in warning the freshmen against overdoing physical exercise, he
casually mentioned that in weeding his garden he had
strained a testicle, an admission which fastened on him
an amusing but undignified nickname.

Whatever President Hill did accomplish was in the
right direction. Courses of 'University Lectures' by distinguished scholars, many of them from outside the University, and all open to the public, led eventually to the
Graduate School and University Extension. Standards
of admission were raised, to the detriment of enrolment
at a time when revenue was hard to come by; and in 1865
the first real progress in twenty years toward an elective
system was made. When new appointments were to be
made, President Hill combed the country for candidates;
for the new chairs of Geology and Mining that were provided for the Scientific School by Samuel Hooper's gift
of fifty thousand dollars in 1865, Josiah Dwight Whitney
(A.B. Yale 1839) was called from Iowa State University,
and the young giant Raphael Pumpelly was induced to
pause at Cambridge in the midst of his restless researches
on two continents. Wolcott Gibbs, the greatest chemist
in America, who had failed to obtain an appointment
from his alma mater Columbia because of his Unitarian
faith, received the Rumford chair of Natural Science,
which Charles W. Eliot wanted. The Lawrence Scientific School was full of sparkle, with Agassiz denouncing
and Gray defending Darwinism, and Jeffries Wyman giving a course of lectures on Comparative Anatomy and
Embryology with the facts so cunningly arranged that
the audience supplied the 'missing links.' In the College,
Benjamin Peirce was 'giving instruction which nobody
understood, to a select audience of students who were

trying to become mathematicians'; but they could go for guidance to the great man's son, James Mills Peirce (A.B. 1853), who had just given up the ministry to be Assistant Professor of Mathematics. Lowell was helping Long- fellow and Norton to translate Dante, and discussing it with a delighted if somewhat hand-picked class of seniors. 'Fanny' Bowen was delivering rather deadly lectures on his own textbooks in Logic and Economics. 'Stubby' Child was devoting what energy he could spare from correcting themes to Anglo-Saxon; Lane, Goodwin, Gur- ney, James B. Greenough, and Evangelinus Apostolides Sophocles sustained the classical programme; and the Divinity School counted among its lecturers George Rapall Noyes the orientalist and the Reverend Frederic H. Hedge (A.B. 1825), transcendentalist, hymn writer, and exponent of German culture and of Biblical criticism. Sibley and Ezra Abbot were the librarians. 'There has never been in any American college a corps of teachers equal to this one,' declared an old member of the Class of 1866; and a perusal of the University Catalogue for his senior year bears him out. Excluding the medical and law professors, proctors and stewards, there were thirty- two 'officers of the University'; and twenty-six of them have attained a certain immortality in the Dictionary of American Biography. One naturally asks: Why, then, was the University so comparatively ineffective? Why did it so need reform? A '69 man has given the answer:

These competent and learned instructors did not give us of their best, but having listened to our stumbling recitations and inscribed an estimate of our blunders, would then withdraw to the congenial companionship of erudite neighbors, contented if collegiate discipline had been reasonably secured. . . . We realized that we were in the presence of distinguished men, but they moved in a higher sphere and tolerated undergraduates as the unruly subjects of official disci- pline. . . .

And there was no graduate school or other means for training scholars.

When Darwin's 'Origin of Species' began to rock the western world in 1859, his friends Asa Gray and Jeffries Wyman, who were already evolutionists, became (with some reservations) converts to natural selection, but Louis Agassiz continued to assert the permanence of type inculcated by his master Cuvier. Agassiz promptly became a hero to the clergy, and until his death in 1873 he remained the rallying point of the opposition. Josiah Parsons Cooke and 'Fanny' Bowen were also anti-Darwinians. It is said to have been a combination of clerical and classical influence that prevented John Fiske, the brilliant young convert to Darwinism who graduated in 1863, from obtaining a Harvard tutorship. Young Nathaniel S. Shaler, however, was appointed University Lecturer in 1864, although satisfied by geological evidence of the essential truth of Darwin's theories; the fear that 'Darwinism' would contaminate undergraduate morals was responsible for this discrimination. Unitarians found evolution no more palatable at first than did any other sect, and Harvard was very touchy on the matter of 'infidelity.' John Fiske, as a junior, had been 'publicly admonished' (which in those days meant simply sixty-four points off the Scale of Merit) for reading Auguste Comte during Sunday service in Christ Church; and it seems significant that Felton, Bowen, and Cooke wanted a more severe punishment, while Gurney, an early convert to Darwinism, and Dr. Andrew P. Peabody, defended young Fiske. President Felton wrote to the lad's mother: 'We never attempt to control the religious opinions of young men. But I consider it a great and lamentable misfortune to a young man, when, in the conceit of superior wisdom, he openly avows himself an infidel. . . .' And he adds that 'any attempt to spread the mischievous opinions which he fancies he has established in his own mind' will require his removal. There is something deliciously ludicrous in the picture of President Felton, member of a cult that had almost reduced Christianity to an inspired system of ethics, looking down his nose at a disciple of Comte.

It was in April, 1865, during President Hill's administration, that the complete separation of the government of the University from the government of the Commonwealth was effected. The moment was propitious; the war, in which Sons of Harvard had rendered distinguished service, was over; both state government and college government were overwhelmingly Republican. The Act of April 28, 1865, accepted by the Governing Boards the same year, abolished all *ex officio* members of the Board of Overseers except the President and Treasurer of the University, and shifted the election of the thirty Overseers provided by the Act of 1851 to Bachelors and Masters of Arts of the University and holders of honorary degrees, voting at Cambridge on Commencement Day.[1] On July 19, 1865, a Governor of Massachusetts presided over the Honorable and Reverend the Board of Overseers for the last time; but his successors have continued to honor Commencement by their presence, and even in a motorized age drive out with the traditional escort of scarlet-coated Lancers.

Professor Hedge chose the occasion of the first alumni election at Commencement, 1866, to deliver an address on university reform, calling on the graduates so to use their new power that their alma mater might take her place 'among the universities, properly so called, of modern times'; John Fiske, now a free-lance writer, followed it up. But poor President Hill was not the man to carry out the needed reforms. Cast down by personal bereavements, he offered his resignation in 1868, expecting to be

[1] An act of 1902 enabled the Governing Boards to extend the franchise; and by 1916 it had been extended to all holders of Harvard degrees. An act of 1921 permitted the Governing Boards to adopt new rules and regulations for voting for Overseers without further reference to the General Court.

granted a year's leave of absence; but to his surprise (and subsequent gratitude) the resignation was promptly accepted. In 1873 he became minister of the First Church in Portland, Maine, and there passed eighteen happy and fruitful years, adored by his parishioners and beloved by the entire community. Late in life, President Eliot declared that he had always been thankful for Hill as a predecessor, since it was he who set the University on the path that she was destined to follow.

College life in the twenty-three years between Quincy and Eliot changed more than in any similar period, except perhaps in that which followed. The clubs changed least. Many of the older societies, such as the Porcellian, Hasty Pudding, Institute of 1770, and Alpha Delta Phi (which gave up its fraternity charter and became the A. D. Club in 1865), hired rooms for their headquarters and library in the college buildings or outside; but none of them yet owned a building, and only the Porcellian served meals. Several national college fraternities established Harvard chapters: Delta Kappa Epsilon (1852), which had no connection with the Institute until much later; Zeta Psi (1852), Psi Upsilon (1856), Theta Delta Chi (1857), and others. Fraternities became such a nuisance that the Faculty abolished them about 1857, the then junior class pledging themselves to join none; but when the ban was removed in 1865 it was discovered that several had been leading a surreptitious life.

The Hasty Pudding, which took in over one-third of each class, held its first theatricals in 1844, in the club rooms on the top floor of Stoughton Hall; but during this period the Pudding's activities were still mainly social, and the initiation was literary in character. On successive nights the candidate had to make an oration, declaim a poem, sing an original song, and present an English, a Latin, and a Greek essay. Hasty Pudding's fame and

popularity were so great that from time to time rivals
were formed by men who were not chosen, some of them
short-lived like the Ydel Cruth, others, like the Pi Eta
(1865), still flourishing. Similarly, the Everett Athe-
naeum rivalled the Institute of 1770 as a sophomore
society.

'Modern conveniences' began to make their timid appearance. Holworthy was lighted by gas from 1855, and
the other halls followed suit. Grays Hall, built in 1863,
was the first college building to have water taps in the
basement; other denizens of the Yard had to obtain their
water from the Yard pumps, or hire one of the college
porters — Big Mike, Little Mike, or Dirty Mike — to lug
it in. Fastidious youths who wanted plumbing had to
room in private houses. For heating, there were only coal
fires in the chambers or living-rooms, to take the edge off
the cold in a bedroom or alcove. The few pictures we
have of college rooms at this period show rather sparse
furniture, student lamps (the kind with a reservoir that
gurgled periodically, and emitted an oleaginous stench,
if one used sperm oil, or exploded occasionally, if filled
with the more expensive precursor to kerosene), a few
prints and pictures on the wall with club medals hung on
them, and a trophy of crossed foils, boxing-gloves, or a
long sweep.

The annual football fight between the freshmen and
sophomores was suppressed by the Faculty in 1860, and
replaced by 'Bloody Monday.' Hazing of freshmen
reached its height in the sixties. The average freshman
was literally afraid for his life at the beginning of the college year, for the sophomores took care to spread horrify-
ing accounts of what would happen on the first Monday
of term. What generally did happen was a visitation by a
band of sophomores armed with huge water syringes,
who, after squirting the freshmen and their belongings,
formed a ring about the wights and forced them to box

and to perform various antics. They were then led blind-folded to the college boat-raft and swung head-and-heels; but the final indignity of ducking was given only to very fresh freshmen. The worst features of hazing were abolished around 1870, or, rather, transferred to the Hasty Pudding initiations; but Bloody Monday continued to be an institution until the turn of the century, when it attracted such gangs of 'muckers' into the Yard that it was abandoned. Harvard never imposed a special badge or uniform on freshmen, but until the World War there were certain things that they must not do, such as sport a cane before Christmas, wear a high hat, smoke a cigar, or frequent Leavitt and Peirce's smoke shop and billiard parlor. Smoking in public was still forbidden to all students.

Early morning chapel was moved forward first to seven and then to seven-thirty; it was still compulsory, and attended by sleepy lads in nightgowns, rubber boots, and ulsters with the collars turned up. Monitors ticked off the attendance; tardiness was punished by a deduction of eight points from the Scale of Merit, absence by but two points, in order to prevent late entries; nineteen cuts per term were allowed free. After chapel came breakfast. Commons closed in 1849, after being degraded to one room in University Hall, for there were now many excellent women in Cambridge who owned or hired houses (including Wadsworth House) and took boarders for two dollars a week up — mostly five dollars up during the Civil War. The landlady presided at the head of a general table, where the 'scrubs' and 'digs' sat; but the jolly fellows had club tables to which one had to be elected. In 1850 a Harvard Branch Railroad was opened; it left the Fitchburg line halfway between Union Square and Porter's Station, followed the present Museum Street, crossed Oxford Street between the Museum and the Palfrey house, and terminated in a small depot on the site of

Austin Hall, next the old Holmes house. In spite of a ten-cent fare, frequent service, and an imposing Board of Directors, the Harvard Branch did not pay, and was abandoned in 1855. Ten years later the depot was fitted up as a commons hall for the poorer students, through a gift from Mr. Nathaniel Thayer. The students who ate in 'Thayer Commons' managed it themselves, an arrangement later adopted in Memorial Hall.

'The passage of horse-cars to and from Boston, nearly, if not quite, a hundred times a day, has rendered it practically impossible for the Government of the College to prevent our young men from being exposed to the temptations of the city.' So President Hill declared in his report for 1863, about the year when Artemus Ward reported that Harvard College was 'located in the Parker House bar.' A ride of forty minutes in the tinkling tram took you to Charles Street or Bowdoin Square; you could then dine in a restaurant and attend the theatre, or call on a girl; it was about this time that Boston society began its slavish dependence on 'Harvard men' for dancing partners. A sly college song of the period, 'On Shawmut Avenue,' suggests that the young ladies of Beacon Hill and the Back Bay did not monopolize the attentions of the young men; old graduates of the period have told me of the terrible ravages of disease among heroes of these nocturnal forays into regions of ill repute.

Cantabrigian isolation had gone. A city government was adopted in 1846. Cambridgeport, once a trading station for country farmers, and East Cambridge, to which the courts had lately been transferred, were now important manufacturing centres, growing out from the bridges toward the College. Suburban villas began to fill the fields and pastures along Harvard Street and North Avenue; new streets were cut through, and for real country one had to go to Fresh Pond or Arlington. As late as 1856 there were only a dozen shops around the Square, which was shaded by a great elm tree where the subway station now offers a brief island of safety from motor traffic; but every year more brick blocks with shops on the ground floor replaced wooden dwellings. Old Cambridge 'grows a little more citylike every day,' wrote Charles Eliot Norton to his cousin Charles W. Eliot in 1864. 'I confess I do not like this process of suburbanization, — or the results of it. The old town was better in the days when we were boys, my dear Charles!'

Urbanization was doubtless one factor in transforming the old college life of the Quincy era; but organized athletics were far more important. Boating (as rowing was called until the late seventies) was the first and most popular of these sports. Oxford and Cambridge had boated since Waterloo; but it was not until 1844 that Harvard discovered the Charles. A boat club was formed among members of the Class of 1846, the six-oared *Oneida* (a plumb-stem, undecked lapstreak, thirty-seven feet long, three-and-a-half-foot beam) was purchased in 1844, and a race arranged with two Boston crews on the Back Bay. It proved such fun that other boat clubs were soon organized; in September, 1847, a senior recorded in his diary: 'This evening went down to see two of the boat-clubs go off in their race-boats. It is really a beautiful sight to see them start, all dressed in their uniforms. There are four boat-clubs here, owning as many boats. Each class is represented. Now and then they have races, which certainly must be very exciting.'

'Boating' is the proper name; for each club was named *Huron*, *Halcyon*, *Ariel*, *Undine*, or the like, after its boat, which differed very little from the captain's gig of a man-of-war. There was a great deal of spit-and-polish and navy form about the college boats — bright-work and gleaming brass, Turks'-heads on the tiller ropes, natty uniforms, colors bow and stern, snappy navy commands and tossed-oar salutes to warships in the harbor or ladies on the riverbank. Racing was but an incident to rowing, most of which was for the mere joy of it, or to get somewhere: upstream with the flood to the Spring Hotel at the Watertown dam; downstream with the ebb to Braman's baths at the foot of Chestnut Street, followed by a visit to the Parker House or the theatre — and perhaps half the crew stretched on the floor boards all the long pull home. Saturdays the boats made for Boston Harbor, and dinner at Taft's on Point Shirley; one heroic crew even attained Nahant, and was nigh swamped by a northwester pulling home. At a Navy Yard celebration, a Boston City Regatta, or a clipper-ship launching in East Boston, all the college boats turned out in full regalia, with colors flying.

There was a decline after 1850, when the *Ariel* club had a brawl with the Boston police and spent the night in jail; and in 1852 the old *Oneida* was the only boat left. In that year she was challenged by a Yale boat club 'to test the superiority of the oarsmen of the two colleges.' The race was rowed on Lake Winnepesaukee on August 3, 1852. There were two races; in the morning the Harvard boat beat three Yale boats, and in the afternoon the ever-victorious *Oneida* won by four lengths in a three-mile race. 'The clubs with other students afterwards passed a very pleasant week at the Lake, and returned together to Concord, New Hampshire, where, amid much good feeling and fraternal adieus, they finally separated.' At the next intercollegiate race, on the Connecticut River at Springfield in 1855, the Harvard *Iris* and *Y. Y.* beat the Yale *Nereid* and *Nautilus*. That fall, the Harvard University Boat Club was organized, and thenceforth, excepting the three war years, 1861–63, rowed in at least one annual race regatta, although not invariably with Yale. The heavy navy gigs were abandoned in 1856, and the first real racing boat, an eight-oared lapstreak with outriggers but fixed seats, was built for the Varsity that year in St. John, New Brunswick.

It was at a Boston City Regatta of June 19, 1858, that crimson was first used as the Harvard color. A Harvard boat club composed largely of graduate students, and including Tutor Eliot, agreed that on account of the large number of entries they must have some distinguishing mark other than the underclothes in which they customarily raced. Captain Crowninshield and Eliot chose at Hovey's store six China silk handkerchiefs of a brilliant crimson, which were tied around their heads. The Harvard boat beat six others from Boston, New York, and St. John in a three-mile race on June 19, and repeated their victory over seven boats in a six-mile race on July 5. The winning color naturally became the Harvard rowing color, and from the crews it spread to the teams. One of the original handkerchiefs is preserved in the University archives; in 1910 its color, officially described as that of arterial blood, was formally adopted by the Corporation as the official livery color of the University.

The races with Yale were resumed in 1864 on Lake Quinsigamond, Worcester; and a year or two later class races began. The first international regatta was rowed with Oxford on the classic Putney-to-Mortlake course on August 27, 1869, in fours, and lost by about three lengths.

Baseball began at Harvard during the Civil War, when a group of boys entering College from Exeter brought to Cambridge what was known as the 'New York game.' A diamond was laid out on Cambridge Common, and several games played with local clubs; the first intercollegiate game was played with a Brown class team at Providence on June 27, 1863, and won by a score of 27 to 17; the first varsity game was played with Williams in 1865, and won by a score of 35 to 30. The first Yale game was played in 1868, and won, 25 to 17.

This was the heyday of 'class spirit.' Around 1840 the numbers of graduating classes began to rise perceptibly for the first time in a hundred years (the Class of 1762

numbered forty-seven, and the Class of 1841 one less); [1]
the Class of 1860 was the first to pass the hundred mark.
Yet the classes of this period, and perhaps down to 1885,
seem to me to have had more fraternal affection for one
another than their predecessors — certainly more than
their successors. Athletic contests offered new occasions
for emulation, and bonds for class feeling. The lads of
the eighteen-sixties had glorious times on class outings
and class dinners — as the appended menu suggests. The
wine-list (not here reprinted) includes nine brands of
Champagne, 'Madame Clicquot' at $2.50 being the dear-
est; Schloss Johannisberger, Fürst von Metternich, 1846
($6.00); Château Lafitte, 1844 ($3.50); Madeira from
Daniel Webster's cellar, and numerous clarets, sherries,
and ports. Taft's was a famous hostelry; his food and
wines were justly famous, his cooking was superb, and
never since has Boston seen the like of his game. 'Birds
of Paradise' was one of Taft's euphemisms for birds that
were out of season; and the 'one fish ball' refers to the
famous ballad by Professor George Martin Lane about
one of his adventures in a low eating-house. For fifty
years it was a favorite Harvard song; and when a benefit
performance was wanted for war sufferers in 1862, John
Knowles Paine built up around the 'lone fish ball' the
burletta *Il Pesceballo*, with Italian libretto by F. J. Child
and English 'translation' by J. R. Lowell.

College journalism entered its new and permanent
phase with the first number of *The Advocate* in 1866; and
old Mother Advocate was a sprightly wench in those days.
Her first name was *The Collegian*, a fortnightly quarto for
'light and bright articles,' fathered by a board of editors

---

[1] Numbers are a difficult matter in the nineteenth century on account
of the practice of granting A.B.'s long subsequent to graduation (sometimes even after the recipient's death) to members of the class who failed to
graduate, and then entering their names in the next catalogue with their
classmates. Thus the Class of 1841 stands 46 strong in the 1930 Quinquennial; but only 42 graduated in 1841.

TAFT'S HOTEL

SUPPER FOR THE

Class of 1860

Point Shirley, June 11th, 1860

BILL OF FARE

FISH

Boiled Salmon

Tautog   Scrod

American Plaice   American Sole

LOBSTER SALAD

ROAST

Bremen Goose   Bremen Ducks

Mongrel Goose   Mongrel Ducks

Wild Goose   Wild Ducks

Spring Chickens

Pig

BIRDS OF PARADISE

GAME

Peeps

Sickle-Bill Curlew

Dough Birds   Jack Curlew

Black Snipe   Wild Squabs

Sand Snipe   Grass Plover

Red-Breast Plover   Yellow-Leg Plover

ONE FISH BALL

JELLIES

Current   Cranberry

PASTRY

ICE CREAMS

Vanilla

Strawberry

Sherbet

Roman Punch

CHARLOTTE RUSSE

DESSERT

ALL THE FRUITS OF THE SEASON

COFFEE

including Thomas Sergeant Perry (A.B. 1866). The motto *Dulce est Periculum* was well chosen, for *The Collegian* proved too light and bright for the Faculty, who suppressed it after the third number; but after five weeks it reappears as *The Advocate*, whose editors protest to the Faculty against 'strangling free speech,' and by a narrow vote get off with a caution to be good. In *The Advocate*, for the first time, one has a periodical mirror of college life — complaints of the curriculum, squib on the 'Bowdoinomaniacs' who are whacking up essays for the Bowdoin prizes, smart reviews of new books and plays, discussion whether the traditional 'dancing on the green' at Class Day be kept up or abandoned for waltzing (as was done), complaints of mud in the Yard, detailed accounts of boat races and baseball matches, devastatingly sarcastic exchange of letters between Harvard and Yale boat clubs about a proposed intercollegiate class regatta that failed to come off, and advertisements of bookstores and Boston tailors, of Harvard Square drug stores and 'Levy, Gentleman *Poco*,' who 'will attend to any business pertaining to the profession, in his most winning manner, provided that it be *sub rosa*, and after twilight.' [1]

Herein, as in other sources, we may discern that Harvard had come through her medieval period and was trembling on the verge of modern times. A new young Captain was ready to take the helm.

[1] 'Poco' was the nickname of this old-clothes-man and money-lender; the word does not appear in Hall's *College Words and Customs* (1856), and died around 1906, when the reign of Max Keezer began.

THE OLYMPIAN AGE

1869–1933

PRESIDENTS

1869–1909   CHARLES WILLIAM ELIOT
1909–1933   ABBOTT LAWRENCE LOWELL

First, universities are teachers, store-houses, and searchers for truth. . . . In addition to these three direct functions, a university has less direct, but still important purposes to fulfill. It should exert a unifying social influence. It should set an example of religious toleration, and cultivate mutual respect between diverse churches. A university which draws its students from a large area has also a unifying influence in regard to political discussions and divisions. A true university is a school of public spirit for its governors, benefactors, officers, graduates, and students. Again, it stands for intellectual and spiritual forces against materialism and luxury. It should always be a school of good manners, and of independent thinking. Finally, universities should be always patriotic in the best sense. . . .

— CHARLES W. ELIOT

XIV

PRESIDENT ELIOT

IN the year 1869, America was in the midst of the most roaring, spectacular material development that she had ever known. Exploitation and expansion were the order of the day. A golden spike forged the last link in the railway chain from Atlantic to Pacific. The mining empire in the Rocky Mountains, the cattle kingdom on the Great Plains, and the westward-striding army of homesteaders were wiping out the frontier. Steel mills in Pittsburgh were running full-blast; cotton and woollen mills in New England were hanging up new annual records of production. In the rapidly growing cities of the East, politicians and financiers, railroad barons and merchant princes, were stepping wide, high, and handsome. Even the prostrate South was beginning to look up again and call the land her own. Ulysses S. Grant was inaugurated President of the United States in 1869, and the Knights of Labor were organized. Everyone was making money and expecting to make more; the inevitable post-war depression was not even suspected; the clank of machinery and the clink of dollars silenced religion, letters, and the arts.

Harvard must expand with the country, must save something for the advancement of learning out of this scramble for wealth, or the age would pass her by, and the ghosts of Dunster, Leverett, and Kirkland would rise to reproach her. There were plenty of rival universities ready to carry the caduceus, if Harvard slowed up or stumbled. Yale already had a graduate school, and better scientific instruction than Harvard; James McCosh, that energetic Scots metaphysician, had just been made

President of Princeton; Frederick A. P. Barnard was ready to make Columbia into a great university, with the teeming wealth and immense population of New York to draw upon; and of the newer universities, Cornell under Andrew D. White and the state universities of Michigan, Wisconsin, and California were coming along rapidly, unhampered by age, tradition, and vested interests in making themselves serviceable to the new era. Engineering schools and institutes of technology were attracting the lads eager to build bridges, to apply chemistry to industry, or to extract the mineral wealth of the country; Johns Hopkins was almost ready to bid against Germany for the patronage of young scholars. Yet Harvard College was hidebound, the Harvard Law School senescent, the Medical School ineffective, and the Lawrence Scientific School 'the resort of shirks and stragglers.' It was an ominous fact that relatively fewer New Englanders were attending College in 1869 than in 1838: .051 per cent of the population in the one year, as against .075 per cent in the other. Had a college of Liberal Arts any future, except as a fashionable finishing school for young gentlemen?

Age was no safeguard to an institution of learning in this pulsating young America; history had seen plenty of cold and deserted academic hearths; something must be done, and that quickly, or Harvard would degenerate to a mere cultural backwater: desire under the elms, and not much desire at that. The foundation for a great university was there; but another twenty years of presidential promises and failures would make Harvard seem merely quaint. More than at any age in our history, a leader was wanted. The leader was ready and waiting. He was thirty-five years old, and his name was Charles William Eliot.

For several years, some of the oldest and most devoted members of the Governing Boards, men like Dr. Walker the former President, John Amory Lowell, and Judge Hoar, had kept an eye on young Mr. Eliot. As assistant professor of Chemistry he had been an unpopular though conscientious teacher, and as a scholar he had shown no great promise; but in everything connected with university administration, from devising written examinations to overseeing the construction of a new building, the President was apt to ask Mr. Eliot to do it, and it was done. Since 1863, when Wolcott Gibbs beat him to the Rumford Professorship, he had been unconnected with Harvard. Two years abroad were devoted more to intensive investigation of the educational system and methods of France, Germany, and England than to study or research in his own subject. In 1865 there came to him at Rome the offer to become superintendent of a cotton mill at Lowell, with a salary of five thousand dollars — more than twice what he could expect for many years as a professor. He had a growing family, and slender means. But the firm belief that the world had work for him to do in education (although the educational world had as yet given no sign of it) compelled him to decline; and then, almost by return mail, arrived a letter from President Rogers offering him a chair of Chemistry in the new Massachusetts Institute of Technology. This he promptly accepted; and at the Institute on Boylston Street, Boston, Eliot passed three happy years, teaching in the lecture room, organizing the laboratory method of instruction, and writing the first textbook in English on Inorganic Chemistry. At Commencement, 1868, he was elected an Overseer of Harvard College; the following September, President Hill resigned.

Shortly after, there appeared in the *Atlantic Monthly* two articles on 'The New Education,' which expressed Eliot's ripe views of how American universities should develop. They coincided, in the main, with recommendations made in a report of a Committee of the Over-

seers headed by James Freeman Clarke, and including
James Walker and Edward Everett Hale. This report
was accepted by the senior Governing Board on February 11, 1869, and printed. The Overseers believed that
something must be done; but that something depended,
in their minds, more on obtaining money than on a
leader. They emphasized the need of more instruction
in the natural and social sciences, and proposed to sweep
away the prescribed curriculum after freshman year, and
widely to extend the elective system. With the Law and
Medical Schools, however, they were almost smugly satisfied; and of a graduate school they dropped no hint. Yet
the concluding paragraphs show that the nineteenth-century German conception of a university, the standard
to which Eliot would constantly refer Harvard, was
already the ideal of the Overseers before Eliot was elected.

The emancipation of Harvard from its confused relation to the
State, and its new basis, resting on the love and help of its Alumni,
opens to it a prospect of great progress and usefulness. The common
aim of all its friends should be to second the movement now taking
place, by which it is gradually changing from a gymnasium or college
into a true university. The distinction between a college and a university is, that in one all the students are taken through the same
prescribed curriculum; in the other they have many and various departments of knowledge offered to them. A college is a place to which
a young man *is sent* to go through an appointed list of studies; a university, one to which he *goes* to get instruction and help in his pursuit
of science. A university should give opportunity for universal culture;
it should provide faculties in language, science, law, theology, medicine, engineering architecture, and all the arts. It ought also to be
furnished with museums, cabinets, libraries, botanic garden, observatory. . . . By bringing together such varied apparatus for study, and
so many teachers and students, a literary atmosphere is created as well
as a tone of thought favorable to learning. Teachers have more of
enthusiasm, and gain a larger, freer style of thought, in such a generous atmosphere. Pedantic narrowness is less likely to appear. Professors are more interested in what they teach, and so are better able to
inspire interest in others, when surrounded by an opinion favorable to
the most thorough investigations. A university attracts students by

the reputation of its professors, and by obtaining a number of great names it becomes conspicuous at a distance. . . .

We should all labor together to make Harvard a noble University, — a seat of learning which shall attract the best teachers and most ardent students, — a University which shall retain all the good of the past, and go forward to welcome the advancing light of the future. So may the priceless gift of our fathers be transmitted to our children, not only unimpaired, but constantly renewed and bettered. Let each generation do its part to make it more worthy of this great country, this advancing civilization, this ripening age. In the largest sense, let it be devoted to Christ, the great teacher of truth, and to his Church, the great means of human education.

Nevertheless, it required many months and much discussion to bring the Overseers to accept young Mr. Eliot. On March 10, 1869, both Governing Boards met in the grim old Medical School on North Grove Street. Eliot attended the Overseers, heavy with anxiety for his beloved wife, whose life was fluttering to a close. From the Corporation came a message that they wished to elect him to the presidency. He consulted Dr. Walker, and his friend and cousin Theodore Lyman; his youth, his duty to the Institute, the opposition of Agassiz, the birthmark on his face which (touching fancy!) he imagined would detract from presidential dignity, made him hang back. Both men persuaded him to accept; and on March 12 he was elected by the Corporation.

Then the opposition developed. The fact that Eliot was not a clergyman troubled nobody, for the clerical tradition had been broken by Quincy's election; and although Everett, Sparks, Walker, and Hill had been Unitarian ministers at one time in their lives, no one since Kirkland had been called from the pulpit to Harvard. Yet there was consternation in the College Faculty (as the last surviving member of it told me) at the thought of Eliot; the classicists feared him, the scientists despised him; and both groups communicated their feelings in no uncertain terms to the Overseers. One group feared, in view of Eliot's pronounced views in favor of new subjects, that all the subtle values of a liberal education, accumulated over two centuries, would be dissipated; Dr. Andrew P. Peabody, the acting president, or Professor Gurney, who had been a classical scholar before he turned historian, was their choice. Others represented that Eliot would turn Harvard into a rival institute of technology — a fear wholly unwarranted, as a paragraph in one of Eliot's *Atlantic* articles might have assured them:

> The whole tone and spirit of a good college ought to be different in kind from that of a good polytechnic or scientific school. In the college, the desire for the broadest culture, for the best formation and information of the mind, the enthusiastic study of subjects for the love of them without any ulterior objects, the love of learning and research for their own sake, should be dominant ideas. . . . The student in a polytechnic school has a practical end constantly in view.

Eliot's nomination was returned to the Corporation, as good as rejected, on April 21. The Corporation replied on May 11 that, remaining unanimously of the opinion that their 'electing Mr. Eliot to the Presidency' was to 'the best interests of the University,' they ventured to lay his name again before the Overseers. Peirce and Agassiz, assured by John A. Lowell that if it was not to be Eliot it must be Peabody, withdrew their objections, and Francis Parkman the historian became Eliot's warm advocate in the Overseers. Eliot's own comment was characteristic: 'As far as I have heard the objections to me, I quite agree with them.'

On May 19 the Overseers finally voted to concur, 16 to 8; and a joint committee of which Mr. Emerson was 'the youngest and least imposing member' informed Mr. Eliot that he was President of Harvard College. 'His administration will prove a turning point in the history of Harvard,' predicted the *Boston Post*, 'producing a body of accurate, trained and practical scholars whose influence will be powerfully and permanently felt in the entire variety of professions and avocations.'

President Eliot finished his task at Technology and then set to work on his inaugural address. His only advisers were George J. Brush and Daniel Coit Gilman of Yale, meeting him discreetly on neutral ground at Springfield. The inauguration on October 19, 1869, in the meetinghouse of the First Church, Unitarian, was the simplest and the most musical that anyone remembered; and few of those present lived to witness another. John Milton's 'Let us with a gladsome mind' was sung as a chorale; prayer by Dr. Peabody; Latin Gratulatory by John Stuart White '70, hailing Eliot's youth as *faustum omen*, predicting great things of his *animi fortitudo perseverantiaque*. Heavy and hortatory speech by the President of the Board of Overseers, the aged ex-Governor Clifford, who hands over the Keys, Charter, and Seal. Crisp reply by President Eliot, who then takes the ancient chair. The chorus breaks out with *Domine salvum fac Praesidem nostrum*, composed by John K. Paine for the previous inauguration. Then, one of the greatest addresses in modern educational history, delivered with a precise diction and in a deep mellow voice that lent weight, and even beauty, to the speaker's simple, muscular English. The delivery lasted an hour and three-quarters, during which one 'might have heard a pin drop, save when the old arches rang with thunders of applause.' The three opening sentences smote like a sharp, clean sword through the controversy between the 'old' and the 'new' education that had caused so many weary hours of discussion since 1825:

> The endless controversies whether language, philosophy, mathematics, or science supplies the best mental training, whether general education should be chiefly literary or chiefly scientific, have no practical lesson for us to-day. This University recognizes no real antagonism between literature and science, and consents to no such narrow

alternatives as mathematics or classics, science or metaphysics. We would have them all, and at their best.

Here are a few of the crackling sentences that followed:—

The only conceivable aim of a college government in our day is to broaden, deepen, and invigorate American teaching in all branches of learning.

The practice of England and America is literally centuries behind the precept of the best thinkers upon education.

The actual problem to be solved is not what to teach, but how to teach.

Philosophical subjects should never be taught with authority.

The worthy fruit of academic culture is an open mind, trained to careful thinking, instructed in the methods of philosophic investigation, acquainted in a general way with the accumulated thought of past generations, and penetrated with humility. It is thus that the university in our day serves Christ and the church.

The vulgar conceit that a Yankee can turn his hand to anything we insensibly carry into high places, where it is preposterous and criminal.

To lose altogether the presence of those who in early life have enjoyed the domestic and social advantages of wealth would be as great a blow to the College as to lose the sons of the poor. Inherited wealth is an unmitigated curse when divorced from culture.

Two kinds of men make good teachers — young men and men who never grow old.

It is very hard to find competent professors for the University. Very few Americans of eminent ability are attracted to this profession.

With the exception of the endowments of the Observatory, the University does not hold a single fund primarily intended to secure to men of learning the leisure and means to prosecute original researches.

The Overseers should always hold toward the Corporation an attitude of suspicious vigilance.

A reputation for scrupulous fidelity to all trusts is the most precious possession of the Corporation.

To see every day the evil fruit of a bad appointment must be the cruellest of official torments.

A university is the last place in the world for a dictator. Learning is always republican. It has idols, but not masters.

Momentous as were Eliot's words, prophetic as they proved to be, his personality was even more impressive; all who saw and heard this young man just turned thirty-five, tall, well-formed, virile, his immobile face wearing a placid smile of confidence and determination, realized that they were listening, not to a statement by an academic theorist as to what ought to be done, but to the declaration by a man of character and energy of what was going to be done, whether they liked it or not.

With singular appropriateness, the inaugural ceremony concluded with the great chorus from Sophocles' Antigone:

> Πολλὰ τὰ δεινὰ κοὐδὲν ἀνθρώπου δεινότερον πέλει
> What a thing is man! Among all wonders
> The wonder of the world is man himself.[1]

The inaugural address said not a word on buildings; and in that field of expansion it was Lowell rather than Eliot who proved to be Harvard's Augustus; but much overdue building and addition of grounds was accomplished the first few years. The old buildings, as Dr. Holmes wrote, had long 'sat still and lifeless as the colossi in the Egyptian desert'; then about New Year's, 1870, they began to spawn progeny in brick and stone. The 'building in the rear of University Hall' was summarily removed, and plumbing installed in the basement of all Yard buildings. Four residential halls, 'dormitories' as they were then called — Thayer Hall, given by Nathaniel Thayer; Matthews Hall, 'the finest college dormitory in America,' designed by Peabody and Stearns and given by Nathan Matthews; Weld Hall, given by William F. Weld in memory of his brother Stephen M. (A.B. 1826); and Holyoke House, built by the College — were provided for by 1870 and completed by 1872. A new physical laboratory was installed in Harvard Hall, and served until

[1] John J. Chapman's translation. The chorus sang the Greek words to Mendelssohn's music.

the Jefferson building (largely the gift of T. Jefferson Coolidge, A.B. 1850) was completed in 1884. Massachusetts was done over into lecture rooms; and, on the Overseers' initiative, an undergraduate reading room, managed by the students themselves, was installed there in 1872. The interior of Appleton Chapel was remodelled and enlarged. The old Holmes estate was purchased by subscription in 1871, and with Jarvis Field, which was given to the University in 1869 in exchange for releasing the Delta for a war memorial, provided ample space for games until Soldiers Field was presented by Major Henry L. Higginson in 1890. On the Delta the cornerstone of Memorial Hall, the most ambitious building ever attempted by the University, an immense Victorian Gothic pile designed by Ware and Van Brunt, was laid by the Reverend Phillips Brooks (A.B. 1855) on October 6, 1870. A memorial to the men of Harvard who died to preserve the Union, paid for by contributions from alumni and other friends of the University, it was dedicated the day before Commencement, 1874. The great Hall, 164 feet long, and seating over a thousand students, was given over to a dining association managed by the members; and the name 'commons,' of unhappy memory, was not revived. Sanders Theatre, occupying the apse of the building, built largely from the bequest left by Charles Sanders in 1864, was ready for the Commencement exercises in 1876. By that time the graduates of 1869 and earlier, as they returned for their class reunions, were already complaining that they 'didn't know the place'; and if they could have re-entered as undergraduates, they would have found it still stranger.

The celerity of the transformation may be gauged by the Corporation Records of January 28, 1870, three months after President Eliot was inaugurated. On that day there were either appointed, or reported confirmed by the Overseers, the following men:

Ephraim W. Gurney, Dean of the College Faculty, and the first dean in Harvard history. His duties, defined a few days before, were to 'administer the discipline of the College,' keep records of admission and of grades, and submit recommendations of scholarships.

Christopher C. Langdell, Dane Professor of Law.

John Chipman Gray, Jr., Lecturer in the Law School.

Oliver Wendell Holmes, Jr., Instructor in Constitutional Law.

Edwin P. Seaver, Assistant Professor of Mathematics.

John Fiske, Instructor in History.

Eighteen series of 'University Lectures' were authorized, including:

Ralph Waldo Emerson, on the Natural History of the Intellect.

Ferdinand Bôcher, on the French Language and Literature.

William Dean Howells, on the New Italian Literature.

Charles Sanders Peirce, on Logic.

Chauncey Wright, on Psychology.

John Fiske, on Positivist Philosophy.

These University Lectures were a modified continuation of President Hill's scheme for higher instruction in the Arts and Sciences. They were grouped in two courses, one on Philosophy and the other on the Modern Languages and Literatures, with six or seven distinguished lecturers each. A fee of $150 was charged (the same as undergraduate tuition), 'reading was required, examinations were held, and honors were granted.' 'Teachers and other competent persons,' both men and women, were admitted; but the total enrolment was only nine: three of the one sex and six of the other. The next year, thirty-five courses of University Lectures of small scope were offered, with fees reduced to as little as three dollars, and undergraduates admitted free; but the takers were few.

President Eliot used to exercise himself almost daily on horseback, until he took up the bicycle at the age of sixty. One spring day when he was riding up Sparks Street, his horse fell and threw him in the mud opposite Dr. Walker's house. That good old gentleman — best of advisers to four presidents, though not a great President himself — inquired how many times that horse had fallen. 'This is the third time,' said Eliot. 'The first time,' said Dr. Walker, 'it was the horse's fault, the other two falls were your fault.' President Eliot sold the horse, and applied the lesson to many things besides. No man ever failed him more than once. University Lectures had to go.

The alternative, a Graduate School of Arts and Sciences (or Graduate Department, as it was first called), was established by the Governing Boards in January, 1872. Up to that time there were no facilities at Harvard for the training of men in the Liberal Arts after taking their first degree, although advanced instruction in the Natural Sciences had been given in the Lawrence Scientific School for over twenty years, without a degree to reward the students' efforts. Harvard men who wished to be trained as scholars in the humanities and the social sciences had to study abroad. It was now provided that the M.A. should be given in future for not less than a year's postgraduate study in approved subjects, and after examination; the Class of 1869 was the last whose members were allowed to take the M.A. for 'keeping out of jail five years and paying five dollars,' as the saying was. The Ph.D. was to be conferred after a more advanced examination and the acceptance of a dissertation deemed a 'contribution to knowledge'; William E. Byerly (A.B. 1871) took the first Harvard Ph.D. in Mathematics, in 1873; and James O. Averill (A.B. Amherst 1870) took the first M.A. of the new dispensation the following year. Corresponding S.M.'s and S.D.'s for scientific students were also provided. Already a few professors, like Henry Adams, had established seminaries of the German type for graduate students and competent undergraduates. Courses 'primarily for graduates' first appeared in the Catalogue for 1875–76, and special instruction from individual professors, the sort of study for which a graduate school properly exists, came two years later. From the first, the College and the Graduate School overlapped; and Harvard University, unlike many of her American rivals, has never walled off graduate students from undergraduates. The instruction is given by the same people; and no course, however advanced, is closed to undergraduates deemed competent by the instructor.

The establishment of the Graduate School was one of Eliot's most vital and far-reaching reforms; yet it was pushed through against opposition, in and out of the Faculty. One member said: 'Yale after twenty years has a graduate school of thirty students; I hope we may do as well!' The weaker brethren knew they could never teach graduate students, and did not wish to be put to the test. Johns Hopkins University, with an endowment of three and a half millions for a graduate school of Arts and Sciences, was about to open; why should Harvard set up a rival school, when she had insufficient funds to teach undergraduates properly? Would it not merely weaken the College? To one such objector President Eliot replied: 'It will strengthen the College. As long as our teachers regard their work as simply giving so many courses for undergraduates, we shall never have first-class teaching here. If they have to teach graduate students as well as undergraduates, they will regard their subjects as infinite, and keep up that constant investigation which is necessary for first-class teaching.'

No prophecy of Eliot's has been more amply fulfilled. More than salaries (which Eliot induced the Corporation to raise), more than libraries and laboratories, the opportunity to train disciples in an atmosphere of professional study and creative scholarship has drawn great scholars to Cambridge, or retained them there. But it was many years before the new school bore much fruit; not until 1900 did Harvard become the premier American Ph.D. mill. Graduate students liked the adventure of studying abroad, or of attending a university, such as Johns Hopkins, that catered to their kind alone. From the other point of view, undergraduates grumbled in the eighteen-eighties, and grumble still, at the presence of earnest aspirants for the M.A. and Ph.D. in their courses, and at the personal attention that these students received from the professors; yet, with few exceptions, the great teachers of the last sixty years, from the undergraduate point of view, have been the very scholars who attracted graduate students and through them spread the influence of Harvard throughout the entire educational system of America.

Eliot's mind was Roman rather than Greek or Hebraic; and that was fortunate for the University. She had had her fill of Hellenic and Hebraic presidents in the last twenty-five years. As Bliss Perry aptly remarked, Eliot 'was primarily an organizer and administrator with an imperial grasp of fact.' As such, he quickly grasped the fact that the Law School badly needed reform. Nothing had changed in twenty years. All instruction was by the three professors, Joel Parker (whom Nathaniel Holmes succeeded in 1868), Emory Washburn, and Theophilus Parsons, all of whom had private practices. Less than half the students were college graduates. They studied the same subjects from textbooks, entered or left at any period of the year, and were granted the LL.B. without examination after eighteen months' residence, even though they might have missed courses on fundamental subjects that were given only every other year.

As a junior in College, Eliot had met in a friend's room a law student from New Hampshire named Christopher Columbus Langdell. In 1870 he recalled the remarkable quality of that young man's conversation, sought him out in an obscure New York office, shoved his appointment as Professor of Law through the Governing Boards, and attended the first recorded meeting of the Law Faculty — Nathaniel Holmes, Washburn, Langdell, and himself — and informed them that a dean must be chosen. Washburn proposed to make the newcomer dean. Eliot put the motion, Holmes and Washburn voted *aye*, and the deed was done. Momentous it was, because Langdell regarded the law as a science to be mastered only by investigation of its sources — decisions and opinions — and because from the first he insisted on the students' learning the law as a growing organism, by studying cases. Nathaniel Holmes resigned in protest against the newfangledness in 1872, but young 'Wendell' Holmes (the future Justice) and John Chipman Gray had already been appointed lecturers, and in 1873 James Bradley Thayer (LL.B. 1856) and James Barr Ames (LL.B. 1872) were appointed professors. The last had never practised law. Written examinations were established, and a progressive three-year curriculum adopted. Thus the last remnants of the old apprentice or lawyer's-office school vanished, a new method (for all the new appointees adopted the case system) was applied, standards were raised, and a profession of teaching law was begun. 'That an experiment so out of line with the Anglo-American professional tradition should ever have been even tried, shows the courage of Langdell, and of Eliot who stood behind him.

That it succeeded is a testimony to the foresight of Lang-dell, and the wisdom of Eliot. The one saw the type of teacher that would be called for by the increasing special-ization, and by the changed conditions of practice then beginning. The other saw the connection of the proposal with the whole problem of academic professional edu-cation in all fields.'

Years of trial, but not of doubt, followed. Langdell was unpopular; students wished to be told what the law was, not to search it out for themselves; the bar was dis-trustful; enrolment declined. By 1880 revival was under way, and in 1883 the Law School moved out of Dane Hall into the new Richardson Romanesque building pro-vided by Edward Austin, and named after his brother. By 1886 it was clear that the new régime was a success. The number of students, after a sharp decline, had doubled; the *Harvard Law Review* was founded, the Har-vard Law School Association organized, and in 1893 the Law Faculty took the bold step of excluding from the School anyone not a college graduate. The Harvard Law School was already the first in any common-law country when Ames succeeded Langdell as dean in 1895.

One of Eliot's earliest, most difficult, and most im-portant reforms was that of the Medical School. This department of the University had almost broken its con-nection with the parent College. Located in Boston since 1810, it had gone its own way, asking for no funds (as the professors were all active practitioners and paid by stu-dents' lecture fees), making its own rules, never seeing the President of the University. 'There is more bad blood in the Medical Faculty than in all the rest of the University put together,' wrote Eliot to one member of it. A vicious system of medical instruction was strongly intrenched. The students, many of whom had not even a good high-school education, were rowdy and illiterate. They merely attended lectures and clinical demonstrations for a minimum of sixteen weeks, although they had to wait three years for a degree. The only examination, at the end, was a *viva voce* of each candidate by nine different professors for ten minutes each; whoever passed five subjects out of the nine, received the M.D. degree. Yet the Harvard was no worse than any other American medical school. 'The ignorance and general incompetence of the average graduate of American Medical Schools . . . is something horrible to contemplate,' wrote Eliot. Dr. Henry J. Bigelow and Dr. Holmes, the senior professors in the School, regarded Medicine as an art rather than a science, and the institution as a recruiting ground rather than a training school. Fortunately some of the younger members, such as Dr. James C. ('Skinny') White, wanted reform; and Eliot, who had inspected medical schools in France and Germany, quickly showed that he meant to have it. In his first annual report he declared bluntly that the Harvard Medical School and its younger satellite, the Dental School, 'were the worst equipped departments of the University.' And Dr. Holmes, who had long been 'under Dr. Bigelow's thumb,' promptly came out from under, and took a sporting delight in observing this 'cool, grave young man' turning over the venerable institution 'like a flapjack.'

The Corporation needed little persuasion to adopt the reforms that Eliot and the younger medicos considered necessary: regular tuition fees and salaries; a progressive three-year course for all; stiff entrance examinations, written examinations, all of which must be passed, at the end of each year. The Medical Faculty was difficult to convert. Dr. Bigelow fought every step, even with the argument that the students should not be expected to pass written examinations, since half of them could hardly write! He was finally outvoted, but there remained the Overseers, where the influence of the elders was strong.

For three meetings the Overseers inconclusively debated the reforms. When the final vote was imminent, the President of the Board, Charles Francis Adams, relinquished the chair in order to speak. 'There was a fierce glare in his eyes, and his face grew red,' remembered Eliot, as Mr. Adams told how a recent graduate of the Medical School, a practitioner in Quincy, had killed three poor patients in succession by an overdose of sulphate of morphia. Such was the result of granting degrees for the passing of five out of nine ten-minute examinations. The vote was taken almost immediately, and the reforms were adopted by a large majority.

The new system went into effect in the fall of 1871, and entrance examinations were first required in 1877. In addition to the basic reforms, new facilities were provided for medical research by laboratories for Physiology and Microscopic Anatomy, the former under the young and enthusiastic Dr. Henry Pickering Bowditch (A.B. 1861), fresh from European study, the first full-time professor in the history of the School. A course for graduates was established. The immediate result of the reform was a drastic curtailment in the number of students; but from a low level of 170 in 1872, numbers rose to 251 in 1879. The proportion of college graduates had greatly increased, that of students from outside New England more than doubled, and the Medical Schools of the Universities of Pennsylvania and Michigan soon fell into line with the new Harvard regulations. 'The only way to drive people out of a school permanently,' said Eliot, 'is to let it be a poor school.' As 'Harvard Medical College' on North Grove Street was already outgrown, two hundred thousand dollars was raised by subscription for new quarters, and the new building on the corner of Boylston and Exeter Streets (sold to Boston University when the School moved to Longwood Avenue in 1906) was occupied in the fall of 1883. The same year, Dr. Thomas Dwight

(A.B. 1866), equally distinguished as Catholic layman and anatomist, who had learned in Germany the new technique of frozen microscopical sections, succeeded Dr. Holmes in the Parkman Professorship of Anatomy. Two years later Dr. Harold C. Ernst (A.B. 1876) was appointed Demonstrator of Bacteriology, and a laboratory was fitted up for the study of this new science. Thus another professional school was brought up from a low level to a position where it fulfilled young Ephraim Eliot's prophecy of 1783.

Eliot had completely reformed the two oldest professional schools of the University, and established a third, before he had been President three years, before he had reached the age of forty, and at a time when the power and prestige that we now associate with his name were all to come.

The elective system was of much slower growth; for in reforming Harvard College President Eliot had to deal with the core of the University, with an institution already one of the best in the country, with vested academic interests, sentiments and emotions, and Governing Boards composed of elders who, theoretically well disposed toward broadening the curriculum, had to be persuaded to take any practical step. Here there could be no flapjack policy, nor could the intrusion of a Langdell, even if a college teacher of his type had been available, convert a stiff-necked faculty that was largely hostile to change. Eliot himself said in 1894, 'The development of the elective system . . . has proved to be the most generally useful piece of work which this university has ever executed.' And whatever verdict the future may render as to its value, no principle in American higher education has ever spread so rapidly or gone so deep as did the elective principle in the hands of this indefatigable advocate, using Harvard College as an experimental laboratory.

The elective system, as Eliot understood it, meant a free choice by the undergraduate of the studies that he would pursue to the completion of his course for the first degree. A free choice, that is, among such subjects as the University could provide; and that provision, in Eliot's view, must be limited to subjects that were cultural in character, non-vocational, and therefore properly comprehended under a nineteenth-century definition of the Liberal Arts and Sciences. The principle that animated the system, in his mind, was that of liberty — and how he loved that word, and rolled it out, every syllable so carefully enunciated; and how bravely and consistently he lived up to it! He firmly believed that a young man of eighteen or nineteen could choose his course, even among infinite combinations, better than anyone else could do it for him; and he subscribed to what many still regard as heresy, that all non-vocational subjects have an equal cultural or disciplinary value, provided they are equally well taught and studied. Realizing the force of this proviso, he used to advise undergraduates to elect professors rather than subjects — a shrewd bit of wisdom that made the heresy much less execrable.

How radical the elective system was, few Americans of the present day can realize. Curricula in the Liberal Arts had changed through the centuries, but one idea had been constant since the Age of Pericles: an educated man was one who knew certain things. It was assumed that in the process of acquiring these things his mind had gained a power, richness, and openness to ideas which made him a liberally educated man. And now the head of the oldest American university insisted that it did not really matter (within the limits of cultural subjects) what you studied, provided you were interested.

Eliot furthered the elective system for two secondary reasons besides the central and animating one of liberty. It was the only practical method that he could devise of domesticating the new science and learning in the College, or of recruiting pupils for teachers of those subjects. University benefactors were not willing to found chairs in subjects such as American Archaeology and Icelandic Literature, and few would have cared to accept such chairs, unless instruction in those subjects would be 'counted' for the first as well as the second degree, and therefore be elected by undergraduates. This free competition for pupils, and the complete liberty of pupils to sample and experiment without loss of credit, and to develop their tastes to the full once they had found them, gave the Harvard of Eliot's day a splendid freedom and spaciousness. It might have been better — I for one believe that it would have been better — had the Faculty required courses to be taken in coherent groups, like the studies for the Oxford honor schools, or Jefferson's Virginian system, or Ticknor's Modern Language department in Augustan Harvard. That Eliot attempted nothing similar in the College was probably due to practical exigencies — the small teaching staff in 1870, and the unwisdom of introducing new subjects faster than competent instructors could be found, or money provided to support them. But he finally came to rationalize 'spontaneous diversity of choice,' declaring briskly in his Report for 1884–85, 'Groups are like ready-made clothing, cut in regular sizes; they never fit any concrete individual.' He wished every man's curriculum to be tailor-made, and by 1886 it was so, subject only to the limitations imposed by conflict of hours, and the requirement that an introductory course precede an advanced one.

Eliot's belief in freedom of choice of studies has variously been attributed to Unitarianism, democracy, utilitarianism, and even romanticism. Eliot was a Unitarian (of the Channing and Parker rather than the Norton and Walker shade), and a democrat in the Jeffersonian, not the Jacksonian, sense; he leaned toward utilitarianism, and may be blamed for minting two coins, 'leadership' and 'service,' that were promptly clipped and defaced when they left his hands. But what he wished to do in higher education was to apply in that field the shift in control that Jefferson wished to apply in government, and Emerson in society as a whole — the shift from external compulsion and discipline to internal compulsion and discipline. Eliot was poles apart from a Rousseau romanticist. He had few illusions about human nature, and expected that many students would make a hash of the elective system; but he regarded these educational misfits and cripples as of very slight importance. Dean Briggs might fuss with them if he liked; Eliot's interest stopped at the middling sort of college student who might, if he 'made an effort' (a good old puritan phrase that he loved), educate himself at Harvard. He intended liberty primarily for the strong and able who knew what they wanted, and were willing to work for it. Like Wotan in the second act of Siegfried, Eliot struck his staff vigorously on the ground, and declared, 'Helden nur können mir frommen!'

Eliot's achievement in broadening the curriculum — one phase of the elective system with which nobody can quarrel — may best be appreciated by a comparison between college studies in 1869 and 1886. He was a true *amplificator imperii*, an enlarger of the intellectual empire. In the year 1868–69 the Faculty of Arts and Sciences consisted of twenty-three members, and there were 529 undergraduates in College. All freshman studies (Latin, Greek, Mathematics, French, Elocution, Ethics, and Duruy's *Histoire Grecque*) were prescribed. Sophomores had to take Physics and Chemistry, German, Elocution, and themes, and recite twenty chapters of Gibbon's 'Decline and Fall' and 'about 350 pages' of Dugald Stewart; for the rest, they must choose at least eight hours a week from four different classes of Latin (mostly in Cicero and

Terence), two of Greek, four of Mathematics, one of Italian, and one of English (Child's Anglo-Saxon). Juniors had a similar list of electives, with the addition of Chemistry, German, and Natural History to choose from, and were required to take Philosophy and Physics; their prescribed studies were Herschel's Astronomy, Lardner's Optics, Bowen's Logic, Walker's editions of the Scots metaphysicians, lectures in Chemistry, and writing forensics. Spanish and Italian could be taken by juniors as extra subjects without credit, but must be so taken if they wished credit for senior Spanish and Italian — an obvious attempt to discourage students from dropping the ancient and taking up the modern languages. Seniors had five hours a week of required History (Guizot, Arnold, Hallam, Story), Philosophy, Bowen's textbook on Economics, and writing themes; they took two or three electives from a list similar to the junior one. Lectures on Geology and Anatomy by Agassiz and Wyman were 'extra studies' open to seniors, but could not be counted as electives. Each study was rigidly attached to a certain class. If a good Greek scholar wished to read the Antigone and the Alcestis, he had to wait until senior year to do it; nor was the boy who had studied Latin for eight years at school permitted under any circumstances to taste the joys of Juvenal before senior year. And the offering in the modern languages was, if anything, inferior to that of forty years earlier.

In 1870–71 these 'studies' became 'courses' with Arabic numerals attached, and were divorced from the classes; in 1872–73 the student was informed for the first time who would give the course. Every year thereafter, some of the required courses became electives, and every new subject added became an elective automatically. Naturally, professors of the required subjects endeavored to retain the prescription, as 'necessary to a gentleman's education' or 'an indispensable means of broadening the mind and disciplining the intellect.' The elective principle advanced by a series of persuasions in faculty meetings; for Eliot was no dictator, and he had too much common sense to impose a reform in which he believed before those who must administer the reform were ready for it. The Governing Boards, a vigorous minority of the College Faculty, old graduates, and rival educators viewed with alarm the progressive abandonment of prescribed Classics, Philosophy, and Mathematics. But Eliot was young, and could wait. He had the patience of an Indian and the persistence of a beaver. He wore down and outlived all his opponents. And in 1883–84 he was able to announce the 'practical completion of a development which began sixty years ago.' There were now no required courses except freshman English and French (or German), sophomore and junior themes and forensics (which were dropped in 1897), and two easy half-year lecture courses in Physics and Chemistry, which were dropped in 1890 and 1894, respectively. By 1886 the Bachelor's degree could be earned by passing eighteen courses, no two of which need be related, one-quarter of them with a grade of C (sixty per cent) or better; the number of units from which these eighteen could be chosen had expanded to 153 full and 61 half-courses, exclusive of seminars; the Faculty of Arts and Sciences now numbered 61, and the undergraduate body 1080.

Parallel with this enrichment and subdivision went a gradual change in method. The system of deducting demerits from the Scale of Merit was abandoned in 1869; and in 1871 the Faculty voted that 'every instructor may assign his marks in such a manner as he shall judge most equitable and effective.' The rank list thus modified, with the publication of the names of the first to the tenth scholar, and finally the assignment of Commencement parts to them, lasted through the Class of 1887; thereafter three grades of honors at graduation (*cum laude, magna cum laude, summa cum laude*) were assigned automatically by the course grades. A similar latitude was allowed in teaching methods; but as President Eliot strongly disapproved of the old-fashioned daily recitation, he was able to report in 1880 that recitations had 'well-nigh disappeared' except for elementary languages and mathematics courses. Lectures (sometimes with required reading, sometimes not), discussions, and 'Socratic' colloquies between teacher and taught, had become the prevailing methods. At the Commencement dinner in 1886, James Freeman Clarke announced, with delicious irony: 'Formerly, the only business of a teacher was to hear recitations, and make marks for merit. Now, he has the opportunity of teaching. This is one of the greatest educational discoveries of modern times, — that the business of a teacher is to teach.'

We may now glance at some of the more significant details in the widening of the college and graduate-school curricula. History and the Social Sciences were one of the first objects of Eliot's solicitude, and proved to be, after English Literature, the favorite field for undergraduate election, rather than (as had been expected) the natural sciences. When Eliot came in, there was no such thing in America as an academic profession of history: darkness had succeeded the false dawn of Sparks. Ancient, Medieval and Modern, and American Constitutional History were taught out of textbooks by Professor Torrey, an excellent representative of the school of dear old gentlemen who taught history as an avocation. A new university professorship of history was created for Gurney in 1869; but Eliot, who saw an administrative rather than an historical scholar in Gurney, had him elevated to the new deanship in 1870; and as a trial substitute young John Fiske was appointed 'instructor in History for the ensuing term' at a salary of five hundred dollars.

Over Fiske, President Eliot had his first contest with the Overseers. A strong party there objected to a reputed Comtist's being afforded contact with the undergraduate mind; they did not so much object to his University Lectures on Positivism, as these were for advanced students and the public — although that course was described by the religious press as 'Harvard's drive on religion.' The nomination of Fiske as Instructor in History created intense feeling among the Overseers, who confirmed him by the close vote of 12 to 10. Fiske ended his course in June, 1870, amid the applause that always greeted his genial eloquence; but the future author of 'The Critical Period' was not reappointed to his thousand-a-year post. Two years later, he was made assistant librarian, at an assistant professor's salary; and from that point began his career as a popular writer and lecturer on history.

Eliot and Gurney made up their minds to drop Fiske, and net Henry Adams, too long on the loose; and in September, 1870, the famous conversation took place:

'"But, Mr. President, I know nothing about Medieval History." — "If you will point out any one who knows more, Mr. Adams, I will appoint him."'

So, at twenty-four hours' notice, Henry Adams began a new career; and although he was a more advanced 'infidel' than John Fiske, there was no opposition to his appointment, since by long use and wont Adamses were expected to say and do the most outrageous things. Henry Adams had no formal 'equipment' for his task save Latin, French, and German, but the event proved that he needed no more. The account of his brief professoriat in his 'Education' is characteristically headed 'Failure.' Subjectively it was that, because Adams became bored with Cambridge, colleagues, and pupils; and the teasing thought that he should be a power in Washington would never down. Objectively, his teaching was a superb success. He interested and stimulated the average undergraduate, and culled some of the best of them for history; he gave the first historical seminar in this country, and by threatening old Sibley, the Librarian, he inaugurated a simple system that nobody had thought of before, of reserving on a special shelf in the College Library the books needed by students in his course. 'He was the greatest teacher that I ever encountered,' wrote Edward Channing — epitaph enough for any man.

By 1877, when Adams had decided to renew his quest for an education elsewhere,[1] he had founded a department, and a school. And by 1886 his pupils Ephraim Emerton (A.B. 1871), Ernest Young and Freeman Snow (A.B. 1873), Edward Channing (A.B. 1878), and Albert Bushnell Hart (A.B. 1880), two of them after postgraduate study in Germany, were offering nine or ten courses on American and Modern European history, besides seminars. This was little enough in comparison with the historical programme twenty years later; but it was a great deal for that time. When President Eliot reproached Princeton for having but one professor of history, who held recitations on Freeman's 'Outlines,' President McCosh replied testily that one was quite enough — 'I think the numerous narrative histories of epochs is just a let-off to easy-going students from the studies which require thought.'

'At Harvard especially, where so great an interest is taken in all historical and economic studies,' said the undergraduate *Harvard Herald* in 1882, a Civil Service Reform Club should be formed — and it soon was. Already 'Ec. 1' was one of the most popular, though the hardest of courses. Economics, curiously enough, began to expand in Harvard from a branch of Moral Philosophy into a separate discipline, in connection with another incident like the Fiske affair that verged on an

[1] See *Development of Harvard University*, p. 156, for a correction to Adams's own account of the reasons for his resignation.

abuse of academic freedom. The subject had for many years been taught by our old friend Professor Francis Bowen, with recitations on his own 'American Political Economy.' Around 1868, 'Fanny' Bowen, to the consternation of the solid men of Boston, went 'Greenbacker' and advocated the payment of the national debt in paper dollars — as it is being paid today. The solid men first raised a lecture fund to bring to Harvard sound-money men who would inculcate the rising generation with correct Hamiltonian principles. Next, through the Governing Boards, they procured the establishment in 1871 of a university professorship of Political Economy (the first in the country), and the appointment to it of Charles F. Dunbar (A.B. 1851), an authority on the monetary question and for many years editor of the most conservative Boston newspaper. Dunbar became one of Eliot's righthand men, and from him stems the Department of Economics. Two recent Harvard Ph.D.'s, J. Laurence Laughlin and Frank W. Taussig, were appointed instructors in this no longer 'dismal science' in 1878 and 1882, respectively. In 1886–87 they offered a programme of Economic Theory, Economic History, Economic Effects of Land Tenures, History of the Tariff, Public Finance and Banking, and Financial History, besides the introductory courses and several seminars.

In his articles, reports, and inaugural address, President Eliot frequently expressed the idea that if one subject of collegiate study should be emphasized over another, it was English Literature and the writing of our mother tongue. It is therefore a puzzle why it was not until 1876 that his friend Francis J. Child was relieved of the Boylston Professorship of Rhetoric and allowed to bequeath his chore of Freshman English to Adams Sherman Hill (A.B. 1853) of Hill's Rhetoric fame. During the remaining twenty years of his life, Child gave courses on Shakspere, Milton, Bacon, Dryden, Anglo-Saxon, Middle English, and Chaucer. 'I have come here to study Anglo-Saxon,' said a very superior young Harvard graduate to the Master of Balliol, in the early seventies. 'Then,' said Jowett, 'you have come to the wrong place. Professor Child at Harvard knows more on that subject than anyone in Oxford.' 'What? "Stubby" Child! I didn't know *he* knew anything!' By the time Child was ready to retire, his most distinguished pupil, George Lyman Kittredge (A.B. 1882), was already taking over his work. LeBaron Russell Briggs (A.B. 1875) began assisting Hill in 1883; Barrett Wendell (A.B. 1877) launched the famous English 12, the advanced composition course, in 1884; this new development came as a result of agitation in the Overseers over the miserable quality of writing by Harvard students — an obvious result of slighting the classics, which was the very reason why the English Department fought a losing fight for twenty-five years against dropping prescribed classics. And though increasing attention was paid to writing English, instruction in spoken English declined. Elocution became an optional subject in 1872, and student debating lamentably failed to make up the deficiency that had existed since medieval disputations disappeared.

The other modern languages recovered the ground lost since Ticknor resigned. Professor Frederic H. Hedge (A.B. 1825) descended from the Divinity School to be Professor of German in 1872; and the distinguished young German historian Kuno Francke joined the Faculty in 1884. Ferdinand Bôcher returned with Eliot from Technology to teach French; and with his compatriots Adrien Jacquinot and Adolphe Cohn, and Charles Hall Grandgent (first scholar of 1883) and another young instructor, the French Department was covering the language and literature of that country by ten courses in 1886. Grandgent and Edward S. Sheldon were offering four graduate courses in Provençal and Romance Philology the same year. Sheldon (A.B. 1872) undertook the Italian and Spanish instruction; for James Russell Lowell was in the diplomatic service from 1877 to 1885, when he gave his famous courses on Dante and Cervantes for the last time. This chapter is fast becoming a potted catalogue; but how else may one convey the amazing expansion of instruction during Eliot's first seventeen years? The President inherited little aesthetic sense from his ancestors, and had acquired less in his education — he regretted that Romney had ever painted a hussy like Lady Hamilton, and regarded cathedrals as inconvenient and obsolete. But he was distinctly not a philistine; and had no illusions of omniscience; and when his friend and cousin Charles Eliot Norton urged him to find a place in Harvard for the Fine Arts, he responded. That Department opened with a bang in 1874, when one of the most broadly cultured gentlemen of his day received the cautiously worded appointment of 'Lecturer on the History of the Fine Arts as Connected with Literature.' Charles H. Moore, Instructor in Drawing and Water Color, was soon translated from Scientific School to College; and Norton's famous lectures for twenty-four years were the principal means of inculcating in our 'young barbarians at play' an urbane and civilized point of view. Norton was also the moving spirit in organizing the American School of Classical Studies at Athens, one of whose earliest students, Harold N. Fowler (A.B. 1880), offered the first Harvard course on Greek Archaeology, in 1885. Ten years more, and the first Fogg Art Museum was built.

Music, whose surreptitious curricular overture was played under President Walker, made its formal début among the electives in 1871, and four years later John Knowles Paine became full professor; by 1886 he was offering five courses, and had already trained such well-known musicians as William F. Apthorp, Arthur Foote, and Walter R. Spalding, his successor. The Sanders

Theatre concerts of the Boston Symphony Orchestra began in 1881, under Eliot's warm patronage; for this 'opened-out puritan' regarded music as one of the finest disciplines for all-round culture and mental training. Yet these subjects that we have just mentioned aroused the greatest criticism from outsiders. President McCosh amused a New York audience in 1885 by describing the education of future Harvard divines, doctors, and lawyers as dilettante reading of French novels (Bôcher's French 8), dabbling in water-color (Moore's Fine Arts 1), listening to lectures on the English Drama (Child on Shakspere), and piano-playing!

In Philosophy, it is doubtful whether President McCosh approved of any of Eliot's appointments, although he shared a taste for Scots philosophers with 'Fanny' Bowen, who hung on until 1889, long enough to oppose furiously the appointment and promotion of William James. Before that, one of 'Eliot's mistakes' had been eliminated. This was a classmate of his who had been teaching since graduation in the Boston public schools. His attempts to apply public-school discipline to the undergraduates were disastrous, especially after he had been seen leading across the Yard a calf that he had won in a charity bazaar! And so from the ridiculous we mount to the sublime; for Eliot the Roman, with a mind impervious to Greek Philosophy, was directly responsible for the appointment of three out of four of Harvard's matchless philosophical foursome.

George Herbert Palmer (A.B. 1864) was translated from the Greek Department to the vacant instructorship in 1872; William James, after a haphazard Jamesian education (schools and private tutors in three or four countries, painting with La Farge under William Morris Hunt, chemistry and anatomy in the Lawrence Scientific School, medicine in the Harvard Medical School), became Instructor in Physiology the same year, established the first American psychological laboratory in 1876, and became Assistant Professor of Philosophy four years later; Josiah Royce, of California, Göttingen, and Johns Hopkins, substituted for James in 1882–83, and remained at Cambridge for the rest of his days; George Santayana graduated from the College in 1886, and shortly after began the second stage of his captivity among the puritans. Each of these four contributed his peculiar and extraordinary gifts to the University, to learning, and to letters. There was no need to prescribe Philosophy when they were teaching at Harvard, for there were few varieties of undergraduates that one of them at least failed to attract; and graduate students flocked to them from all parts of the country, and from overseas.

The classical discipline already had a distinguished staff in 1869: Sophocles of the ambrosial locks; George Martin Lane of fishball fame; Goodwin of the Greek tenses; James B. Greenough, forever to be associated with Joseph H. Allen (A.B. 1840) as Liddell with Scott; William ('Piggy') Everett, President Everett's brilliant but erratic son; and Clement L. (nickname deleted) Smith. Latin and Greek were both prescribed subjects for freshmen until 1884, and three years later Greek was dropped as an absolute requirement for entrance. As if to make up for his hostility to the classicists' immemorial privilege, Eliot lent vigorous aid in maintaining the fame of their department and in building up the philological side of classical studies. Frederic DeForest Allen, of Oberlin and Leipzig, became the first Harvard Professor of Classical Philology in 1880; John W. White, of Ohio Wesleyan, became Tutor in Greek in 1874, three years before taking his Ph.D., and in 1881 produced the first of our Greek plays, the *Œdipus Tyrannus*, in Sanders Theatre; and Charles P. Parker, a 'first' in Oxford 'Greats,' joined the staff in 1883. These younger men, besides offering a respectable training in Classical Philology for graduate students, began to teach Greek literature to the undergraduates; and when Greek began to be dropped from high schools, they met the challenge by the famous course for beginners that covered in one year what schoolboys stumbled through in three or four.

Mathematics lagged until the nineties; but the biological and natural sciences forged ahead with their rivals in the Social Sciences. To his own subject, Chemistry, Eliot unconsciously dealt a severe blow in exiling Wolcott Gibbs to Physics for purposes of economy. It was the worst mistake that he ever made. Josiah Parsons Cooke carried on; the famous 'Chem. 1' was inaugurated in 1870 by Charles Loring Jackson; Henry B. Hill (A.B. 1869), son of President Hill, introduced the first course in Organic Chemistry in 1873. In Physics Professor Lovering, already a College character of many years' standing, one who regarded the growing interest in electricity as 'only a spurt,' lasted through Eliot's first nineteen years; but Wolcott Gibbs, with courses on the Spectroscope and Thermodynamics, and John Trowbridge (S.B. 1865), a great electrical physicist and one of the most beloved teachers of his day, provided new voltage. Robert W. Willson (A.B. 1873), the astronomer, and Benjamin Osgood Peirce (A.B. 1876) were among Trowbridge's earliest and greatest pupils, and the Jefferson Laboratory was one of the first fruits of his efforts. The Department was offering seven whole and four half courses, besides seminars, in 1886, and was ready to take its part in the astounding development of physical science during the next twenty-five years.

Turning now to the Natural Sciences, Shaler's vivacious and picturesque personality, the excursions on which he took the students, and his advice that they read no geology lest they imbibe wrong notions, made 'Geology 4' the favorite introductory course in the College;

but his pupil William Morris Davis (s.b. 1869) and Josiah D. Whitney, stranded by the collapse of the Mining School in 1875, probably did more for the training of geologists and for the development of the science. Their pupil the mineralogist John E. Wolff (a.b. 1879) was already assisting them in 1886. The Botanical Department, since 1842 carried on by Asa Gray alone, was given four young men of distinguished promise in 1872–74, three of them (George L. Goodale, Charles S. Sargent, and William G. Farlow) from Harvard, and Sereno Watson from Yale. Unfortunately, no one of the three Harvardians could abide the other two. Each intrenched himself in his special herbarium, laboratory, or arboretum, and spent a disproportionate amount of time and energy trying to bag all available students and funds; despite brilliant individual work in research (especially by Farlow in Cryptogamic Botany and by Sargent at the Arnold Aboretum, a department of the University that attained the very highest reputation), this jealousy prevented a well-rounded programme, and hampered Botany at Harvard for almost half a century. Closely allied to these botanical subdivisions in subject-matter, and impartially detested by them all, was the Bussey Institution in Jamaica Plain, established in 1870 with the bequest of Benjamin Bussey as a school of agriculture and horticulture. The competition of land-grant colleges and the want of funds left this institution languishing, despite its distinguished faculty, throughout the Eliot administration; it has only lately begun to flourish as a biological and research station in subjects related to agriculture.

Zoölogy received a double blow in the deaths of Louis Agassiz and Wyman in 1873–74. Eliot wrote that the want of Americans worthy to take their places, or those of Asa Gray and Benjamin Peirce, was a significant proof of the failure of American universities to breed scholars, and the strongest possible argument for a graduate school.

Huxley declined an invitation; and although Hermann Hagen the entomologist was imported from Königsberg,[1] and an American with German training, Edward L. Mark and Walter Faxon (s.d., 1878), were appointed instructors, the glory had departed. Alexander Agassiz, however, continued to enlarge and enrich the Museum, in order to fulfil his father's generous plans for that institution.

'For the past twenty years,' announced Dean Smith in his Report for 1885–86, 'the function of the Faculty . . . has been to watch over' the growth of the elective system, 'and to determine when the time was ripe for each successive stage in its development. For the next few years our problem will be to devise and apply such checks and regulations as experience has shown to be needed.'

'As it is the principal function of a University to train leaders, — men who have originating power, who reach forward, and in all fields of activity push beyond the beaten paths of habit, tradition, and custom, — it is evident that a large measure of liberty is essential for its students.' So Eliot declared in his Report for 1876–77. In that year the Statutes and Laws of Harvard College, the last printed edition of which (1866) had 16 chapters and 204 articles, became so meagre from aggressive pruning that it was replaced by a new set of University Statutes, occupying less than five pages of the Annual Catalogue, and so general in nature that few revisions have been required since. By this time students were on the average a year and a half older than they had been when Eliot was in College, and the meticulous regulations in the old 'College Bible' against smoking in public, walking on Sunday, 'grouping in the Yard' (the Faculty is said to have defined a group as 'two students and the pump'),

---

[1] Hagen was a great scientist, but he never learned enough English to become an effective teacher here. One of his declarations in faculty meeting was long remembered. Demanding a stiffening of entrance requirements, he exclaimed, 'We haf too much *pons asinorum* better *als gut!*'

visiting Boston, and attending the theatre, were abolished. Students began to behave less like boys and more like men. Not that they liked their President. To the average undergraduate he seemed a pretty grim person; his reserve and nearsightedness they mistook for indifference or coldness; his justice for severity. All that he had done to make their studies more varied and pleasant and their life more free, they took for granted. Every Class Day there were loud cheers for Dr. Peabody, but few and feeble for 'Prexy'; the average Harvard man of the period rather envied rival colleges their nice old clerical presidents with white beard and a genial manner.

As one looks back on Eliot's reforms after fifty years, they seem obvious, timely, and necessary. Yet, like most reforms, they created friction, aroused hostile criticism, and required uncommon fortitude and perseverance on the part of the reformer. 'In the first twenty years of my service here,' recalled Eliot on his seventieth birthday, 'I was generally conscious of speaking to men who, to say the least, did not agree with me.' An understatement! President Hyde of Bowdoin declared that 'for the first twenty-five years President Eliot was misunderstood, misrepresented, maligned, hated.' Any outsider who heard the conversation of Boston clubs and drawing-rooms in those days might well have concluded that President Eliot was 'Public Enemy No. 1.'

Eliot's personality enabled him to get things done, but there was nothing in that personality to make his way easier, and much to make it harder. Only the impenetrable armor of the righteous, an intellectual and emotional detachment so rare that few could comprehend it, a belief in God so simple and so deep that few suspected its existence, saw him through. If at any time before 1886, perhaps before 1890, his policies had been referred to a plebiscite of Harvard Alumni, they would surely have been reversed. The Corporation was much less tractable after the appointment of Martin Brimmer, Joseph Henry Thayer, John Quincy Adams, and Alexander Agassiz in 1877–78; it is said that Mr. Brimmer used to pierce Mr. Eliot with a rapier, and Mr. Adams hit him on the head with a bludgeon; but always he came up smiling! In his Report for 1882–83, the President expressed a wish that a few young men might be elected Overseers — there was then nobody on the Board who had graduated later than 1866; the first alumnus even partly educated under Eliot to reach the senior Board was Henry Cabot Lodge (A.B. 1871), in 1884; the first Overseer from outside Massachusetts, Charlemagne Tower (A.B. 1830) of Philadelphia, took his seat the same year.[1]

The years 1885–86 were Eliot's most difficult period, when one false step would have meant the end of his administration. College Faculty and Governing Boards were boiling. The Corporation, it is said, at one point would have asked for his resignation if either of two Fellows could have been persuaded to take the presidency. A committee of the Overseers, led by Moorfield Storey, made a devastating report on the English Department. Another entered upon a fruitless and exhausting investigation of entrance examinations, attendance, and the elective system. Eight New England college presidents, headed by Noah Porter of Yale, begged the Overseers not to drop Greek as a requirement for the Arts degree. There was a strong party among the alumni for awarding a new degree to students who took no classics, forgetting that the content of the Liberal Arts through the centuries had never been constant.

[1] The Reverend Henry W. Bellows (A.B. 1832), then of New York, was elected in 1880, as a result of an effort of the Harvard Club of New York to get representation on the Board; but he was denied a seat on the ground that the Act of 1865 had not repealed the earlier requirement that Overseers be inhabitants of Massachusetts. Before the end of 1880 an act throwing open the Overseers to citizens of any State was passed by the General Court; but it does not appear that Mr. Bellows, who died in 1882, ever took his seat.

There was so much discussion of the President's policies among the alumni that in 1886 the secretaries of several classes sent a questionnaire to candidates for the Board of Overseers selected by the Alumni Association, and circulated among the electors a pamphlet containing their replies, a tabulation of which follows: [1]

1. Should chapel be made voluntary?
2. Should Greek be dropped as a requirement for admission?
3. Should the marking system and rank list be abolished?
4. Should the Medical School be open to women?
5. Should women be admitted to Harvard College?
6. Do you approve of the elective system and its extension?
* Candidates asterisked were elected.
** Defeated in the primary postal ballot, so not on the ballot at the election.

Candidates for Six-Year Term

	1	2	3	4	5	6	Votes
*James F. Clarke '29.....	yes	yes	yes	yes	yes		419
B. Apthorp Gould '44 ...		no		no	no		292
Henry W. Haynes '51 ...	no	no	yes	no		yes	**
Darwin E. Ware '52.....	yes	yes		yes	no	yes	109
Moses Merrill '56.......	yes	no	no	yes			**
Alexander McKenzie '59	yes	yes	yes	yes			227
Charles E. Grinnell '62 .	yes	yes	yes	yes			**
Charles W. Clifford '65 .	yes	yes	yes	yes			**
Thomas S. Perry '66	yes	yes	yes	yes		yes	51
*Henry W. Putnam '69 ..	yes	no	yes			yes	346
Henry Parkman '70	yes	no		yes	no		121

Candidates for Five-Year Term

*T. Jefferson Coolidge '50 .		declined to answer					385
Moses Williams '68	yes	yes	yes	yes		no	236

Candidates for One-Year Term

*Francis C. Lowell '76 ...	yes	no	yes	no		no	507
Henry A. Whitney '46 ..		no answer received					113

[1] I have omitted the three candidates who were re-elected: John O. Sargent '30, Henry Lee '36, and Robert M. Morse '57. Sargent replied evasively, except that he was in favor of voluntary prayers, and the other two did not reply. They received 373, 533, and 509 votes, respectively.

This result may indicate no more than that of most elections of Overseers, when the alumni are apt to vote for the most prominent names; but it is probably significant that the old crusader James Freeman Clarke was the only man who gave an unqualified consent who was elected, and that the one unqualified dissenter, Benjamin Apthorp Gould, was defeated in spite of his world-wide fame as an astronomer. Most significant was the choice of young Lowell, whose letter was a highly intelligent criticism of the new régime. 'I believe that the danger from over-specialization is real and pressing,' he had written. There had not been a Lowell on the Governing Boards since 1877. There was to be one or more, henceforth, until 1933. But if Eliot, like Kubla Khan,

> heard from far
> Ancestral voices prophesying war,

he gave no sign. Disagreement he was so used to, that complete agreement would have made him suspect something wrong; and he looked on no man as a personal rival, much less as an enemy. Even the professors who opposed him most frequently and bitterly in faculty meeting were promptly promoted; and in his successive 'house-cleanings' of the Faculty, when resignations were obtained, or short appointments not repeated, it was apt to be the 'yes-men' who left. Clear in his aims, and confident of their worth, Eliot only hoped to be spared long enough to see them on the way to accomplishment; and it was not until Commencement, 1892, that he permitted himself to approach as near as he ever did to boasting: 'I think we may fairly say we are now well on the way to the complete organization of a university in a true sense.'

The two hundred and fiftieth anniversary of Harvard's founding established a brief 'truce of God.' The College was becoming conscious of her age. Daniel French's ideal statue of John Harvard was presented by Samuel J. Bridge in 1884, and placed in the Delta (whence, twenty-five years later, it was removed to the front of University Hall). A new heraldic seal was adopted, with *Veritas* restored to the three open books, whence it had been banished by President Everett; for the alumni had been fired by Dr. Holmes's sonnet in which he bade Alma Mater cast her 'brave truth on every warring blast.' The anniversary was celebrated on four days, November 5–8, 1886; and great was the preparation, especially in the matter of academic gowns, which for the first time were formally adopted for members of all faculties. Henry Lee, a graduate of the bicentennial Class of 1836, served as Chief Marshal. About twenty-two hundred alumni, and three hundred other guests, including President and Mrs. Cleveland, attended. Forty-two honorary degrees were conferred; but President Cleveland resolutely refused to accept the LL.D. that had been voted by the Governing Boards, on the ground that his education had been scanty, and he could not figure as an eminent lawyer. Complimentary addresses were presented by delegates of the Universities of Cambridge, Edinburgh, and Heidelberg, and by Emmanuel College, represented by Dr. Mandell Creighton. There were reunions of college classes and the Law School Association, and the Scientific School alumni; the students had boat races, a football game, and a jolly procession in which they masqueraded as puritans, Indians, Harvard Washington Corps, Navy Club, and English judges in crimson, ermine, and wig. Oliver Wendell Holmes read one of the last of his occasional poems, including the lines:

> As once of old from Ida's lofty height
> The flaming signal flashed across the night,
> So Harvard's beacon sheds its unspent rays
> Till every watch-tower shows its kindling blaze.
> Caught from a spark and fanned by every gale,

A brighter radiance gilds the roofs of Yale;
Amherst and Williams bid their flambeaus shine,
And Bowdoin answers through her groves of pine;
O'er Princeton's sands the far reflections steal,
Where mighty Edwards stamped his iron heel. . . .

President McCosh took offence at this, and went home early; but that was the only untoward incident.

Phillips Brooks preached a noble sermon on Hebrews xiii. 8. James Russell Lowell delivered a learned and witty oration, as full of quotations from ancient and modern writers as a treatise by Cotton Mather. President Dwight brought the greetings of Yale; Mark Hopkins, those of Williams. President Angell represented the University of Michigan; and for Johns Hopkins, Professor Gildersleeve graciously acknowledged 'We measure everything to-day by the standard of Harvard.' Mr. Justice Holmes, then of the Supreme Judicial Court of Massachusetts, speaking to the Law School alumni, laid down a law of life, of which his own life was the noblest illustration:

Perhaps in America . . . we need specialists even more than we do civilized men. Civilized men who are nothing else are a little apt to think that they cannot breathe the American atmosphere. But if a man is a specialist it is most desirable that he should also be civilized; that he should have laid in the outline of the other sciences as well as the light and shade of his own; that he should be reasonable, and see things in their proportion. Nay, more, that he should be passionate as well as reasonable, — that he should be able not only to explain, but to feel; that the ardors of intellectual pursuit should be relieved by the charms of art, should be succeeded by the joy of life become an end in itself.

But the highest note was struck by President Eliot:

The brief history of modern civilization shows that in backward ages universities keep alive philosophy, and in progressive ages they lead the forward movement, guiding adventurous spirits to the best point of onward departure. They bring a portion of each successive generation to the confines of knowledge, to the very edge of the territory already conquered, and say to the eager youth: 'Thus far came our fathers. Now press you on!'

'Press on! press on!' might have been Eliot's own motto. No one better than he knew that his work was but half accomplished; yet how much had been accomplished in those seventeen fruitful years! The elective system widely extended, the Graduate School founded, the Law and Medical Schools reorganized and given new standards of excellence and efficiency. Many men, deans and professors, had co-operated to bring this about; the generosity of alumni, implementing their loyalty to Alma Mater and their faith in her mission, had met needs readily, even when hardly convinced that they were desirable. Yet Joseph H. Choate spoke the literal truth when he said of Eliot in 1894: 'His brain conceived, his hand had guided, his prudence had sustained, the great advance.'

XV

THE HARVEST SEASON

PRESIDENT ELIOT was only fifty-two years old in 1886, with twenty-three years of service ahead as President of the University. The last man disposed to rest on his laurels, he and the University went on from strength to strength. The first experimental period of the elective system was at an end. Almost everyone on the Governing Boards and the College Faculty agreed that it was a success, in principle, but needed reform in application. During the 1870's, Harvard enrolment had increased only 3.7 per cent, as against 37.3 per cent for Yale, 34 per cent for Princeton, and 61 per cent for Williams. Parents still preferred to send their sons, and schools their pupils, to colleges with the traditional prescribed curriculum. But by 1885, apparently, the public was converted, for numbers at Harvard increased 66.4 per cent in the eighties, and 88.8 per cent in the nineties, — an increase greater than that of any of the larger colleges and universities, except Cornell and Princeton in the former decade, and Brown in the latter. American college education had at last become painless; no wonder that it was popular. Enrolment continued to swell until about 1903, when the progressive advance in numbers stopped, with the immediate result of a deficit, which the graduates made up by subscribing a Teachers' Endowment Fund of over two million dollars.

Of new buildings, there is very little to chronicle in this era, apart from those erected to house new departments and laboratories. Most of the new construction by the University was north of the Yard; and a good beginning was made, mostly by gifts from graduating classes, toward enclosing the Yard with a handsome brick wall and iron fence. The new main gate between Harvard and Massachusetts, designed by McKim, Mead and White, was named after Samuel Johnston (A.B. 1855) of Chicago, one of the first western graduates to remember the College in his will.

Under the new régime of liberty, and with the declining vogue of family prayers, the daily 'college prayers' were becoming more and more irksome to students. After the suspension of them for five months in 1871–72, when Appleton Chapel was being repaired, had produced no apparent moral or disciplinary relapse, Eliot proposed that attendance be made voluntary; but the Overseers' permission was prevented by the unexpected opposition of Ralph Waldo Emerson. In 1881, when Dr. Andrew P. Peabody retired, the experiment was tried of putting the hour forward from 7.45 to 8.45, and having prayers conducted by a series of local ministers representing three or four different Protestant denominations. 'The service is impressive, edifying, and interesting,' Eliot reported; but neither students nor Faculty agreed, and each body repeatedly petitioned the Governing Boards to make attendance voluntary; but for several years these petitions were invariably rejected by the Governing Boards.

The Reverend Francis G. Peabody (A.B. 1869) succeeded his cousin Andrew in 1886 as Plummer Professor, one of whose duties was to conduct prayers. The compulsive feature of this college congregation reminded young Dr. Peabody unpleasantly of his experience in preaching at the State Prison. With the aid of Phillips Brooks, then an Overseer, he persuaded the Governing Boards that the interests of religion in the College demanded an end of this blasphemous parody of worship. For compulsory 'college prayers' there was substituted in the fall of 1886 a daily 'religious service' which nobody was compelled to attend. The stipends of the Board of College Preachers were raised to a figure which made it possible for distinguished clergymen of Boston and other cities to devote a week or two each term to conducting the week-day and Sunday services. The first Board consisted of Edward Everett Hale, Phillips Brooks, Alexander McKenzie, and George A. Gordon; within three years Lyman Abbott had come on from Brooklyn, and Henry Van Dyke from Princeton, and some of the younger clergymen, like William Lawrence, were brought into the Board of Preachers by the sapient Dr. Peabody, who as chairman administered the system admirably. Under Warren A. Locke (A.B. 1869), organist and choirmaster from 1882 to 1910, an excellent choir of boys and men was trained. As this was the first abandonment of compulsory chapel by any American college, it aroused tremendous interest. Almost everyone concerned thought the experiment a success. The cry of 'godless Harvard' was of course raised; but an Edinburgh divine who visited us in 1887 after attending eight other American colleges where chapel was still compulsory, said that Harvard's was 'the most *religious* service, public or private,' that he had seen on his tour. For many years the daily congregations were numbered by the hundred; Appleton was sometimes crowded to the doors, and earnest seekers after spiritual guidance visited the preacher's study in Wadsworth House. The same system still obtains, *diminuendo*; preachers as eminent and inspiring as their predecessors now address daily congregations numbering a bare score or two, in the beautiful new Memorial Chapel.

The abolition of compulsory prayers, the influence of Dr. Peabody's new courses in Social Ethics, and the example of Toynbee Hall (the first social settlement in London) enhanced the religious interest in Harvard College, and gave it a definite turn toward philanthropy. The College Y.M.C.A. had about two hundred members in 1890; the St. Paul's Society of Episcopalians (who by this time numbered more adherents in the College than any other denomination) flourished; but the Christian Brethren, the old evangelical society, died. Volunteer Bible classes attracted many students; settlement work in Boston appealed to others, and two Cambridge night schools, the Prospect Union and the Social Union, were conducted by student volunteers. The College Conferences, a student forum that was organized in 1887, discussed such topics as The Belief in Immortality under Professor C. C. Everett, and Problems of Charity under Arthur Treadway White, besides welcoming a host of lecturers on the uplifting and public-service strains that appealed to youthful idealism as the century drew to a close. Phillips Brooks House, 'dedicated to Piety, Charity, and Hospitality,' was opened in 1900 as a home for the religious and charitable organizations supported by the student body.

In other respects *fin de siècle* marked the zenith of undergraduate liberty at Harvard. It was in 1886 that 'discretionary supervision' of attendance at scholastic exercises, as the Dean discreetly termed it, was adopted. 'Opportunity with responsibility' was the slogan of this hopeful era; all students welcomed the one, but most were quite willing to let the Dean and the Faculty shoulder the other. 'Discretionary supervision' meant in practice that upperclassmen could cut classes at will; and term-time trips to New York, Montreal, and Bermuda became all too common. The Faculty remained in blissful ignorance of this new definition of liberty until it was called to their attention by a careless student and his irate father. The lad had left Cambridge for the more genial climate of Havana, writing a series of post-dated letters, which his chum was supposed to mail to his parents at proper intervals. Unfortunately, his 'goody' placed the lot in the mail; the alarmed father came to Cambridge, and no officer of the University had the remotest idea where the son might be. Shortly after, the Overseers offered the Faculty the choice between holding a daily morning roll-call and checking attendance in classes. They chose the latter.

The year 1886–87 also saw the abolition of the last vestiges of Quincy's old Scale of Merit. No further effort was made to determine the first ten scholars of each class on a numerical scale, and lettered grades were adopted for grading performance in courses. One could graduate with a minimum of C in one-quarter of one's eighteen courses, and D in the rest. Even after the proportion of C's was raised to one-half in 1892–93, Harvard had the reputation of being 'the hardest college to get into and the easiest to stay in.' The first part of this proposition was undoubtedly true. Admission requirements were steadily raised during Eliot's administration by requiring higher attainments in the traditional trinity of Classics, Mathematics, and Modern Languages, and by adding new requirements in such subjects as English (in 1874), History, and Science. What is now called the 'Old Plan' of admission, the accumulation of 'points' in a preliminary and a final entrance examination, like a junior elective system, began in the late seventies and was perfected in 1902. For some years, President Eliot had been urging uniformity in college entrance examinations, without succeeding in bringing our rivals up to what he considered the proper level. Harvard entrance examinations were given at over fifty different places in the United States, at considerable expense. The College Entrance Examination Board, formed without Harvard's participation at the turn of the century, threatened to isolate the College as far as secondary-school preparation was concerned; and it was probably fortunate that in 1906 the Faculty persuaded itself that the Board's standards were sufficiently exacting, and accepted their examinations in all subjects.

One result of raising the entrance requirements was to lift the average age of entering freshman from around eighteen at the beginning of Eliot's administration to nineteen in 1883; and as the Law and Medical and Graduate Schools either had required the Bachelor's degree for entrance or would shortly do so, this meant that a Harvard student could not begin a professional career before the age of twenty-six or twenty-seven. After appeals to parents and schools had failed to lower the age, President Eliot came to the conclusion that the only remedy was to reduce the standard college course to three years. The first move to make this possible was the privilege accorded in 1881-82 of 'anticipating' three out of five of the freshman courses by extra points in the entrance examinations. The Faculty recommended in 1891 that only sixteen instead of eighteen courses be required for the Bachelor's degree, but this, to their great honor, was defeated by the Overseers. Nevertheless, many ambitious students, by 'anticipation,' taking six or even seven courses a year instead of four or five, and picking up a course or two in Summer School, were able to get through in three years. It was also provided that degrees could be conferred at midyears, which allowed seniors to begin looking for a job in January instead of June. Another concession was granted to the classes of 1903 and after: the course requirement was reduced to $17\frac{1}{2}$ (or 17 if English A was passed with a grade of C, or 16 if that course was 'anticipated'), and 'class spirit' was placated by allowing the name of a three-year graduate to be entered in the Quinquennial among those who entered College with him. But at that point the Faculty dug in its heels and refused to allow further reduction in requirements so that the average student could graduate in three years. The top of the curve of three-year B.A.'s was reached with 36 per cent of the Class of 1906; from that point it has fallen to less than one per cent. But a large number of the three-year or three-and-a-half-year men did not leave College immediately, or enter a professional school. Many remained a fourth year and enrolled in the Graduate School of Arts and Sciences, often obtaining their second degree in four years. Franklin D. Roosevelt '04 was one of those who did this; he 'anticipated' four courses, took fifteen — half of them in political science — in the next three years, and graduated B.A., after which he took five more courses as a member of the Graduate School. The medieval *septennium* with which Harvard began was completely shattered; but the average age of taking the M.A. was the same as in John Harvard's day.

During the years 1889–91 there was an administrative reorganization of the College and the Graduate School, and a partial amalgamation of both with the Lawrence Scientific School. This last institution never fulfilled the expectation of its founders. Eliot, realizing from his recent experience at the Massachusetts Institute of Technology that the L. S. S. could never rival the M. I. T. as a polytechnic, made overtures for an amalgamation in 1870, but was repelled. The Lawrence Scientific School was then reorganized, the courses in the natural and physical sciences given over to Harvard College, and a series of three- and four-year programmes offered in different fields of engineering and practical science. These were not a success; and enrolment in the School dropped to fourteen students by 1886. In 1890 the Faculty of the Scientific School was combined with that of the College as the Faculty of Arts and Sciences. Henceforth practically all the courses at the School could be taken by students in the College, or vice versa; gradually the only real distinction between the A.B. and S.B. degrees came to be that candidates in Arts entered the University with, and those in Science without, Latin. A college student might do practically all his work in

Engineering and yet receive the A.B. degree; conversely, a student in the Scientific School might graduate with highest honors in English or History. Two other attempts were made in Eliot's presidency to 'unload' the engineering courses on the Massachusetts Institute of Technology, and convert the Lawrence Scientific School into a graduate school of science; but both failed.

In 1890 the College Faculty (which was also the Faculty of the Graduate School) and the Scientific School Faculty were combined as the Faculty of Arts and Sciences, 62 strong. This Faculty was divided into twelve Divisions, each including all the teachers in one broad field of study; and the larger Divisions into Departments. For instance, the Division of Modern Languages included the Departments of English, German, Romance Languages, and (beginning 1906) Comparative Literature. By 1905 the Faculty of Arts and Sciences had over 150 members. It still functioned as a deliberative body; and the old chapel in University Hall was restored as the Faculty Room in 1896 to accommodate it; but many of its functions were delegated to standing committees on Instruction, Admission, etc., and to three Administrative Boards for the College, the Scientific School, and the Graduate School.

In his early years President Eliot followed the practice of his predecessors in making all appointments himself (subject of course to a favorable vote by both Governing Boards of the University), consulting informally some of the professors and the Dean of the Faculty. For a time he used the Academic Council — a body consisting of all the professors of all faculties — as an advisory board for appointments, and for a time, the College Faculty; but both methods were too cumbersome. After the administrative reorganization of 1889–91 the constitutional practice grew up of the President submitting to the Corporation only those appointments and promotions that had been suggested or accepted by the Committee of Professors in the appropriate department and passed upon by the Dean of the Faculty. The President and Fellows have always reserved the right to make appointments over the heads of the professors; but this right has only been resorted to occasionally, as in the case of departments that distinctly needed gingering up. Unlike those of most American universities, the departments of the Faculty of Arts and Sciences have had chairmen, rather than heads, presiding officers rather than rulers; every professor enjoys an equal power in promoting the younger men, and in calling full professors from elsewhere — but the financial powers of the Corporation have given it a very effective veto on expansion.

In addition to the regular courses, the Corporation in 1897 tried to institute something like the German *Privatdocent*, permitting the Faculty to authorize any Doctor of Philosophy or of Science resident in Cambridge, whether or not connected with the University, to offer a course of his own, and fix and collect the fees. The elective offering was so rich that few doctors and still fewer students availed themselves of this privilege, and by the end of Eliot's administration the practice had died out.

A rapid review of new appointments, new departments, and new departures in departments already established will indicate something of the progressive enrichment of the offering in College and Graduate School during this second part of Eliot's administration.

In the Classics and Classical Philology, this was the era when Morris Hicky Morgan, Clifford H. Moore (A.B. 1889), E. K. Rand (A.B. 1894), and Charles B. Gulick (A.B. 1890) began their fruitful careers of teaching and scholarship; and at the same period, John H. Wright, a Dartmouth graduate, and Minton Warren, a graduate of Tufts, were called to Harvard from Johns Hopkins.

Herbert Weir Smyth, a fellow-member with Paul Shorey of the distinguished Class of 1878, was called from Bryn Mawr to the Eliot Professorship of Greek in 1901 in order to strengthen the literary side of the Classics department, which was now somewhat overloaded on the philological. In English, Wendell, Kittredge, Briggs, and Neilson were the giants of those days; the first two broke many a lance with Eliot in faculty meetings. Bliss Perry, a scholar and man of letters, came from Princeton at the close of the era; gladly did he teach, and eagerly did one learn from him. George P. Baker (A.B. 1887), instructor the year after, got ready for his remarkable though short-lived practical school of the drama. John Hays Gardiner introduced the literary study of the English Bible, against the violent objection of one of his colleagues that he knew no Hebrew; and Charles T. Copeland (of whom more anon) began his long term of unrivalled influence among the students.

Von Jagemann was called from Indiana in 1889, and Horatio S. White from Cornell in 1902, to be colleagues to Francke. William H. Schofield, a Canadian, introduced courses in the Scandinavian languages and organized the Department of Comparative Literature; his fellow-countryman Frederick Caesar de Sumichrast was the popular lecturer in Romance Languages and Literature, but Grandgent, Bôcher, and E. S. Sheldon were the only real scholars in the department until 1895, when Jeremiah Denis Matthias Ford, the year after his graduation, rescued the Spanish damsel from her long and unmerited neglect. Fred N. Robinson (A.B. 1891) began offering courses in the Celtic languages and literatures in 1896; and Leo Wiener, a Russian exile, one of the most remarkable linguists and teachers of languages we have ever had, began teaching Russian the same year. In 1902 Kuno Francke arranged the exchange professorship with Germany, and Barrett Wendell brilliantly inaugurated the

French exchange on the James Hazen Hyde foundation in 1904. The visit of Prince Henry of Prussia in 1902 brought to a culmination Francke's efforts to establish a Germanic Museum; the first collection, in the Old Gymnasium, was opened in 1903. Bliss Perry, reading at the British Museum in the summer of 1887, encountered an old Williams acquaintance, a brilliant Jew named Charles Gross, who had taken his Ph.D. at Göttingen *summa cum laude* and was continuing his researches on English institutional history. Gross had applied for a teaching position at one college after another, without success, and was on the point of returning to his father's clothing business in Troy, New York. On March 2, 1888, Ernest Young (A.B. 1873), a pupil of Henry Adams, of whom great things were expected, fell a victim to overwork only two months after his promotion to a full professorship. President Eliot decided to fill the vacancy by appointing two young instructors instead of one professor, which would allow the department to expand without further funds. For the modern side, George Bendelari (A.B. 1874) was called from Yale to an instructorship; he proved inadequate, and was swept out in the 'housecleaning' of 1893. Gross applied to President Eliot for an opportunity to teach medieval history. At that time he was personally unknown to anyone at Harvard, and only his Göttingen dissertation on *Gilda Mercatoria* and an article or two had been published. But Eliot, with his uncanny flair for men of parts in subjects that he knew nothing about, seized the opportunity and by return mail invited Gross to accept an instructorship for one year, 'as an experiment.' The experiment turned out so well that Charles Gross made his career at Harvard. He continued, with complete professional competence, the study of medieval institutions that Henry Adams had inaugurated with amateur brilliance; his 'History 9,' on the Constitutional History of England, became one of the famous courses in the social sciences; and under his pupil Charles H. McIlwain (PH.D. 1911) it still is.

Channing and Hart at this period made Harvard the American centre for the study of American History. Archibald Cary Coolidge (A.B. 1887) began teaching the history of Northern and Eastern Europe in 1894. The year 1902 is memorable in the annals of History at Harvard, for in that year Roger B. Merriman (A.B. 1896) bounded from Oxford into the hearts of the Harvard undergraduates; Charles H. Haskins, indisputably first among American medievalists, and a man whose energy, erudition, and character inspired the entire department to high endeavor, was called from Wisconsin; and George Foot Moore came to us from Yale, via Andover, to teach the History of Religions. Moore combined in a rare degree scholarship and humanity; no one has ever excelled him as a teacher of undergraduates and a trainer of advanced students.

Government was inseparable from History until 1892, when courses on the former subject were so named; but for another decade Government courses were given by members of the History Department and the Law Faculty. Mr. A. Lawrence Lowell, appointed part-time Lecturer in 1897, was the first to give his entire attention to Government; and William Bennett Munro (PH.D. 1900), who began his famous course on Municipal Government in 1904, was the second. The first course in the College on International Law was given by Freeman Snow in 1886–87.

After the death of Dunbar in 1900, the successive appointments of Carver of Cornell, Ripley of Columbia, Gay of Michigan, and Bullock of Wisconsin made the Harvard Economics Department one of the most distinguished in the country.

Sociology began to be taught at Harvard, like Economics, as a branch of Moral Philosophy; but it remained fast to ethical moorings for some sixty years after the other discipline broke loose. This happened because the subject was first taken up and developed by Francis G. Peabody. His pioneer course of 1883, which after several changes in title became Social Ethics 1, was an approach to contemporary social problems in terms of Christianity. Although nicknamed 'Drains, Drink, and Divorce' by the irreverent, this course did succeed in awakening young men to their social responsibilities; and it expanded into a department, with a share of the new Emerson Hall (1906). At that time Jeffrey R. Brackett (A.B. 1883) was called from Johns Hopkins to establish a school for professional social workers under the joint control of Harvard and Simmons College. The advance of Sociology as a science was making the religious approach somewhat difficult to maintain in a secular university; the Corporation somewhat inconsistently withdrew its support from the School of Social Workers, and then set up a new Department of Sociology.

Psychology was another subject that strained at its Aristotelian leash to Philosophy throughout this period. Hugo Münsterberg, a pupil of Wundt whom James had met and admired, was called from Freiburg in 1892 at the age of twenty-nine to take charge of the psychological laboratory in Dane Hall; the new laboratory in Emerson Hall was opened in 1905. He received a permanent appointment five years later, and soon became a character, one of the 'famous professors' with whom Harvard was identified in the eyes of the public. Although Münsterberg is regarded as a forerunner of the behaviorists, and his pupil and collaborator R. M. Yerkes (A.B. 1898) inaugurated the study of animal behaviorism; the influence of James and Münsterberg has always kept psychology an experimental science at Harvard, with close biologico-medical connections, rather than an art, philosophy, or quack religion. In the main fields of Philosophy the three Olympians of the earlier period, Palmer, James, and Royce, flourished through this; and in 1889 found a Phoebus Apollo in the shape of Santayana.

Mathematics had its renaissance in 1890–91 when William F. Osgood (A.B. 1886) and Maxime Bôcher (A.B. 1888) were appointed instructors, after taking their doctorates in Germany. They established new standards and traditions, more notably the principle to which almost every other department had already conformed, that permanent members must contribute to the advancement of learning, and be willing and able to make themselves clear to undergraduates. Julian L. Coolidge (A.B. 1895), one of the earliest pupils of Osgood and Bôcher, joined the staff in 1899.

In Chemistry, Theodore W. Richards, Nobel prize-winner, began his Harvard career of thirty-seven years in 1891; his pupil and successor Gregory P. Baxter joined the staff in 1897, and Charles R. Sanger two years later; of the older men, Jackson and Henry Barker Hill carried on. The chemical laboratory in Boylston Hall now came into its own as one of the leading centres of chemical research in the New World. Physics took many 'spurts' unanticipated by Lovering, now that the Jefferson Laboratory was in operation; Trowbridge and Edwin H. Hall and B. O. Peirce of the older period were the leading figures; Wallace C. Sabine, like Jackson in Chemistry a recruiter of scientists from the undergraduate body, reached the height of his reputation; the researches into the spectrum inaugurated by Trowbridge were carried many steps further by his pupils Theodore Lyman (A.B. 1897) and William Duane (A.B. 1893). All the scientific teachers at Harvard in this period were much more heavily burdened with teaching duties, especially in connection with undergraduates, than they are today; as Eliot admitted, it required something approaching a 'fanatical zeal' to do research as well, until the very end of the century.

In Geology and Geography, Shaler and Davis reigned supreme; Jay B. Woodworth became instructor in 1893, even before obtaining his S.B. degree; Robert Tracy Jackson (s.b. 1884) took charge of Paleontology from 1899; Meteorology broke off under Davis's pupil Robert DeCourcy Ward in 1895. The same year a Department of Mineralogy and Petrography was organized, with John E. Wolff in charge and Charles Palache as assistant. Botany continued its chosen process of subdivision and specialization, with its numerous laboratories, herbaria, and institutions, to which the Atkins Botanic Garden and Laboratory near Soledad, Cuba, was added in 1900, and the Harvard Forest at Petersham, Massachusetts (under the much-beloved Richard T. Fisher as director), in 1907. The famous glass flowers began to arrive in 1887. Benjamin L. Robinson, who graduated that year, became Curator of the Gray Herbarium in 1892 and Professor of Systematic Botany seven years later; his friends and pupils Merritt L. Fernald (s.b. 1897) and Oakes Ames (a.b. 1898) became instructors at the turn of the century. Both have contributed to the restoration of harmony among Harvard botanists, and have negotiated alliances with the biological sciences.

Instruction in Zoölogy expanded under Edward L. Mark (Hersey Professor in 1885), George H. Parker (appointed instructor in 1888, the year after his graduation from the Scientific School), William E. Castle, who about ten years later began to make his notable contributions to genetics, and Herbert W. Rand, who was of the same vintage. The Museum of Comparative Zoölogy continued to grow under the able if autocratic direction of Alexander Agassiz, and largely through his own munificence — in fifteen years he spent over three-quarters of a million of his own money on the Museum. President Eliot, in a splendid tribute to Agassiz, characteristically included a mild rebuke for not 'making any communication on the subject' of his gifts to the President and Fellows.

Instruction in the Fine Arts, first offered by Norton and Charles Moore in 1874, grew rapidly after 1890. The Fogg Art Museum (lately renamed after its architect, Richard Morris Hunt) was built in 1894–95. The first lectures on the History of Architecture, given by Herbert Langford Warren in 1893, were so successful that within two years a well-rounded programme on the historical and artistic aspects of Architecture was offered, and Frederick Law Olmsted, Jr. (A.B. 1894), introduced Landscape Architecture in 1901. Robinson Hall was built the same year, and a Department of Architecture was created in the Scientific School in 1906, but not until Lowell's administration did we have the Graduate Schools of Architecture and Landscape Architecture. In the residuary Department of Fine Arts, there were seven courses open to undergraduates by 1908. Together with Santayana's Aesthetics, and courses under the Classical, German, and French Departments, and with the Germanic Museum and the Museum of Fine Arts in Boston as 'laboratories,' the department offered a well-rounded curriculum for students preparing for an artistic or architectural career, and a limited programme for those primarily interested in literature or history.

The allied field of Egyptology began with a single course by George A. Reisner (A.B. 1889) in 1896, but was promptly interrupted by Dr. Reisner's departure to direct excavations in Egypt; since that time the introductory course has been offered only once every three or four years, by Dr. Reisner or Dr. Albert N. Lythgoe (A.B. 1892), when they are not occupied with the field work supported jointly by the University and the Boston Museum of Fine Arts. Egyptology was an outgrowth of a belated attempt to restore Harvard to her once unique eminence as the New World centre for Oriental Languages. Since the early nineteenth century these had been studied only in the Divinity School, and not much there; but in 1880 Charles R. Lanman (PH.D. Yale 1873), a forthright and vigorous gentleman, and a scholar of unusual depth, precision, and imagination, was called from Johns Hopkins to be Professor of Sanskrit. For half a century Lanman taught Indic Philology and everything connected with it; the first edition of his famous 'Sanskrit Reader' dates from 1884. Crawford H. Toy (A.M. Virginia 1856, and sometime private of artillery, C.S.A.) was called from the Southern Baptist Theological Seminary to the historic Hancock professorship of Hebrew in 1880, and two years later his pupil David G. Lyon, who had been studying Assyriology at Leipzig under Delitzsche, was appointed to the long-suspended Hollis chair of Divinity. Let us hope that Thomas Hollis was gratified to have at last a Baptist on his foundation, even though his job was to teach Semitic Languages and not Divinity! Unfortunately this division of learning never made much appeal to undergraduates, and therefore did not acquire the funds to build up a school of Oriental Languages comparable to that of Leningrad. Such is one of the unfortunate limitations caused by Harvard's collegiate origin. Except for a brief residence in the seventies by a Chinese professor, who died in Cambridge, no serious attempt to introduce the study of Far Eastern Languages was made before the Lowell administration. Nevertheless, in the Semitic and Indic departments, the Harvard group made some notable contributions to learning. The Semitic Museum, the gift of Jacob H. Schiff, was opened in 1903, and Harvard excavations in Samaria began five years later. Lanman initiated the Harvard Oriental Series, thirty-two volumes of which, almost all edited by him, are one of the glories of the University.

Astronomy, fortunately, is a subject of such widespread popular interest that the Observatory never had to trouble itself with catering to undergraduates. Nevertheless, they became interested as soon as Astronomy was revived as a subject of undergraduate study, by Robert W. Willson of the Physics Department, in 1891. Twelve years later he converted old 'Zoölogy Hall,' the frame building that had been moved to Jarvis Street, into an astronomical laboratory and classroom for the young men. 'Astronomy 1' became a popular introductory course, and the practical course on Navigation attracted amateur seamen in large numbers. At the main Observatory, this was the Pickering era: Edward C. Pickering (s.b. 1865), aided by his brother William, and a corps of expert observers and computers, undertook a complete photometry of the stars, and a photometric survey of the entire heavens, combined with important researches in stellar spectroscopy — a programme that required imagination to initiate, and persistence and the co-operation of many, both as observers and donors, to carry through. In order to extend the work to the Southern Hemisphere, a station of the Harvard Observatory was equipped at Arequipa, Peru. The Meteorological Observatory on the Great Blue Hill was founded by Abbott Lawrence Rotch in 1884, the year that he graduated from the Massachusetts Institute of Technology. The next year it became a department of Harvard University, with Mr. Rotch as director, and served not only as a research station in matters of great practical value for aëronauts, navigators, and farmers, but as a liaison with the great meteorological stations of the Old World.

Although the Peabody Museum of American Archaeology and Ethnology was founded and began its publications in President Hill's administration, and completed the nucleus of its present building on Divinity Avenue in 1877, instruction in those subjects and in Anthropology did not begin until 1891, after Frederic Ward Putnam (s.b. 1862), Curator of the Museum, had been made professor as well. For a few years Putnam had only a few graduate students to teach, but in 1894 he followed the usual trend of research institutions at Harvard in offering a general course that was open to undergraduates. With the aid of pupils (notably Roland B. Dixon, Alfred M. Tozzer, and Herbert J. Spinden), Putnam was offering a full programme on Anthropology, American Archaeology, Ethnography, Somatology, and American Indian Languages and Hieroglyphics by the time that he retired, in 1909; and the collections had been enriched through explorations of members of the Museum staff and their pupils in Africa, Southwestern United States, and ancient Mayapan.

The 'three-group' system of courses went into effect in 1890; the lowest 'primarily for undergraduates,' the middle 'for undergraduates and graduates,' and the highest 'primarily for graduates.' The lowest has tended to diminish, and to be confined to introductory or beginners' courses only. The middle group includes most of the courses that undergraduates take, and is very extensively elected by first-year graduate students. The graduate courses are frequently elected by seniors who are specializing in the field. Counting those of all three groups in the Catalogue for 1907–08, but excluding the personal or '20' courses that were very seldom taken by undergraduates, in that year 189 full and 254 half-courses were actually taken by students in Harvard College or the Scientific School, and in addition 49 whole and 87 half-courses were offered or bracketed. Naturally the student body was unevenly distributed among these courses, and free election was limited both by conflicts in hours and by the requirement, waived only for especially able undergraduates (but not applied to graduate students), that an introductory course in the lowest group must be passed 'satisfactorily' before a student could elect any of the middle group in that subject.

In addition to the courses, there were many special lectures and readings in this era that were open to the university and the public generally. To take the year 1906–07 as an example: Gilbert Murray's lectures that he published as 'The Rise of the Greek Epic'; twelve readings and lectures by 'Copey'; Major Darwin's lectures on Municipal Ownership and another set of lectures on Socialism; Paul Vinogradoff on Constitutional History; Henry Arthur Jones on the Modern Drama; five lectures on 'Der Junge Goethe und Goethe's Faust' by Kühnemann of Breslau; eight lectures in French on the social history of France by the Vicomte d'Avenel; five 'popular scientific' lectures, illustrated, by Wolff, Tozzer, Davis, Goodale, and D. W. Johnson; the Longfellow centenary, celebrated with addresses by Norton, Howells, and others; and at the Harvard Union, T. P. O'Connor, William Jennings Bryan, Dr. Grenfell, Jacob Riis, Booker T. Washington, and President Roosevelt were heard by large undergraduate audiences. All the world seemed to be flowing through Harvard Square.

By the dawn of the twentieth century the 'pure' elective system seemed to be as firmly established as the trivium and quadrivium in the middle ages. Every large college or university in the country had adopted it except Yale (which did so in 1904); the idea had been 'sold' to the American public; there was something spacious and compelling about the fat college catalogues of the period, the Sears, Roebucks of the educational world, that proclaimed to the youth of the land: 'We teach everything. Come and learn anything!' Eliot had outlived most of his early critics; success had silenced others. The students loved the elective system, for it offered the fullest opportunity to those who wished to learn, and interfered very little with the social life of students who did not care to study. But the teachers who gave courses and the deans who administered the system were very uneasy about it;

especially about the large lecture courses in which hundreds of students were enrolled. This tendency of undergraduates to gang up in certain introductory courses had been growing fast; in 1902–03 there were thirteen courses with over 200, and six (the introductory courses in History, Government, Economics, Geology, and English) with over 400 enrolled. In such courses the lecturer had to be an expert to hold his audience, and it was doubtful whether the average attendant did anything more than take notes on the lectures, if that; since, in order to meet the needs of idle or socially preoccupied members of these large courses, the 'Widow Nolen' and other private tutors organized a system of intensive cramming with printed notes, abstracts of required reading, and pre-examination reviews, which completely defeated the object of the College to 'educate' her sons.

A 'Committee on Improving Instruction,' of which the leading members were Dean Briggs, Professors Lowell, Byerly, and Morgan, and O. M. W. Sprague (A.B. 1894), then a young instructor in Economics, was appointed by the Faculty of Arts and Sciences in the spring of 1902. The Committee spent an entire academic year on investigation, compiled over seventeen hundred reports on courses by individual students, and issued a report that is the most complete and searching analysis of our system of instruction in three centuries. It exposed many defects in the elective system that have been remedied in the last thirty years, with some others that are inherent in education and are not likely to be remedied as long as students are students and teachers are teachers. The Committee appeared to be naïvely astonished at their 'discovery' that undergraduates spent only about half as much time in study as the instructors thought they should, and that a student's appreciation of courses and professors varied in direct proportion to the grade that he obtained. But they uncovered an alarming amount of

slipshod teaching, haphazard organization of undergraduates' studies, and dilettantism. The large lecture
course which clearly met a real need was vindicated; but
the Committee recommended that those courses in which
little or no reading was required should be stiffened up,
that the taking of more than five courses in one year be
discouraged, and that the quality of assistants be improved. Yet it deprecated 'any action of the Faculty
which might hamper the individual instructor in teaching as he thinks fit.' A perusal by the instructor of the
students' reports was generally sufficient to bring about
reform; in History 1, for instance, almost all the students
criticized the 'check-up' system of monthly conferences
summoned at a moment's notice, and at their suggestion
it soon after became a two-lecture and one-recitation
course. Professor Shaler, who objected to the committee's
methods, observing that in his native Kentucky 'privates were not invited to criticize their officers,' made
Geology 4 a voluntary course rather than stiffen it up;
and the consequent drop in enrolment almost broke his
heart.

In the main, this report was an endorsement of the existing system, and as such President Eliot regarded it; yet
it marks a distinct turning-point in faculty policy from
expanding liberty, toward tightening-up, integration, and
a discreet modicum of paternalism. Two statements in
the report, both written by Professor Lowell, became the
keynotes of President Lowell's policy: 'There is in the
College to-day too much teaching and too little studying';
'Every serious man with health and ability should be encouraged to take honors in some subject.'

It was in 1903 that the Faculty refused to be pushed
any further toward a normal three-year course for the
Bachelor's degree; and in 1906 an extra tuition charge
for each course over four went into effect. But the most
important outcome of the Report was the new degree of

A.B. 'with distinction' (first granted in 1907), the attainment of which required a grouping of at least eight courses, honor grades (A or B) in them, the submission of a dissertation, and the passing of a general oral examination at the end of senior year. Here was a beginning of Mr. Lowell's modifications in the elective system.

The writer, who had the best of both worlds — entering at the zenith of free electives, taking the first distinction examinations, and teaching in the stimulating and challenging atmosphere of the Lowell régime, feels that something was lost when we turned away from Eliot and liberty; but that more was gained. The old system was haphazard, illogical, postulated on too high an expectation of a young man's will to learn and too low an estimate of the many attractive side-shows outside the main tent. The arrangement by which you received your degree for seventeen or eighteen courses meant piecemeal education, if that; unity of knowledge, or even integration of a subject, was seldom attained. There was too much 'shopping about' for 'cinch courses,' convenient hours, and complaisant instructors; and too many earnest seekers after special knowledge, once their prescribed freshman courses were worked off, took everything in one department. Dilettantism received the same countenance and credit as premature and excessive specialization, provided the grades were the same.

Yet education is the most unpredictable thing in the world, and the last subject to be dogmatic about. The Eliot era was full of stories about youths who chose courses with no more system than the fall of a roulette ball, yet found an unexpected exhilarator. The 'long train of events' that led to my writing this book began thirty years ago, when Professor Albert Bushnell Hart allowed me to build a course around a case of old Federalist correspondence that I found in my grandfather's wine-cellar. Some of the most distinguished American anthropologists and archaeologists today are the young gentlemen who, a generation and more ago, took Anthropology 1 as a reputed 'snap.' They came to loaf, and remained to dig. Professor Toy, a perfect example of the ripe and gentle scholar, chatted twice a week on the History of the Spanish Califate to a divinity student and several undergraduates, seated around a table in the Semitic Museum, at an inconvenient afternoon hour. One of the undergraduates took the course because he had already written a thesis on the Cid, and hoped to use it again. Another was a musician, and wrote a thesis on Arabian music. 'Of course there isn't any,' said Professor Toy, 'but it will do him good to find it out!' And it did. A third had some notion of becoming an historian, and decided that he would, if the study of history made men such as Professor Toy. The fourth was there because he expected number 3 to help him collect a much-wanted C; and he obtained a B from his own efforts. Yet three of the four look back on that course, after thirty years, as one of their finest experiences in College. Under the present system, none of them could have afforded to spend time on so peripheral a subject, with divisionals looming in their field of concentration.

James A. Field took his A.B. *summa cum laude* in 1903 with a straight 'A' record mostly in elementary courses: three in Economics, two in German, two and a half in French, two in Mathematics, one each in Latin, Physics, Chemistry, Philosophy, Hygiene, and Archaeology, and half a course in Geology! There was much wagging of faculty heads over this record, and predictions that a young man who so scattered his studies would come to no good. Actually, Field found his main interest in his freshman year; but as he planned to study Economics in the Graduate School, he spent his time in College getting up the essential languages and the elements of science, and keeping a hand in the classics. Besides, he was the leader of the Glee Club and a member of several societies. In a short time he became a distinguished economist and professor at the University of Chicago.

Of course many other instances could be related of men who floundered about from one subject to another and left Cambridge with a Bachelor's degree, but completely devoid of intellectual baggage.

It must also be remembered that the average student who entered Harvard College before 1900 had already studied Greek for four, Latin for six, and Mathematics for ten years; he had already been given a fair classical education, whether he prepared at an endowed school like Exeter, Andover, and St. Paul's, or at one of the excellent classical high schools of the era; and of mental discipline he had had plenty. It was natural and proper for a young man thus trained to branch out in College and 'browse about,' as the phrase was, until he found something to his liking. The worst effects of the elective system came outside Harvard, and especially in the schools. Eliot advocated the principle of free choice in high schools, overlooking the fact that the normal lad of fourteen to eighteen will always avoid subjects that require hard thought and much expenditure before they yield returns, in favor of those which require no greater mental effort than memory, and pay prompt dividends in achievement. It was due to Eliot's insistent pressure that the Harvard Faculty abolished the Greek requirement for entrance in 1887, after dropping required Latin and Greek for freshman year. His and Harvard's reputation, the pressure of teachers trained in the new learning, and of parents wanting 'practical' instruction for their sons, soon had the classics on the run, in schools as well as colleges; and no equivalent to the classics, for mental training, cultural background, or solid satisfaction in after life, has yet been discovered. It is a hard saying, but Mr. Eliot, more than any other man, is responsible for the greatest educational crime of the century against American youth — depriving him of his classical heritage.

No new graduate schools were established in the second half of Eliot's administration, except the Business School, which came so near the end that it may best be considered in a later chapter. But there were two new developments, which we may consider here. The Harvard Summer School claims priority over all university summer schools or vacation sessions in the United States, by virtue of a special summer course in Botany for teachers offered by Asa Gray as a private venture in 1871. Every year thereafter a similar course for teachers in some scientific subject was offered, but the University had no more to do with them than to lend buildings and apparatus. About 1886 Professor Shaler was appointed chairman of a committee in charge of summer courses; and with that and other titles managed them for twenty years. At first these courses were taught by members of the Harvard Faculty, and by Dr. Dudley A. Sargent, who created a vigorous Department of Physical Education. Gradually teachers from other institutions were invited to instruct, and in 1891 Harvard undergraduates and graduate students were admitted as students, in order to make up a half-course 'flunked' during the college year, or acquire a similar credit toward taking a degree in three years. By the turn of the century over sixty courses were offered, and the average enrolment was between seven and eight hundred. The Scientific School, since 1902, has maintained its own summer school of engineering in a camp of seven hundred acres at Squam Lake, New Hampshire. In the summer of 1900, at the request of the Cuban Department of Public Instruction, a summer session was organized at Cambridge for Cuban school-teachers — a friendly gesture toward the new republic that gave the University much valuable publicity, and afforded more than twelve hundred Cuban teachers their first contact with North American education. The experiment was repeated for Puerto Rican teachers four years later.

It was also in this period that the University began to accept a certain responsibility for the higher education of women. President Eliot devoted a paragraph to the subject in his inaugural address, declaring that Harvard did not wish to face 'the difficulties involved in a common residence of hundreds of young men and women of immature character and marriageable age.' He hoped that admission to the 'University Lectures' would satisfy them; but these proved a dead-end for women's education, as for graduate study. Nor did an invitation to study Horticulture, Entomology, and Agricultural Chemistry in the Bussey Institution prove attractive to the fair sex.

In 1872 Samuel Eliot (A.B. 1839), then headmaster of the Girls' High School, Boston, presented to the Women's Education Association of Boston an account of the examinations for women lately established by one of the English universities. The Association persuaded Harvard to perform a similar service, and in 1872 two sets of papers were prepared: the preliminary, equivalent to the Harvard entrance examinations, and the advanced, covering certain courses of the first two college years. Six candidates presented themselves, and four were passed. The demand soon became so great that in 1877 the examinations were held in New York, Philadelphia, and Chicago as well as in Cambridge. The next year, when there were fifty-nine candidates, the time seemed opportune to offer instruction of collegiate grade to those who passed the examinations. In order to avoid challenging the masculine traditions of Harvard College, a very clever and sensible scheme was set on foot by Mr. and Mrs. Arthur Gilman of Cambridge, supported by Professors Child, Goodwin, and Greenough, with the hearty blessing of President Eliot. A committee of ladies such as Mrs.

Louis Agassiz and Miss Alice Longfellow, who were un-
suspected of seeking 'woman's rights,' formed an association for 'Private Collegiate Instruction for Women,'
raised money, hired a few rooms at 15 Appian Way, and
engaged a few Harvard professors to give courses to young
ladies in their spare time. The 'Harvard Annex,' as this
institution was soon nicknamed, opened in the fall of 1879
with twenty-seven students, of whom ten were given a
certificate in due course that they had completed a
course of study similar to that for the first degree in Arts
at Harvard.

In the meantime so many others had put in for 'private
collegiate instruction' that the association obtained a
state charter as 'The Society for the Collegiate Instruction of Women,' which took over both entrance examinations and instructions, and purchased in 1885 the Fay
mansion under the shadow of the Washington Elm.
Many Harvard professors and instructors consented to repeat their courses at 'The Annex' for a small stipend,
and enrolment reached 250 in 1894. Plans for an official
affiliation with Harvard University were discussed, an
endowment of a hundred thousand dollars was raised,
but Harvard firmly declined to annex the Annex on condition of granting Harvard degrees to the alumnae. A
sensible compromise was worked out by which the Harvard Governing Boards accepted a visitatorial power,
and consented to countersign women's degree diplomas,
on the condition that all instruction be given by members
of the Harvard staff. On this basis, the Society for the
Collegiate Instruction of Women received a new State
Charter in 1894 as Radcliffe College, which was em-
powered to confer all honors and degrees given by any
university in the Commonwealth. Under this charter
Radcliffe has grown and prospered beside her somewhat
supercilious parent; and her graduate students are commonly admitted to some of the seminars and advanced

courses in the Graduate School of Arts and Sciences, and the scientific courses at the Medical School. But women have never been admitted to the regular course for the M.D., although they came very near to it in the 1880's; or to the Law School; and no proposition to make Harvard College co-educational has ever been seriously entertained.

In the Medical School, now located at Boylston and Exeter Streets in Boston, another bold step was taken in 1892 — the course was lengthened to four years; and in 1901 the B.A. degree at Harvard or some other college of high standard was made a prerequisite for admission.[1] Despite the facilities offered by the various hospitals in Boston, the School suffered by not having a single hospital or dispensary under its control; hence School appointments of physicians and surgeons from other cities were contingent on hospital trustees finding a place for them on their staffs, which aroused a certain jealousy among local practitioners. The rapid development of medical science demanded more and more space, equipment, and laboratories for proper instruction and fruitful research; and in 1899 the movement for a new site and buildings was launched. With the aid of princely donors of the houses of Morgan, Rockefeller, and Huntington, the money was finally raised, and the new Medical School on the Longwood site, designed by the late Charles Allerton Coolidge (A.B. 1881), was dedicated with appropriate pomp and ceremony in September, 1906. The new Peter Bent Brigham Hospital, closely affiliated with the School, was completed in 1912.

The close and intelligent interest that President Eliot showed to the end of his administration in the Medical School is shown by a letter that he wrote to Major Henry L. Higginson, Fellow of the Corporation, in 1907.

[1] This was modified in 1909 in favor of men who had had two years of college training; but soon after the increasing number of applicants made the concession nugatory.

We have an opportunity now to make a new declaration of what we expect from that School by appointing a new kind of Dean and letting him select the new kind of Secretary. We want to have a School which is going not only to train men learned and skilful in what is now known and applied, but expectant of progress, and desirous to contribute to new discovery. We want to have the whole atmosphere and spirit of the School a hopeful and expectant one as regards preventive medicine and medical and surgical discovery. To this end the administrative officers of the School ought to be men sympathetic with all laboratory research, and desirous of combining laboratory research with clinical research and hospital practice. To get this sort of man, I think we shall have to take as Dean and Secretary men whose chief interest lies in medical and surgical progress rather than in the cautious application of what is now supposed to be known. In all probability both men will have to be under forty years of age.

Henry A. Christian, a thirty-two-year-old Virginian, M.D. of Johns Hopkins and Instructor in the Medical School, was the man selected by Eliot to be the new Dean and Hersey Professor in 1908; and under his young and alert leadership the Medical School in its new home entered the fresh fields of usefulness outlined by Eliot.

In the Law School, the Langdell reform had been so effective that nothing further was required in this period than to select the proper teachers to instruct the increasing number of students who came from all parts of the country, and to restrict admission to 'graduates of approved colleges' (1899). Langdell was succeeded as Dean in 1895 by James Barr Ames, who carried on until his death in 1910. Ames had a genius for teaching by Langdell's case method, and to him much of the success both of that method and of the School must be attributed. Jeremiah Smith (A.B. 1856) became Story Professor in 1890 after a long career at the bar and on the bench of his native New Hampshire; Joseph H. Beale (LL.B. 1887) and Samuel Williston (LL.B. 1888) joined the Law Faculty the same year; Eugene Wambaugh (LL.B. 1880) was called to Harvard from Iowa State University in 1892;

John Chipman Gray, first in time of the great teachers who made the reputation of the School in the earlier period, served as Royall Professor until 1913; and James Bradley Thayer held the new Weld Professorship from 1883 to 1902. In 1898 the Bemis Professorship of International Law was founded, and the first appointee was Edward H. Strobel (LL.B. 1882), who had been for thirteen years in the diplomatic service. He left in 1903 to become first of a series of Harvard-trained advisers to the Siamese Government. Under John H. Arnold, librarian from 1872 to 1913, the Law Library increased ten-fold in bulk, and more than that in quality; even before the nineteenth century closed, A. V. Dicey called it 'the most perfect collection of the legal records of the English people to be found in any part of the English-speaking world.' Langdell Hall began to rise over the old running track on Holmes Field in 1907.

The Divinity School, humorously described at the beginning of Eliot's administration as consisting of 'three mystics, three skeptics, and three dyspeptics' (actually the students numbered 36), made a gradual progress toward becoming what Eliot wished it to be — a university school of Theology. Degrees were first conferred in 1870, the elective system was introduced, and divinity students had the benefit of the rich offerings under the Faculty of Arts and Sciences; yet the graduating class of 1872, fourteen in number, was the record until 1914. About half the graduates (e.g., Christopher R. Eliot, S.T.B. 1881, and John Haynes Holmes, S.T.B. 1904) became ministers, and the rest (e.g., Earl M. Wilbur, S.T.B. 1890; William W. Fenn, S.T.B. 1887; William J. Campbell, S.T.B. 1907) became theological scholars, teachers, and administrators. In 1908, to the great delight of aged Unitarians, the Andover Theological Seminary, which had been founded as a protest against Harvard liberalism, removed to Cambridge and affiliated with the

University. 'Jonah has returned to the whale's belly,' declared an academic wit.

Justin Winsor, the historian and scholar who became College Librarian in 1877, began a new era in the Library. His 'fundamental principle that books should be used to the largest extent possible and with the least trouble' was revolutionary — and in a majority of the world's libraries it would be revolutionary today. In practice this meant the 'reserved books' system in the reading room for the younger men, and stack privileges for graduate students and faculty. Successive enlargements of Gore Hall, and the creation of special libraries outside, gave space for a series of remarkable gifts from a long line of generous donors — for instance, Thomas Carlyle, who left the books that he had used for writing his Cromwell and his Frederick to the alma mater of Emerson and his other transatlantic friends, as testifying 'a variety of kind feelings, obligations and regards towards New England . . . recognizing with gratitude, how much of friendliness, of actually credible human love I have had from that country.'

Throughout the last twenty-three years of his administration, as in the first seventeen, Eliot kept his finger on the pulse of every department of the University. His essential qualities did not change; he retained all his confidence, resourcefulness, energy, vitality, patience, scrupulous fairness, uncanny judgment of men, and relentless pursuit of his goal of making Harvard a fit instrument to serve the cause of learning and civilization. At his retirement, as at his inauguration, Eliot was devoid of vanity or ostentation, blunt and tactless, incapable of softening or modifying what he had to say in order to please an audience or flatter a possible benefactor. But the estimate of him by the University and the country underwent a complete change. The twenty-fifth anniversary of his election, in 1894, was the occasion of an outpouring of praise and admiration that took him completely by surprise, called forth some of the latent warmth in his nature, and made him more forthgoing and responsive. Within a few years he had established a cordial personal relationship with his faculty associates, and had become a hero to the students. They began to realize that a President who was so highly respected by leaders of public opinion must be a great man, after all! One after the other, the greater universities of the country followed the reforms that Harvard had adopted; it was clear by the middle nineties that the Harvard of Eliot, instead of striking off on an individual line toward Germany, had set new standards for higher education in America. For Eliot did not confine his spoken or written word to higher education, much less to Harvard: his first two books of collected articles and addresses, 'American Contributions to Civilization' (1897) and 'Educational Reform' (1898), covered the entire field of education from the kindergarten to the research institute, in their relation to fundamental problems of democratic society. By the turn of the century he was one of the leading public figures of the country; his opinion and support were sought on every variety of public question.

People did not think of his reputation and his honors when they talked with Eliot, or heard him speak. Listening for him was a form of activity; courteous but insistent questioning was his favorite way of acquiring information. When his time came to speak he was apt to turn his visitor inside out, yet sent him away feeling privileged to be deviscerated by so expert a surgeon. But it was when he arose to address an audience, tall, straight, majestic to his life's end, that one felt most keenly Eliot's character and personality. There was always a strong bond between him and any audience, for in his outlook on life he represented the best of his age — that forward-looking half-century before the World War, when democracy seemed capable of putting all crooked ways straight — the age of reason and of action, of accomplishment and of hope; Eliot recognized no 'spirit that denies.' He always appealed to reason and common sense; never did he resort to passionate utterance or appeal to emotion or prejudice. What he said was dressed with little art; yet he was a powerful orator. His eloquence came from simplicity and strength; an athlete of the platform, he well knew how to apply that muscular English in which he was so skilled. His pellucid sincerity, his deep voice with the quality of old vintage port, lent an oracular force even to commonplace statements of fact. There must be many who remember an address to freshmen that he delivered in the Harvard Union about the year 1906. It was built around one thought, repeated twice or thrice in the discourse, which as he uttered it, seemed to the young men impressive as a voice from Heaven:

'Look forward to being married, and to having a blessed home of your own.'

To the end of his administration, 'Prexy,' as the students called him, was never 'popular' in the general meaning of that word. He never pretended to enter into their ardent desire to 'beat Yale,' and the 'joining' instinct he neither felt nor respected. Yet the students came to regard him not only with veneration, but genuine affection. And when the news of his resignation came out in November, 1908, it seemed to the young men that the glory was about to depart from old Harvard. There was a mass meeting at the Union, and after it was over the students clustered in front of the little mansard-roofed house that was still the presidential mansion, and cheered Eliot repeatedly until he came out on the porch and addressed them, in one of his most characteristic speeches, looking as ever toward the future:

This is a great surprise, and I greatly appreciate your coming. . . . The occupation which has been mine for a lifetime has been a most pleasant one, and I regret that it is about to terminate. Forty years of service has been given me in the pursuance of a profession that has no equal in the world. . . . [But] I don't like to have my coming retirement spoken of with regret. It is touching to find that feeling, but I think it is something to be looked forward to with hope. We must all set to work to find some young, able, active man for the place. He can be found; we shall find him. We need a man who will take up this extremely laborious and extremely influential position with untiring energy and carry this university to a higher plane than it now occupies.

How wonderfully had been fulfilled over those forty years the brave prophecy that Eliot had made at the first Commencement over which he presided, in 1870:

'We mean to build here, securely and slowly, a university in the largest sense.'

XVI

COLLEGE LIFE FROM WAR TO WAR

FRANCIS G. ATTWOOD '78 executed a series of excellent line-drawings in the new *Harvard Lampoon* that embalm the 'Manners and Customs of ye Harvard Studente' of that day. These had not much changed since we last glanced at them in Civil War times. Our 'Harvard Studente' lives in the Yard, and studies by gaslight or student lamp a few days before exams. The more affluent members are accompanied by 'ye Dogge of ye Period,' a huge mastiff; an odd assortment of terriers follow the rest. On summer afternoons the lads lounge about on the grass outside Holworthy, or sit on the fence near Boylston and ogle passing damsels. They dine at club tables in boarding houses or at Memorial Hall, inspected by visitors in the galleries who come to 'watch the animals eat' — it was not until two or three years later that the Holly Tree, the first restaurant in the Square, was opened. Freshmen have to give a punch to the sophomores, who attend in top hats; after Christmas the freshman may sport a cane; 'bowler hats' are coming into vogue. And all who can, grow a moustache and twirl the ends thereof assiduously. At recitations in University Hall, before heavily bearded instructors, the students wear overcoats, sit on benches, prompt each other, and 'bone up' their assignment in class; during examinations, which are held in the bare 'Upper Mass.,' cribbing goes on merrily under the proctors' noses and whiskers. Placards announcing club meetings are posted on the bulletin board in front of University Hall; 'shingles' (notifications of election) decked with club medals and ribbons hang on the walls of rooms. The boat-houses have acquired floats — no longer does one have to lower shells into the water and slide into them down the pilings like a fireman — but the floats are still flanked by coal wharves and unloading schooners. Football and baseball are played on Holmes and Jarvis fields, before a very small group of spectators; the catcher wears the new mask said to have been invented by F. W. Thayer '78. There are fencing matches in the Old Gym, and boxing matches with 'a fashionable private tutor' in college rooms; dancing classes and assemblies in Boston for the swells, 'pick-ups' on Tremont Street for some of the others. 'When a man wishes to pass for a graduate of Harvard,' said the *Boston Post*, 'he has his room decorated with photographs of all the leading burlesque actresses.' On Class Day the seniors parade around the Yard with a band, cheering the buildings, and dance around the Tree in dress suits and toppers.

As athletics increased, riots and disorder faded out. During the years when Memorial Hall and the new dormitories were being built, there was an epidemic of bonfires in the Yard, started with the heaps of lumber that were lying about; and every bonfire was the signal for the proctors and 'Yard cops' to try to extinguish the flames. Lanman's trundling off an old buggy filled with burning hay amid cries of 'Giddap!' was a long-remembered event; and Eliot was once seen pulling a mattress off the flames, with a student at the other end trying to get it back. Finally the President had a bright idea. He ordered proctors to keep to their rooms in the event of a bonfire; and the students, deprived of the delicious spectacle of distracted proctors, took no more interest in that particular form of riot.

A bonfire incident in 1871 indicates the gulf that still existed between students and Faculty. Professor Charles L. Jackson seized a culprit, and asked his name. The student replied, 'What's *your* name?' Jackson gave it. 'No such name in the catalogue!' declared the rash student. For 'insolence to a professor' he was suspended for six months, and that was considered letting him down easy.

As the old marking system was gradually abolished, this gulf between students and Faculty began to narrow; but it was a long time before anyone managed to bridge it. Louis Dyer (A.B. 1874), who taught the classics from 1878 to 1887, tried to, but was laughed at for his pains, and finally found his niche at Balliol. In the late seventies the students began to form societies to discuss serious subjects such as economics with their instructors; but as social occasions, these meetings were rather stiff. The Peirces, Hills, and other Faculty families of the eighties loved music and often had students at their houses for informal concerts; in 1888, when the Cambridge Dramatic Club produced the operetta 'Old King Cole' by 'Allen and Greenough,' students took the chorus parts. But Charles T. Copeland (A.B. 1882), who became Instructor in English ten years after his graduation, was the first member of the Faculty to become friendly with a large number of undergraduates of all sorts. For almost forty years 'Copey' kept open house 'Wednesday evenings after ten' in his successive chambers — Grays 24, Stoughton 7, and (from 1904 to 1932) Hollis 15; and no Harvard instructor has ever accumulated so devoted a following as his. An excellent lecturer and teacher of English composition, he did not confine his instruction to his classes. The lads flocked to him because he liked them; his conversation ranged over all subjects, and brought out the views of his guests; and his readings gave the most illiterate a taste for the English classics. As Jack Reed well said, Copeland 'stimulated generations of men to find color and strength and beauty in books and in the world, and to express it again.' He is the Mr. Fleetwood of Flandrau's 'Diary of a Freshman'; a whole saga has grown up about him. Yet Copey was never properly appreciated by his colleagues; he was not even promoted Assistant Professor until 1910.

The only teacher to be mentioned in the same breath with Copeland is LeBaron Russell Briggs. After the faculty reorganization of 1890, Briggs was given the new post of Dean of Harvard College, to handle student relations. Although he only held it eleven years, Briggs established such a reputation that to the end of his life he was the students' friend. The key to his character was a unique balance of kindness and shrewdness. He believed in human nature without being soft. The old Yankee in him knew that the devil was in you, somewhere; the smile that crinkled all over his face, and a deceptively casual remark, brought out your confidence, and you became friends. Briggs was also an excellent teacher of English composition; but he operated largely on the moral, Copey on the intellectual and aesthetic, natures of the young men.

Sympathetic mentors like Copey and Briggs were the more needed in an era when personal liberty and free election bewildered many students, left them drifting without rudders, the sport of every breeze. The Board of Freshman Advisers was set up in 1889, but they did little except address the entering class *en masse*, approve study cards, and invite the advisee to a pallid luncheon at the Colonial Club. Except for procuring the Stillman Infirmary (1901) from a persistently generous family of benefactors, the Eliot administration refrained from paternalistic gestures. Students even had to found the Harvard Co-operative Society in 1882 (Charles H. Kip '83 was the organizing genius) in order to protect themselves from the rapacity of Harvard Square coal dealers and booksellers. So the new tactics of Briggs and Copey were the more appreciated. Their example encouraged the younger instructors to forget dignity and mingle with their pupils both at work and at play; and by 1900 caste feelings in the Faculty had completely vanished. George H. Palmer told me ten years ago that, of all the improvements in the College since his graduation in 1864, this friendly relation between teachers and taught was the greatest. The increasing staff of tutors after 1917 helped the process; the main barrier now is the fact that so large a part of an ambitious instructor's time must be spent in writing or research, and that the students as well find a twenty-four-hour day too short.

The spontaneous growth of athletics was the most astounding phenomenon of student life, to the old-timers, in the first fifteen years of Eliot's administration. The beginnings of rowing and baseball in the fifties and sixties we have already seen. The old rough-and-tumble football games between freshmen and sophomores were forbidden in 1860; 'Boston football,' a new game, began to be played by class teams in 1871, and the Harvard University Foot Ball Club was organized in Holden Chapel on December 3, 1872, with Bob Grant '73 as president. A committee including Charlie Prince '73 and his brother Morton '75 proceeded to codify the rules that had grown up more or less spontaneously in Boston schoolboy contests. These rules were somewhat like those of English Rugby; but in the meantime Yale, Columbia, and other colleges were developing a rudimentary soccer. It was a toss-up which would become the American game until 1874, when the H.U.F.B.C. received a challenge from the Foot-ball Club of McGill University to play a series of Rugby matches; and it was agreed that the first should be under the Harvard rules, and the second under McGill's modified English Rugby rules. The first match of three games (periods) was played on Jarvis Field on May 14, 1874. Originally there were to be fifteen men on a side, but the number was reduced to eleven because four of the McGill men were unable to leave Montreal.

The Canadians wore neat striped jerseys and caps, shaming the Harvardian dark pants, white undershirt, and magenta handkerchief; but Harvard contributed some 'plays' unknown to English Rugby, which enabled them to win the first match, and to hold McGill to a scoreless tie in the second. The 'gate' of a few hundred dollars was pleasantly spent in giving the Canadians a champagne banquet at the Parker House.

A return match which the H.U.F.B.C. played at Montreal in October weaned Harvard from her peculiar Boston rules to the game from which American football has developed. Tufts College took it up and trounced Harvard the following June; in the fall of 1875 Yale was converted, and defeated. The first Harvard-Yale football game was played on November 13, 1875, at New Haven, where about a hundred and fifty Harvard students were on hand to see their team win by four goals and four touchdowns. It had been better to have been more moderate, for Yale made a determined and successful effort to learn more than her teacher. Walter Camp began to play in 1878; and Harvard did not beat Yale again until 1890. The following description from the *Harvard Herald* of the first half of the Harvard-Yale football game of 1882 is typical:

The eleven played its last game of the season on Holmes field Saturday, and received its first defeat. Although a cold wind blew down the field promising much inconvenience to spectators, about 2,500 people were grouped around the lines at 2.15 when the teams came on the field. Yale won the toss and chose the wind, Harvard kicking off. The ball was passed back and sent on to Yale's ground by Mason's kick and Morison's rush. Soon, however, Yale's half-back, taking advantage of the wind, sent the ball by a high punt far into Harvard's territory, and Hull receiving the ball from a down carried it over our line by a pretty rush and scored a touchdown, but no goal was kicked.[1] Yale now commenced the contemptible game she re-

[1] A touchdown in those days did not count unless followed by a goal. Yale won this game by one goal.

sorted to last fall, and in a few minutes nearly every man in her rush line was warned and threatened with disqualification either for foul tackling or for jumping on and fouling the backs. It was an exhibition which will be long remembered at Harvard and by the outsiders as well, who came expecting to see a scientific game of foot-ball. Wessel-hoeft sprained his ankle in one of the roughest scrimmages, and Adams, '86, took his place. Yale soon scored a touchdown through Beck, from a fumble by one of our rush; but Richards again failed in the goal. Harvard then rallied, and brilliant rushing by Morison and Appleton carried the ball into the middle of the field, when time was called.

The 'fouling the backs' complained of was the beginning of interference; but Harvard had no right to 'kick,' because her initial victory over McGill had been won by springing new plays that were neither forbidden nor anticipated by the Rugby rules. This constant innovation has been the genius and the bane of the American game, for the almost invisible line between clever tactics and foul play made the temptation to unsportsmanlike conduct almost irresistible, and hard feeling between contestants an inevitable concomitant.

But the boat races as well engendered ill feeling. The surviving reports, protocols, and *pièces justificatives* on the Harvard-Columbia 'race' of 1882, when, owing to a dispute as to the hour, Columbia rowed down the Thames alone, were worthy of a peace conference; the question of what to do about the Yale shell being a foot longer than the Harvard one was for long the great Eastern Question. The essential cause of this unsportsmanlike bickering — which Oxford and Cambridge had already outgrown — was the desperate desire for notoriety and victory that still trails its slimy track over American intercollegiate athletics. Harvard at this period was consistently successful on the river and the diamond; the crew won twelve out of seventeen races with Yale in 1866–82 inclusive, and twenty-one out of thirty-five baseball games with Yale, in the same period. Defeats in baseball occasioned no great grief; but a Yale victory on the river or the football field was a subject for mourning, from the early seventies. Organized cheering — a staccato yelp, not the now classic three long Harvards and three times three — was noticed in the Montreal papers as early as the McGill game of 1874; and the slogan 'Support the team!' was coined not long after. 'Encourage the team this fall in every way we can,' declared the *Harvard Herald* in its opening number of 1882. 'Let us help the captain get all the desirable candidates on the field regularly, let us encourage them in their practice games every afternoon by becoming interested spectators.' 'Our athletics suffer more from this very same carelessness of her prominent men than from any other cause.' Herein is an allusion, though not by name, to the famous 'Harvard indifference,' a quality attributed to the undergraduates from the early eighties to the present because they never did 'support the team' anything like one hundred per cent. Their athletes did not water track or sod with tears of bitterness when defeated; and a mask of indifference had to be cultivated to hide the chagrin of successive drubbings by Walter Camp's teams. Harvard felt a certain loss of manhood in not winning a single football game with Yale in the eighties and only two in the nineties; it was no consolation to have President Eliot prove that the College gained the most students in these valleys of humiliation.

Athletics properly so called, the classic games and contests of the ancient world,[1] began at Harvard as a sideshow to the boat races. At the intercollegiate regatta at Saratoga in 1874 there were four running races, and a seven-mile walk. In October, 1874, the Harvard Athletic Association was formed, with Benjamin R. Curtis '75 as president. This body, made up entirely of undergradu-

[1] The word was used in that sense only — for track and field sports, boxing and wrestling — at Harvard until about 1880, and is still so used in England.

ates, took charge of running, leaping, boxing, wrestling, and gymnastic competitions for almost twenty years. By that time American usage had extended 'athletics' to include all manner of games and contests; athletics in the Greek sense were given the ugly qualification 'track.'

Informal track meets were held by the H.A.A. on Jarvis Field from 1874; A. Lawrence Lowell '77 hung up the first mile and half-mile records. Oarsmen and others competed in the regatta game; but the great event was the formation of the Intercollegiate Association of Amateur Athletes of America in 1876. That summer the Association conducted the last regatta track meet at Saratoga; the next year the winged sandal broke away from the sweep and rudder, and the intercollegiate meets at Mott Haven began. Princeton won the first, and Columbia the next two; there was not much interest in running at Harvard until Evert J. Wendell '82 entered College, and the first cinder track was built around Jarvis Field in 1879. Wendell was not only a remarkable performer (he ran the 'hundred' in ten flat before the crouching start was invented), but a born leader; and Harvard won the intercollegiate meet of 1880 by an overwhelming margin, Wendell alone scoring three firsts. Then, and for ten years more, an amusing feature of these meets was high-wheel bicycles. There was a bicycle club in College from around 1875 to 1890 that made long runs into the country on high wheels — even to Peterborough, New Hampshire, on one occasion.

Cricket was played at Harvard into the present century. Lacrosse and lawn tennis were introduced in the seventies; but as these never became 'major sports,' little of their history has been preserved.

The University began to take the physical welfare of her students more seriously. The Hemenway Gymnasium, the gift of a student only three years out of College, was completed in 1878, and the year following Dudley A.

Sargent (A.B. Bowdoin, M.D. Yale) was appointed Assistant Professor of Physical Training and Director of the Gymnasium. 'During the forty years in which he held the position he exerted a greater influence on the development of physical training in American colleges and schools than any other man.' Under his impetus, and with the new equipment, the H.A.A. went in strongly for gymnastics. At the spring meet in 1881, state the newspapers, 'every available position in the huge building was taken,' and the performance had to be repeated to serve public curiosity. There were fifty-six entries in ten events, and some of the aërial acts, especially Dr. Sargent's famous stunt of sitting in a rocking-chair on a swinging trapeze, 'were thrilling enough to blanch the cheeks of the ladies.' That year, Dr. Sargent organized his famous private school of physical culture, which after his death became a department of Boston University.

President Eliot in his report for 1881 declared games and sports to be 'of great advantage to the University,' not only because 'the ideal student [had] been transformed from a stooping, weak, and sickly youth into one well-formed, robust, and healthy,' but because 'the perseverance, resolution and self-denial necessary to success in athletic sports turn out to be qualities valuable in business and other active occupations of after life.' The H.A.A. and the University Baseball, Football, and Boat Clubs chose their own student officers, engaged professional trainers, took in the exiguous gate receipts of the period, expended them as they chose, and made their own schedules. There were no eligibility rules, except that a player must be enrolled in some department of the University; of the numerous law students on the Harvard baseball teams in the eighties a number were professionals, whose tuition fees as 'law students' were paid by 'patriotic' old grads., but who never opened a law book. 'We had four professionals on our baseball team in 1888,'

an old grad. told me. 'Yale had five, and Princeton, six.'
Men played on the varsity for six or seven years. But it
was the alarming length of the baseball schedule of 1882
— twenty-eight games, nineteen of them away from Cambridge — that precipitated a reluctant Faculty into a
policy of oversight and regulation that for nigh fifty years
afforded that learned body more grief than any learned
subject. They appointed a committee of five, under the
chairmanship of the aesthetic Norton, but including Dr.
Sargent and Adams and Agassiz of the Corporation, to
regulate athletic sports; and this committee adopted five
rules that are the basis of our athletic regulations today:

1. College teams and athletic clubs to compete only with amateurs.
2. No trainers or coaches to be employed without authority from
the Committee.
3. Nobody to take part in contests except after examination by the
Physical Director.[1]
4. All games outside Cambridge to be played on Saturday.
5. All oarsmen to pass a swimming test before going on the river.

The first thing that the Athletic Committee did was to
send the professional football trainer packing and forbid
coaching except by amateurs. This did not please the
players; and in the winter of 1890–91 the H.U.B.B.C.
hired Kelley and Clarkson, the Boston Nationals' '$10,000
battery,' to coach them secretly in the loft over the police
station in Brattle Square. By the turn of the century the
Faculty had been brought around to the viewpoint that
Harvard students were entitled to professional teaching
in sports as in studies; and from that time there has been
an increasing staff of competent professional coaches in
all major sports.

Our first Athletic Committee was discharged in 1885,
and a new one constituted by the Governing Boards, to

---

[1] Dr. Sargent had already begun his famous 'strength tests,' which
were a part of the examination and which, however faulty in conception,
induced many pindling youths to build up their physique.

consist of the Physical Director as chairman, a physician (Dr. Henry P. Walcott, A.B. 1858, held that seat for many years), a young graduate who had been an athlete (James J. Storrow, A.B. 1885, was the first), and two undergraduates (Charles Francis Adams '88, the future Secretary of the Navy, and Walter B. Phillips '86 were the first two). Except for the addition of more members in 1888 to make three each from Faculty, graduates, and undergraduates, the organization of this committee has been unchanged to the present day. Over the H.A.A. (reorganized in 1893 to include all undergraduates who paid a dollar a year) the Athletic Committee appointed a salaried graduate manager (later called graduate treasurer) as executive officer. He, in turn, was superseded in 1926 by a Director of Athletics (William J. Bingham, A.B. 1916), appointed by the Corporation, and now a member of the Faculty of Arts and Sciences. The H.A.A. no longer exists, although the term is still used for 'Bill' Bingham and his clerical staff; the Athletic Committee, which is his constitutional cabinet, approves all captains, coaches, and schedules; finances are handled through the College Treasury.

Until 1890, the athletic centre of Harvard was the area north of Kirkland Street and east of Massachusetts Avenue: Holmes Field (now almost completely covered with buildings) and Jarvis Field (the free part of which is now laid out in tennis courts). Additional football grids and baseball diamonds are laid out behind Divinity Hall; the Carey (now called the Rotch) Building, erected in 1889, contained an indoor baseball cage, hand-ball courts, and a rowing tank. But in 1890 the University received a new site for her sports, the magnificent gift of thirty-one acres from Major Henry L. Higginson (1855), named Soldiers Field in memory of six of his Harvard comrades who fell fighting for the Union.[1] It was dedicated on June 10,

---

[1] Nine acres adjoining on the north were purchased by the University at the same time, and they connected with thirty acres of marsh given by

1890, with one of the Major's simple, manly addresses, concluding with words that we need constantly to remember:

Mates, the Princeton and the Yale fellows are our brothers. Let us beat them fairly if we can, and believe that they will play the game just as we do.

Gentlemen, will you remember that this new playground will only be good if it is used constantly and freely by you all, and that it is a legacy from my friends to the dear old College, and so to you?

Major Higginson was a great gentleman, and a noble benefactor to Boston and to his University. Let us spare a thought for him, whenever we play on or visit 'that great lovely plain, bordered by the sunset and other irreclaimable gifts of the sky and landscape, and set forever there in memory of valor and of love.'

Unconsciously men were training to be soldiers on Soldiers Field. The first war flurry in twenty years came with President Cleveland's Venezuela message in 1895. Harvard students at that time were not particularly interested in public affairs, but the prospect of war brought a flood of meetings, pro- and anti-administration, and a notable exchange of views in the *Crimson* between Theodore Roosevelt and William James. The one wrote down the President's critics as victims of 'stock-jobbing timidity' and 'colonial dependence on England.' The other replied, in the true Harvard tradition:

May I express a hope that in this University, if no where else on the continent, we shall be patriotic enough *not* to remain passive whilst the destinies of our country are being settled by surprise. . . . Let us refuse to be bound over night by proclamation, or hypnotized by sacramental phrases through the day. Let us consult our reason as to what is best, and then exert ourselves as citizens with all our might.

---

the poet Longfellow and his family and friends in 1870. These areas have been gradually reclaimed from marsh as needed for playing fields, and for the Harvard R. O. T. C. The first Weld Boat House was given by George W. Weld (A.B. 1860) in 1890, and replaced in 1907 by the present house; the present University or Newell Boat House was given by the Harvard Club of New York in 1900.

Of the war with Spain, Harvard might say, as the Empress Eugénie is reported to have said of the Franco-Prussian, 'C'est ma guerre, c'est ma petite guerre à moi!' The three political musketeers who did the most to bring it on were Henry Cabot Lodge (A.B. 1871), William Randolph Hearst (1886), and Theodore Roosevelt. John D. Long (A.B. 1857) was the honest and effective Secretary of the Navy; Leonard Wood (M.D. 1884) commanded the Rough Riders. Yet, as on other public occasions, Harvard spoke with no single voice. Charles Eliot Norton, addressing the students shortly after the outbreak, declared that the war was needless, inglorious, and criminal, and advised them to consider carefully whether the best use they could make of themselves in their country's service was to enlist. For this he was abused by politicians, newspapers, and even clergymen, through the length and breadth of the land. His prompt dismissal was demanded, although his resignation had already been accepted, and certain local politicians went so far as to suggest that he be tarred and feathered, or even lynched. And his classmate Senator George F. Hoar, who later struggled against the consequences of the war, wrote to Norton: 'All lovers of Harvard, and all lovers of the country, have felt for a long time that your relation to the University made your influence bad for the college and bad for the youth of the country.' William James, addressing his class at the Jefferson Laboratory, made a speech concluding with a sentence they never forgot: 'Don't yelp with the pack!' President Eliot, however, offered no discouragement to public service, and in the short four months' war about a hundred students enlisted, and ten made the supreme sacrifice. There is a tablet to their memory in the Harvard Union.

Returning to athletics, we have no space for a chronicle of contests. Football was a constant subject of discussion among alumni, students, and the Governing Boards.

By 1904 (the year that Dartmouth dedicated the new Stadium, inauspiciously) it was clear that if the game and its surroundings were not reformed, the Governing Boards would forbid the College to play it; so a determined effort was made to change the rules of play and of eligibility. In 1906, freshmen, special students and students in the graduate and professional schools were first barred from varsity teams and crews; and the 'new football' began. And in the fall of 1908 the glorious Haughton era opened. Percy D. Haughton (A.B. 1899) as head coach built up a football machine that in the next twelve years of play (there were no games in 1917 and 1918) gave us eight victories over Yale (culminating in 41 to nothing by Eddie Mahan's team in 1915), two scoreless ties, and only two defeats. Haughton was the first of the modern 'big-time coaches,' and he certainly 'delivered the goods'; but it may be questioned whether his talent for picturesque profanity made the game more enjoyable, or whether his strategical and tactical developments turned football in the right direction. Later coaches of other colleges, building on what Haughton began, have made successful football playing a full-time, almost a professional job; and the public have responded with such keen delight that college players are now subjected to the unpleasing publicity that attends a movie star. Gate receipts mounted, so that various expensive developments were undertaken and minor sports became dependent on them; schedules had to be made with a view to the 'gate' rather than the game. Except from the viewpoint of 'grand-stand quarterbacks' and professional sports writers, the last state of football is worse than the first; and a fresh move for Harvard to withdraw from a game no longer suitable for amateurs was only prevented by the transfer of public attention to professional football.

Until the end of the Eliot administration, the principal emphasis in Harvard athletics was on developing winning teams and crews; others were supposed to look on and cheer. There was no form of exercise open to the physically ungifted student except tennis and its derivatives, indoor gymnastics, and paddling in a wherry. The ten years from 1907 to the World War brought a great improvement in this respect; and the man to whom it is mostly due is William F. Garcelon (LL.B. 1895), volunteer track coach and graduate treasurer of the H.A.A. Mr. Garcelon, observing that 'many men . . . needed only a word of encouragement and a bit of instruction to transform them from lookers-on and pipe-smoking idlers to enthusiastic participants,' gave the same help to gangling hobbledehoys as to 'varsity material,' improving beyond all measure their physique, their morale, and their enjoyment of College. His success, and the intelligent interest of Dr. Roger I. Lee (A.B. 1902), Professor of Hygiene since 1914, brought about the policy of 'athletics for all.' Compulsory exercise for freshmen was instituted in 1919, and by the second decade of the present century it became an exception for Harvard students not to be engaged in some regular form of physical activity.

The growth of athletics tended to integrate college life in the Eliot era; participation in them, both as players and as managers, brought together men of the widest social origins, and victory over Yale in the four 'major' sports of football, rowing, baseball, and track was something that the entire College prayed for.[1] But parallel with this development came a strong disintegrating force — the increase in numbers and in social diversity.

The first graduating class that passed the hundred mark was that of 1860. The Class of '77 (that of James Byrne, A. Lawrence Lowell, E. S. Martin, Governor

---

[1] Ice hockey was first played at Harvard in 1896; four years later came the first game with Yale; and in 1913 hockey was promoted to the class of 'major sport,' which means that contestants in games or races with Yale may wear the H without qualifying letters or emblems.

Russell, E. H. Strobel, Barrett Wendell, and G. E. Woodberry) was the first to enter over two hundred strong. Fifteen years later entered a class with over three hundred students, that of '92 (including William T. Brewster, Governor Forbes, Senator Hollis, Thomas W. Lamont, Robert Morss Lovett, William MacDonald, Bishop Perry, and Jeremiah Smith, Jr.). Four years more and we had a freshman class of over four hundred — that of '96, with Governor Bass, Walter B. Cannon, Sidney B. Fay, Jerome D. Greene, Gilbert N. Lewis, Roger B. Merriman, John Lord O'Brian, J. S. P. Tatlock, and Bruce Wyman. Another four years, and the five-hundred mark was passed by President Roosevelt's Class of 1904, and the Class of 1906 was over six hundred strong. From that point until a few years before the World War numbers remained stable.

This almost astronomical progression would not have been so damaging to class unity but for two disruptive factors — the elective system and Boston society. So long as Harvard classes studied mainly the same subjects, and recited to the same professors, they were forced to be together several hours in the day, and learned each other's strengths and weaknesses very quickly. But with everyone pursuing an individual tailor-made curriculum, and being passively lectured to rather than actively reciting, studies ceased to be a social bond.

The other disintegrating force was social. Harvard has never been socially homogeneous since President Dunster's day, nor sectionally so since President Willard's; but the 'constant' of middle-class New England students has always been able to assimilate most of the others, leaving a little aristocracy apart. The new 'variables' were both sectional and social. Southerners avoided Harvard after the Civil War because it admitted negroes on the same terms as whites, allowing them to eat at Memorial Hall, room in college dormitories, and participate in debating and athletic contests. The principal accessions of students from outside New England were from the Middle States, the Pacific Coast, and (a poor third) the Middle West, which much preferred Yale. As early as 1864 and 1865 there were enough Harvard graduates in Philadelphia and New York to form Harvard Clubs in those cities. By 1870 there was a similar nucleus in Chicago, by 1880 in Minneapolis; and in 1892 there were counted over 650 Harvard graduates in the West. These loyal Harvardians *in partibus* naturally made it a point to recruit promising lads for Alma Mater. If such boys were sent to a school that especially prepared for Harvard, they entered College with friends and immediately 'belonged'; but the sole graduate of a mid-western high school was apt to pass a lonely freshman year in the Eliot era, unless he became prominent in athletics, or promptly 'made' a college journal. In an even less favorable situation were representatives of the new racial stocks in New England. It was long before the Irish Catholics came to Harvard in considerable numbers, as their hierarchy directed them to the excellent Jesuit colleges; but by 1893 there were enough of them to form the St. Paul's Catholic Club, which in 1912 acquired Newman House for a gathering place. Students of Scandinavian descent formed an Edda Club around 1910. The first German Jews who came were easily absorbed into the social pattern; but at the turn of the century the bright Russian and Polish Jewish lads from the Boston public schools began to arrive. There were enough of them in 1906 to form the Menorah Society, and in another fifteen years Harvard had her 'Jewish problem.'

In the face of this infiltration, the old spirit of class solidarity stood up remarkably well — far better, for instance, than in most of the great state universities. Most classes of the nineteenth century, at least after they graduated, became mutual benevolent societies, of which no member need suffer as long as any were well off, and knew of his need. But the possibility of being one's brother's keeper declined when the family numbered over nine hundred. Class spirit took care of itself until around 1890; after that there began a conscious cultivation of it by athletic contests, beer nights, smokers, and other get-togethers, 'in order that pure and perfect democracy might be promoted' as 'At Good Old Siwash'; but these efforts bore little fruit until the class graduated, when classmates at last met one another on common ground, and vied with other classes in generosity to the University.[1] Major Higginson in 1901 founded the Harvard Union, which he hoped would prove a 'house of fellowship' and bring democracy to Harvard. The Union is a noble building. It provided club facilities (excepting a bar) for the unclubbed, a place for hearing visiting speakers and for holding football rallies and junior class dances (started in 1904, and studiously *not* called 'proms'); but it did not notably make for democracy, and after 1908 the membership declined to less than two thousand.

It is easy to be wise after the event. Before the total enrolment in the College had reached a thousand, new residential colleges, co-ordinate with Harvard College, should have been established; and doubtless in fifty years they would have been as desirable as the old. Certain farsighted persons recommended this as early as 1871, and in 1894–95 plans for an 'Oxford system' were publicly discussed. But President Eliot did not listen. He was too busy increasing the intellectual opportunities at Harvard to care much for the social life. He shared the expansionist philosophy of the era. Why should not Harvard College expand indefinitely like the United States?

---

[1] The Class of 1879 inaugurated the practice of making the University a twenty-fifth birthday gift of $100,000 — theirs went toward the new stadium.

And as the faculties and Governing Boards shared his point of view, their attitude toward the increasing social problem within the College was one of unsalutary neglect. The 'collegiate way of living,' for which our forefathers made such sacrifices, vanished.

The Corporation even left the housing of the new increment to private capital. Beck Hall, built in 1876, was first in a long series of 'private dormitories' with single and double suites of bedroom, study, and bath. King's 'Guide to Cambridge' grows lyrical over the high ceilings, ash trim, handsome chandeliers, steam-heating apparatus, and marble mantels of Beck, whose janitor, the admirable Eckert (with whom, as perfect of their kind, only 'Jimmy Claverly' and John Donovan may be compared), catered to the sons of millionaires. Beck was so promptly filled with gilded youth that another building of the same sort, Felton Hall, was cannily placed in 1877 just outside the quarter-mile 'prayer-limit,' so that its denizens need not attend chapel; but Claverly Hall, built in 1893, began the trend to Mt. Auburn Street. Dunster (now Dudley Hall), Russell, Fairfax, Apley, Dana Chambers, Randolph, and Westmorly were built along or near that 'Gold Coast' by 1900. Sundry run-down dwellings and three-deckers in the neighborhood were remodelled and let out at land-office prices; Soldiers Field naturally helped this *Drang nach Süden*; and when the Institute of 1770 transferred the opening stages of its initiation to Claverly, Mt. Auburn Street very definitely became the centre of college life. Claverly in fact was so popular that freshmen had to be elected as candidates for rooms. The Corporation did nothing to meet this competition in the way of providing modern conveniences in the Yard (as late as 1908 some of the halls there had no central heating, and no plumbing above the basement), and the only residential halls that the College erected — the highly unattractive Conant, Perkins, and Walter Hastings

— were so far from the new centre that only freshmen, law, and graduate students would live in them.

This cleavage between 'Yard' and 'Gold Coast' was the more unfortunate because it was financial as well as social: the rooms in the private dormitories were more comfortable and expensive than those provided by the College, and some of the buildings had swimming pools and squash courts. At the same time three other axes were hewing on the same line — Boston society, the private schools, and the club system.

Harvard may well say of Boston, *non possum vivere sine te nec cum te*. Boston gave the first funds for expansion from College to University; Boston has always provided students and faculty with society, music, drama, drink, and excitement. But Boston has been a social leech of Harvard College. Formerly, the College was permitted to live her own life; but in the eighties, when the supply of eligible young men in Boston was decreased by the westward movement, the Boston mammas suddenly became aware that Harvard contained many appetizing young gentlemen from New York, Philadelphia, and elsewhere. One met them in the summer at Newport or Beverly or Bar Harbor; naturally one invited them to Mr. Papanti's or Mr. Foster's 'Friday evenings' when they entered College, to the 'Saturday evening sociables' sophomore year, and to coming-out balls thereafter. What was more natural than to ask your brother's college friends to your coming-out dance?

This was very nice for the right young men, and pleasant for the girls; but it cut a deep chasm in the College. Santayana, who saw everything, signalled it in 1892: 'Divisions of wealth and breeding are not made conspicuous at Yale as at Harvard by the neighborhood of a city with well-marked social sets, the most fashionable of which sends all its boys to the College. These boys . . . form the most conspicuous masculine contingent of

Boston Society, and the necessity falls upon them of determining which of their college friends are socially presentable.' Obviously, you could not room with a man in College, or be very intimate with him, unless you could invite him home; consequently you were careful not to be too intimate with those you could not well ask to meet your sister, and naturally you got your friends into your club in preference to others. Presently the hostesses of Winchester, the Newtons, and the South Shore were reaching out to Harvard for dancing partners of their own kind; and as modern transportation lessened the time between Cambridge and the surrounding towns (Harvard Bridge built, 1893; subway opened, 1912), the social sets of metropolitan Boston became increasingly the dictators of social sets in Cambridge. This has baulked all attempts to make Harvard a social democracy. In vain are freshmen tossed onto the same heap; freshman fellowship, brisk enough in the opening days of College and the first elections of committees, blows away in a whiff of invitations to dances and week-end house parties. The social cleaver widened the chasm that a mistaken laissez-faire created between Yard and Gold Coast; and not even the Houses or the depression have bridged that gap.

Closely integrated with the Harvard clubs and Boston society were the preparatory schools. It has always been an advantage in every college to enter with a crowd of schoolmates. From Ezekiel Cheever's day to about 1870 the Boston Latin School graduates had a privileged position in the freshman classes at Harvard, shared by Phillips Exeter and the Boston private schools. During the period 1870–90 the proportion of freshmen entering from public high schools fell off from 38 to 23 per cent, and the graduates of Exeter and Adams Academy, Quincy, became dominant socially.[1] About 1890 the Episcopal Church schools, together with Milton Academy and one

[1] The high-school proportion has since recovered to 49 or 50 per cent.

or two Boston private schools, secured the social leadership. With the addition of graduates of the various country day schools from Newton to Winnetka, of the newer boarding schools such as Brooks and Middlesex, and an improved social rating of Exeter, Andover, and the Roxbury Latin, this situation has continued to the present day. Since 1890 it has been almost necessary for a Harvard student with social ambition to enter from the 'right' sort of school and be popular there, to room on the 'Gold Coast' and be accepted by Boston society his freshman year, in order to be on the right side of the social chasm. Family and race did not matter: an Irish-American, Jew, Italian, or Cuban was not regarded as such if he went to the right school and adopted the mores of his fellows; conversely, a lad of Mayflower and Porcellian ancestry who entered from a high school was as much 'out of it' as a ghetto Jew. Nor did wealth matter: men who worked their way through College were respected, and eligible; but too much spending damned a freshman — a now prominent multimillionaire who came to Cambridge with a retinue of cars and servants, and hired a whole apartment, had no notice taken of him, and soon departed.

These factors of school, site, and the Boston hall-mark determined the socially eligible class, which was always from 25 to 50 per cent greater than the number of places in the clubs. Consequently ambitious freshmen had to watch their steps very carefully. No 'Harvard individualism' for them! You must say, do, wear, the 'right thing,' avoid the company of all ineligibles, and, above all, eschew originality. Athletic success, except possibly a place on the freshman crew, was not much help. Intellect was no handicap, provided it was tactfully concealed, and all the social taboos observed. Once having 'made' a club, you could reassert your individuality; often by that time you had none.

Except for two rowdy societies, the Polo and Fencing, which flourished for about thirty years, there have been no social clubs for freshmen at Harvard. The basic society from which the smaller clubs have chosen their members during the last seventy years has been the Institute of 1770. In 1875 the Institute ceased to make any pretense of cultivating literature, and became merely the first social sifting of the sophomores. From the Class of 1877 it elected sixty-three members, or about 30 per cent; for the Class of 1888 the number elected was raised to one hundred, which was 40 per cent of that class; but as enrolment grew in the College the hundred-member limit declined to less than 20 per cent of the total class by 1906. When the Institute and Pudding combined in 1926, the joint membership was increased to 150 from each class, which maintains a ratio of 15 to 18 per cent of the whole; but this complement of 150 is not reached until the middle of senior year. In May, 1936, the Institute-Pudding included 418 members, about 16 per cent of the three upper classes.

Elections were then organized in 'fifteens,' but from around 1880 to World War I, in 'tens.' The whole membership from each class, either at the end of its sophomore or the beginning of its junior year, chose the first 'ten' from the next class; this 'first ten' chose the second, these two the third, and so on until the limit had been reached. Until 1904 the names were printed in the college and Boston papers in the exact order of their election, and the whole list served as an index of social rating, somewhat like the colonial order of seniority in the era 1730–72. On the night when the initiation began, the Institute used to march around singing its lilting song — said to have been of Hawaiian origin, imported by one of our Island Withingtons around 1871 — pulling the neophytes out of their rooms with savage roars, and dragging them about in the procession.

The first seven or eight tens of the Institute belonged automatically to the D.K.E., 'Dickey' or 'Deeks' (the 'secret society' of Santayana's novel 'to which everybody of consequence belonged'). 'Running for the Dickey,' the public part of the initiations, was taken over from the Pudding around 1880. For six days the neophyte had to attend all his classes, yet keep on the run, and be absolute slave to his tormentors, who invented all sorts of public stunts humiliating to his self-esteem; latterly these have been commuted by burlesque performances in the Yard, or divertissements between the halves at football games. The private part, which has always been kept secret, included sundry terrifying ordeals. Dickey initiations were often denounced as barbarous, ungentlemanly, and indecent; actually they were an excellent character test both of initiated and initiators. Of those socially eligible it was a major catastrophe not to make the Dickey, or at least the Institute; whilst to be chosen in the top tens meant assured social success in College, a lion's rôle in Boston débutante society, prompt election to the best clubs of New York and Boston after graduation, and a job at Lee Higginson's or a New York brokerage house.

Having 'made the Dickey,' the climber on the social ladder next thought of a 'waiting club.' Between 1875 and 1900 these were mainly chapters of national fraternities; but the Harvard chapters found their obligations to brethren from other colleges onerous, surrendered their charters, and became local clubs. Each maintained rooms or a house, the essential features of which were a bar, a billiard table, a card-room, and a dining-room. At the top of the club pyramid are the 'final' clubs.[1] In 1875 there were but two of these: the Porcel-

---

[1] 'Final,' in Harvard club lingo, means mutually exclusive; you can belong to but one final club, but are not restricted from joining clubs of other groups.

lian, which almost from its origin had been the goal of social ambition, and whose practices and postures were imitated by all the rest; and the A.D., a survival of the old Harvard chapter of Alpha Delta Phi. Around 1898 the 'waiting clubs' began to vote themselves 'final'; and at present there are only two of the waiting, as against nine final clubs. These begin taking in members from each class sophomore year, and complete the number senior year; few receive more than ten from any one class, and the present total membership of the nine final clubs is 278, about 12 per cent of the three upper classes. From 1878, when the A.D. purchased a house of its own, every final club has shaken down its graduates for a house, each new one surpassing the last in size and luxurious appointments.

The evolution of a fraternity chapter to 'waiting' and 'final' club is well illustrated by the story of the Delta Phi. There had been a chapter of that national fraternity at Harvard in 1846, but all memory of it was lost when in 1885 the Grand Council sent a committee to Cambridge to start a new one. Living in Beck Hall they found five wealthy New Yorkers who had not 'made' a club, and wanted one badly. Chapter Zeta of the Delta Phi was promptly organized, and rooms on Brattle Street hired. It was difficult to induce the 'right people' to join something new; but success was assured when James Gore King '89 and his classmate 'Jack' Morgan became members. By virtue of a remarkable financial operation they procured land and built a clubhouse, of which the new steward was so proud that he kept every room brilliantly illuminated, giving rise to the club's nickname, 'the Gas House.' The election of Guy Lowell '92, Gordon Bell '93, Winthrop Ames '95, and two faculty members, Santayana and William ('Kid') Woodworth, brought in a Bohemian breeze that dissipated the fog of heavy-swelldom and made the 'Gas House' the jolliest waiting club in College. It surrendered the Delta Phi charter, and officially adopted the humorous nickname. Around 1898 began a new era. Athletes like Ben Dibblee '99 and all the Milton clans began to predominate; the club went final, built itself a handsome new clubhouse, and was re-named the Delphic.

In junior and senior years all members of the Institute still in College (and some who were not), together with those whose talents were needed for the annual show, were elected to the Hasty Pudding Club. The Pudding theatricals were private and of varied nature until 1882, when Owen Wister's brilliant opera bouffe 'Dido and Aeneas,' the music a potpourri of Offenbach, Suppé, Sullivan, Bizet, Meyerbeer, and Wagner, went 'on the road,' and took Philadelphia, New York, and Boston by storm. That established a precedent that has since been followed; but as the eligible group seldom produces anything approaching Wisterian wit, the Pudding shows of the last forty years have mostly been poor imitations of Broadway musical comedies. There have been several exceptions, such as Lewis S. Thompson's *Sphinx* in 1892; Edward Burlingame Hill and Daniel Gregory Mason's *Granada* in 1894; D. W. Streeter and Edward Ballantine's *Lotus-Eaters* in 1907; and *Diana's Debut* in 1910, memorable for Jack Reed's lyric:

> At the Somerset things were rather wet,
>   Big exclusive affair!
> From the lack of heat all of Beacon Street
>   Surely must have been there.
> Berkeley Copley's son had a lovely bun,
>   So did all of the rest;
> For of many ways you can enjoy your days
>   A gentle Boston dance is best.

Outside the Institute-Pudding-waiting club-final club crowd, recruited from the graduates of fashionable schools and the socially eligible, there are very few social clubs at Harvard of any permanence. The Signet, organized in 1870 by Charles J. Bonaparte '71 as a protest against the class politics in the Pudding, and to maintain the literary traditions that the Pudding had abandoned, occasionally elects the unclubbed intelligentsia. It acquired an attractive clubhouse in 1900, and is still one of the pleasantest societies in College. The Pi Eta, and chapters of the Acacia, Sigma Alpha Epsilon, and Delta Upsilon fraternities, elect about seventy-five members of each class, from outside the Institute circle. Except for these and other unpretentious clubs and fraternity chapters that died in the War or the depression, there have been no clubs at Harvard since 1870 to which graduates of high schools and the sons of country lawyers and ministers, who used to fill the Institute and the Pudding before the Civil War, could hope to be chosen. And, strange as it may seem, nobody seems to care. The proportion of each class in the clubs has been so small that they do not dominate the social life of the College; and there is so much going on outside them. Some form of social exclusiveness exists in every American college of any size, and there is something to be said for a system that is geared to American society itself, and which inflicts no 'inferiority complex' on outsiders, as against societies based on success in puerile activities, or fraternities which take in so many that it is a badge of shame not to belong. If colleges must have clubs, why not have clubs that are 'clubby,' and not fortuitous assemblages of fundamentally uncongenial adolescents?

The Harvard clubs have been very important to those who belonged (Theodore Roosevelt, announcing the engagement of his daughter to Nicholas Longworth, informed Kaiser Wilhelm that 'Nick' and he belonged to the Porcellian), but supremely unimportant to those on the other side of the social chasm. They have always included a considerable number of the men in each class who subsequently became famous; even some of the 'Harvard Heretics and Rebels' recently enumerated by Roger Baldwin '05 and Corliss Lamont '24 — both clubmen themselves. The clubs are not the best preparation for living in a democratic society; yet many of their graduates have been faithful servants to the University, to the Republic, and to learning. The split between Yard and Gold Coast that the clubs helped to create had often resulted in bitterly contested class elections; but this hard feeling vanished at graduation, and anything like fraternity or senior society politics in after life is unknown among Harvard men.

Outside clubdom, though participated in by many club members on a level with others, was the real college life of the period, where originality and individualism were formed, small congenial groups were easily formed and dissolved, and all manner of societies flourished for every possible taste, from trap-shooting to art-collecting. For this larger college world there was no pressure to conform, no standard mould; the genius of the place, as it had been since President Leverett's day, was to encourage each individual to develop his peculiar tastes and talents. A lad who came to Harvard with the makings of genius did not have his little spark quenched or his ambition trampled upon; conversely, the boy who entered a fool was very apt to graduate a damned fool. You might not belong to a single social club, yet cover half a wall with framed 'shingles' of membership in this or that society, with Harvard and school banners; with photographs of athletic teams, foreign travel, and actresses; with world's fair souvenirs, posters, and stolen signboards; with steins, pewter mugs, empty bottles, and nude statuettes adorning the mantelpiece and bookshelves, from which dangled dance programmes, knicknacks, and beer advertisements; a winning oar fastened to the cornice, and charts of summer cruises to the ceiling; and to this agglomeration there might be added the black strip with your name in white letters which delicately proclaimed your membership in D.K.E., or the rope, bar, and bandanna used in the Pi Eta initiation. The decorations and furnishings of students' rooms from 1880 until after the War were pretty dreadful, especially after the 'mission style' furniture came into fashion.

The societies, shop clubs, political clubs, and other student associations such as the religious and philanthropic groups that had headquarters in Phillips Brooks House, were generally open to anyone, undergraduate, graduate, law, or divinity student, who was interested; yet we were not much infested by the 'activity man,' that pest of American colleges. Special places were provided for practical young men by the managerships of the various teams, and the 'business editorships' of the college papers, which relieved the 'literary editors' from sordid care. Santayana was right in saying that the undergraduate 'does, except when the pressure or fear of the outer world constrains him, only what he finds worth doing for its own sake.' Moreover, none of these activities was a microcosmos. An editor-in-chief of the *Monthly* might, and often did, stroke a class crew, belong to a final club, teach his sub-editors boxing when proofreading palled, and act in a play. This state of things used to puzzle our visitors from other colleges. With them an 'aesthoot' stuck to his book, brush, or pen, and drank tea; an 'athloot' took exercise instead of culture, and drank high-balls when not in training. But that the same 'stude' should row, attend 'pink teas,' box, discuss philosophy, and graduate *magna cum laude* seemed to our neighbors something outside the order of nature.

College journalism after 1870 largely took the place of the literary societies of earlier eras. The *Advocate* continued without a break, though its function of humorous commentator on college affairs was usurped in 1876 by the *Lampoon*, founded by Edward S. ('Dan') Martin '77, Ralph W. Curtis, Samuel Sherwood, John T. Wheelwright, and other wits of '76. The *Lampoon* bred some of the cleverest cartoonists and columnists of the present day, such as Gluyas Williams '11 and Bob Benchley '12; but after acquiring a needlessly luxurious clubhouse in 1910, it has tended to become a mere social club, with the paper a side issue. The *Advocate* went in heavily for short stories in the nineties — and no wonder, with lads such as Arthur S. Pier '95, Arthur C. Train '96 and Arthur B. Ruhl '99 on the board; criticism revived with Van Wyck Brooks '08; but the *Advocate's* poetry was pretty feeble compared with that of the *Harvard Monthly*. Founded by Santayana and his friends in 1885, the *Monthly* has been edited by such men as Mark Howe and Bernhard Berenson '87, Norman Hapgood '90, William Vaughan Moody '93, Robert Morss Lovett '92, Lucien Price '07, and John Hall Wheelock '08. In it was printed some of the early poetry of Moody, Bliss Carman (Graduate School '88), Edwin Arlington Robinson '95, and Swinburne Hale '05. The *Illustrated Magazine*, founded in 1899, was innocuous until Gerard C. Henderson '12 became managing editor; but, like the *Monthly*, it died in World War I. The weekly *Magenta*, founded in 1873, when the athletic teams had adopted that unpleasantly aniline color, changed to the *Crimson* when the proper color was restored in 1875, and united with the daily *Herald* in 1883. Among its editors were Lloyd McKim Garrison '88, Henry James '99, Dan Sargent '13, and Edward A. Whitney '17. Until it acquired a building in 1915 the 'Crime' was a paying proposition, cutting handsome dividends for the editors.

Societies like the History Club and the Boylston Chemical Club (founded by Theodore W. Richards in 1885), fostered by members of the Faculty, continued to flourish; the old Natural History Society was still going strong, with such men as Thomas Barbour '06, future Director of the Museum, and John H. Baker '15, future head of the Audubon Society, as presidents. Jerome D. Greene, Arthur C. Train, and others founded the Harvard Memorial Society in 1895 to preserve the records of the past; they celebrated John Harvard's birthday, put up bronze tablets on historic spots, and compiled the records of occupants of rooms in the older halls.

From the Civil War to World War I Harvard undergraduates had an insatiable thirst for theatricals. The Pudding and Pi Eta, in addition to their public musical show, gave three or four private plays a year, besides impromptus (known in Pudding mythology as 'spoops') put on by the neophytes. The Dickey, the Signet Society, and most of the college journals produced plays (mostly very scurrilous and indecent) in their rooms or houses. Even the University Boat Club and Baseball Club gave public performances for their own benefit at Horticultural Hall in the seventies. And the social workers coached theatricals given by the settlement houses in Boston.

Of a different order were the plays produced by the four associations formed for the cultivation of foreign languages — the Cercle Français, Deutscher Verein, Sociedad Española, and Circolo Italiano, each of which had from forty-five to eighty members by 1908. The French club began its theatrical annals in 1888 with *Le Misanthrope*, and followed it the next year with a modern play by Labiche; these (says M. Gafflot in *Le Théâtre au Collège*) were the first performances of French drama in any college or university since the expulsion of the Jesuits from France in 1762. In 1899 the Cercle Français gave the first production in history of *Le Pédant Joué* by Cyrano de Bergerac, for which Professor Ferdinand Bôcher provided a revised text, with a biographical introduction by

Horace B. Stanton '00. James Hazen Hyde (A.B. 1898), president of the Cercle in his undergraduate days, became the Cercle's Maecenas upon graduation, paid the deficits, and provided the professional coach. This gave the Frenchmen a considerable edge on their rivals, although all four produced plays, and the Deutscher Verein was stimulated into great activity by the imperial visit of 1902 — the famous Ernst F. Hanfstaengl '09 was president of it his senior year.

Besides an occasional Greek play or Terentian comedy, produced by students of the classics, there were classic English dramas sponsored by the English Department. The Delta Upsilon fraternity, with the aid of Professor George P. Baker, began in 1898 to produce annually a play by Beaumont and Fletcher, Dekker, or some other Elizabethan dramatist long since forgotten by the commercial theatre; and the Harvard Dramatic Club was founded in 1908. Mr. Baker's 47 'Workshop,' a graduate-school course that became a training school for players, producers, and managers, began its notable career in the same decade. The students in this course wrote, acted, and produced their own plays; a picked academic audience had the privilege of witnessing them, and the duty of submitting critiques. English 47 was one of those rare opportunities afforded by a university for a co-ordination of thought, art, and action; and Yale's greatest victory over Harvard in the present century came in 1925, when Professor Baker, after long discouragement by the Harvard Corporation and failure to obtain the long-desired theatre, translated English 47 to New Haven. Until that date, Harvard was the premier theatrical college in the country; and it was most fitting that the largest and most important theatrical collection in the world should have been presented to the University by Robert Gould Shaw (A.B. 1869) in 1915.

Music was in the air for those attuned to receive it:

serious study with the Department; the Pierian Sodality orchestra, which had Philip G. Clapp '09 and Chalmres D. Clifton '12 for conductors toward the end of our period; and the Instrumental Clubs (banjo, mandolin, and guitar). The Glee Club, which in the seventies and eighties had a series of inspiring leaders, such as Arthur Foote '74 and Thomas Mott Osborne '84, fell off in the nineties, but more than recovered under Professor Archibald T. ('Doc.') Davison (a.b. 1906), who enlarged the repertoire of traditional light opera and 'college songs' with sacred music by the early Italian composers, and profane music of the English madrigalists. The Boston Symphony Orchestra began its series of Cambridge concerts in the early eighties, and the five annual Arthur Whiting Chamber Concerts began in 1905. Daniel Gregory Mason (a.b. 1895) has lately given us a charming picture of one of these literary-musical groups in the nineties — Pierre la Rose, William Vaughan Moody, Edward Burlingame Hill: constant piano-playing and trying out scores borrowed from the College Library; the thrilling discovery of Brahms and Dvořák; hot rum toddy over an open coal fire in Matthews; walks in bleak sunset across Harvard Bridge, to dine at Billy Parks', or Marliave's famous fifty-cent table d'hôte, *vin compris*. . . .

As spring came on there were mint juleps in Boston, or boating at Riverside, or long afternoon trudges; and in the evenings there were magical walks up Brattle Street, fragrant with lilacs, or to Fresh Pond, ghostly in mist and moonlight. And always there was the fascination of Moody's imagination-releasing figures of speech, his fertile silences, his irresponsible humor, comical slang, and shouting gusto of laughter, his deep, contagious sense of the infinite mystery and richness of life.[1]

And after describing the influence of Norton and the great philosophers, he concludes that Harvard

---

[1] Mason, 'Harvard in the Nineties,' *New England Quarterly*, ix. 48–49.

was more than stimulating, it was mellowing, ripening. This was because we students had not only the provocation of these contacts with truly great men, of a surprising diversity of interests, characters, and personalities, but, what is even more precious, we had liberty in the choosing of these influences, time to digest and assimilate them, leisure to grow from our centres as well as absorb at our points of contact. We were not regimented, standardized, herded, and labelled. We were not intimidated into imitativeness, browbeaten into conformity, or nagged into efficiency. Our healthy nutrition was as little in danger from forced feeding as from starvation; for while we had set before us the feast of the whole of human civilization, what we should take was determined only by our own tastes, appetites, and powers of digestion. No doubt we became less specialized than we might have become under less generous systems. Hill and I have often compared notes on how much more rapidly we might have progressed in our purely technical musical skill had we gone to a good conservatory instead of to Harvard. Technical skill, however, is not all there is in art; nor is even intellectual power of a purely impersonal kind. Musicians are especially likely to be narrow, unimaginative, devoid of mental nuances. Ripeness, fullness, richness of nature come only from many interests, freely followed, and allowed to cross-fertilize.

For one more example of the multifarious patterns that individuals wove out of these rich materials, read what Jack Reed '10 wrote of his experiences when seven years out of College:

All sorts of strange characters, of every race and mind, poets, philosophers, cranks of every twist, were in our Class. The very hugeness of it prevented any one man from knowing more than a few of his classmates, though I managed to make the acquaintance of about five hundred of them. . . . What is known as 'college spirit' was not very powerful; no odium attached to those who didn't go to football games and cheer. There was talk of the world, and daring thought, and intellectual insurgency; heresy has always been a Harvard and a New England tradition. Students themselves criticized the faculty for not educating them, attacked the sacred institution of intercollegiate athletics, sneered at undergraduate clubs so holy that no one dared mention their names. No matter what you were or what you did — at Harvard you could find your kind. It wasn't a breeder for masses of mediocrely educated young men equipped with 'business' psychology; out of each class came a few creative minds, a few scholars, a few

'gentlemen' with insolent manners, and a ruck of nobodies. . . .
Things have changed now.[1] I liked Harvard better then.

Toward the end of my college course two influences came into my
life, which had a good deal to do with shaping me. One was contact
with Professor Copeland. . . . The other was what I call, for lack of a
better name, the manifestation of the modern spirit. Some men,
notably Walter Lippmann, had been reading and thinking and talking
about politics and economics, not as dry theoretical studies, but as live
forces acting on the world, on the University even. They formed the
Socialist Club, to study and discuss all modern social and economic
theories, and began to experiment with the community in which they
lived.

Under their stimulus the college political clubs, which had formerly
been quadrennial mushroom growths for the purpose of drinking beer,
parading and burning red fire, took on a new significance. The Club
drew up a platform for the Socialist Party in the city elections. It
had social legislation introduced into the Massachusetts Legislature.
Its members wrote articles in the college papers challenging undergraduate ideals, and muckraked the University for not paying its
servants living wages, and so forth. Out of the agitation sprang the
Harvard Men's League for Women's Suffrage, the Single Tax Club,
[and] an Anarchist group. The faculty was petitioned for a course in
socialism. Prominent radicals were invited to Cambridge to lecture.
An open forum was started, to debate college matters and the issues of
the day. The result of this movement upon the undergraduate world
was potent. All over the place radicals sprang up, in music, painting,
poetry, the theatre. The more serious college papers took a socialistic,
or at least progressive tinge. Of course all this made no ostensible
difference in the look of Harvard society, and probably the clubmen
and the athletes, who represented us to the world, never even heard
of it. But it made me, and many others, realize that there was something going on in the dull outside world more thrilling than college
activities, and turned our attention to the writings of men like H. G.
Wells and Graham Wallas, wrenching us away from the Oscar
Wildean dilettantism that had possessed undergraduate littérateurs
for generations.[2]

Reed does not exaggerate. Hundreds of students
wanted just what he did, and Lee Simonson '09 provided

---

[1] Not so much as he thought! It is amusing to find Reed taking on the
standard 'old grad.' attitude toward Alma Mater.

[2] *New Republic*, LXXXVI. 332–33.

the spark with an essay in the *Advocate* for January, 1908, of which these are a few of the provocative sentences:

> The virtues here are the contented, unassertive virtues of middle-age, tact and deference, easy comradeship and slipshod kindliness. . . . But there is no effective sign here of the boisterous virtues of youth. . . . The very air is heavy with urbanity. The ideal of gentility sooths us like a warm blanket. . . . The poor are knocking at our doors. Socialism can no longer be passed by with a shrug. But are we facing it? . . . We accept the poor as there, as providentially provided to exercise our morality upon. . . .
>
> Of course there is great intellectual capacity here but it is never converted into intellectual enthusiasm. . . . Why not organize our intellectual enthusiasms? . . . our most crying need at present is a dramatic club. The few more or less trivial operettas, and more or less tiresome revivals we are accustomed to, are an altogether inadequate expression of the serious and permanent interest here in the modern drama. . . . What we need also is a reform club where we can hear from the constructive social theorists, socialists, communists, and even the exponents of the single tax. . . .

Things began to happen. Clubs of a new sort sprang up like mushrooms — and some of them even outlasted World War I. There was the Speakers' Club 'to maintain an open Forum at the University,' and get away from the blight of 'college debating.' For a time the Speakers' was a training ground for young men such as A. A. Berle '13; but it acquired a clubhouse and became purely social after the War. There was the Cosmopolitan Club, for bringing together men of different nationalities, races, and colors (Mr. Aab '13, the Siamese who appears likely to head the roll of Harvard men for eternity, was an early president); and the Socialist Club, of which Walter Lippmann '10, A. Jaretzki '13, and R. W. Chubb '15 (the last two now members of conservative law firms in New York and Saint Louis) were the leading spirits. The Social Politics Club, founded in 1909 'to bring together men who believe the world is not finished,' was composed half of Faculty (such as Edwin F. Gay, Lewis J. Johnson, and Comfort Avery Adams) and half of undergraduates (such as Gerard C. Henderson '12 and Arthur Fisher '15). They attempted to carry into the field of political science and sociology the intimate teacher-student relation that Copey had established in the literary field. The future 'white-spat boys' founded a Diplomatic Club in 1912; others, thinking that too stuffy, started the International Polity Club 'to promote the thoughtful discussion and study of modern international problems.' George W. Nasmyth of the Graduate School, the first president, invited men like Norman Angell to discuss ways and means of consolidating peace, and arranged conferences with similar clubs in other colleges. As soon as the World War broke out, the discussions became exceedingly lively.

A similar ferment was going on in letters and the drama. Only two months after Simonson asked for it, the Dramatic Club was founded with Edward B. Sheldon '08 as president; in December came its first production: 'The Promised Land,' by Allan Davis '07. The next few years plays by Hermann Hagedorn '07, Hiram K. Motherwell, and others were produced from scores submitted by members; and with David Carb's 'Voice of the People' (1912) it was clear that the Dramatic Club had arrived. It was the first Harvard club to admit Radcliffe girls. The Corporation, however, drew the line at its presenting 'Mrs. Warren's Profession' with Radcliffe providing the women's rôles.

The poets were naturally slow to organize themselves, but in 1915 the Harvard Poetry Society was founded by S. Foster Damon '14, e. e. cummings '15, John Dos Passos '16, Robert Hillyer '17, and others, with the blessing of Dean Briggs. The members met irregularly to read their own poems and take the rap of vigorous criticism, or to listen to readings by poets such as Robert Frost, John Gould Fletcher, and Amy Lowell. One memorable occasion was when Jack Wheelwright asked the lady,

'How do you write, Miss Lowell, when you have nothing to say?'; another, the costume punch, where Hillyer appeared as Cupid. *Eight Harvard Poets* (1917) and *Eight More Harvard Poets* (1923) preserve some of the best work of these young men, who scorned to be called a 'school' of poesy.

These activities attracted the earnest, the artistic, the seekers after truth; but there were other things in the air, in this pre-war generation, than reform and literary expression. The dance mania — turkey-trotting and the like — hit the College hard, and more students acquired cars, since Henry Ford had invented Model T for the impecunious; whilst Nationals, Renaults, and Mercedes began to be seen parked along the Gold Coast. Boys who a few years before would have been content to lounge about their clubs now began to tear about the country with 'hot mammas,' dancing and drinking in roadside 'clubs'; you had to drink deeply in order to keep awake dancing, and the more you danced the thirstier you became.

Never was College so exciting, or drunks so drunken, or the generous feelings of ardent youth so exalted, as in those last golden years before World War I. Here, as in the European universities, Sarajevo and what followed shattered illusions, postponed indefinitely high hopes, and obscured the democratic vision. Undergraduate opinion on the war passed through the same phases as American opinion: incredulity, discussion, and a gradual hardening of pro-Ally feeling. By the time war came to America there were very few Harvard men who did not believe it to be a holy and righteous war, the successful conclusion of which would permit democracy to advance to new **triumphs.** *Dis aliter visum.*

XVII

THE LOWELL ADMINISTRATION

'THE history of Harvard University has now been brought down to our own times; to a period too near to be viewed in just historical perspective.' So remarked Josiah Quincy, historian of Harvard a century ago, when he reached the year 1780. We have now long passed the corresponding date in the last century; and as this story approaches our own times, the difficulty of threading one's way among the mass of material increases. It will be best to consider the rest of this book as a personal impression, subject to correction in fact, and to revision as perspective lengthens.

Abbott Lawrence Lowell was born in Boston on December 13, 1856, of a family that had served University and Commonwealth for several generations.[1] He entered Harvard College from Mr. Noble's School in 1873, graduated *cum laude* in 1877, with highest honors in Mathematics, took the LL.B. three years later, and practised law in Boston with great success. In 1897, as a consequence of his treatise on 'Governments and Parties in Continental Europe,' he became a part-time lecturer on Government at Harvard, proved to be a stimulating teacher, and in 1900 was promoted full professor. His *magnum opus*, 'The Government of England,' came out in 1908. Mr. Lowell's character, talents, background, and activity in university reform made him the one logical candidate for the succession; he was elected by the Corporation on January 13, 1909, promptly confirmed by the Overseers, entered upon the duties of the office when

[1] See genealogical table on page 159.

President Eliot retired in May, and was formally inaugurated in October.

President Lowell, like President Eliot, was a 'Boston Brahmin' and a Unitarian. He had the high ambition to promote scholarship in Harvard University and to raise the standards of higher education in America. He had definite aims, and a tireless energy in seeking their translation into action. There the likeness to his predecessor ceased. Mr. Lowell's mind has the Greek agility that Eliot's lacked; it acquires knowledge easily and imparts it eagerly. His personality is outgoing and vivacious; he converses rapidly and listens little, yet what he says is always worth hearing. His temper is more autocratic than that of Mr. Eliot, and with opposition he has less patience. A brilliant member of a gifted family (Percival Lowell the astronomer was his brother, and Amy Lowell the poet his sister), he is impatient of intellectual mediocrities, 'C men,' plodding graduate students, and merely useful members of faculties; he is inclined to draw conclusions from limited observations of his own, rather than from the prolonged research of an expert. Under stresses to which Eliot was never subjected, Mr. Lowell has been tolerant and just. He not only believed in academic freedom, but practised it through trying circumstances, defending the right of instructors to teach the truth as they saw it, and in their public relations to express unpopular opinions with which he fundamentally disagreed. The knowledge that he could be depended upon to defend these rights made the members of the several faculties more responsible and cautious in their utterances than they would have been under a President likely to let them down. His positive and incessant efforts to improve instruction, and to convince undergraduates of the worth of intellectual effort, made the Harvard of his day an exciting place in which to study or to teach, and attracted the devotion of the younger generation.

Mr. Lowell's aims were often misrepresented twenty years ago, and to some extent are still misunderstood. He did not undervalue the graduate schools, but paid less attention to them than to the College, because it was the College that needed reform. He had no desire to turn out a uniform, standard product stamped with the Harvard hall-mark, or to undo anything that Eliot had done. He did not propose to serve business, or any lesser interests than learning and the nation. But he did propose to consolidate the advance of the Eliot era, much as the Federal Constitution had consolidated the gains of the American Revolution: to balance liberty with order. He proposed to put back into the academic basket some of the things that had fallen through the mesh during the process of expansion. Of these, the most important was education. Mr. Lowell was distressed at the large number of able youths, some of them of high standing in school, who entered Harvard only to have their enthusiasm directed to the side-shows, and to treat their studies as an inconvenient ritual. 'C is the gentleman's grade' was a slogan of the Eliot era that he detested. Academic honors, still largely based on course grades, were regarded with indifference by both students and public, and not even entered in the Quinquennial Catalogue.

An intellectual aristocrat himself, Mr. Lowell disliked the social divisions that he found in the College, because they were based on wealth, schooling, and Boston society, rather than on intellectual ability. The 'collegiate way of living' that our founders in their poverty established had vanished in the sprawling College of twenty-two hundred students, increasing every year. The traditional union of religion, learning, and social life no longer existed; even in the clubs, which had salvaged the social side, there was no religion and little learning. Of the students, some were living in luxurious private dormitories, and eating in clubs or at restaurants; others were rooming in the shabby Yard, and feeding in a mob at Memorial Hall; the poor and struggling lived in College House or cheap lodgings; and another group lived at home in Greater Boston, commuting forlornly in trains and trolleys. Before the degree formulas were anglicized in 1896, the President used to certify to the Overseers that the *juvenes* presented to them were sufficient *tam doctrina quam moribus* (in learning as in manners) to be admitted to the first degree in Arts. As for knowledge, it was possible to obtain a degree for cramming, unloading, and forgetting seventeen courses; and what had become of the *mores*? It could hardly be said that Harvard men had bad manners, for they had none save what they brought with them. And although there were sagas of unknown farmer boys, like Marshall Newell '94, who began by knowing nobody, yet 'made' everything, there were too many youths who became pocketed freshman year, and never rubbed shoulders with anyone. There was a terrific social wastage going on. Harvard, wrote John Corbin (A.B. 1892) at the end of the Eliot era, had become 'a social orphan asylum.'

Mr. Lowell had studied the social system of the English universities, which, rising from their deep cultural slough in the eighteenth century, had somehow managed to make learning fruitful by grafting it to the natural enthusiasm of youth. Oxford and Cambridge had no elective system, except for the 'pass men'; the key to their success was in the 'Honour Schools' or 'Tripos' in a number of broad subjects, prepared for under the direction of a tutor, and tested by a stiff general examination before graduation — a plan that had earned the respect of the public. A beginning of this had already been made at Harvard with the new regulations for degrees with distinction, especially in History and Literature. Barrett Wendell had almost dragged some of the bright lads of social distinction into that new field, in order to make honors fashionable. Might not more be done, by insisting that every student in Harvard College integrate his curriculum (once he had chosen a general subject), providing him with a tutor to help him in the process, and setting up a comprehensive examination as a goal? President Wilson had already done some of this at Princeton, yet omitted the indispensable goal.

On the social side, Mr. Lowell observed that at Oxford and Cambridge there was a union of learning with the fine art of living; and that, without there being any pretense of democracy, the poorest student in a college was within reach of the best that his college had to give. Was Harvard past reconstructing according to the collegiate pattern of the founders? If the 'Gold Coast,' the 'Yard,' and the 'rooming houses' were blown up, could the pieces be reassembled in any decent or socially potent pattern? Mr. Lowell thought that they could, provided we avoided President Wilson's mistake of running headlong on vested interests. Not many agreed with him. Harvard College had been pretty vigorously reformed by President Eliot, and wanted repose; but repose was not a posture that Mr. Lowell found agreeable himself, or that he rendered comfortable for members of the several faculties.

Mr. Lowell's inaugural address challenged the academic world, as Mr. Eliot's had forty years before. Delivered from a stage on the west front of University Hall, and carried by the speaker's own voice clear across the Yard, it opened with Aristotle's saying that man is by nature a social animal, and that American colleges exist to develop his powers as a social being. Yet 'college life has shown a marked tendency to disintegrate, both intellectually and socially.' It was ominous that neither the community nor the College valued high proficiency in college studies. The College was in danger of being pinched out, as in Germany, between secondary education (or 'junior colleges') and professional schools. It would be suicide to further this process by shortening the college course. 'The most vital measure for saving the college is not to shorten its duration, but to ensure that it shall be worth saving.'

To make it worth saving,

the college ought to produce, not defective specialists, but men intellectually well rounded, of wide sympathies and unfettered judgment. At the same time they ought to be trained to hard and accurate thought, and this . . . requires a mastery of something, acquired by continuous application. Surely the essence of a liberal education consists in an attitude of mind, a familiarity with methods of thought, an ability to use information rather than in a memory stocked with facts, however valuable such a storehouse may be.

In the relation of undergraduates to one another, 'might there not be more points of intellectual contact among the undergraduates, and might not considerable numbers of them have much in common?' And he goes on to sketch out his ideal of a college course: an integrated curriculum like that of an Oxford honors school, supplemented by 'a number of general courses on wholly unrelated fields.'

'The social relations of the undergraduates among themselves are quite as important.' Under present conditions 'the college itself falls short of its national mission of throwing together youths of promise of every kind from every part of the country.' College society reflects the divisions outside, 'on the basis of wealth.' But 'one object of a university is to counteract rather than copy the defects of the civilization of the day.'

America has not yet contributed her share to scholarly creation, and the fault lies in part at the doors of our universities. They do not strive enough in the impressionable years of early manhood to stimulate intellectual appetite and ambition; nor do they foster productive scholarship enough among those members of their staffs who are capable thereof. . . . The university touches the community at many points, and as time goes on it ought to serve the public through ever increasing channels. But all its activities are more or less connected with, and most of them are based upon, the college. It is there that character ought to be shaped, that aspirations ought to be formed, that citizens ought to be trained, and scholarly tastes implanted.

It was a favorite simile of Mr. Lowell's that you cannot lift a blanket by one corner. There must be effort at several points in order to raise the general standard. Consequently, his programme for the College included four points: the Freshman Halls, concentration and distribution, the tutorial system, and honors. These left the centre sagging, to be sure; but when opportunity came the house plan raised that as well. Each distinct lift required money, and it was found. Mr. Lowell had a way of doing that, and in the grand manner, as a Prince of the Church in the Renaissance accepted tribute from condottiere and merchant-banker for civilized objects. Edward W. Forbes (A.B. 1895), Director of the Fogg Art Museum, with a number of friends, had already purchased most of the land between Mt. Auburn Street and the Charles, and was holding it until such time as the Corporation should have the good sense to use it. The building of the Charles River Dam in 1910, raising the water permanently to high-tide level, made the river-front far more attractive than in the days of marshes and mud flats. The Corporation now took over the land; and the firm of Coolidge, Shepley, Bulfinch and Abbott made plans for the new Freshman Halls. Standish Hall, given by Mrs. Russell Sage, and Gore Hall (perpetuating the name of the superseded Library), provided by subscriptions of alumni, were open quadrangles facing the river; the Smith Halls, provided from a long-accumulated bequest from George Smith (A.B. 1853), was a closed quadrangle on Boylston Street. These, holding almost five hundred freshmen, were completed by the fall of 1914; and McKinlock Hall, given after the war by the parents of one of its victims, made a fourth. Each contained a dining hall and a common room; the suites, for from one to five persons, had all modern comforts and conveniences; and the rooms were priced at various levels so that all but the very poorest could afford to live with their classmates, and enter into the social activities of freshmen.

'Concentration and distribution' first went into effect for the Class of 1914. This was the system commonly known as 'majoring and minoring' in other American universities. It was required that every undergraduate 'concentrate' at least six of his sixteen elective courses in one Division; and 'distribute' at least six of the rest among three general groups of studies outside his field of concentration. 'The object to be attained was two-fold,' wrote President Lowell. 'First, to require every student to make a choice of electives that will secure a systematic education, based on the principle of knowing a little of everything and something well. . . . Second . . . to make the student plan his college curriculum seriously, and plan it as a whole.' In practice, more than six courses in the field of concentration have generally been taken, and the distribution requirements have lately been reduced to four courses, distributed as the student wishes.

As this integration of the student's course would mean little so long as he was enabled to win a degree by counting off courses, Mr. Lowell early recommended that he be given something to concentrate on. The divisional examinations, three written papers to be passed before graduation, were adopted in principle in 1912, but so revolutionary a step as requiring a student to remember something until he graduated was wisely left optional with each Division of the Faculty. Mr. Lowell, in other words, adopted the same persuasive tactics as Mr. Eliot; he knew his academic community too well to force new burdens on unwilling professors. The first Division to adopt the general examination was that of History, Government, and Economics for the Class of 1917. Others followed after the war, until all divisions of the Faculty of Arts and Sciences, excepting those of Engineering and Chemistry, had taken it up. There are now some twenty-five fields of concentration that require 'divisionals,' including several cross-sections between departments such as the pioneer History and Literature, and History and Science.

In order to prepare the students for these general examinations, each Division as soon as it adopted them was given a corps of tutors, proportionate to the number of concentrators.

A tutorship in Harvard College now signifies a function, not a rank. Instructors of every grade up to and including full professor may be tutors as well; and if they are, a proportionate amount of their course work is remitted. Even with this relatively easy method of introducing the system it was very expensive, and difficult to gear to courses. Most students and alumni were against it, partly as a new burden, partly because it seemed a retrograde step from the free election of the Eliot era. Not many members of the Faculty cared to undertake tutorial instruction, and new men had to pick up tutorial technique as best they could. Some divisions made the mistake of appointing as tutors worthy graduate students who were mainly interested in winning a Doctor's degree. There was so much tutorial turnover in the first fifteen years (as in the early days of Harvard College) that a student seldom had the same preceptor for three years. There have been constant, and on the whole constructive, criticisms of the system from the Student Council, the *Crimson*, and the tutors themselves. Gradually the personnel has improved, and, especially since the Houses have been built, a close personal and friendly relation between tutor and 'tutee' has been established. One tendency at the present time is to lessen the student's course work and give him more time for reading under his tutor's direction; another is for tutors to give less attention to 'C men' who are merely trying to 'get by,' and concentrate on making ambitious scholars better.

The most surprising improvement has been the increasing number of undergraduates who undertake additional study in order to obtain honors at graduation. Mr. Lowell urged the worth of academic honors in and out of season; the tutors, and now the Houses, vie with each other to induce properly equipped students to make the extra effort; and the public, after twenty-five years, is beginning to appreciate the value of a young man who has given this evidence of ability and intelligence. The honors candidate has to pass his divisionals with distinction, submit a 'thesis' (dissertation) of at least 'B' grade in his senior year, and make a good course record as well. The only special privilege he receives is the remission of a half or a full course in his senior year in order to give him time to prepare his dissertation.

These new regulations halted the trend toward the three-year course. For many years divisionals were also given at mid-years, but that additional burden on the examiners has ended, and of the Class of 1934 less than one per cent got through in three years, while a considerable number, after failure either in courses or divisionals senior year, passed successfully later.[1]

These few and simple reforms have made an immense difference in the average college student's attitude toward his studies, that is only faintly expressed in statistics. About forty per cent of each graduating class take honors in special fields at graduation.[2] In some fields, such as His-

---

[1] The Class of 1934 entered 897 strong. Of these 6 graduated in less than 4 years (3 with honors), 566 in 4 years (244 with honors), 77 in $4\frac{1}{2}$–$5\frac{1}{2}$ years (19 with honors). Of those who as yet have obtained no degree, about 100 withdrew, 100 were dropped or fired, 7 died, and the remainder stayed four years in College but did not receive a degree.

[2] The highest number of Bachelor's degrees with honors in special fields granted in any one year before the World War was 87 out of 517,

tory, the examination has been divided between junior and senior years, in order to give the student more opportunity for specialization his last year; and we often have honors dissertations for the A.B. nowadays that would have been thought worthy of a Ph.D. thirty years ago. Study, as the Director of Athletics recently remarked, is now Harvard's principal indoor sport — game schedules have to be arranged so as not to interfere with it! Harvard students are more responsive and responsible, and easier to teach, than they were before the war. This was Mr. Lowell's greatest achievement; he 'sold' education to Harvard College!

Mr. Lowell was the greatest builder of any Harvard president; and during the last twenty years of his presidency, more new construction was completed than in all Harvard history previous to his day. Yet the new construction has done less violence to the old Harvard than might have been expected, since most of it was entrusted to the firm of architects headed by Charles A. Coolidge (A.B. 1881, ART.D. 1906), which, instead of going in for the 'collegiate Gothic' or 'imperial Elizabethan' that have so transformed the appearance of our ancient contemporaries, stuck consistently to Georgian. Consequently, our newer buildings appear to have grown out of the most ancient, and our former excursions into Richardson Romanesque and Victorian Gothic are much less obtrusive.

This building activity set in around 1911, and for twenty-two years the sound of the steel-riveter, the carpenter, and the mason was never absent from Cambridge. Mr. Lowell could be seen almost any day in-

---

in 1915. Numbers rose both relatively and absolutely after the war, reaching a high point in 1935, when 266 Bachelor's degrees out of 623 were conferred with honors in special fields (statistics prepared by Miss Magruder). The old regulation awarding *cum laude* on course grades only has continued; and in addition to the figures cited above, 57 students in 1915 and 39 in 1935 graduated '*cum laude* in general studies.'

specting operations, deciding details with quick and accurate judgment, and leading perspiring and trembling celebrities across swaying planks and up builders' ladders. In 1912–14 in the northern section of the college grounds much-needed laboratories (the Cruft High Tension, the Wolcott Gibbs, and the T. J. Coolidge, Jr.) were built for the departments of Physics and Chemistry; the Peabody Museum was wedded to the Museum of Comparative Zoölogy by a ring of steel and brick (as their Peabody, Putnam, and Agassiz parents had long ago planned), nearly doubling the space available for the ethnological spoils that our field expeditions were bringing home; the Larz Anderson Bridge provided a worthy approach to Soldiers Field; the Paine Music Building arose modestly behind the skirts of Lawrence Hall; three Freshman Halls were completed; and over all (except Memorial) bulked Widener, the new home of the Harvard College Library. This great building, presented by Mrs. George D. Widener in memory of her son Harry of the Class of 1907, and built around his remarkable collection of first editions, unfortunately dwarfs everything else in the Yard, but is almost perfect for interior arrangements; both the building and the books which the Director (Professor A. C. Coolidge) and sundry donors have poured into it have made an immeasurable contribution to scholarly achievement.

As early as 1915 one can snuff the approach of war in President Lowell's reports. At the western university where I was teaching when the war broke in Europe, it seemed to the average student as unreal as the Wars of the Roses; returning to Harvard early in 1915, one was on the outskirts of battle. The first ambulance and hospital units had gone over from the Harvard Medical and Dental Schools; scores of young graduates were enlisting in the Canadian and the British expeditionary forces, the Foreign Legion, the Lafayette flying squadron; sympathy for the allied cause was unconcealed; not for a moment was the Harvard community neutral in thought or deed. There is some reason to believe that the German Emperor's gift of the casts that made the nucleus of the Germanic Museum, coincident with the visit of Prince Henry in 1902, was not a purely disinterested gesture; but if he expected Harvard to become a centre of German influence, he was disappointed. Most of our graduates who studied at the German universities after 1900 reported a decline both in learning and in *Lernfreiheit*; Kuno Francke, the most eminent German on the Harvard faculties, became a naturalized American, loyal to the country of his adoption; and by 1914 our relations with the universities of France and Great Britain were closer than with those of Germany. The 'Manifesto of the German Intellectuals' and the military destruction of the University of Louvain threw American university opinion definitely on the side of the Allies; and Harvard called two of Louvain's exiled professors to her faculty early in 1915.

The inflamed feeling that arose after the sinking of the *Lusitania* raised in an acute form the problem of academic freedom; and on this subject Mr. Lowell thought clearly, acted vigorously, and stood his ground with firm courage. The issue had hardly been raised in the administration of President Eliot. As soon as the Darwinian storm had passed, everyone appeared to approve of complete freedom for students to study and professors to teach in the manner that the professors deemed best; and few took exception to professors' taking an active part in political and social controversies. On the Harvard faculties were members of all political parties, including the Socialist, just as there were members of many Christian sects and other religions; but these matters, which were once considered of great pith and moment, were no longer regarded as anybody's business in 1909.

Around 1914 the intensification of social issues in politics revived the notion that universities should either (*a*) 'point out that the insidious teachings of the agitators ... cannot change the great laws of nature' (Howard Elliott), or (*b*) align themselves with the forces of light against the forces of darkness (almost any 'Bull-Moose' of 1912). The attempt to avoid committing themselves on either side gave the universities in that era much embarrassment. Trouble first arose at Harvard over student organizations inviting contentious speakers to Cambridge, and demanding the use of college buildings for public meetings to hear them. There the Corporation drew the line. Students might have anyone they pleased for a meeting that was open only to members of the University, or hold a public meeting outside the College; but the halls of the University were not to be used for public meetings that presented but one side of a contentious contemporary question. Otherwise, the University's hospitality would be interpreted as approval. This ruling was made when the Social Politics Club demanded Emerson Hall for presenting the Misses Pankhurst, English suffragettes, to the Cambridge public. When the Corporation refused, Brattle Hall was hired, and the 'standing room only' sign was put out early.

The next thorny question was raised by Mr. Morris Llewellyn Cooke, Director of Public Works in Philadelphia, who was invited to deliver two lectures in a 'composite lecture course' on industrial management at the new Harvard School of Business Administration. Mr. Cooke desired publicity for his lectures by releasing them in advance to the press; but as the course was a university one, open to students only, he was warned by Dean Gay against doing this, although there was no bar to his publishing the lectures subsequent to their delivery. Mr. Cooke did release the lectures beforehand, and consequently was not invited to the School again. These are the essential facts in the case; but Mr. Cooke claimed to be a martyr to the 'utilities'; and, according to Upton Sinclair, he was 'fired' for supporting public ownership 'in opposition to the electric lighting interests which control Harvard University and gave President Lowell his job.' The Harvard of that time cannot have been very much afraid of 'the interests,' since a Professor of Law was dismissed in 1914 when it was discovered that he was receiving a secret retainer from the New Haven Railroad to write articles and make speeches opposing the regulation of public utilities, which were supposed to be the results of purely academic research.

The first issue raised by the war was that of Professor Münsterberg, one of the most eminent and popular Harvard professors. He had served the community well through his researches in psychology, and had performed innumerable acts of kindness to individuals. But all this availed him nothing when, as a loyal German subject, he undertook (completely within his rights in a supposedly neutral country) to present the German case to the American public; and this he did with dignity and good taste. There were also rumors that he was in the German Secret Service; the pigeons that the Professor's daughter was accustomed to feed in the professorial backyard became, in the imagination of Cambridge neighbors, carrier pigeons taking messages to spies! The public let Münsterberg alone, but old friends and colleagues would no longer speak to him, and a vociferous minority of alumni demanded that he be dismissed, as a poisonous pro-German influence on the students. This the Corporation steadfastly declined to do, and Münsterberg died a professor of Harvard University in December, 1916.

When America entered the war, it soon became clear that the demand for Münsterberg's scalp was but a sample of what we were to expect. President Lowell,

anticipating this, made in his Report for 1916–17 a definition of Academic Freedom that has become classic:

Experience has proved, and probably no one would now deny, that
knowledge can advance, or at least can advance most rapidly, only by
means of an unfettered search for truth on the part of those who devote
their lives to seeking it in their respective fields, and by complete freedom in imparting to their pupils the truth that they have found. This
has become an axiom in higher education, in spite of the fact that a
searcher may discover error instead of truth, and be misled, and mis-
lead others, thereby. We believe that if light enough is let in, the real
relations of things will soon be seen, and that they can be seen in no
other way. . . .

The teaching by the professor in his class-room on the subjects
within the scope of his chair ought to be absolutely free. He must
teach the truth as he has found it and sees it. This is the primary
condition of academic freedom, and any violation of it endangers
intellectual progress. In order to make it secure it is essential that the
teaching in the class-room should be confidential. This does not mean
that it is secret, but that what is said there should not be published.
If the remarks of the instructor were repeated by the pupils in the
public press, he would be subjected to constant criticism by people,
not familiar with the subject, who misunderstood his teaching; and,
what is more important, he would certainly be misquoted, because his
remarks would be reported by the student without their context or
the qualifications that give them their accuracy. Moreover, if the rule
that remarks in the class-room shall not be reported for publication
elsewhere is to be maintained, the professor himself must not report
them. Lectures open to the public stand on a different footing; but
lectures in a private class-room must not be given by the instructor to
the newspapers. That principle is, I believe, observed in all reputable
institutions.

This brings us to the next subdivision of the inquiry, the freedom
of the professor within his field of study, but outside of his class-room.
It has been pointed out that he ought not to publish his class-room
lectures as such in the daily press. That does not mean a denial of
the right to publish them in a book, or their substance in a learned
periodical. On the contrary, the object of institutions of learning is
not only the acquisition but also the diffusion of knowledge. Every
professor must, therefore, be wholly unrestrained in publishing the
results of his study in the field of his professorship. It is needless to add
that for the dignity of his profession, for the maintenance of its privileges, as well as for his own reputation among his fellows, whatever

he writes or says on his own subject should be uttered as a scholar, in a scholarly tone and form. This is a matter of decorum, not of discipline; to be remedied by a suggestion, not by a penalty. . . .

The gravest questions, and the strongest feelings, arise from action by a professor beyond his chosen field and outside of his class-room. Here he speaks only as a citizen. By appointment to a professorship he acquires no rights that he did not possess before; but there is a real difference of opinion today on the question whether he loses any rights that he would otherwise enjoy. The argument in favor of a restraining power on the part of the governing boards of universities and colleges is based upon the fact that by extreme, or injudicious, remarks that shock public sentiment a professor can do great harm to the institution with which he is connected. That is true, and sometimes a professor thoughtlessly does an injury that is without justification. If he publishes an article on the futility and harmfulness of vaccination, and signs it as professor in a certain university, he leads the public to believe that his views are those of an authority on the subject, approved by the institution and taught to its students. If he is really a professor of Greek, he is misleading the public and misrepresenting his university, which he would not do if he gave his title in full.

In spite, however, of the risk of injury to the institution, the objections to restraint upon what professors may say as citizens seem to me far greater than the harm done by leaving them free. In the first place, to impose upon the teacher in a university restrictions to which the members of other professions, lawyers, physicians, engineers, and so forth, are not subjected, would produce a sense of irritation and humiliation. In accepting a chair under such conditions a man would surrender a part of his liberty; what he might say would be submitted to the censorship of a board of trustees, and he would cease to be a free citizen. The lawyer, physician or engineer may express his views as he likes on the subject of the protective tariff; shall the professor of astronomy not be free to do the same? Such a policy would tend seriously to discourage some of the best men from taking up the scholar's life. It is not a question of academic freedom, but of personal liberty from constraint, yet it touches the dignity of the academic career.

That is an objection to restraint on freedom of speech from the standpoint of the teacher. There is another, not less weighty, from that of the institution itself. If a university or college censors what its professors may say, if it restrains them from uttering something that it does not approve, *it thereby assumes responsibility for that which it permits them to say.* This is logical and inevitable, but it is a responsibility which an institution of learning would be very unwise in assuming.

It is sometimes suggested that the principles are different in time of war; that the governing boards are then justified in restraining unpatriotic expressions injurious to the country. But the same problem is presented in war time as in time of peace. If the university is right in restraining its professors, it has a duty to do so, and it is responsible for whatever it permits. There is no middle ground. Either the university assumes full responsibility for permitting its professors to express certain opinions in public, or it assumes no responsibility whatever, and leaves them to be dealt with like other citizens by the public authorities according to the laws of the land.

All this refers, of course, to opinions on public matters sincerely uttered. If a professor speaks in a way that reveals moral obliquity, he may be treated as he would on any other evidence of moral defect; for character in the teacher is essential to the welfare of the students.

Every human attempt to attain a good object involves some compromise, some sacrifice of lesser ends for the larger ones. Hence every profession has its own code of ethics designed to promote its major objects, and entailing restrictions whose importance is often not clear to outsiders. . . . But it must not be forgotten that all liberty and every privilege implies responsibilities. Professors should speak in public soberly and seriously, not for notoriety or self advertisement, under a deep sense of responsibility for the good name of the institution and the dignity of their profession. They should take care that they are understood to speak personally, not officially. When they so speak, and governing boards respect their freedom to express their sincere opinions as other citizens may do, there will be little danger that liberty of speech will be either misused or curtailed. . . .

As the war approached America, the question came up as to what part the University should take in preparedness. Mr. Lowell from the first encouraged students to enroll in the Plattsburg training camps, and in the second half of 1915–16 a course in Military Science, given by General Leonard Wood and two other regular army officers, was offered to Plattsburg graduates and members of the National Guard. This was the nucleus of the Harvard Reserve Officers' Training Corps. The Corporation was convinced, somewhat earlier than the War Department, that Harvard students were officer material, and should be given an officer's training; for that reason the course provided in the National Defense Act of 1916, including an unnecessary amount of drill with a modicum of theory, was too elementary. The War Department consented to modify the provisions of this Act for Harvard and other colleges; Captain Constant Cordier, U.S.A., was detailed to Cambridge; and 864 students enrolled under him in 'Military Science 1' during the fall of 1916. Most of the actual instruction was done by Harvard professors, such as Theodore Lyman, William B. Munro, and Julian L. Coolidge, who had had Plattsburg training. The course counted for a Harvard degree, and, in connection with work in the training camps, prepared students for commissions in the United States Army.

Ten weeks before the declaration of war on Germany, President Lowell made a move that put the University in a very enviable light. He requested the French Government to send us a few disabled officers to train our R.O.T.C. in the methods of warfare lately developed in Europe. They responded; and in April, 1917, the French mission, headed by Commandant Azan (author of 'The War of Positions,' 1917), and including Lieutenant André Morize, who has since remained with us as a Professor of French Literature, was formally welcomed at the Harvard Club of Boston. It was a memorable and uplifting occasion; but the speeches, full of high hopes for a really lasting peace, read rather sadly now.

The Harvard R.O.T.C., increased to 1227 men, promptly began intensive training under the French officers, using the Freshman Halls as barracks, and furrowing the land about Fresh Pond with trenches. After a 'Battle of Fresh Pond,' they adjourned to camp at Barre, whence most of the members proceeded to a regular officers' training camp. The French officers were in too much demand to be retained for the summer of 1918, when a greatly depleted R.O.T.C., under two United States army officers and Lieutenant Morize, trained at the Smith Halls and Lancaster. This second R.O.T.C.

was for men below the draft age; almost all over that were by this time in the government training camps or on active service.

The World War, presented to us as the pursuit of a high ideal, made a peculiar appeal to American youth. Practically all undergraduates who were old enough and physically fit got into some form of war service. Both the Government and College encouraged them to enter officers' training schools and thus to continue their education to the age of twenty-one, when they would be eligible for commissions. President Lowell urged the younger men not to 'mistake excitement for duty,' as they could serve their country much more effectively by taking officers' training than by enlisting in the ranks. Hundreds who were too impatient to wait enlisted as 'gobs,' 'dough-boys,' or marines. Special finals were held in April-May, 1917, when most of the student body left for active service or joined the R.O.T.C. The University conferred 'war degrees' on all who completed twelve courses satisfactorily, and gave members of the faculties who entered national service the difference between their government pay and their former salaries.

In the autumn of 1917 the Cadet School for the First Naval District was established in Holyoke House and Standish Hall, and the University offered a special course leading to an ensign's commission. A government Naval Radio School was established in Pierce Hall and the Cruft Laboratory in the spring of 1917, under the command of Lieutenant Nathaniel F. Ayer (s.b. 1900). It expanded so fast that within six months almost all the University buildings north of the Yard, including Memorial Hall, had become 'ships'; and by the end of the war the Naval School had covered Cambridge Common with temporary barracks.[1] Men were constantly joining and

[1] The Gordon McKay Laboratory on Oxford Street is a relic of the Naval Radio School.

leaving, and the total enrolment at one time reached five thousand.

In other ways the University adapted itself to war service. The Chemistry Department, notably Professor James B. Conant, became practically a section of the War Department, producing masks for our troops and poison gas for those of the enemy. The Harvard Surgical Unit under Dr. Hugh Cabot (A.B. 1894) continued its service in France with the British Expeditionary Force; another hospital unit was organized by Harvey W. Cushing (M.D. 1895), Moseley Professor of Surgery at the Medical School. Many other professors and graduates of the Medical and Dental Schools served with the American Expeditionary Forces; the Law School contributed professors to the Judge Advocate General's department; the Bussey Institution became headquarters of the Botanical Raw Products Committee; the Psychological Laboratory devised tests for aviators; the German Department worked at decoding German messages and translating documents. Early in 1918 several members of the History Department began preparing data for the Peace Conference under Professor A. C. Coolidge, and most of them were later attached to the American Commission to Negotiate Peace.

Yet all departments of the University opened in the autumn of 1917, and offered regular instruction to an enrolment which by May 1, 1918, had tapered off to about one-fifth normal. Most student activities except intercollegiate sports were continued, especially by the freshmen.

During the summer of 1918 the Government decided to put all college students into uniform, and College opened in the fall with everyone but the near-sighted, the flat-footed, and the very young in the Students' Army Training Corps. The S.A.T.C. proper was quartered in the Freshman Halls and Randolph and Westmorly. The

Naval unit took over Weld, Grays, and Holyoke House; the Naval Ensigns' School was in Matthews, and the Junior S.A.T.C. in Hollis, Stoughton, and Holworthy. Fortunately the war ended before the S.A.T.C. could be proved a successor failure. All student units were demobilized by Christmas, 1918, and a regular college year began on January 20, 1919, with a scant enrolment of 1756 in the College and 1000 more in the University. Veterans kept returning in order to complete the twelve full courses necessary to obtain a war degree. By April 1, 1919, when the last of the naval radio students disappeared, the University had resumed its pre-war appearance, except that the older Yard buildings were filled with freshmen late of the Junior S.A.T.C.

Over eleven thousand Harvard students and former students had enlisted in the armed forces of the United States and her associates; and of these 375 were killed or died in service. The Memorial Chapel, erected in 1931–32, commemorates their sacrifice, as well as that of the three Harvard men who died in the German service.

Post-war Harvard was faced by an increasing enrolment, 'flaming youth,' higher costs, a big deficit, and the imperative necessity of raising salaries and tuition. An endowment drive conducted by the alumni yielded the enormous sum of $13,789,746.74, and put the University on a sound financial basis. Tuition had been $150 in the College and most other departments of the University through the Eliot administration; it was raised to $200 in 1913, $250 in 1921, $300 in 1925, and $400 in 1928. Yet the enrolment increased.

The highest professor's salary under the Faculty of Arts and Sciences had been set at $4000 in 1869; in 1918 it had only reached $5500; in 1919 it was raised to $8000, in 1928 to $9000, and in 1930 to $12,000. The young instructor in the Faculty of Arts and Sciences is probably harder-worked now than before the war, for in every department except Chemistry and Engineering he has to begin as a tutor with twenty or more students to look out for, yet also give a course or two and produce writing or research acceptable as evidence of his qualification for a permanent appointment. The lot of the professor, however, has become happier. His stint of courses has tended to become less, he may look to the Milton and other research funds for additions to his salary to employ a secretary, or for research expenses; a new Faculty Club, given by Allston Burr (A.B. 1889) and the Corporation, caters to his comfort and convenience; and not infrequently he is granted a term's exemption from teaching in order to complete a bit of research. The reading period of two and one-half weeks before midyears, and three and one-half weeks before finals, adopted in 1927 for all but freshman and introductory courses, has been a great relief, for in this period lectures and tutoring cease. Still, a more busily occupied and less otiose body of men than the members of the Harvard faculties would be difficult to find.

Peace brought embarrassments, no less than war. To most of us, the post-war student seemed more seriously interested in his studies than his pre-war fellows. Improved preparation in the schools, and the prospect of better supervision of freshmen in College, brought down the average age at entrance a whole twelvemonth in the last twenty years; and the new provision of admitting the 'first seventh' of a class from accredited schools without examination widened the College's recruiting ground. Compulsory physical training for freshmen — which in practice meant participation in games or sports — took a good deal of mischief out of them; generous sports equipment, and the great new Indoor Athletic Building with swimming tank, provided by the anonymous *Alumnus Aquaticus*, offer new facilities for healthy recreation; but cars, roadhouses, and bootleggers multiplied, and the new corps of assistant deans had plenty to do in endeavoring to keep students on the straight-and-narrow. A progressive tendency to stiffen minimum requirements for study, and an increasing readiness, in view of the large enrolment, to eliminate students unable or unwilling to meet them, gave the young men less time for their amusements; 'activities' suffered in consequence. The Student Council (organized as far back as 1908) once made the naïve proposal that 'going out for something' be counted as a half-course!

With these exceptions, the pre-war social pattern of college life was resumed. Before the war the College had exchanged College House, whose forlorn chambers had possibilities for business development, for Randolph Hall, one of the best of the private dormitories; and during the war the owners of the other private halls on the Gold Coast sold out to the University. The Freshman Halls did not, as President Lowell had hoped, succeed in 'breaking up groups of similar origin.' Freshmen love to go about in gangs. Groton continued to consort with St. Mark's, Andover with Exeter, and B. L. S. with C. L. S.; but the Halls did afford friendless freshmen an opportunity to 'get acquainted' promptly, engage in class activities, and form congenial groups. More and more Yard buildings were engaged by members of the senior class, a movement that began as far back as 1908. But for most of the three upper classes the cliquishness and chaos of the pre-war years became worse, and numerous fly-by-night clubs and fraternity chapters sprang up to meet the social need. Eating places multiplied in Cambridge, and the student body became so restless that commons in Memorial Hall, operated at a loss by the University since the war, had to be closed in 1924. Everyone but freshmen and those who boarded in the Union had to 'eat around' for the next six years.

The war brought a shift in the standpoint from which

American universities in general and Harvard in particular were publicly criticized. Before, it was generally charged that colleges were subservient supporters of capitalistic society, purveyors to Wall Street, recruiters of reaction, obstacles to democratic progress, and the like; Upton Sinclair's 'The Goose Step,' though written after the war, is a sample of what one used to read on the Hearst editorial pages, and hear in liberal and progressive circles. But within a year of the conclusion of peace, the colleges began to be pilloried as cells of sedition, foyers of revolution, and Little Brothers of the Bolsheviki! University faculties had kept their heads; and nobody is more unpopular than a cool-headed man in a riot. The war ended just at the point when the American public had been whipped up by patriotic propaganda to a state of exaggerated nationalism, and their hatred was promptly transferred from the Germans to Russians, Communists, Socialists, supporters of international co-operation, and everything not '100 per cent American.' Professors who had done their duty in the war, and were proud of it, now considered it a duty equally imperative to speak out against the denial of civil liberties, the lawlessness of public authorities, and the intolerance of public opinion. The student body, deeply affected by post-war disillusion and the decline of moral standards, in part took refuge in work, in part in dissipation; but a saving remnant engaged in serious discussion of the issues of the day. Professors naturally encouraged an intellectual activity which was geared to the spirit of youth, and helped the young men form their Liberal Clubs, League of Nations Unions, and so forth. Wishing to hear all sides, and having a natural curiosity about Russia, these student organizations sometimes invited Communists and other radicals to speak, as well as men and women of conservative views; the first was 'news,' while the second was not; and before long professional red-baiters, and to some extent the ultraconservative press, began stirring up the public to believe that the colleges were centres of disloyalty and sedition. Although persons so exalted as Calvin Coolidge allowed themselves to be drawn into these attacks on the colleges,[1] Harvard kept a dignified silence, hoping that the storm would pass. It is now doubtful whether this policy was wise, for (with some let-up in the money-mad twenties) constant repetition of the same perverted and malignant propaganda for over fifteen years has made a deep impress on public opinion. We are just beginning to experience the effects of it in teachers' oaths of loyalty, and other efforts to limit freedom in education.

While most Harvard alumni had faith in their alma mater, as shown by their magnificent addition to the endowment in these troublous times, a vociferous minority felt that he who pays the academic piper should call the tune — that, if private capital provided the money for our academic band, they must play nothing but patriotic songs. Whenever a Harvard instructor was quoted as criticizing some of the reactionary tendencies of the day, or saying a good word for Russia, or advocating a socialized control of wealth, President Lowell was certain to receive a sheaf of letters from indignant alumni crying 'Throw him out!' The two foremost cases of this sort were those of Mr. Chafee and Mr. Laski.

It was in the Faculty of Law, naturally, that the greatest uneasiness developed about the lawlessness of law-enforcing agencies during and immediately following the

[1] When the articles signed (though not, it is said, written) by Vice-President Coolidge on 'Enemies of the Republic' (in the women's colleges) began coming out in *The Delineator* in 1921, the writer called on President Emeritus Eliot in the hope that he might prepare or at least counsel a rejoinder. 'Mr. Coolidge's views on the women's colleges, if they are his, are completely insignificant, and not worth the trouble of refutation,' was Mr. Eliot's typical reply. Unfortunately the American public estimated Mr. Coolidge's oracular platitudes somewhat more highly than Mr. Eliot did. Mr. Hearst did not wheel his press into action against the 'Reds in the colleges' until later.

war, and the denial of constitutional rights such as freedom of speech. As these matters came within their field, Dean Roscoe Pound, Professor Felix Frankfurter, Professor Zechariah Chafee, Jr., and others had published a 'Report upon the Illegal Practices of the United States Department of Justice' in the days of Mr. A. Mitchell Palmer. This stimulated indignation over 'radicalism in the Harvard Law School' on the part of its more conservative New York graduates, a feeling which culminated in a printed 'Statement for the Information of the President and Fellows . . . with respect to Certain Teachers in the Harvard Law School,' which was mainly an indictment of Mr. Chafee's article on the Abrams case in the *Harvard Law Review* for April, 1920, since reprinted with corrections in his book 'Freedom of Speech.' Mr. Lowell, observing that this was not the first attempt in Harvard history to exempt from academic freedom the subject over which people were momentarily excited, induced the Overseers to refer this complaint to their Visiting Committee. The Visiting Committee gave 'complainants' and 'defendants' a hearing on May 22, 1921, at the Harvard Club of Boston. The Committee, which was presided over by Judge Francis J. Swayze (A.B. 1879), and included Judge (now Mr. Justice) Cardozo, Judge Augustus N. Hand (LL.B. 1894), and his classmate Judge James M. Morton, Jr., voted unanimously 'that Professor Chafee made no statements in his article which were consciously erroneous.' The majority voted that 'the errors, if any, were in matters of opinion only'; the minority, that the article did contain errors of fact that should have been corrected. Mr. Chafee admitted certain minor errors, and printed these in the *Harvard Law Review*. The Law School was not disturbed again.

The other important case was that of Harold J. Laski. This brilliant young Oxford graduate at the age of twenty-three was appointed instructor and tutor in political science. His mind was alert and original; he had a great capacity for friendship with old as well as young, and proved to be a devoted and effective teacher. After three annual appointments, he was promoted Lecturer and Tutor for three years, beginning September 1, 1918. Mr. Laski, as Governor Winthrop remarked of Sir Harry Vane in troublous times some three centuries earlier, was 'a young man tossed about by new opinions.' The Boston police strike of 1919 — the one that elevated Governor Coolidge to the Vice-Presidency — illustrated, in Mr. Laski's opinion, a principle of pluralistic liberty that he held dear; and, addressing the wives of the striking policemen in a public meeting, he praised their husbands' contribution to political science in philosophical language, the drift of which both they and the reporters caught. Then, things broke loose! Harvard was supporting the police strike (actually, some two hundred students had joined the temporary police force, at Mr. Lowell's suggestion); Laski was a traitor and a Bolshevik; he must be fired. It was a real test of the principles that Mr. Lowell had announced; for Mr. Laski was not *persona grata* to Mr. Lowell, nor an American citizen; he had not yet made a reputation as a scholar, and his dismissal would have been very popular outside the University. Yet the President stood firm, and told the Governing Boards that if they chose to exercise their legal right to dismiss Mr. Laski, he would resign himself. Shortly after, Mr. Laski received a call from the University of London, and resigned from Harvard at the end of the year, greatly to the regret of his colleagues.

Mr. Lowell and the deans and Governing Boards, at a time when discussion was being muzzled and the free expression of opinion stifled in many American universities, acted so as to make every member of the teaching faculties feel that he could teach, write, and say what he believed to be the truth, with due regard to decency in utterance, and appropriateness in occasion. No reasonable man could breath the air of Harvard at this time and not feel free.

In this administration there was a tendency for the graduate schools to recover some of the autonomy that they had lost in the Eliot era. President Lowell continued to preside at meetings of the several faculties or administrative boards; but questions of policy and personnel were generally decided by the respective deans and administrative boards.

In the Law School this was an era of growth and expansion under Deans Thayer and Pound. The number of students more than doubled, the faculty was increased in proportion, and Langdell Hall grew clear across the field where Oliver Wendell Holmes and his brother had once struggled to raise vegetables in a sandy soil. Professors Beale, Williston, and Wambaugh taught during the last half of the Eliot, and the whole of the next administration. Of the new appointments, to mention but a few: Roscoe Pound (A.B. Nebraska 1888) was called from Chicago to the Story Professorship in 1910, and continued to profess law, to study botany, and to ride his numerous other hobbies during his tenure as Dean of the School; Felix Frankfurter (LL.B. 1906) was made Professor in 1914, and six years later appointed to the new chair of Administrative Law founded by James Byrne, Fellow of the Corporation; Joseph Warren (A.B. 1897), of the old medical family, had been teaching in the School since 1909; Austin W. Scott (LL.B. 1909) never left; Manley O. Hudson (LL.B. 1910) divided his time between Geneva and the Bemis Professorship of International Law; Thomas Reed Powell (LL.B. 1904) was called from Columbia in 1925, Josef Redlich from Vienna in 1926, and Edmund M. Morgan (A.B. 1902) from Yale the same year. A graduate department of the Law School was organized in

1911 in order to train men for teaching and research in law, seminars were provided, the degrees of Doctor of Juridical Science, and, for those who could not spend the time, of Master of Laws (1924), offered. And as the fame of the Harvard Law School became world-wide, students came from South America, Europe, India, and China, as well as all parts of the United States, for graduate study and research. Since 1912 about 150 S.J.D.'s have been conferred, on men such as Dean Charles A. Huston of the Law School of Stanford University; Pierre Lepaulle, Director of the Seminar on Anglo-American Law at the University of Paris; Armistead M. Dobie, Professor of Law at the University of Virginia; and James M. Landis, head of the National Securities Commission. The Law School was no longer satisfied to train college graduates to become practitioners, and perhaps judges; it contributed to our knowledge of the history and philosophy of law, and brought sociological concepts to bear on the interpretation thereof, much as had been done by theological concepts in the middle ages.

A law school is capable of quick and almost indefinite expansion, because it needs no other equipment than professors and books; but in a medical school this is impossible. Harvey W. Cushing, Milton J. Rosenau (M.D. Pennsylvania), Richard P. Strong (M.D. Johns Hopkins), George R. Minot (A.B. 1908, winner of the Nobel Prize in Medicine), Elmer E. Southard (A.B. 1897), Charles MacFie Campbell (M.D. Edinburgh), Alice Hamilton (M.D. Michigan), Hans Zinsser (M.D. Columbia), and M. N. Smith-Petersen (M.D. 1914) were among those appointed to the Faculty of Medicine during the first and second decades of the century. New departments such as Preventive Medicine (out of which a separate School of Public Health developed), Neuropathology, Tropical Medicine, the Harvard Medical School in China, and, not least, the service performed by members of the School and its graduates throughout the whole of World War I, enhanced the School's already great reputation; but until 1918, when David L. Edsall (M.D. Pennsylvania) became Dean, it was hampered by lack of funds. Immediately after the war, bequests, benefactions, and grants from the Rockefeller Foundation and the General Education Board began to flow in. But the apparatus and installations necessary for instruction in a modern medical school are so expensive, complicated, and spendthrift of space that it was necessary in 1914, only eight years after the School acquired its new buildings, to limit the size of each entering class to 125. The 'block system' of instruction was introduced in 1909, and a general examination before graduation in 1911, and, shortly after, tutors were provided and required work was reduced in order to give the students time to think, read, and correlate their knowledge. Until 1926 medical students had to find their own board and lodgings; in that year Harold S. Vanderbilt (A.B. 1907) and others presented the School with a residential hall, complete with common-room, dining facilities, and gymnasium. Except for this, the outward aspect of the Medical School has been practically unchanged in the last thirty years; but the scope of its activity has been greatly widened, and the methods and facilities improved. It has, in fact, become a national institution, the faculty and selected student body being recruited from all parts of the country and from abroad. A large proportion of graduates become specialists, teachers of medicine, and medical researchers. Yet a large part of the teaching staff are still active practitioners; and the old 'medical dynasties' of Boston — Cheever, Fitz, Minot, Mixter, Shattuck, and Warren — if no longer 'in charge,' are still represented on the Faculty of Medicine.

The Faculty of the Dental School became part of the Faculty of Medicine in 1899, retaining its own administrative board; and ten years later the School moved into its own new building adjoining the Medical group. The Dental School had an important share — especially through the brilliant reconstructive surgery of V. H. Kazanjian (D.M.D. 1905) — in medical war work. In 1917 the course was lengthened to four years; in 1925 two years of college study were required as prerequisite for admission; and in 1929 the school began, through the bequest of Charles A. Brackett (D.M.D. 1873), who taught there for half a century, and the gift of John T. Morse, Jr. (A.B. 1860), to acquire a long-overdue endowment fund. Until that time, the teaching staff in the Dental School gave their services gratis. Almost half the students in the School by 1936 were college graduates.

The Lowell administration saw the establishment of new graduate schools, the roots of which go back to courses given under the Faculty of Arts and Sciences in President Eliot's day. The study of Education (with a capital E) at Harvard begins in 1891, when Paul H. Hanus (S.B. Michigan) was called from the State Normal School of Colorado to profess the History, Art, and Technique of Teaching. In 1906 Professor Hanus and his colleague Arthur O. Norton (A.B. 1898) became a Division under the Faculty of Arts and Sciences, and recruited Henry W. Holmes (A.B. 1903), who became the Dean of the Graduate School of Education, established in 1920 with an endowment of two millions. This was the first department of the University to admit women on the same terms as men; but men students have predominated. For four years the School catered mostly to active teachers eager to improve their technique and equipment, but able to study only for part of their time; for the last ten years it has admitted as candidates for the degree of Ed.M. and Ed.D. only college graduates able to concentrate on the work of the School. In 1936, in conjunction with the Faculty of Arts and Sciences, the new degree of Master of Arts in Teaching was established — a necessary innovation in order to enable the School's graduates to meet modern State requirements of training in Education, and yet acquire a grasp of the subject to be taught.

The School of Education is housed in Lawrence Hall, the original home of the Lawrence Scientific School. The successive reorganizations of that School well illustrate what Barrett Wendell called the Harvard tradition of constant change. Renewed wooing of M. I. T., with the great Gordon McKay bequest as dowry, resulted in 1914 in a marriage which was dissolved three years later by that stern moralist, the Supreme Judicial Court of Massachusetts. Both an undergraduate and a graduate School of Engineering were conducted in Pierce Hall and the McKay and other laboratories until 1934. The undergraduate courses were then unloaded on Harvard College, and a new group of graduate courses in ten or twelve different branches of Engineering, open only to college graduates, and leading to the degrees of Master and Doctor of Science, was provided by the Graduate School of Engineering. Over a hundred students registered in this School during its opening year, 1935–36.

The Harvard School of Business Administration began as the inconspicuous appendage to Professor A. C. Coolidge's project for a School of Political Science. After thirty years the donation of Lucius N. Littauer (A.B. 1878) brought the original plan into actual effect; but in 1906–07, in view of the probable difficulty of placing trained men in government service, the economic tail was lopped off behind the ears of the political dog. After the panic of 1907 it seemed more important for the University to try to make a profession of 'the oldest of the arts' — business.

Accordingly the 'Business School' was established in the fall of 1908 as a department of the Graduate School of

Arts and Sciences, with a two-year programme for the degree of Master of Business Administration. It met with strong opposition on the assumption that it was to be a mere school of successful money-making; and although that motive has not been absent from the students' minds, the object of Dean Gay and his staff was to create a practice, a profession, and an ethic of business management. Unlike business schools in most American universities, it was open only to college graduates, who flocked in such numbers as to crowd the top floor of Widener to the point of bursting. Mr. George F. Baker, banker, industrial director, and father of our like-named alumnus of the Class of 1899, then presented the University with five million dollars for a group of buildings. The suggestion came from Bishop Lawrence; the purpose was to 'give a new start to better business standards.' The new School, in the Georgian style though not by the University architects, arose rapidly on the south side of the Charles, east of Soldiers Field, and was dedicated in 1927. It was a complete 'plant' from the beginning, including a central library, a dining hall, faculty club, class-rooms, and students' residential halls, named after the great Secretaries of the Treasury (including Hamilton) and Mr. Baker and Mr. Morgan. The School suffered in its early years from part-time instructors who were better at conducting business than at teaching it; but this quasi-apprentice stage was surmounted more quickly than in the Law School and the Medical School. In spite of the great depression, the School has worked out its own technique of teaching, acquired a competent professional staff, a library rich in economic history, research institutes, and an enthusiastic body of students.

The School of Architecture emerged from the chrysalis stage in 1914 together with the School of Landscape Architecture; these two, with the School of City Planning (established 1929), are under the Faculty of Architecture.

When George H. Edgell, Dean of this faculty from 1922, became Director of the Boston Museum of Fine Arts, he was succeeded by Joseph F. Hudnut (S.M. Columbia). Of the faculty of sixteen, Jean-Jacques Haffner (Grand Prix de Rome, 1919) has been Professor of Architecture since 1922, Bremer W. Pond (M.L.A. 1911) has succeeded James Sturgis Pray (A.B. 1895) as Charles Eliot Professor of Landscape Architecture, and Henry V. Hubbard (A.B. 1897) is the Chairman of the Council of the School of City Planning.

It must not be supposed that the College and the Graduate School of Arts and Sciences stood still while these new developments were taking place. Old graduates complained (as did their predecessors in 1836 and 1886) that the great teachers of the past were gone; but as each Olympian dies or retires, his place is filled, sometimes not so well, sometimes better; and no doubt in 1986 the old grads. will be asking, 'Where are the great men we venerated in the Lowell and Conant era?'

Rapidly running over the departments: the four great philosophers have gone; but Alfred North Whitehead of the University of Cambridge began a new and fruitful career at Harvard in 1924, while Raphael Demos (PH.D. 1916), William E. Hocking (A.B. 1901), and R. B. Perry (PH.D. 1899) have grown to professorial stature. In the Classics, E. K. Rand and C. B. Gulick were still going strong; Arthur S. Pease (A.B. 1902) had been called from Amherst, and Joshua Whatmough from the University of Cairo; and some brilliant younger men were ministering to a number of 'concentrators' that is unfortunately diminishing. In English, George P. Baker and 'English 47' were lost by a bad fumble, and Neilson became President of Smith in 1917; but John L. Lowes (PH.D. 1905) came back to us from St. Louis, and Hyder E. Rollins (PH.D. 1917) from New York; Kirsopp Lake, for almost ten years a professor at Leyden, raised the old courses on the

English Bible to new heights of excellence; Chester N. Greenough (A.B. 1898) and Kenneth B. Murdock (A.B. 1916) introduced the study of American Literature; F. O. Matthiessen (PH.D. 1927) was recruited from Yale, Theodore Spencer (PH.D. 1928) from Princeton, and Robert Hillyer (A.B. 1917) from Trinity. The Charles Eliot Norton Chair of Poetry, endowed by Charles Chauncey Stillman (A.B. 1898) in 1925, has an annual tenure; two of the incumbents so far have been Gilbert Murray and T. S. Eliot (A.B. 1910). Samuel H. Cross (A.B. 1912) succeeded Wiener in Slavic, and Harry A. Wolfson (A.B. 1912) and Walter E. Clark (A.B. 1903) in Semitic and Indic languages and literatures; and new departments of Chinese and Japanese were established. In the Fine Arts, this was the era of Chandler R. Post (A.B. 1904), Arthur Pope (A.B. 1901), Paul J. Sachs (A.B. 1900), and Arthur Kingsley Porter, who came to us from Yale, the source also of Wilbur C. Abbott (B.LITT. Oxford) in English History. Clarence H. Haring (A.B. 1907) undertook the new chair in Latin-American History in 1923; Frederick J. Turner, the father of the frontier interpretation, came to us from Wisconsin in 1910, and retired in 1924; he was succeeded by Arthur M. Schlesinger (PH.D. Columbia). Robert H. Lord (A.B. 1906), Sidney B. Fay (A.B. 1896), and William L. Langer (A.B. 1915) have been the high lights in Modern, William S. Ferguson (PH.D. Cornell) and Robert Pierpont Blake (PH.D. 1916) in Ancient, History. George Sarton (SC.D. Ghent), the editor of *Isis*, and Lawrence J. Henderson (A.B. 1898), persistent 'rover' between Chemistry, Physics, Medicine, and Sociology, have introduced the new subject of History of Science; George Grafton Wilson (PH.D. Brown) taught the International Law since 1907; and two Wisconsin Doctors of Philosophy, Allyn A. Young and John D. Black, and John H. Williams (PH.D. 1919) have been some of the new appointees in Economics. A Department of Sociology has been organized under Dr. P. A. Sorokin, with help from other social scientists. In Mathematics the Peirce dynasty has come to an end, but George D. Birkhoff (A.B. 1905) and William C. Graustein (A.B. 1910) have come up from the ranks, and E. B. Van Vleck (PH.D. Göttingen) has come from Wisconsin. In Chemistry, E. P. Kohler (PH.D. Johns Hopkins), Arthur B. Lamb (PH.D. 1904), and James B. Conant (A.B. 1914) took the places of Cooke, Jackson, and Richards; and the father of Edward Mallinckrodt (A.B. 1900) of St. Louis gave the new laboratory (begun in 1927) that replaced the long-antiquated quarters in Boylston Hall. In Physics, Theodore Lyman (A.B. 1897) carried on through the Lowell administration; and Percy W. Bridgman (A.B. 1904), F. A. Saunders (PH.D. Johns Hopkins), and G. W. Pierce (PH.D. 1900) are still with us. Harlow Shapley (PH.D. Princeton), appointed Director of the Astronomical Observatory in 1921, has transformed, broadened, and deepened the work of that institution. Geology, Geography, and allied subjects have been strengthened by the Institute for Geographical Exploration, founded by Professor A. Hamilton Rice (A.B. 1898) and Mrs. Rice (the former Mrs. Widener) in 1931. Reginald A. Daly (PH.D. 1896) held the Sturgis-Hooper chair since 1912; Kirtley F. Mather (PH.D. Chicago) stepped into Shaler's shoes; Charles Palache (PH.D. California) became Professor of Mineralogy in 1912; and Oceanography has been introduced to the curriculum by Henry B. Bigelow (A.B. 1901).

The increasing interest of botanists and zoölogists in living organisms has brought a new orientation of these disciplines, and of Physiology, around Biology. The Biological Institute, the largest building owned by the University, completed in 1931 from a gift of three millions from the General Education Board, provided ample laboratories and classrooms for Professors G. H. Parker (s.b. 1887), Oakes Ames, W. H. Weston (ph.d. 1915), W. J. Crozier (ph.d. 1915), Leigh Hoadley (ph.d. Chicago), C. T. Brues (s.m. Texas), Jeffries Wyman (a.b. 1923), W. E. Castle (a.b. 1893), and William Morton Wheeler (ph.d. Clark) the entomologist, who has recently retired after bringing the long-derelict Bussey Institution into port. Roland Thaxter (a.b. 1882) carried on to his death in 1932 the work of Farlow on Cryptogamic Botany in the small building adjoining the Biological Institute; the new Gray Herbarium by the Botanical Garden, the first piece of modernist and purely 'functional' architecture put up by the University, was completed in 1915.

The last of Mr. Lowell's reforms was the House Plan. Although the freshmen had their own halls, and seniors generally roomed in the Yard (which in 1923–25 began to be 'cloistered' by the erection of Mower, Lionel, Straus, and Lehman Halls), there was a gap of two years in which students roomed anywhere; and only the clubmen had decent dining places after freshman year. By 1926, when practically all divisions of the Faculty had a corps of tutors, the time seemed ripe to decentralize Harvard College, house the upper three classes with their tutors in residential units, each with its dining hall and common-room, and see if some of the old social values of a college education could not be restored. An able report of a committee of the Student Council, written by E. C. Aswell '26, recommended that this be done; but an application to the General Education Board for the wherewithal to build one experimental house for honors students was turned down. It looked as if Mr. Lowell would have to end his administration without realizing his dearest ambition for the College, when, one day in the fall of 1928, Mr. Edward S. Harkness (a.b. Yale 1897) walked into the President's office and offered him three million dollars to build and endow an 'Honor College' with resident tutors and a master, the members to be picked from the three upper classes. Mr. Harkness had already proposed this plan, or something similar, to his alma mater, but had been discouraged by arguments and delays. It took Mr. Lowell about ten seconds to accept; and the *fait accompli* was announced to the Faculty of Arts and Sciences on November 6, 1928. The Governing Boards took up the plan with such alacrity and enthusiasm that Mr. Harkness in a few weeks increased his offer to ten millions for equipping no less than seven houses for the bulk of the three upper classes, three houses to be built from the ground up, and the others to be created out of existing halls, with suitable additions and alterations. Thus a Yale man became the greatest benefactor to Harvard in our entire history, making a noble return for the part that Harvard men had taken in founding his alma mater.

This stupendous plan aroused much enthusiasm, and almost as much opposition. It seemed more revolutionary at first than it really was. The Faculty did not like the way it was 'railroaded through' without consulting them, and thought that an experiment should be made of two or three houses, so that inevitable mistakes could be put to profit in designing the rest. The students, on the whole, were hostile. The *Crimson* denounced it; clubmen did not like the idea of being herded with the majority, who in turn preferred the traditional social flexibility of Harvard, the liberty to sink or swim, and dreaded boarding-school discipline or Oxford 'gating.' As it turned out, Mr. Lowell did well to accept the complete plan and push it through, for if time had been taken for experimenting, the depression might have postponed completion to the Greek Kalends.

The first two houses, appropriately named Dunster after the first President, and Lowell after the dynasty, were ready for occupancy in the fall of 1930, and promptly filled. The one was built on the river just east of the furthest freshman hall; the other, with two quadrangles, in the space formerly covered by old dwellings and gardens south of Holyoke Place. Professor C. N. Greenough and C. H. Haring have been the successive masters of Dunster, and Professor Julian L. Coolidge, Master of Lowell House. The other five were ready the next year: Eliot House, under Professor Roger B. Merriman as master, was built on the site of the old power house in the angle between Boylston Street and Memorial Drive. Winthrop House included Gore and Standish Halls, with additions, and was placed under Professor Ronald M. Ferry (A.B. 1912) as master. Kirkland House was made out of the Smith Halls, with the old Hicks house for library; the successive masters have been Professors E. A. Whitney (A.B. 1917) and W. E. Clark. Leverett House was formed out of McKinlock Hall, with a new dining hall, and a new quadrangle (Mather Hall) across Mill Street, and Professor Kenneth B. Murdock as Master. Adams House is a combination of Randolph, Westmorly, and a new residential and dining hall on the site of Russell, with Apthorp House for the Master, Professor James Phinney Baxter 3rd (PH.D. 1926). Each House has single, double, and quadruple suites for students; suites for residential and non-residential tutors; a dining hall, common-rooms for students and tutors, and a house library — a feature insisted upon by the masters, which has proved one of the most useful in the plan. Adams has a swimming pool, and several have their own squash courts; but the land available was not sufficient to provide the greens and gardens of English colleges. The freshmen have been installed in the Yard, the cloistering of which has been completed by Wigglesworth Hall along the southern edge; and the Union fitted up for their meals, library, and game rooms.

There has been no compulsion on the upperclassmen

to live in the Houses; but most of them do, and a certain number of graduate students fill the vacancies. In order to prevent social segregation and certain houses becoming more fashionable than others, students have been allotted to Houses by the 'cross-section' plan, which has prevented any house from maintaining a distinct character for more than a few years.

Interhouse athletics were promptly organized; in 1935 there were championship contests in fifteen different sports, and the winning outfit plays the champion of the Harkness Colleges at Yale. All sorts of House activities have grown up, and a new social pattern is gradually being evolved. It cannot be said that they have furthered democracy, any more than the Harvard Union and the Freshman Halls. The Gold Coast is no more, but the old social chasm between the clubbed and the unclubbed still exists, as in the nineties of the last century. For the great majority in the College the Houses mean a vast improvement in living conditions and social opportunities; for the tutors, fellowship with each other and with their pupils. Indeed, the advantages have been so great that in the year 1935, on the demand of the 'commuters,' a dining hall and common-room were provided for them in Dudley Hall. If the members of the Graduate School of Arts and Sciences, who have had the Union taken from them and nothing substituted, could be given a House, the system would be complete, for the Business School is well provided for, and the Law School apparently does not want one.

Another dream of Mr. Lowell's was realized in 1933. Endowment was obtained, from a source not far away, for a 'Society of Fellows,' a group of seven members chosen from the faculties and Governing Boards, and twenty-four Junior Fellows, elected for three-year terms. The Junior Fellows may be graduates of any College, and must not be more than twenty-five years old at their appointment; they may engage in any approved writing or research, and receive an annual stipend of $1250 to $1500; but they must not take courses or study for a degree. This institution is intended to free exceptional graduate students from the necessity of teaching or doing prescribed studies, and to enable each to contribute his peculiar gifts to the cause of learning when still young and vigorous. The Society has a dining hall and common-room in Eliot House, and dines together weekly; the Fellows may live in the Houses, or outside.

Although for want of space a financial history of the University has not been included in this volume, a brief tribute must be paid to Mr. Frederick S. Mead (A.B. 1887), who introduced the budget system around 1925; to Charles Francis Adams (A.B. 1888), Treasurer of the University from 1898 to 1929, and Henry L. Shattuck (A.B. 1901), his successor. Through their conservative and wise management of the University's investments, and their realization that lean years are apt to succeed the fat ones, Harvard was able to survive the depression without salary cuts, or serious curtailment of its staff or its services.

President Lowell announced his intention of retiring in the fall of 1932. The usual discussion of his successor went on in the University, among the alumni, and in the Boston and New York press. There was no obvious candidate as in 1909, and about fifty members of the faculties, the Governing Boards, and prominent alumni were 'mentioned.' The *Lampoon* produced a 'fake *Crimson*' announcing the election of a mythical Chicago business man, and fooled the Associated Press. The Corporation, taking its time, elected James B. Conant (A.B. 1914), Sheldon Emery Professor of Organic Chemistry, President of Harvard College on May 8, 1933; and he was unanimously confirmed by the Overseers on June 21.

Mr. Lowell, becoming President in the shadow of the

greatest holder of that office, proved an educational statesman of the first rank. His defense of academic freedom maintained the great liberal tradition of the University; his wisdom and energy invigorated its many departments; his devotion restored to Harvard College the ancient 'collegiate way of living.'

'THE AGE THAT IS WAITING
BEFORE'

PRESIDENT

1933-   JAMES BRYANT CONANT

Beneath these specifically religious forces and permeating the whole community there is, I think, a vaguer but deeper religion — the faith in enlightenment, the aspiration to be just, the sympathy with the multiform thoughts and labors of humanity. This is surely the noblest inspiration, and one which unites us to all ages and places in which men have cultivated reason. No one, I am sure, who has felt this high passion and freely fostered it in these halls, will put any place above Harvard in his affection. Some universities have greater beauty and a richer past, some have maturer scholars and more famous teachers, Yale herself has more unity, more energy, and greater fitness to our present conditions. Harvard, instead of all these advantages, has freedom, both from external trammels and from the pleasant torpor of too fixed a tradition. She has freedom and a single eye for the truth, and these are enough to secure for her, if the world goes well, an incomparable future.

— Santayana, in *Harvard Monthly*, 1892

XVIII

'TO ADVANCE LEARNING'

JAMES BRYANT CONANT was one of the famous organic chemists in America when elected President of Harvard College. Born in Boston in 1893, a descendant of the early settler Roger Conant but without immediate Harvard forbears, he prepared for College at the Roxbury Latin School, and graduated A.B. *magna cum laude* in 1913, as of the Class of 1914. He took his Ph.D. in 1916, and received his first appointment in the Department of Chemistry that year. In 1921 he married the daughter of Professor Theodore W. Richards. This election gave great satisfaction to the Faculty of Arts and Sciences. To them he was known as a man of limpid sincerity, strong character, and broad interests outside the field in which he had won distinction.

Mr. Conant entered upon the duties of his office on September 1, 1933, and his first annual report, dated January 8, 1934, declared what he considered to be the most pressing needs of the University. After observing that universities were the residuary legatees of many of the spiritual values that had formerly been guarded by the churches of New England, he declared:

If future generations are to have that high regard for the achievements of the human mind which is essential to civilization, there must be a true reverence for learning in the community. It is not sufficient to train investigators and scholars, no matter how brilliant they may be; a large body of influential citizens must have a passionate interest in the growth of human knowledge. It is our ambition to inspire the undergraduates in Harvard College with an enthusiasm for creative scholarship and a respect for the accumulated intellectual treasures of the past. This is one way in which we today perpetuate learning to posterity.

Learning must be advanced as well as perpetuated. Indeed, in the last analysis it is only by advancing learning that it is possible to perpetuate it. When knowledge ceases to expand and develop, it becomes devitalized, degraded, and a matter of little importance to the present or future. The community loses interest, and the youth of the country respond to other challenges. Able young men enlist in an enterprise only if they are persuaded that they, too, may contribute by creative work. A zest for intellectual adventure should be the characteristic of every university. In the future as in the past, our teachers must be scholars who are extending the frontiers of knowledge in every direction. I hope there will never be a separation of our faculty into those who teach and those who carry on creative work. No line should be drawn between teaching and research. Our strength in the past has lain in the fact that the spirit of scholarship has pervaded our teaching and our scholars have seen the importance of perpetuating the ideals of scholarship as well as advancing knowledge in their own specialty.

A university is a group of men — a community of scholars and students — and here lies the real problem in regard to the future of all institutions of higher learning. Harvard's success will depend almost entirely on our ability to procure men of the highest caliber for our student body and for our faculty. . . .

The new President accepted the framework of Harvard University that he inherited from Mr. Lowell. Except for minor administrative changes, he had no desire to alter the structure, or even to add to the buildings. But he knew, and was willing to admit, that while Harvard had been expanding and growing, other American universities had been pushing ahead even faster; and in certain departments of knowledge, a chair in Harvard University was no longer necessarily regarded as an academic first prize. Mr. Conant believed that the University should seek, not only the best professors, but the best students; not by increasing the difficulty of entrance examinations, but by offering scholarship stipends sufficient to cover the entire expenses of a college education. Financial conditions have so radically changed in the United States in the last twenty years that the heroic figure of the past, the poor young man who enters college with five dollars in his pocket and works his way through by stoking furnaces and waiting on table, can no longer be considered the ideal scholar. Opportunities for student self-help have decreased, and the demands of the University on a student's time for study have increased; the only solution seems to be scholarships sufficiently generous to relieve the scholar of financial worries.

Mr. Conant's third academic year had not been concluded before there was considerable progress to chronicle. Besides the usual number of promotions, several distinguished professors accepted calls from other places. Serge Elisséeff (D.LITT. Tokio) arrived as Professor of Far Eastern Languages; Wilhelm Köhler (D.PHIL. Vienna) from the University of Jena, as Professor of Fine Arts; Henry J. Cadbury (PH.D. 1914) from Bryn Mawr, as Hollis Professor of Divinity; Karl S. Lashley (PH.D. Johns Hopkins) from Chicago, as Professor of Psychology; Morris B. Lambie (PH.D. 1924) from Minnesota, as Professor of Government; Elmer D. Merrill (M.S. Maine) from Columbia, as Professor of Botany; Gaetano Salvemini (PH.D. Florence), formerly of the University of Florence, as De Bosis Lecturer on the History of Italian Civilization; Dr. Fernand Baldensperger from Paris as Professor of Comparative Literature; Robert Ulich (D.PHIL. Leipzig) from Dresden as Lecturer on Comparative Education; Howard Mumford Jones (M.A. Chicago) from Ann Arbor as Professor of American Literature. President Conant, believing that knowledge is in process of becoming too departmentalized, wishes to establish what he calls 'roving professors,' who may lecture in two or more departments and have at their disposal a considerable budget for research. Mr. Thomas W. Lamont has already founded one professorship of this nature.

In order to aid in the recruiting of promising scholars from all parts of the country, the Corporation has established a group of Harvard College Prize Fellowships to be awarded to ten students entering the College from the 'Old Northwest,' Iowa and Kentucky being included in 1935–36, when eleven students entered. These are awarded on the basis of merit, as determined by character and 'scholastic aptitude,' the stipend paid (up to a maximum of $1000) being adjusted to the winner's financial need. The first recipients completed their freshman year with highly creditable records, and were then awarded scholarships for their remaining three years in College, with a maximum stipend of $1200. It is hoped, out of the tercentenary and other contributions, to establish many more such scholarships, for other regions, as their benefit to the College is not confined to attracting the winners. Many of the runners-up have also entered the College; and as other universities fall in line, there will be something like the competition to recruit scholars that there now is, among some of our contemporaries, to recruit football players.

There have also been administrative changes. The Faculty of Arts and Sciences, which had long since become too large for deliberation, and whose functions in practice had been reduced to ratifying the decisions of committees, delegated its powers to a Faculty Council, consisting of one-fifth of the membership of each rank, elected by the whole Faculty. A similar delegation has taken place in the large Faculty of Medicine. In the Graduate School of Arts and Sciences the Master's degree requirements have been stiffened; the reorganization of the Engineering School and the new 'combined' degree in the Graduate School of Education have already been noted. In the College, a reaction from the quasi-paternalism of the Lowell administration toward the liberty of the Eliot era has already set in; the dreaded November and April grades have been abolished for all but freshman courses, attendance of upperclassmen is no longer taken, distribution requirements have been reduced, language requirements have been changed, and in other respects the upperclassmen are encouraged to take more responsibility for their own education. But there is still too much cramming and forgetting in our system of college education, as the prosperity of Harvard Square tutoring schools witnesses.

Thus, her three-hundredth birthday found Harvard University in a normal state of self-dissatisfaction, thinking of numerous things she would like to do better, rather than boasting of what she had done well. It was a matter of bright promise for the future that President Conant and the thousand or more teachers and administrators of the modern University were critical of themselves and eager to be of greater service, as were President Dunster and his five fellows in 1650. Inspiring is the continued generosity of the body of Harvard alumni, to whom the support of their alma mater has been delegated by the Commonwealth. Challenging is the note of freedom that still rings out from the Harvard Yard, into a world by no means so eager to hear it as a century ago. The University is a school of liberty as well as of learning; and events of the last few years have driven home the lesson that only in an atmosphere of liberty, and in a body politic that practises as well as preaches democracy, can learning flourish. Standing on the threshold of her fourth century, the University asks of the State, freedom; of her sons, loyalty; of God, grace that she may be saved from the besetting sin of pride, wisdom to do his will, and power 'to advance *Learning*, and perpetuate it to Posterity.'

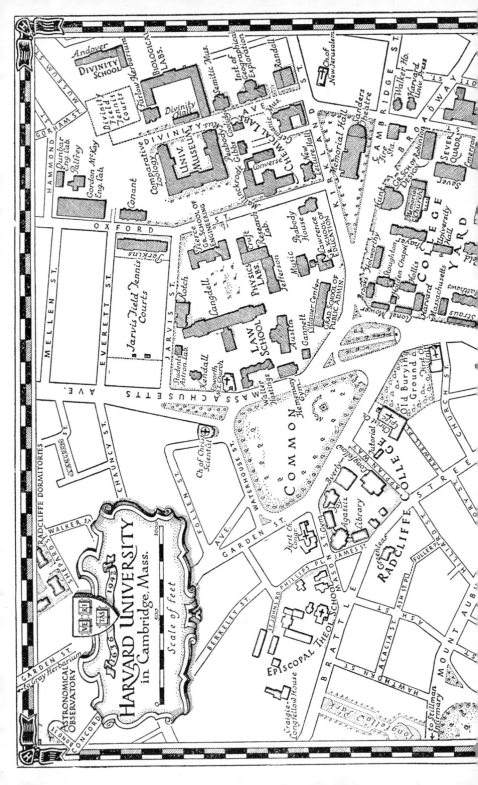

HARVARD UNIVERSITY in Cambridge, Mass.

1636   1942   VE RI TAS

Scale of feet
0   500   1000

Erwin Raisz
Inst. of Geogr. Exploration

HARVARD

CHARLES RIVER

Baptist Ch.

MASSACHUSETTS AVENUE

Faculty Club
Warren
Varsity Club
Harvard Union

St Pauls Catholic Ch.

ADAMS HOUSE

LEVERETT HOUSE

DUNSTER HOUSE

MEMORIAL DRIVE

Univ. Squash

LOWELL HOUSE

Psychol. Clinic

Hicks

McKinlock

Gore

JOHN WINTHROP HOUSE

Van
dish

Louise Squash Courts

KIRKLAND HOUSE

Shannon Athletic
Bldg

Indoor Athletic
Bldg

Smith Halls

Dudley

Hygiene

Apley

Holyoke

Univ.

Littauer Library

Palmer

WEEKS MEM BRIDGE

Boston Elevated
Railway Yards

BOYLSTON ST

ELIOT ST

ELIOT HOUSE

Weld Boat House

ANDERSON BRIDGE

SOLDIERS FIELD ROAD

MEMORIAL DRIVE

UNIVERSITY

Newell Boat House

Tennis Courts

Dillon
Briggs

Carpenter

Field House

SOLDIERS FIELD

NORTH HARVARD ST

Soldiers Class

Students Club

McCulloch

Chase

Gallatin

Baker Library

Mellon

Hamilton

Faculty Club

Sherman

Morris

Morgan

Dean

SOLDIERS FIELD ROAD

to Schools of Medicine,
Dentistry & Public Health,
Arnold Arboretum, etc.

Tennis
Courts

Cowie

GRADUATE SCHOOL OF BUSINESS ADMINISTRATION

Stadium

Maintenance
Shops

BANKS

STERLING ST

COWPERTHWAITE ST

McCARTHY RD

GRANT ST

ATHENS ST

DE WOLFE ST

PLYMPTON ST

MILL ST

DUNSTER ST

HOLYOKE ST

MT AUBURN ST

BOW ST

ARROW ST

WINTHROP ST

GRANT ST

APPENDIX

STATISTICS OF GROWTH, 1869–1936

		College	L.S.S.[1]	Graduate School of Arts and Sciences	Medical School	Law School
Number of Faculty	1869–70	23	9[2]	Same	13	4
	1886–87	61	19[3]	faculty as	22	6
	1908–09	165		Harvard	57	17
	1919–20	180		College	86	12
	1935–36	332			147	33
Number of Students	1869–70	563	43	28[4]	306	120
	1886–87	1077	14	70	271	180
	1908–09	2238	39	403	328	684
	1919–20	2534	112	538	419	879
	1935–36	3726	..	736	529	1466
Number of College Graduates among Students	1869–70	..	5	26[4]	78	61
	1886–87	12	..	69	154	138
	1908–09	17	6	390	254	648
	1919–20	..	37	525	327	835[5]
	1935–36	..	..	726	497	1466
Number of States and Foreign Countries represented by Students	1869–70	26	13	9[4]	21	19
	1886–87	42	7	11	23	26
	1908–09	65	6	44	53	45
	1919–20	61	22	60	46	53
	1935–36	59	..	55	50	58

[1] Lawrence Scientific School from 1869 through 1910; undergraduate Engineering School in 1919–20. Engineering students are in Harvard College in 1935–36.

[2] Five of these nine are also included in the College Faculty.

[3] All but one also included in the College Faculty. These two faculties were combined as the Faculty of Arts and Sciences in 1890. There are, on the average, 20 per cent more teachers in the College and Graduate School — assistants, one-year instructors, visiting lecturers, temporary appointees — than there are members of the Faculty of Arts and Sciences.

[4] These Graduate School figures are for 1872–73, the first year of the School.

[5] In addition, 37, who had been in military or naval service, had completed three years of college work.

INDEX

The first degree of Harvard graduates is given to facilitate identification, or when not provided in the text. The year of the degree is that given in the Quinquennial Catalogue, the Harvard practice being to place a graduate with his original Class, even if his degree was conferred many years later. See, for instance, the case of John Adams on p. 231. Dates in parentheses without degree abbreviation indicate the Class of men who did not graduate, and who never subsequently were granted a Bachelor's degree. The name Harvard on such titles as Harvard Athletic Association, Harvard Law School, is omitted.